My Calabria

Town of Scilla, site of the sea monster Scylla of Greek mythology, on the Tyrrhenian Sea

My Calabria

Rustic Family Cooking from Italy's Undiscovered South

Rosetta Costantino with Janet Fletcher

WINE SUGGESTIONS BY SHELLEY LINDGREN
Photographs by Sara Remington

W. W. Norton & Company
New York London

For information about permission to reproduce selections from this book,
write to Permissions, W. W. Norton & Company, Inc.,
500 Fifth Avenue, New York, NY 10110

For information about special discounts for bulk purchases, please contact
W. W. Norton Special Sales at specialsales@wwnorton.com or 800-233-4830

Manufacturing by Toppan Printing Company
Book design by Jan Derevjanik
Production manager: Andrew Marasia and Anna Oler
Map on page xii by Adrian Kitzinger

Library of Congress Cataloging-in-Publication Data

Costantino, Rosetta.
My Calabria : rustic family cooking from Italy's undiscovered
south / Rosetta Costantino with Janet Fletcher ; wine suggestions
by Shelley Lindgren ; photographs by Sara Remington.
p. cm.
Includes bibliographical references and index.
ISBN 978-0-393-06516-9 (hardcover)
1. Cookery, Italian—Southern style. 2. Cookery—Italy—Calabria.
I. Fletcher, Janet Kessel. II. Lindgren, Shelley. III. Title.
TX723.2.S65C67 2010
641.5945'78—dc22
2010004806

W. W. Norton & Company, Inc.
500 Fifth Avenue, New York, N.Y. 10110
www.wwnorton.com

W. W. Norton & Company Ltd.
Castle House, 75/76 Wells Street, London W1T 3QT

4 5 6 7 8 9 0

To my mother, Maria,
and to all the Calabresi in the world.

*Questo libro e dedicato alla mia mamma Maria
e a tutti i Calabresi nel mondo.*

Contents

Chiesa Santa Maria, an operating Catholic church in Tropea, on the Tyrrhenian Sea

Acknowledgments

My thanks to my agent, Carole Bidnick, for her advice and encouragement, and for helping me from the beginning and seeing this book through to the end.

I would like to give special thanks to my editor, Maria Guarnaschelli, who loved the idea of my book from the minute she met me, believed in it, and was persistent in wanting to make it the definitive cookbook on Calabria. I am also deeply grateful to Melanie Tortoroli, Maria's assistant, for going out of her way to help me on many occasions.

Thanks to Sara Remington, the photographer, who worked so hard with the food stylist, Katie Christ, and the prop stylist, Kami Bremyer, to make the food look great. And to Italian wine authority Shelley Lindgren, who did such a careful job of pairing my recipes with wines from Southern Italy.

Thanks to Randy Hicks for being my assistant from my very first class, testing and editing my recipes from the beginning, and for his advice and friendship; to Miss Linda for assisting in my cooking classes and for her enthusiasm and encouragement; and to all my students for their helpful feedback on recipes.

Thanks to Agnes Lord for pushing me to write a cookbook and helping me with the initial book proposal.

Thanks to Francesca Nudo, our dear Calabrian friend, who supported me along the way and helped with researching the history of Calabria, and who has provided sound advice and friendship.

Thanks to Linda Carucci, without whom I probably would have never embarked on this journey. She encouraged me to start teaching Calabrian cooking classes and allowed me to teach with her so that I could get my foot in the door.

Linda introduced me to Janet Fletcher, my coauthor, whose article on my family's Calabrian culinary traditions in the *San Francisco Chronicle* got me started in this new career. Janet also encouraged me to teach Calabrian cooking classes and accepted the challenge to work with me and write this book. It was a pleasure working with her from day one. She kept on asking questions that pushed me to learn so much more about my native land.

I would like to give special thanks to the following people and establishments in Calabria for their warm hospitality and for sharing recipes: Roberto Ceraudo,

Azienda Agrituristica Dattilo; Rita Callipo, Agriturismo Casa Janca; Pasquale Vacca, Villa San Domenico; Agriturismo Santo Janni; Agriturismo Le Colline del Gelso; Denise and Pietro Lecce, San Lorenzo si alberga; Agriturismo Contrada Guido; and Agriturismo Le Carolee. Italian food importer Cesare Gallo; Rolando Beramendi and Brooke Thornton of Manicaretti; and Italian food marketer Gisella Isidori helped us arrange producer visits during our trip to Calabria. Andrea Sertoli of Select Italy also assisted with our travel plans. In the United States, Italian food marketers Richard Armanino of ItalFoods, Gianluca Guglielmo of A. G. Ferrari, and Martina Kenworthy and Beatrice Ughi from Gustiamo have helped with ingredient needs. Thanks also to Nino Delfino, who drove Janet and me around Calabria to meet the region's artisans and producers.

I also want to thank the following producers who allowed us to visit their facilities and generously shared their expertise: Giuseppe Falcone at Fratelli Falcone; Christine Conrad at Pittaffo A&C; Francesco Sergi at Colavolpe; Vincenzo Cundari at Cundari; Prof. Vittorio Caminiti of Alla Degusteria; Domenico Scalise of Delizie di Calabria; Rosa Fanfulla of Salagione San Francesco; Domenico Alagna and M. Carmela Spanò, Alagna & Spanò Pesce Stocco; Natale Aiello of Pasticceria Aiello; Lucia Lombardo of Pastificio La Porta; Angelo Minisci and Anita Minisci of La Molazza; Francesco Martino at Laratta; Antonio Paese at Caseificio Paese; Saverio Grillo, Azienda Agricola Saverio Grillo; Francesco Madia, Caseificio Villafiore; Fortunato Amarelli of Amarelli; Alfonso Maiorano, Francesco Rizzo, and Francesco Laudari at Azienda Agricola Maiorano; Cinzia Ieracitano and Francesca Rombola at Callipo; Giuseppe Riggio of Salumificio Riggio; Santino Rinaldi of Mirti & Zagare; Giuseppe Sarubbi of I Magnifici del Mezzogiorno; and Verbicaro shepherd Pasquale Di Giorno.

Many thanks to the following Calabrian chefs and restaurant owners, who generously shared recipes with me: Enzo Filardi, La Kamastra; Carminuccio Longo, La Capricciosa; Margarita Amasino, Ristorante Dattilo; Antonio Napoli, Pantagruel; Salvatore Murano, Max Trattoria; and to Vittorio Riga, Bar Gelateria Chez Toi, for sharing the technique for shaping the famous Tartufo di Pizzo. Sincere thanks also to Prof. Dott. Ottavio Cavalcanti, Università della Calabria, who shared his deep knowledge of Calabrian culinary history.

My thanks to the following wine experts, who educated me about Calabrian wines and welcomed me warmly: Paolo Librandi of Librandi; Pietro Andricciola; Gregorio Odoardi of Azienda Agricola Odoardi; Francesco Tramontana of Criserà; Antonio

Tramontana of Azienda Vinicola Tramontana; Fattoria San Francesco; Verbicaro Viti e Vini; Vintripodi Cantine; and John Battista of Winebow.

I am grateful to Maria Woodley and Augusto Marchini of the Italian Trade Commission for their assistance with our research trip to Calabria; and to Christine McDonald and Rick Smilow of the Institute of Culinary Education in New York City for underwriting the class that helped me secure the book contract.

Thanks to my cousins Alberto and Vincenzo Celia and their wives, Rosangela and Filomena, for always welcoming me into their homes and sharing recipes. Many thanks to all my other cousins in Calabria for their support of this project.

I would have never started this book without the encouragement of my husband and my children. They put up with me during the five years I worked on this project, which sometimes seemed endless. My children inspired me to write this book, as they wanted me to record all the recipes my mother carried in her head so they could pass them on to their own children.

This book would not exist without my mom and dad, Maria and Vincenzo Dito. My mother put in endless hours teaching me the recipes and testing them with me, and she has been beside me at every one of my cooking classes. My dad takes care of my garden so that I can always have the best homegrown vegetables, and he has shared his knowledge of how to live from what Mother Earth gives you. Thank you, Mom and Dad, for teaching me how to grow and cook my own food.

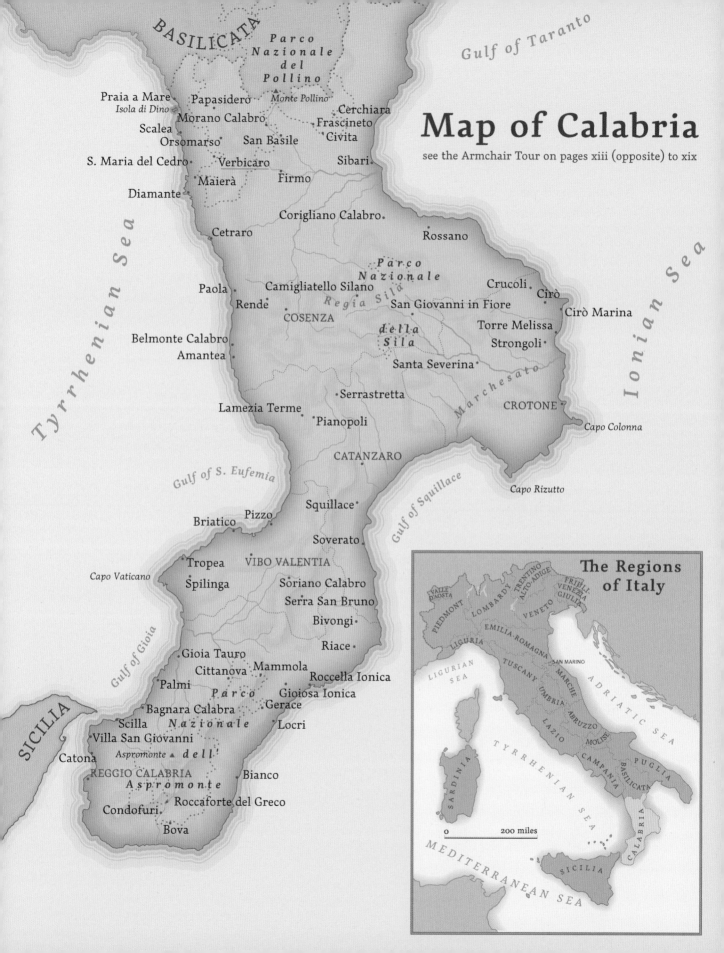

Un Viaggio Virtuale in Calabria

AN ARMCHAIR TOUR

The home that so many Calabrians once had to abandon is a painfully beautiful place, a remote land of majestic castles and ancient fortresses; snow-covered highlands that resemble Switzerland; markets proffering salt cod, unusual *salumi*, and fresh ricotta cheese; and miles of beaches and unspoiled coastline, the longest in all Italy.

Rural Calabria remains a lush green much of the year, with fields of wild raspberries and wild strawberries in the hills where goats roam; high mountain pastures and dense chestnut forests; and vast coastal plantings of fragrant citrus.

With six major mountain chains, Calabria has limited arable land. In places, such as near Bagnara Calabra and Capo Vaticano, on the Tyrrhenian coast, the coastline is so narrow that the steep mountains seem to rise from the sea. Calabria's extreme geography, in such a narrow peninsula, explains its extraordinarily varied climate, agriculture, and landscape.

This armchair tour of Calabria is not an itinerary in the conventional sense as it pays little heed to the most efficient route through the region. Instead, it aims to highlight the main attractions of each region from the perspective of the food-loving traveler.

LA PROVINCIA DI COSENZA

The largest and northernmost of Calabria's five provinces, the province of Cosenza borders the region of Basilicata. Its landscape could hardly be more varied, ranging from the rugged, remote Pollino mountains to the wide, cabana-covered beaches of the Riviera dei Cedri; from the mushroom-rich forests of the Sila Grande to the piana di Sibari (plain of Sibari), a broad, fertile basin blanketed with citrus and stone fruits.

From the visitor's perspective, it makes sense to divide the province into more manageable parts:

La Riviera dei Cedri and Tyrrhenian Coast

La Riviera dei Cedri (the Citron Coast) has no fixed borders but extends roughly from the towns of Praia a Mare to Cetraro, and from the coast to the foothills. Although citron plantings have given way to beachfront development in much of the region, this balmy, frost-free zone is where citron thrives (page 329). You can still see the low-growing trees along the coast, especially around the town of Santa Maria del Cedro.

Just south of the Basilicata border, Praia a Mare welcomes visitors to Calabria with splendid beaches, clear sea waters, pedestrian-only streets, and fine shopping. The Isola di Dino, Calabria's largest island, sits just opposite the Praia beach and is easily accessible by boat for those who want to tour its natural grottoes, the result of erosion.

Scalea, south of Praia, is a bustling beach town that swells with sun-worshippers in July and August. Dozens of *gelaterie* (ice cream shops) vie for customers here, catering to the Italians' insatiable appetite for gelato. The hilly old quarter has good seafood restaurants and arresting sea views.

Farther south along the coast is the picturesque town of Diamante, which owes its modern renown to the *peperoncino* (hot pepper), a key ingredient in the regional cooking and the agriculture of the surrounding province. The annual *Festival del Peperoncino*, an enormous food fair held here in September, draws heat-seeking tourists from all over Europe. The nearby hilltown of Maierà has a Museo del Peperoncino, a museum that is a must-stop for hot pepper fans, and virtually every food shop in Diamante is crammed with pepper-laden souvenirs. Built on a rock, Diamante has steep, alley-like streets that are delightful to roam (in the proper shoes); roughly 150 vivid murals, initially painted in 1981 by artists from around the world, adorn many of the buildings' stucco walls. Diamante boasts a wide beach and a charming *lungomare*, or boardwalk, where locals and visitors take their evening stroll and restaurants set up outdoor tables for diners feasting on local seafood.

Continuing south along the coast, you enter the realm of the fig tree. Belmonte Calabro is headquarters for Colavolpe, a century-old firm famous for its dried fig confections. Its beautiful shop offers many elegantly packaged temptations, from the classic dried-fig wreaths, or *coroncine*—figs strung in a ring, like beads on a necklace—to modern fantasies such as chocolate-dipped dried figs stuffed with hazelnut cream. If you visit in summer, check local markets for the *pomodori di Belmonte*, also known as *cuore di bue* (ox heart), enormous heart-shaped tomatoes that can weigh three pounds each. Amantea, just south of Belmonte Calabro, has dried-fig enterprises, too, but is better known for its anchovies and *rosamarina* (newborn anchovies), which cooks dip in batter and fry to make fritters known as *pitticelle.*

Between Diamante and Belmonte Calabro, the town of Paola lures thousands of pilgrims every May to a procession in honor of San Francesco di Paola, a fifteenth-century ascetic and the patron saint of fishermen. Fervid religious processions featuring mechanized floats, bands, chanting, torchlights, and fireworks are an almost weekly occurrence all over Calabria, but the one commemorating San Francesco is among the largest.

Il Parco Nazionale del Pollino

The Parco Nazionale del Pollino, a national park, draws outdoor enthusiasts such as hikers, cyclists, and mushroom foragers. My native village of Verbicaro is on the western edge of the park, on the Abetamarco River, an area with numerous picnic sites. Many tourists and city people come here to picnic in summer after buying fresh ricotta from one of the shepherds in the area. Another worthwhile stop is the remote mountain village of Papasìdero, where history-minded visitors come to tour the grotta del Romito (page 8).

The breathtaking town of Morano Calabro looks two-dimensional as you approach it, so steeply is it pitched on its hillside. An energetic tourist can climb the town's steep main street to the thirteenth-century Norman castle at its peak. In town, a museum displays the artifacts of everyday life for Calabrian sharecroppers and shepherds in earlier times. If you visit in late June, the town's mulberry trees will be laden with fruit, and you will be able to sample these luscious berries at the local farmers' market.

San Basile, Frascineto, and Civita are all Arbëresh towns in the national park, populated largely by Calabrians of Albanian descent (page 62). In Civita, a tiny village with a spectacular mountain setting, you can visit the small Arbëresh ethnic museum and dine well at Kamastra, a restaurant specializing in Arbëresh dishes, such as *dromësat* (page 60), a type of handmade pasta that resembles couscous. Bread enthusiasts will want to make a detour for Cerchiara di Calabria, on the southeast edge of the park. There, in a handful of bakeries in this self-proclaimed Città del Pane (city of bread), women still prepare the traditional *pane di Cerchiara.* This enormous, round, part-whole-wheat loaf weighs five pounds or more (two to three kilos) and requires four hours to bake in a wood-fired oven.

The Piana di Sibari and Olive Country

The eastern side of the province encompasses one of the only significant plains in Calabria, a broad expanse of productive land known as the piana di Sibari. Here, clementines and peaches, the latter trellised like grapevines, cover thousands of acres. Perhaps if more of Calabria were as arable as the piana di Sibari, people would not have had to struggle so hard to survive.

Visitors to the area can see the remains of ancient Sibari (Sybaris), considered among the most beautiful cities of Magna Graecia, the area of Southern Italy colonized by the ancient Greeks. South of Sibari is olive country with production centered around Corigliano Calabro. Olive trees blanket the hillsides here, climbing so high that one wonders how they are ever harvested.

The isolated Byzantine hill town of Rossano, southeast of Corigliano Calabro, is one of the most picturesque in all Calabria. A prosperous town in the 1800s, Rossano has many lovingly restored buildings and stately homes, as well as an eleventh-century Byzantine cathedral. The cathedral's museum houses the Codex Purpureus, discovered in the cathedral's sacristy in 1879 and one of the oldest pictorial Gospels known, written in gold and silver on parchment. The esteemed licorice firm of Amarelli (page 350), established in 1730, is located on the outskirts of Rossano.

The Interior and La Sila

Home to the Università della Calabria, the modern town of Rende has no particular charm, but its *centro storico*, or historic quarter, on a high bluff above the new town, merits a stop. Well-preserved medieval buildings and *palazzi* (grand private homes) serve as a reminder of this area's prosperous past as a center for wheat, olive, fig, chestnut, and mulberry production for the silk trade. Have lunch at Pantagruel, a superb seafood establishment in an elegant old townhouse, then stroll around the old quarter and admire the view of the valley below.

East of the city of Cosenza, another mountain range—the Sila—rises majestically, and several large lakes make this region a vacation destination. Dairy cows thrive on the emerald-green high plateau of La Sila—one of the only parts of Calabria that is hospitable to cattle. Consequently, most of Calabria's cow's milk cheeses—including Caciocavallo Silano (a DOP cheese) and Provola—come from this zone.

The Sila Mountains are snow covered in winter, luring skiers and other winter-sport enthusiasts to what some Calabrians proudly call "Little Switzerland." Charming mountain towns like Camigliatello Silano have an alpine feel, with timbered buildings and hotels bearing names like Edelweiss. And when the snow melts, the mushroom foraging begins. Porcini and other wild fungi lurk in the forests here and find their way to the local restaurants in season. For those wanting an edible souvenir, the upscale food shops in Camigliatello Silano sell dried porcini of flawless quality.

Thanks to its cool mountain air, the Sila has long been known for its fine *salumi*. Although commercial producers have modern plants now and no longer depend on nature to cool them, the tradition of artisan *salumi* production remains strong here. Farther east, the town of San Giovanni in Fiore is known for its *pitta 'mpigliata* (page 338), a strudel-like coiled pastry stuffed with raisins, cinnamon, and nuts.

LA PROVINCIA DI CROTONE

Carved out of the province of Catanzaro in the early 1990s, the province of Crotone encompasses Calabria's most famous wine region, some of its best-preserved castles, and one of its most inviting small cities.

The Greeks founded the coastal city of Crotone in the eighth century B.C. Indeed the old Greek acropolis still remains within the massive castle that King Carlos V built in the sixteenth century to protect the city from invaders.

Today, the outskirts of Crotone are lined with factories and industrial buildings—not a pretty sight—but the *centro storico*, or old quarter, is delightful. Its heart is the Piazza Pitagora, named for Pythagoras, who lived much of his life in Crotone. In the maze of small streets near the *piazza* are the beautiful seventeenth- and eighteenth-century homes of long-ago nobility. A lively food market takes place in these streets during the day, and at night, the action moves to the *lungomare*, the promenade along the sea, which is lined with cafés and seafood restaurants. Among the regional food specialties are *covatelli Crotonese*, small ridged pasta shaped like gnocchi and sauced with a meat or fish *ragù*; and *quadaru*, a fish soup made with the local catch.

West of Crotone is the vast expanse of rolling hills known as the Marchesato, so named because it belonged to the local *marchese* in feudal times.

Sheep graze its grassy knolls, providing the rich milk for fresh ricotta, ricotta salata, and Pecorino Crotonese. The specialty food shops in nearby Crotone carry the best of these local cheeses. The southern end of the Marchesato is farm country, with vast plantings of asparagus, fennel, and other vegetables.

At Santa Severina, at the north end of the Marchesato, stands a magnificent eleventh-century Norman castle with watchtowers at four corners, a sight well worth the torturous mountain drive to get there. Other architectural traces of the region's tumultuous past include the splendid remains of an Aragonese castle at Le Castella, built on a small island connected to the coast by a sliver of land; the single soaring Doric column at Capo Colonna, all that remains of an ancient Greek temple devoted to Hera; and the many watchtowers that still stand symbolic guard on the coast in places like Capo Rizzuto, Torre Melissa, and Cirò Marina.

Calabria's finest wines come from the Cirò DOC, from coastal vineyards in the vicinity of Cirò and Cirò Marina. The vines march straight down to the sea here and climb the hills, taking advantage of the ocean breezes to cool the grapes at night.

Crucoli has a claim to fame: as a center for the production of *sardella*, the fiery spread made from salted baby anchovies and sardines and hot peppers (page 42). In and around Crucoli, which bills itself as *la Città della Sardella*, the spicy condiment rarely leaves the table. Locals slather it on crostini, stir it into tomato sauce, and spread it on pizza.

LA PROVINCIA DI CATANZARO

The province of Catanzaro was established in 1816. In the 1990s, its land mass shrunk by half when the new provinces of Crotone and Vibo Valentia were carved out of it. It covers roughly the center of Calabria, with Cosenza and Crotone to the north and Vibo Valentia and Reggio Calabria to the south.

The city of Catanzaro, at about 1,000 feet (350 meters) above sea level, was established in the Byzantine era and enjoyed a strategic fortified position between Calabria's two seas. Today, the city is the administrative capital of Calabria, with many of its one hundred thousand residents employed in government service. For the food-loving traveler, the main reason to pause here is for a lunch of *morseddu*, a spicy braised-tripe sandwich that is a specialty of Catanzaro's restaurants and hard to find elsewhere. Another local specialty is the *tiella d'agnello* (page 227), an Easter dish of braised lamb, artichokes, and peas baked with breadcrumbs.

Chestnuts from the foothills of the Sila Piccola are a major crop for the region, the raw material for France's elegant *marrons glacés* (glazed chestnuts). In restaurants in towns like Serrastretta, in the heart of the chestnut forest, you can dine on tagliatelle made from chestnut flour, followed by pork braised with chestnuts, and chestnut mousse for dessert.

West of Catanzaro, near the Tyrrhenian coast and the town of Lamezia Terme, wine grapes and olives flourish. The olive oil made here, largely from the Carolea olive, carries the DOP Lametia, a name protected by the European Union.

On the Ionic side, the town of Squillace, south of Catanzaro, has been a ceramics center since Greek times, and skilled artisans there continue to produce decorative ceramics using Byzantine techniques. For sun lovers, the best beaches on this side are between Squillace Lido and Gioiosa Ionica, the latter in the province of Reggio Calabria. The sea is flat and calm here, but tourism and development are minimal compared to the beach resorts on the Tyrrhenian. Soverato, with its lovely white-sand beach, does draw many visitors in summer and has the hotels, restaurants, and night life to accommodate them.

LA PROVINCIA DI VIBO VALENTIA

Like Crotone, the province of Vibo Valentia is a latecomer, created in the early 1990s from land that was formerly part of Catanzaro province. Its namesake city on the Gulf of Saint Eufemia, like many in Calabria, has upper and lower parts: the old town, situated inland and perched on a hill to provide protection from raiders; and the modern town on the coast, Vibo Marina. The old town has the Duomo, the cobbled streets, and the Greek and Roman ruins; the new town has some beach tourism, along with a port for commercial fishing and pleasure boats. Throughout Calabria, the "marina towns"—Marina di Paola, Cirò Marina, Marina di Gioiosa Ionica, and dozens more—arose mostly in the twentieth century, when the fear of malaria faded and people could move down from the hills to be closer to their farmland.

The northern and eastern sections of Vibo Valentia province are sparsely populated, with few attractions for the traveler. This is thickly forested country, hospitable to wild mushrooms but not to most agriculture. In the eleventh century, Cistercian monks established their first monastery in Italy, in the remote mountain village of Serra San Bruno. It survives today, and although you can't tour the monastery, you can buy the monks' products—honey, jam, and the like—at the monastery shop. The scenery en route is beautiful, but as befits a hermetic society, the monastery is a long way from anywhere.

Soriano Calabro, a tiny village on the road from Vibo Valentia to the monastery, is the center of Calabria's commercial *mostaccioli* production. At the pastry shops in the village, you can buy these long-lasting honey cookies (page 326), similar to gingerbread but harder, in dozens of whimsical and decorative shapes. With some protection, they travel well and will make it home in one piece.

The western edge of the province presents a vastly different picture from the interior. The scenic coastal stretch from Briatico to Capo Vaticano—billed as the Riviera degli Dei, or Riviera of the Gods—is heavily patronized beachfront, with elbow-to-elbow resorts, several of them deluxe. At the spectacular Capo Vaticano, the mountains come right down to the sea, leaving only slivers of sandy beach.

Pizzo has an active fishing fleet, with tuna the most valuable catch. Predictably, the restaurants here prepare tuna expertly, in many guises and using every part. Sample *scilatelli* (fresh pasta) with tuna *ragù*, and spaghetti with *bottarga* (salted tuna roe) or *lattume* (the tuna's sperm sac, a local specialty). The many shops on Pizzo's quaint back streets have good prices on *bottarga* and canned tuna under oil.

History buffs know Pizzo as the place where Joachim Murat, Napoleon's brother-in-law and former King of the Two Sicilies, was executed by firing squad in 1815 for having tried to retake his kingdom. But Italian food lovers know it as *la città del gelato*, with arguably more ice cream shops per capita than any other town in Italy. The Piazza Belvedere, the town's heart, is ringed with *gelaterie*, each with outdoor tables and scurrying waiters, and each claiming to make the best *tartufo di Pizzo* (page 355), a cocoa-dusted frozen dessert with chocolate and hazelnut ice creams encasing a flowing chocolate sauce.

Tropea is Calabria's St. Tropez, with luxury resorts and a lively night scene. The town perches dramatically on a promontory overlooking crystal-clear water and a wide, sandy beach. Souvenir shops line the main street and narrow side streets, offering every conceivable foodstuff spiked with hot red pepper, as well as the sweet red onions that are a specialty of the local farms. 'Nduja, a spicy pork spread from the nearby town of Spilinga, also lines the shelves in Tropea's shops, but you will pay less for it in Spilinga, just a few kilometers south. There, you can sample 'nduja in the local restaurants, stirred into tripe stew, tossed with tomato sauce and homemade *filej* (long noodles formed around a knitting needle, known elsewhere in Calabria as *fusilli*), or simply spread on bread.

Sheep thrive around Spilinga and the gentle hills to the east, providing milk for the highly regarded Pecorino del Monte Poro and ricotta. The aged pecorino, hard enough to grate, makes an easily packable and nonperishable souvenir.

LA PROVINCIA DI REGGIO CALABRIA

Surrounded by water on three sides, Reggio Calabria is the region's southernmost province and its most populous. The province encompasses Calabria's largest city, Reggio di Calabria (Reggio for short), some of its major fishing towns, and a large national park—the Parco Nazionale dell'Aspromonte—at its heart.

For centuries, Reggio has been the entry point for ingredients and ideas from Sicily, with the result that many dishes in Reggio show an obvious Sicilian imprint. You can find *arancine*, the Sicilian fried rice croquettes, in the shops and restaurants of Reggio, just as in Palermo. In fact, some people from Reggio will insist that *arancine* are their invention. In Reggio's numerous pastry shops and cafés, you can have your gelato stuffed inside a split brioche, the same way Sicilians enjoy it. Ricotta-filled cannoli and cassata, the signature pastries of Sicily, are ubiquitous in Reggio. Sicily's fingerprints are also on Reggio's *caponata*, a sweet-and-sour eggplant dish, and on its swordfish and *stoccafisso* (stockfish, or air-dried cod) prepared *alla ghiotta* (with tomatoes, capers, and olives).

The town has a picturesque, palm tree–lined *lungomare*, or boardwalk, where locals take their evening stroll, and good shopping on the Corso Garibaldi. But for many visitors today, the chief lure of Reggio is the Museo Archeologico Nazionale, or archeological museum, one of the finest in Italy. The museum's most splendid treasures are the *Bronzi di Riace*, a pair of enormous bronze statues of unidentified men—warriors, perhaps?—found off the coast of Riace, near Reggio, by a scuba diver in 1972. They are thought to date from the fifth century B.C., and although scholars can only speculate on how and when they ended up in the ocean, they seem virtually unscathed by their long submersion.

Southeast of Reggio, in tiny villages on the southern edge of the Aspromonte, one finds the heartland of Greek Calabria. In this handful of villages—Bova, Condofuri, Roccaforte del Greco, and a few others along the Amendolea River—people maintain linguistic and cultural links to the ancient Greeks. Fewer than two thousand people in the area, most of them elderly, still speak *grecanico*, or *Greco di Calabria*, a language—some say a dialect—that has some commonality with early Greek but is incomprehensible to Italians. After decades of discouraging *grecanico* and punishing students

who spoke it, the Italian government has reversed itself and the endangered tongue is being taught in schools. Here one can taste the *lestopitta*, considered "the pizza of the ancient Greeks": an unleavened dough, flattened like a pizza and fried, then topped with tomato, eggplant, peppers, or other condiments.

The Ionian coast of Reggio Calabria draws history enthusiasts, who come to see Gerace, a well-preserved medieval town in the mountains of the eastern Aspromonte; and the remains of the ancient Greek colony of Locri, on the coast. Just north of Locri but inland is the charming medieval hill town of Mammola, famous among food lovers for its *stoccafisso* (stockfish), "*il pesce che arriva dove il mare non c'è*" (the fish that comes where there is no sea). The stockfish isn't caught here, of course, or even dried here—it comes dried from Norway—but it is reconstituted in shops here, and the Mammolesi credit their clean mountain water with producing superior results. Naturally, Mammola's restaurants specialize in *stoccafisso* and *baccalà* (salt cod) prepared in every imaginable way: as carpaccio; in fritters and pasta sauce; as a marinated salad with oil and vinegar; or braised with tomato, green olives, and potatoes. Cittanova, on the northwestern edge of the Aspromonte, is equally famed for its preparation of stockfish. Throughout Reggio Calabria, the popular vote goes to stockfish over salt cod, although the same recipes are used for both.

The Tyrrhenian coast of Reggio Calabria will reward visitors who love fishing villages, the sight of working boats in a harbor and men mending nets on shore. The stretch between Palmi and Villa San Giovanni is known as the Costa Viola for good reason: the setting sun casts a violet glow on the water here. No Costa Viola town is more enchanting than Scilla—the dangerous Scylla of Homer's *Odyssey*—its harbor filled with *passerelle*, the traditional swordfish boats (page 174), its narrow streets connected by steep staircases. A lunch here at Ristorante Glauco, overlooking the port, showcases the region's freshest seafood: swordfish carpaccio, tiny fried *gamberetti* (baby shrimp); fried sardines; octopus salad; and pasta with swordfish and zucchini.

To the north of Scilla, the fishing town of Bagnara Calabra is worth a stop for fans of *torrone*, or almond nougat. Several shops in town specialize in this honey-and-almond confection, an Arab legacy that Calabrians relish, especially at Christmas. Bagnara is also a center for the commercial swordfish catch and the host of an annual swordfish *sagra*, or festival, that draws attendees from all over Italy. Swordfish Bagnara style (page 167) is steamed in a water bath; many restaurants here serve it, along with many anchovy and octopus dishes.

Between the coast and the Aspromonte is rich agricultural land, much of it devoted to olives, terraced wine and table grapes, and citrus. The olive trees around Gioia Tauro are so immense they take one's breath away; they do not produce high-quality oil, but no one talks of removing these giants and replanting. Nor do the wine grapes from this area produce Reggio's best wines—those come from Bivongi, in the northeast corner of the province, and from Bianco in the southeast, where the *passito di Greco di Bianco*, a much admired dessert wine, is made.

Lemons, oranges, and clementines thrive along this stretch of the Tyrrhenian coast, but the most exotic citrus produced in the region is the fragrant bergamot (page 323), prized for its essential oil. It grows in a U-shaped band that hugs the coast and extends from Catona, just north of Reggio, to Roccella Ionica on the Ionian side. Cherimoya, a heart-shaped subtropical fruit with pale green skin, has also become an important coastal crop in recent years

Reggio's pastry repertoire is larger than that of any other Calabrian province, with the city of Reggio in particular offering a trove of sweets in its numerous *pasticcerie* (pastry shops). Specialties to try include *sospiri di monaca*, or "nun's sighs," a glazed cake with a cream filling; *pignolata*, tiny fritters glazed with lemon icing or chocolate, similar to *cicirata* (page 316); *petrali*, pastry turnovers filled with dried figs, almonds, and candied citron; *martorana*, marzipan skillfully shaped to look like fruits; *pitta di San Martino*, a glazed bun with dried fruits and nuts; *stomatico*, a dry spice cookie made with caramelized sugar; cakes, tarts, and jam flavored with bergamot; and a large range of almond cookies and cakes. Throughout the province of Reggio Calabria, a tempting pastry is never far away.

An apartment building in the town of Tropea

Introduction: From the Land of the Bergamot

At the southern tip of the Italian peninsula lies an Italy that few people know: a land of fragrant citron and bergamot orchards, ancient olive groves and terraced vineyards; a place of persistent tradition and ritual, where the annual swordfish catch and hot pepper harvest are celebrated with elaborate festivals, and where women still roll pasta dough around knitting needles.

In Calabria, this scenic and storied region at the "toe" of the Italian boot, cooks maintain a food culture unique in Italy. Rooted in the garden and enlivened by the *peperoncino* (hot pepper), Calabrian cooking is rustic and spicy, deeply flavorful but devoid of ornament, a daily demonstration of ingenuity.

I was born and raised in this rugged landscape, in Verbicaro, a small wine-producing hill town above Scalea, near the Tyrrhenian Sea. My father was a shepherd and winemaker, my mother his tireless assistant, and I grew up with food that was almost entirely homegrown and homemade. Although we are Californians now, my family still clings to the foods of Calabria, the ancestral home of many Italian-Americans.

Separated from the region of Basilicata, its northern neighbor, by the Pollino mountain range, Calabria faces water on all other sides—the Tyrrhenian Sea to the west, the Ionian Sea to the east, and the Strait of Messina that separates it from Sicily to the south. Until the rail line connecting Naples to Reggio Calabria was completed in 1895, the region remained hard to reach and hard to leave. Some of Calabria's hill towns and mountain villages didn't see paved roads until the 1960s; until then, commerce and communication were slow and difficult. My father recalls that a horse-drawn carriage brought the mail to Verbicaro until the late 1930s.

This remoteness hampered economic progress but preserved a distinctive Calabrian cuisine. Although similarities exist with the kitchens of the surrounding regions of Campania, Basilicata, Sicily, and Puglia, Calabrian cooks have a repertoire all their own.

On a typical day, if you were to join my family for breakfast, we would serve you homemade bread with fresh fig preserves (page 277); or *i visquotti*, barely sweet breakfast cookies that we dip in coffee. Stay for lunch and we might have *pitta*, the Calabrian stuffed pizza (page 131), filled with chard from our garden and dill; or a platter of whole fried sweet peppers stuffed with anchovies (page 241) along with the oil-preserved tuna (page 288) that I prepare in summer, when albacore is in season. For dinner, we might start with a *minestra*, or thick soup, of fava beans and red onions (page 97), followed by baked sardines stuffed with breadcrumbs (page 166); or we might have *fusilli*, homemade "knitting-needle pasta," with a goat sauce (page 85) or a spicy pork-rib *sugo* (page 88).

These are the dishes I grew up with in Verbicaro, before my parents emigrated when I was fourteen. They are the dishes I continue to make in my Northern California home, using the eggplants, tomatoes, and peppers from my garden; fresh ricotta made from scratch; and pasta fashioned by hand.

When I was young, I didn't appreciate how clever Calabrian cooks were in making so much from so little. With limited ingredients, they created a collection of dishes of remarkably complex flavor. Simplicity is the cuisine's hallmark, resourcefulness the Calabrian cook's signature and strength. The food is bold and substantial, and it speaks directly to hunger. In its artlessness, it is the opposite of the refined and baroque cooking of Emilia-Romagna.

This is not to say that Calabrian cooks are unskilled—far from it. With only flour and water—no egg—they make an astonishing number of pasta shapes by hand. Their *ragùs* are deeply flavorful, their homemade ricotta finer than anything you can buy. They are master preservers, sun drying their garden vegetables for the winter, preserving tuna under oil, and transforming tree-ripened figs into jam and mandarin oranges into fragrant homemade liqueurs.

Calabria is the kingdom of the eggplant and tomato, where every cook knows dozens of ways to prepare these vegetables, together and separately. Pork, lamb, and goat are the dominant meats, roasted simply with wild herbs and potatoes, or made into rustic, slow-cooked pasta sauces. The sea yields incomparable tuna and swordfish, anchovies and sardines, as well as octopus, clams, and mussels. The swordfish may be steamed in a water bath with parsley, olive oil, and garlic in the method of Bagnara (page 167); the sardines baked with breadcrumbs (page 166); the tuna or swordfish prepared *alla ghiotta* ("glutton's style") with tomato, olives, and capers (page 175). Despite the abundant fresh fish, Calabrians have never lost a taste for salt cod, and the Verbicaro preparation with dried sweet peppers (page 184) is sublime.

Like the neighboring Sicilians, Calabrians have a sweet tooth and countless ways to satisfy it. Many of the *dolci* are associated with saint's days and other special occasions, when people would allow themselves a small indulgence, such the *chinule*, or sweet chestnut ravioli (page 319), a Christmas specialty. Ice creams and frozen *semifreddi* turn up in flavors Americans may never have imagined: chocolate gelato with a pinch of hot red pepper (page 348); ricotta gelato (page 345); or gelato flavored with Calabrian licorice (page 349).

These frugal people long ago learned how to make their summer abundance last through the winter—by drying, salting, or fermenting the harvest, or preserving it under oil. These preserves became treasured ingredients, essential in some dishes; they are not "second best." Braised rabbit with dried sweet peppers can be made with fresh peppers (page 222), but it is just as tasty with the sun-dried sweet peppers that my mother and I preserve in summer.

For much of my adult life, I mostly watched my mother in the kitchen and lent a hand on occasion. I had a busy engineering career and no time for handmade *fusilli*. But as she and my father aged, I began to realize how much would be lost if I didn't master these techniques and recipes and record them for others. Many Calabrians and Calabrian-Americans of my generation have not maintained the old ways and don't know how to make the dishes their mothers and grandmothers made. Motivated by love for my native region and a desire to preserve its vanishing culinary customs, I undertook the joyous task of assembling this book. I hope it will encourage the immigrant sons and daughters of Calabria to be proud of their heritage, to return for a visit, and to keep the food traditions alive. And I want to introduce others to a region that merits exploring, for the beauty of its landscapes, the appealing simplicity of its way of life, and the allure of its cuisine.

A LONG LOOK BACK

On September 8, 1905, my paternal grandfather and his father boarded a ship in Naples bound for New York. My grandfather was all of nineteen and was leaving three younger siblings and his mother behind in Verbicaro. They landed in New York City almost two weeks later, found rooms to rent at 28 Mulberry Street, in the heart of Little Italy, and secured work as manual laborers. Like many of their immigrant compatriots from Calabria, the two had no intention of staying in America. My great-grandfather's plan was to make just enough money to return home and buy a herd of goats.

By Calabrian standards of the day, they were not poor. My great-grandparents owned a small amount of vineyard and farmland, so they weren't sharecroppers, as many others were. Every year they grew enough olives, wheat, corn, grapes, figs, and potatoes to feed the family and to have enough olive oil and wine to sell. But with goats, whose milk could be turned into cheese, they would have yet another income source.

After four years in America, the two men had accumulated the necessary funds, but by then my twenty-three-year-old grandfather did not want to leave. Perhaps he believed America offered more opportunity than Verbicaro, but in the end, it didn't matter what he thought. In those days, a young Italian man submitted to his father's wishes, so the two returned home to Verbicaro and purchased their herd. They made goat cheese and continued growing wine grapes, a modest farming enterprise that my father and his brother inherited, a venture that America financed and that America would eventually bring to an end.

In 1959, my father married Maria Torrano, a young Verbicaro woman from another farming family. In keeping with tradition, the bride's family provided a house for the young couple, along with a trunk full of linens. The groom's family supplied the furniture and the kitchen staples, such as flour and *salumi*. Vincenzo Dito and Maria Torrano had a promising start on married life, with more means than many Calabrians. They had a parcel of mountain property for their goats with a two-room stone farmhouse; a vineyard on the outskirts of Verbicaro and a modern flat in town with no space for gardening; and another vineyard and coastal plot for their vegetables near Orsomarso, a ninety-minute walk from Verbicaro.

I was born the following year, the only child. My parents are enterprising people, with little education but boundless energy, and they worked incessantly to squeeze a decent living from their assets. There was no finished road between our Verbicaro home and the mountain property, so my father had to make the steep two-hour trip on foot, his horse and donkey loaded with supplies. He and his brother spent alternate weeks at the farmhouse there, moving their goats from one pasture to the next and making ricotta and aged pecorino in the farmhouse. The lack of roads made it impossible for my father to get fresh ricotta to market, so he salted and smoked the ricotta to make it last until he got back to town.

In the summer, when I was out of school, my mother and I would accompany my father to the simple mountain house on occasion. To me, the trek was an adventure-filled hike, with wild strawberries to pick and streams to cross on the way, but for my mother and father, the trip was more arduous. My mother walked the six miles up the mountain with a basket filled with food on her head, with a coiled cloth rope underneath to soften the weight; she walked down carrying cheese or vegetables. Repeatedly, local officials would announce that a road was imminent. But every trip up and down that mountain was an aggravating reminder of yet another broken government promise.

Still, my parents persisted with farming, and my childhood was a happy one. At the mountain house, which had no electricity and no running water, I would fetch our drinking and cooking water from a nearby stream in tin jugs. My mother cooked in the fireplace in big copper pots, the smoke from the fire infusing my father's cheeses, which he stored on a rack above the hearth. From the age of nine or ten, I had my own little vegetable plot and proudly tended it in imitation of my father. I recall the thrill of finding warm eggs under the chickens and the pleasure of drinking fresh goat's milk for breakfast, still warm and frothy from the morning's milking. I had a swing under the walnut tree, the riverbank to explore, and an army of crickets to keep me amused.

Sometimes, my father would bring me wild raspberries from the distant pastures where he took his goats. When that happened, I would beg to go with him the next day so I could pick more raspberries myself. No, he would say, you're a girl and your legs will get scratched. Finally I persuaded my mother to make me a pair of pants so I could accompany my father to the wild raspberry patch.

We kept rabbits and chickens, raised a pig every year, and made our own olive oil. My father's land produced goat and lamb for our table; ricotta cheese and pecorino; wine and vinegar; figs and nectarines, some of which we preserved; wheat for bread and pasta; and endless vegetables. Neighbors in Verbicaro would buy the cheese my mother hauled down the mountain. Remnants of the prewar barter economy persisted in our community, with people trading oil for wine, or cheese for shoes. Many people, my family included, were all but self-sufficient.

Although we had few material luxuries, our table was a daily source of pleasure and abundance. My mother was a master of all the regional pasta shapes, from *fusilli* (spaghetti-like strands fashioned around a knitting needle) to *cavatelli* (small curled pasta shaped with two fingers). She made our bread—dense, sturdy loaves baked in our wood-burning oven—and *pitta*, Calabria's signature stuffed pizza. With the relentlessness of someone who remembered the hunger of the war years, when even people with money could find no food to buy, she preserved all the fruits and vegetables we couldn't eat fresh, either by packing them under oil or vinegar, or by sun drying. She made golden frittatas with fresh eggs from our chickens, their

My hometown, Verbicaro. On the right is the old town, which is now largely abandoned. The new buildings, on the left, were built after the 1960s. Many of these, too, are empty because it is difficult to make a living in Verbicaro. My father's farmhouse, where my mother and I stayed with my father in the summer, was located behind the mountain, pictured here.

yolks the color of the sunrise; prepared thick bean soups flavored with pork skin; and simmered tender Savoy cabbage from the garden with succulent pork ribs. On holidays, we ate like royalty: baby goat or lamb for Easter, roasted to a turn with rosemary and garlic; and the traditional salt cod feast at Christmas, ending with a parade of honey-drizzled desserts and confections.

The 1960s, my childhood years, were relatively prosperous in Calabria, especially compared to the war years that both of my parents had endured. With the men away in the military, Calabrian women had to maintain the farms, and suffering was widespread. Basic supplies from beyond the region, like sugar, boxed pasta, and flour, became increasingly scarce. The German army destroyed farms and vineyards, and by 1944, the year my mother refers to as *l'anno della fame* (the year of hunger), many Calabrians were able to prevent starvation only by foraging for wild greens, mushrooms, and herbs. The experience left people like my parents with a deep aversion to waste and a profound respect for what nature provides.

In the grim postwar years, Calabrians left for America in droves, one of several waves since Italy was unified in 1861. Many, like my great-grandfather, came at the turn of the century, frustrated that the Italian South had not benefited economically from unification. They felt deceived, because they had been told so often that unification would bring investment in infrastructure, a fairer distribution of land, and a decline in corruption.

After resettling and finding work, they would call their brothers and cousins and urge them to come, too, sometimes lining up a job for them in advance, as my uncles did for my father. As a result of this mass exodus, entire towns were practically erased from the face of Calabria. Verbicaro, my hometown, was once famous for its red wine and its Zibibbo grapes, which were dried for raisins. But so many people walked away from their vineyards that, by the 1950s, Verbicaro's glory days had passed. By the 1960s, even the local cooperative, to which my dad sold his grapes, was on the verge of collapse. Today, the historic quarter of Verbicaro, where we lived, is essentially a ghost town, occupied largely by elderly women and cats.

It is hard to imagine how difficult it is for people who have hardly ever left their town to leave their country. In Calabria, separated from the rest of Italy by mountains and with more impenetrable mountains down its spine, families remained for generations in the same place. Nevertheless, my parents began to consider leaving Calabria. It seemed that the road into the mountains would never get built (they were wrong about that), that they worked too hard for too little, and that their only child would have a brighter future in America.

In 1974, when I was fourteen, they decided to join my mother's brothers, who had emigrated to California a decade before. By the standards of a Calabrian farmer, who relied every year on the kindness of nature, my California uncles enjoyed the good life. Each had a car and a comfortable home and a nine-to-five job with a guaranteed paycheck. So my parents abandoned their land—there was no hope for a sale—and we left for America, as my ancestors had done seventy-five years before.

Resettled in Oakland, our family quickly adapted, but we never abandoned our traditional ways. My mother still makes her bread with the starter she brought from Calabria in her purse, shapes *fusilli* by hand (and has taught my children), cures olives and fresh anchovies, and, with my help, puts up dozens of quarts of homegrown peeled tomatoes every summer. My father maintains a garden behind my house that provides virtually all the fruits and vegetables we had in Calabria, including *peperoncini* and golden figs.

As I have discovered in the cooking classes I teach, many people are eager to taste these Southern Italian family dishes and to participate in some of these kitchen rituals. And as my students have learned, a platter of homemade *fusilli*, and the immense pride that comes from making it, is within everyone's reach. You don't have to have a garden to reproduce the essence of Calabrian cooking. A farmers' market or well-supplied supermarket can provide the ingredients. But these recipes speak to all those interested in recapturing the pleasures of an era before fast food and the flavor of a place where "natural food" was all anyone had. Anyone willing to make some modest effort can experience the gratifying aromas of Tropea's red-onion soup (page 101) or the revelation of homemade tomato paste (page 299). Calabrian cooking is never complicated, and our way of eating accords with the growing preference for wholesome food based on local ingredients.

CALABRIA'S STORY

The history of Calabria is a tale of successive invasions and its people's stubborn resistance to their conquerors. Among the few fortunate legacies from this unsettled past are the many foods and cooking methods introduced to the region by its occupiers.

Archaeologists continue to find evidence in Calabria of an early human presence. In 1961, just outside the mountain village of Papasìdero, northeast of Scalea, researchers discovered a prehistoric cave—the grotta del Romito. At its entrance was a large boulder finely incised with the image of a now-extinct bull, a drawing believed to be twelve thousand years old and one of the earliest examples of Paleolithic art in Italy.

By the Iron Age (1000 B.C.), the Enotrians had become the most powerful tribe in the area. Recent archaeological finds suggest that the Enotrians made wine and olive oil, well before the arrival of the Greeks, who often get the credit for bringing the grape and the olive to Southern Italy.

But it was surely the Greeks who first brought Calabria to the forefront of history. Beginning in the eighth century B.C., they founded many powerful cities all along the Adriatic, Ionian, and Tyrrhenian coasts and gave this area the name of Magna Graecia ("Greater Greece"). The modern cities of Reggio Calabria, Locri, Crotone, and Sibari were all established by the Greeks and were major settlements of that era. Pythagoras, the eminent Greek mathematician and philosopher, settled in Crotone and founded a school there. The Greeks brought honey, chick peas, and figs to Calabria, expanded the planting of grapes and olives, and introduced many grape varieties.

Calabria passed from the Greeks to the Romans, then successively to the Byzantines, Lombards, Normans, Swabians, Angevins, and Aragonese. In 1504, the French and the Spanish divided Italy between them, with Spain getting Calabria. The Spanish conquest brought many evils, but it did introduce important foods to Calabria from the Spanish territories of the New World, such as tomatoes, potatoes, peppers, beans, sweet potatoes, prickly pear, and maize.

The Spanish ruled for two hundred years and sowed much discontent in Calabria through their feudal system, which kept the landed gentry wealthy and the peasants impoverished and virtually enslaved. Bourbon kings succeeded the Spanish and ruled, with some interruptions, until 1860, when Garibaldi led the uprisings that abolished the monarchy and helped unite Italy.

Over many centuries, since the fall of the Roman Empire, Calabrians had gradually abandoned the Greek settlements on the coast and moved to the mountains. They were fleeing malaria and the repeated incursions of marauding invaders. As late as the nineteenth century, the isolation of these mountain dwellers remained profound. At the time of Italy's unification, in 1861, only one road traversed Calabria from north to south, and the vast majority of towns were inaccessible by paved road.

Under a unified Italy, Southerners dared to hope for investment and progress, but those hopes were soon dashed. Calabrians, for good reason, had long been suspicious of government promises, but in the wake of unification, the disillusionment was deep indeed, as the government appeared to do little to address the South's economic troubles. In the last quarter of the nineteenth century, more than 275,000 Calabrians left Italy, many for North and South America. An even larger exodus occurred in the first fifteen years of the new century, when more than 600,000 Calabrians emigrated.

Many of these immigrants were married men who expected to work for a few years in the New World and eventually return to their families with a nest egg for a farm or a business venture. In reality, few did return. The wives they left behind were known as "white widows" because they effectively had no husbands, although they weren't consigned to the dreary black garments of the true widow. Some small Calabrian villages in the early twentieth century were virtually devoid of able-bodied men. Occasionally, a husband would return for a brief family visit, staying just long enough to become reacquainted with his young children and to leave his wife pregnant again.

Immigration slowed during the war years but picked up again after World War II. More than 400,000 Calabrians left between 1946 and 1961.

And then, gradually but inexorably, conditions began to improve. Completed in 1974, a new 500-kilometer (310-mile) *autostrada*, or highway, connected Reggio di Calabria to Naples, making it possible to transport goods and people quickly. Roads were built to the mountain villages, ending the isolation of the highland residents. For lack of roads, my father could not get his fresh cheese to market easily in the 1960s. Today, city people drive into the hills to buy fresh ricotta from the shepherds, who are often sold out by noon.

With the highway in place, investors saw new potential in Calabria's scenic western coast. Many developers snapped up property and built condominiums and beach resorts in Scalea. The construction boom brought jobs, and the tourist influx lured restaurants and services that have brought a measure of prosperity to Calabria.

In recent years, the growth of *agriturismi*, or farms welcoming overnight visitors, has helped bring income to Calabria's rural areas, providing the impetus and the funds to restore some lovely properties. Some *agriturismi* are simple farmsteads, offering rustic accommodations and perhaps the chance to watch a shepherd milk his goats or make cheese. Others are more polished, with a hired chef in the dining room and a swimming pool for guests. Dattilo in Strongoli Marina, Le Colline del Gelso near Rossano, and Le Carolee in Pianopoli, near Lamezia Terme, are just three of the many agricultural estates that house guests comfortably and treat them to good local cooking. Some of the recipes in the book, such as Rita Callipo's Creamy Red Onion Soup (page 101) and Spaghetti with a Creamy Potato and Pancetta Sauce (page 66), have been inspired by dishes I tasted at an *agriturismo*.

Every one of Calabria's five provinces has charming towns and villages to visit, unusual food specialties to sample, and signature dishes rarely seen elsewhere. It delights me to see my native region thriving and becoming a rewarding and hospitable destination for the food-loving traveler.

Key Ingredients

Included here are a few essential seasonings and ingredients in the Calabrian kitchen, and some guidelines on how to select and use them.

ANCHOVIES

Among store-bought anchovies, my preference is whole anchovies layered in salt, such as those packed by Agostino Recca in Sicily. Anchovy processors tend to put their best-quality fish under salt. The second-tier fish are filleted and packed in olive oil, and everything else becomes anchovy paste. Anchovies packed in salt remain firm, moist, and meaty; they aren't at all fishy when fresh from the tin. But the Recca tins are large—about three pounds—and most home cooks can't use all the anchovies before they go rancid from exposure to air. To prevent rancidity, after opening the tin, repack the anchovies in a clean, wide-mouth glass canning jar, sprinkling sea salt or kosher salt between the layers. Covered and refrigerated, the anchovies will keep indefinitely.

CANNED TOMATOES

I am fortunate to have a garden where I can grow my own tomatoes for canning, but I realize that most people must rely on commercially canned tomatoes for much of the year. I have sampled many brands of canned tomatoes in search of some I can recommend. Most brands contain citric acid to lower the pH so the tomatoes can be processed faster. Many also contain calcium chloride to keep the tomatoes firm and attractive. But for Calabrian-style sauces, you don't want firm tomatoes; you want them soft, so they collapse quickly into a sauce. Nor do you want the tart taste of citric acid. I also dislike the thick tomato puree that surrounds most canned tomatoes, preferring instead a tomato canned in its natural juices.

In my experience, the best-tasting canned tomatoes with the best texture are Italian San Marzano tomatoes. These are the ones I have used when testing any recipes that call for canned tomatoes. Become a label reader: look for brands without citric acid or calcium chloride. They should also say "San Marzano DOP" on the label, a sign that the can contains true San Marzano tomatoes that merit the European Union's protected designation of origin status. The San Marzano tomato is an elongated plum-type tomato with a thin skin and meaty flesh. You will find that the recipes in this book work with any canned plum-type tomato, but they will taste best if made with San Marzano DOP tomatoes with no additives. Seek them out in specialty food stores and well-stocked supermarkets.

September in Oakland means canning San Marzano tomatoes from my garden for the winter with my mother.

When using canned tomatoes, place them in a bowl and break them up well with your fingers. Remove any fragments of skin or tough bits around the core. Unless the recipe directs otherwise, use the entire contents of the can—the tomatoes and the juices or puree surrounding them.

CANNED TUNA

Calabrians adore canned tuna. In markets there, the best-quality canned tuna is costly and held in high regard. At the store, look for tuna packed in olive oil, preferably from Calabria, Sicily, Spain, or Portugal. The Callipo brand from Calabria is superb (see Resources, page 370). Top of the line is the *tonno di tonnara*, identified on the label as bluefin tuna, famous for its rich, dark meat. Callipo's yellowfin tuna—what Americans call ahi and Italians simply call *tonno*—is also excellent, identified on the label as "light tuna."

If you can find it, buy tuna packed in glass jars so you can see for yourself that the chunks are thick and firm. Lesser-quality tuna in tins may be mushy and reduced to flakes. For an occasional indulgence, invest in a jar of *ventresca*, or tuna belly, the most succulent part of the fish. Save *ventresca* for salads, where you can appreciate its silky texture.

Don't discard the oil from the tuna jar or tin without tasting it first. If it tastes good, you can use it to replace some of the oil in a dish, such as in a dressing for tomato salad or in a pasta sauce with tuna. Water-packed tuna is unsuitable for Calabrian recipes.

CAPERS

The unopened flower buds of a Mediterranean shrub (*Capparis spinosa*), capers are harvested from spring through fall and processed with brine or salt to make a pungent seasoning. Calabrian cooks value capers for the piquant, lightly salty taste they add to seafood salads, pasta sauces, and breadcrumb-based stuffings for swordfish and tuna. Caper use is greatest in the southernmost province of Reggio Calabria, reflecting the influence of neighboring Sicily, a caper producer.

Some manufacturers pickle capers in brine; others pack them in salt to preserve them. I prefer salt-packed capers as they have a pure, floral taste, unadulterated by the vinegar in the brine. Salt-packed capers must be rinsed thoroughly or they can make a dish too salty.

Both brined and salt-packed capers last indefinitely in the refrigerator. Rinse brined capers well to minimize the vinegar taste; if they are large, chop them coarsely before using.

DRIED OREGANO

In Calabria, no one grows oregano in a home garden, as it proliferates in the wild. Foragers harvest the oregano when it flowers in July, dry it on the stem, and sell it in large bunches at farmers' markets and in local shops. Many Calabrians dry their own oregano, collecting a year's supply while on a hike or a summer picnic in the country, then tying the stems together in bundles and hanging them upside down in a shady spot to dry. Because the herb remains on the stem, it retains far more aroma than the musty loose leaves available in jars in supermarkets.

If you grow oregano and would like to dry your own, harvest the herb while it is in full flower, cutting it at the base so you have long stems. Bundle the stems and tie them together with kitchen string. Hang the bundle upside down outdoors in a shady spot, away from direct sun. Depending on the weather, the leaves will be fully dry in two to four weeks. They should be stiff and dry enough to crumble.

Keep dried oregano stems in a sealed plastic bag in a cool, dark pantry. To use, pull the flowers and leaves from the stem, crushing them with your fingers to release their aromatic oils. Alternatively, you can pull all the flowers and leaves off the stems, discard the stems, and store just the flowers and leaves in an airtight bag or glass jar. Calabrians do not consider dried oregano a second-best alternative to the fresh herb. In fact, we rarely use fresh oregano, preferring the intense aroma of the herb after it is dried.

Drying fresh oregano in my backyard in Oakland

FLOUR

I use unbleached all-purpose flour for all my pasta and bread doughs and pastry making. I prefer to weigh flour for these recipes because it is more accurate than measuring the volume, but I have provided both weight and volume measures. To measure flour accurately, spoon it into a measuring cup, overfilling the cup slightly, then use a table knife to scrape off the excess. Don't use the cup to scoop flour out of a bag, or you will pack the flour and your measure will not be equivalent to mine in weight.

OLIVE OIL

Extra virgin olive oil is the flavor base of the Calabrian kitchen. We use it liberally as an ingredient, not in drizzles as a finishing oil. Olive trees cover almost 25 percent of the arable land in Calabria, so the oil from these widespread trees is not considered precious or something to use with restraint.

In my California kitchen, I use only extra virgin, whether I am sautéing, deep-frying, or making a salad dressing. Although many people think you can't deep-fry in extra virgin olive oil—that the oil will break down when heated high enough for frying—that is not true. You can heat extra virgin olive oil to 375°F (190°C), the temperature I use for virtually all fried foods, and it does not break down. Its smoking point is between 400°F and 420°F (205°C to 215°C).

Extra virgin olive oil, which is extracted without heat or chemicals, does cost more than refined olive oil, but I believe the extra money is well spent. Extra virgin olive oil has considerably more flavor and more antioxidants, which means it delivers more health benefits. You don't need to pay a fortune for it, as you would if you bought only the fancy 750-milliliter bottles at specialty stores. Ethnic markets often sell extra virgin olive oil from Italy or other Mediterranean countries at an affordable price, typically in three-liter tins. Keep olive oil in a cool, dark place. It deteriorates quickly when exposed to heat or light.

Calabria produces more olive oil than any other Italian region except for Puglia, but only 30 percent of its production is extra virgin. Until recent times, most Calabrian growers managed their orchards for quantity, not quality, and few growers bottled their own oil. Instead, they sold it in bulk and it vanished into a blend—no doubt labeled, in some instances, as the more prized Tuscan oil.

Today, the Calabrian olive oil industry is in transition, with many producers putting quality first and planting new orchards accordingly. The old indigenous Calabrian olive varieties—Carolea, Tondina, and Dolce di Rossano, among others—produce a sweet, buttery oil with little piquancy. The progressive producers are now planting varieties from other parts of Italy, such as the Coratina from Puglia and the Frantoio from Tuscany, that are capable of yielding a more perfumed and piquant oil with longer shelf life.

The European Union has granted two areas of Calabria the coveted DOP (*denominazione di origine protetta*, or protected designation of origin) status for extra virgin olive oil, similar to an appellation for wine. The two DOP zones are Bruzio (from the province of Cosenza) and Lamezia (from the province of Catanzaro), and as the region's oil quality improves, I expect that America will see more of these smooth and mellow oils.

PECORINO CHEESE FOR GRATING

By far the dominant cheese used for grating in the Calabrian kitchen is aged pecorino, a hard sheep's milk cheese with a pale ivory interior and a sharp, salty taste. Calabria's mountainous landscape, with its limited pasture, is more hospitable to sheep than to cows, so the regional preference veers naturally to sheep's milk cheeses. Although Calabrians enjoy pecorino cheese as a sliceable table cheese when it is young and mellow, the cheese used for grating over pasta and soups comes from an aged wheel. These wheels may be anywhere from three to twelve months old, becoming progressively drier, saltier, more piquant and concentrated in flavor as they age. For a Calabrian, many pasta and vegetables dishes taste incomplete until they are showered with freshly grated aged pecorino.

The pecorino romano sold in the United States can be excessively salty, so taste before you buy, if possible. If you can't find Calabrian pecorino, look for the widely available Locatelli brand; it is less salty than most and a good choice for Calabrian cooking.

The fine holes on a four-sided box grater are ideal for grating aged pecorino. A Microplane grates the cheese too fine for my taste.

POLENTA

Most Calabrians use fine cornmeal for polenta, not the coarse cornmeal that is commonly labeled as polenta in the United States. Any American brand of fine cornmeal, white or yellow, stoneground or not, will work well in Calabrian recipes. I successfully tested recipes with Albers, a brand widely available on the West Coast. With Italian brands such as Moretti (page 369), look for packages labeled as "corn flour." Despite its name, this product has the texture of American cornmeal and is suitable for the polenta recipes in this book.

RED PEPPER, HOT AND SWEET

My Calabrian kitchen in America could not function without *peperoncini* (hot peppers) and *pepe rosso* (sweet red pepper). When my parents first settled in California in the mid 1970s, they could not find either hot peppers or sweet peppers with the characteristic Calabrian taste, so they began growing their own. We have done so ever since, although I have now found readily available substitutes for both.

The *peperoncino* my father grows is a small, very hot pepper slightly larger than a Thai bird pepper. We use it fresh in summer, in both its green (unripe) and red states, and we sun dry the fresh ripe peppers for winter use. We leave some of these

Homegrown *peperoncini*, our beloved Calabrian hot peppers, from our garden in Oakland

dried red peppers whole, and we grind some (see page 303). The ground hot red pepper available at Indian markets, often labeled simply "ground chili," is the closest substitute. Red pepper flakes are too coarse; cayenne pepper would be a better choice. Thai bird peppers, red and green, or fresh cayenne peppers are the best approximation of the fresh hot peppers in my garden. We use the same word—*peperoncino*—for a fresh hot pepper, a dried hot pepper, and ground hot red pepper. Throughout this book, I have used the phrase "ground hot red pepper" rather than "ground chili" for fear that people might mistakenly use chili powder, a seasoning blend that is not appropriate.

Pepe rosso—literally, "red pepper"— resembles mild Spanish paprika but it is sweeter. It contributes a mellow pepper flavor and rich, brick-red color to many dishes, such as Spicy Braised Rabbit with Sweet Peppers and Oregano (page 222). My mother and I make it ourselves (page 304) from the long sweet Italian peppers that my father grows. Mild, unsmoked Spanish paprika is the closest substitute. For the recipes in this book, I have translated *pepe rosso* as Calabrian paprika.

SALT

I use only Diamond Crystal kosher salt in cooking, as it contains no additives and has a clean, unadulterated taste. Sea salt, also additive free, is another good choice, but it tends to be more expensive. Table salt contains additives to prevent it from clumping, and it is finer than kosher salt, so 1 teaspoon of table salt will be saltier than 1 teaspoon of kosher salt.

All the salt measurements in this book are based on Diamond Crystal kosher salt and may not be accurate for other salts that are finer or coarser.

SALT COD

The thick, meaty salt cod (*baccalà*) that Calabrians adore comes primarily from Norway and Iceland, prepared from fish caught in the frigid waters of the North Atlantic. Perhaps because Calabrians are such avid consumers and thus discriminating about quality, they get excellent salt cod—thick, moist, white fillets that take only two or three days to rehydrate (see "To soak salt cod," page 184). If you travel to Calabria, leave room in your suitcase for salt cod, as it is much finer than the products available in the United States—and less costly, too. You can freeze it in a heavy-duty plastic storage bag without loss of quality for up to one year.

I am often disappointed by the salt cod I purchase in California, which comes mostly from Nova Scotia or other parts of Canada. Packers tend to put a single attractive piece on the top of the package, and scraps or thin tail pieces underneath. I have found the best quality at Italian, Spanish, and Portuguese markets, where you can often buy a whole side and examine it for quality—difficult when the salt cod is packed in a wooden box. In my experience, the best salt cod comes from Norway and still has the skin attached. I usually leave the skin on when I cook salt cod, as it has a gelatinous quality and contributes body to the sauce, but you can remove it after soaking the fish and before cooking if you like.

Good salt cod is white, not yellowish, and the center fillet should be thick. Read the label carefully or ask the merchant to make sure you are buying cod. I have seen packages labeled as *baccalà* but identified as haddock on the ingredient list.

WILD FENNEL SEED

Similar in shape to the cultivated fennel seed available on supermarket spice racks, wild fennel seed is smaller and has a more pungent, licorice-like taste. My mother, the forager, harvests it every summer (page 215); it thrives in vacant lots near her home and abandoned fields throughout Northern California. I add it to fresh Calabrian sausage and use it to season the green and ripe olives that I cure in the fall. For the recipes in this book, I highly recommend purchasing wild fennel seed from Calabria, available by mail order (page 370). You can substitute supermarket fennel seed, but its flavor is more dilute, a difference you can't erase by using more.

A NOTE ABOUT THE WINE SELECTIONS

Shelley Lindgren, co-proprietor of A16 and SPQR restaurants in San Francisco, developed the wine suggestions for the recipes in this book. Lindgren restricted her selections to wines from Southern Italy that are available in the United States, a category that is rapidly growing. Even so, many of these wines have limited distribution, so Lindgren has also suggested a more widely available alternative. Although she is deeply knowledgeable about the region, many readers may be confused by the unfamiliar winery names, grape names, and appellations. For clarity, here is the format she followed in listing the wines:

Winery or producer name
Wine name (proprietary wine and vineyard names are in quotes)
Appellation
Region

Antipasti

Antipasti as we know them today were not part of the traditional Calabrian meal of the past. For most of the region's history, its people have been primarily farmers and shepherds, accustomed to strenuous physical labor and the appetite that goes with it. When these hard-working rural people sat down to a meal, they went straight to pasta or *minestra* (thick soup), belly-filling foods that quelled their hunger quickly. Even well-to-do Calabrians—the major land owners, barons, and counts—did not launch their meals with antipasti, judging from the eighteenth- and nineteenth-century accounts of the British on their European Grand Tour.

But since the 1970s, tourism has mushroomed in Calabria, bringing people from all over Europe on holiday, most of whom expect to dine in a more relaxed fashion than farmers do. Consequently, modern Calabrian restaurants, even the simplest ones, will usually offer an assortment of antipasti. Home cooks, too, now prepare antipasti, albeit only when guests are coming or on Sundays and feast days.

For the most part, the Calabrian antipasto table today includes dishes that Calabrians have always eaten but in another context, typically as a snack or side dish. The region boasts an impressive repertoire of *polpette*, a word for which there is no adequate English translation. Made with meat, *polpette* are certainly meatballs, but Calabrians make many meatless *polpette*—with tuna, salt cod, eggplant, or ricotta. *Polpette* traditionally appear on the home table as a second course, but today, you may find them on a restaurant's antipasto platter. Fritters (*frittelle*) made with fresh or dried sweet red peppers, anchovies, zucchini blossoms, or salt cod would, in a typical Calabrian home, constitute a second course, along with a vegetable. But many restaurants have moved them to the antipasto category.

Pictured on left: A Calabrian antipasti table (clockwise from top): crostini with *bottarga*; preserved zucchini; crostini with fresh sardines; cracked green olives; preserved green tomatoes; eggplant meatballs

Even the *salumi* (cured meats), cheeses, and vegetables preserved under oil or vinegar that commonly comprise an antipasto course today were not used in that way historically. Calabrians of my father's generation would have a little sliced prosciutto or cured sausage for their second course at dinner, alongside a frittata perhaps, with a salad to follow. Even today, my parents and their contemporaries view their home-preserved vegetables as a room-temperature side dish or salad to have with their second course, not as an antipasto.

When I was a child, my mother would give me a slice of homemade bread spread with warm tomato sauce to keep me quiet until dinner was ready. In summer, I would fetch a ripe tomato from the garden, cut it in half, and rub it all over a slice of bread until only the skin remained in my hand. With a pinch of salt on top, it made a snack I love to this day. Sometimes my mother would appease her hungry only child with homemade *friselle* (Calabrian rusks) topped with olive oil, oregano, and garlic (page 35), a wholesome nibble that I often make for my children today when they come home from school. We didn't think we were eating antipasti in those days, but any of these snacks would be appropriate on a Calabrian antipasto platter today.

Traveling through Calabria, you will see some regional variation in the antipasti being offered. In the mountainous region of La Sila, a typical platter might include wild mushrooms preserved under oil (page 283); local prosciutto, *soppressata*, or *salsiccia Calabrese* (cured spicy sausage); cracked green olives; breadcrumb-stuffed zucchini; and a slice of the local Caciocavallo cheese. On the east coast, around Crotone and Cirò, an antipasto platter is almost certain to include *sardella* (page 42), a fiery seafood and red pepper condiment typically spread on crostini. On the west coast, in the region of Vibo Valentia, crostini are topped instead with *'nduja* (page 199), a preserved pork spread similar to French rillettes but spicy. *'Nduja* is a specialty of Spilinga, a village just south of Tropea, and you should go out of your way to try it in Calabria because you will probably not find it in the United States.

The restaurants on the Tyrrhenian coast are the place to sample a variety of ocean-based antipasti, such as fritters with anchovies, seaweed, or the tiny newborn fish known as *neonate*; buttered crostini with *bottarga* (page 42), preserved tuna roe; and the now trendy carpaccio made with swordfish or octopus. *Fragaglia* is another dish to look for on restaurant menus on the Tyrrhenian coast. It's a *fritto misto* of small whole fish—whatever the sea provides—presented hot, crisp, and crunchy, and eaten whole, bones and all.

In addition to the antipasti in this chapter, many of the traditional Calabrian preserves make appropriate additions to an antipasto course. Don't hesitate to borrow from that collection to enhance an antipasto platter or buffet. Consider Green Tomatoes Preserved in Oil (page 279); Pickled Eggplant Preserved in Oil with Hot Peppers, Wild Fennel, and Garlic (page 281); or Fresh Tuna Preserved Under Oil (page 288). Some recipes from this book's vegetable chapter also make excellent antipasti, such as Sun-Dried Zucchini with Calabrian Paprika (page 248) and Fried Cauliflower (page 266).

Accompany your antipasti with My Family's Everyday Bread (page 119) or another dense and crusty loaf, and your Calabrian meal will be off to a fine start.

Olive Verdi Schiacciate

CRACKED GREEN OLIVES WITH FENNEL AND HOT PEPPER

All fresh olives are green when unripe, darkening to purple, reddish-brown, or black when fully ripe. Whether green or ripe, most varieties are intensely bitter, and that bitterness must be extracted to make the olives edible.

To cure green (unripe) olives, most Calabrians crack them and remove the pits, then use daily changes of water to leach out the bitter compounds. Pitting them accelerates the leaching, which might otherwise drag on for weeks. Once most of the bitterness is gone, the olives spend a day in salt water to season them. Then they are drained and weighted to remove the excess water that would hasten their spoilage.

In the old days, Calabrians would dress them at this point with olive oil, wild fennel seed, hot peppers, and garlic, and keep them in the pantry with a weight on top so the olives were submerged in oil. Even so, they were only enjoyable for a few weeks, as they would gradually soften. Most people would consume their green olives by Christmas and then move on to their ripe black olives (page 27).

Today, I freeze the cured olives in plastic freezer bags and thaw them only as I need them. You can freeze them dressed or undressed; it makes no difference. Once dressed, these glistening green olives are firm, even a little crunchy, and infused with their spicy seasoning. They have a clean, faintly bitter taste, without the lush oiliness of a ripe olive. Compared to store-bought green olives, which often taste too briny and overdressed with tired herbs, these homemade olives have a fresher taste, with more vivid seasoning. Because they don't have pits, we don't eat them one at a time, as you would consume an unpitted olive. Instead we scoop them onto a slice of bread or eat them by the spoonful, as you might eat marinated chick peas. Although American markets

Cracked Green Olives

sell so-called cracked olives that have merely been slashed, not pitted, to a Calabrian an *olive schiacciate,* or crushed olive, has had the pit removed.

In both Calabria and California, green olives are usually ready to pick in October, depending on the year. They should be fully green and unblemished, with no sign that they are beginning to ripen to black. In California, you can sometimes find fresh green olives in the fall at farmers' markets and specialty produce markets. You can also order them online (see Resources, page 369). Choose a medium to large variety, such as Manzanilla. Extra-large California olives, sometimes identified as "Colossal," are hard to pit without crushing them and are not typical of what you would find in Calabria. If you can't locate fresh olives or don't want to bother curing them, you can use the same dressing on cracked and pitted Picholine or Lucques olives or other store-bought green olives.

SUGGESTED WINE: Cantine Lento Greco Bianco, Lamezia, Calabria
A white wine with tropical and mineral aromas.
ALTERNATE: New Zealand Sauvignon Blanc

---

3 pounds (1½ kilograms) fresh (uncured) green olives, such as
    Manzanilla, see Resources (page 369)

Kosher salt

¾ cup (175 milliliters) extra virgin olive oil

1½ teaspoons wild fennel seeds (page 215) *or* store-bought fennel seeds

6 small fresh hot red peppers, such as cayenne or Thai, sliced

6 garlic cloves, sliced

WITH A HAMMER or meat mallet, crack each olive just enough to remove the pit; you want to keep the olives as intact as possible. Remove the pits and place the olives in a plastic container full of cold water. If you are curing a large quantity of olives, use a plastic food-grade bucket. The olives must be placed in water immediately after you crack them or they will turn dark.

Keep the olives submerged by placing a plate directly on top. One easy way to keep the olives together and submerged is to pack them in a mesh bag like the ones that onions and oranges are often packed in at the supermarket. Tie the bag shut, submerge in the water, and place a weight on top.

Keep the olives at room temperature, changing the water every day until the olives no longer taste bitter when you sample them. This process can take ten to twelve days. On the final day, drain the olives in a sieve set over a bowl. Measure the volume of water. Fill a bowl with the same volume of fresh water and add kosher salt in the ratio of ¾ cup (105 grams) salt to 1 gallon (4 liters) of water, stirring until the salt dissolves. Discard the previously used water. Submerge the olives in the freshly mixed salt water and let stand for 24 hours to season them.

Drain the olives and place in a colander. Top with a weight, such as a heavy plastic bucket filled with water, and let stand for 8 to 10 hours to extract as much water from the olives as possible.

At this point you can dress them or freeze them in plastic freezer storage bags for future use. Thaw frozen olives before dressing them.

To dress the olives, place them in a small bowl and toss with olive oil, fennel seeds, peppers, and garlic. For best flavor, let the dressed olives stand for a few hours before serving.

MAKES ABOUT 6 CUPS CURED OLIVES (1 POUND 14 OUNCES/850 GRAMS)

Olive Nere Secche con Peperoncino
DRY-CURED BLACK OLIVES WITH HOT RED PEPPER AND FENNEL

The olives on my parents' trees in Calabria would ripen fully in December, turning black and beginning to fall from the tree. My mother remembers them being mild enough to eat without curing, but that is not the case with the fresh ripe olives I find in California. They are bitter and must be salted to leach out the bitter juices.

Dry curing is a method of de-bittering ripe olives with dry salt, as opposed to a wet brine. Over a period of about two weeks, the salt draws out the moisture, the olives shrivel, and the bitterness diminishes. When I am satisfied with the way they taste, I put them in the freezer. I thaw a cup or two as needed, then season them with olive oil, garlic, fennel seeds, and hot pepper. Despite being cured in salt, these olives aren't overly salty; they are mellow, oily, soft, and rich. With a platter of sliced cured meats, such as *soppressata* or prosciutto, they make an instant antipasto.

California markets sometimes carry ripe olives in the late fall. You can also mail-order them (see Resources, page 369). You can cure any variety, but if you have a choice, choose a medium-size olive, not the so-called jumbo or colossal types, which may take a long time to cure. You can also use this marinade on store-bought dry-cured olives as long as they are not already seasoned with herbs and spices.

SUGGESTED WINE: Santa Venere Cirò Rosato, Calabria
A dry, fruity rosé with aromas of tomato water and dried oregano.
ALTERNATE: any dry rosé

---

3 pounds (1½ kilograms) freshly picked black (ripe) olives

¼ cup (35 grams) kosher salt

SEASONING

1 cup (150 grams) homemade dry-cured black olives, thawed if frozen, *or* store-bought dry-cured black olives

1 tablespoon extra virgin olive oil

1 large garlic clove, halved crosswise, then thinly sliced

½ teaspoon Calabrian paprika (page 304) *or* Spanish sweet paprika

¼ teaspoon ground hot red pepper, or to taste

¼ teaspoon fennel seeds, preferably wild fennel seed

TO DRY-CURE FRESH OLIVES: Rinse the olives well. Drain and place in a bowl without drying them so they are still moist. Add the salt and toss to coat well. Keep the olives at room temperature, uncovered, and toss them two to three times a day over the next five days to encourage the salt to dissolve. After five days, place the olives in a single layer on a piece of plain cardboard or on a baking sheet lined with the heavy brown paper from a deconstructed grocery bag. Do not use an aluminum baking sheet as the salt will etch it.

Once a day, turn the olives to help the drying process. Continue drying and turning them daily until the olives have shriveled and no longer taste bitter, a process that may take two weeks.

Transfer the olives to heavy-duty freezer bags and store in the freezer. To season and serve, thaw only as many as you need, allowing one day to thaw. After seasoning, the olives can be kept at room temperature for two days.

TO SEASON DRY-CURED OLIVES: Place the olives in a bowl and toss with the olive oil, garlic, paprika, and hot pepper. If using store-bought fennel seeds, crush them lightly in a mortar before adding to the bowl. If using the smaller wild fennel seeds, add to the bowl without crushing them. Let stand for at least 4 hours or up to one day before serving.

MAKES ABOUT 6 CUPS CURED OLIVES (1 POUND 14 OUNCES/850 GRAMS)

A Winter Antipasto Menu

Coppa, Soppressata, Prosciutto
Young pecorino or Caciocavallo cheese
Favas and Olives (page 29)
Mushrooms Preserved in Oil with Hot Peppers, Wild Fennel, and Garlic (page 281)

Fave Arrappate
FAVAS AND OLIVES

The tiny mountaintop village of Civita, near Castrovillari, is a required stop for anyone who wants to know more about the history of the Arbëresh people in Calabria. A small museum in the town preserves costumes, tools, and photos that help illuminate the way of life of these Calabrians of Albanian descent (page 62). Just around the corner from the museum, Ristorante Kamastra serves excellent local food, including a few Arbëresh dishes and this unusual appetizer. *Fave arrappate* means "wrinkled favas," although only the olives are wrinkled. The dried favas are boiled, then cooled and tossed with dry-cured olives, olive oil, garlic, and hot red pepper. I think the combination is a nice change of pace from the predictable bowl of olives before dinner.

SUGGESTED WINE: Clelia Romano "Colli di Lapio," Fiano di Avellino, Campania
A crisp white wine with aromas of honeydew melon, peach, and flint.
ALTERNATE: Chablis with no oak

½ pound (225 grams) dried unpeeled fava beans, soaked overnight

2 tablespoons kosher salt

1 cup (150 grams) dry-cured olives

4 garlic cloves, coarsely chopped

3 tablespoons extra virgin olive oil

¼ teaspoon ground hot red pepper, or more to taste

DRAIN THE BEANS and put them in a 4-quart (4-liter) pot with 2 quarts (2 liters) cold water. Bring to a simmer over medium heat, then reduce the heat and simmer until the beans are barely tender; they should still be firm but not chalky. Begin testing them after about 40 minutes. Add the salt and let the beans cool in the liquid.

Drain the beans and put them in a bowl with the olives, garlic, olive oil, and hot pepper. Toss to coat the beans and olives with the seasonings. Taste and add salt if desired. Cover the bowl and let stand at room temperature for 12 to 24 hours before serving. Stir occasionally to redistribute the seasonings.

MAKES 4 CUPS, TO SERVE 8 TO 10

Alici Marinate

MARINATED FRESH ANCHOVIES WITH RED ONION AND PARSLEY

Many summer meals in Calabria start with a plate of marinated fresh anchovies in olive oil and some sturdy sliced country bread. These are not the familiar tinned anchovies but fresh fish that have been filleted, lightly pickled in vinegar until they turn white, then bathed in olive oil and garnished with chopped onion, parsley, and other seasonings. To make them successfully, you need absolutely fresh anchovies, no more than a day out of the water. Fish markets don't carry them often, but some fishmongers will order them for you.

SUGGESTED WINE: Alois Falanghina "Caulino," Terre del Volturno, Campania
A white wine with bright lemon-lime and pineapple aromas; crisp and nervy.
ALTERNATE: Sancerre or Albariño

1 pound (450 grams) fresh anchovies

2 teaspoons kosher salt

½ cup (125 milliliters) white wine vinegar

½ cup (125 milliliters) fresh lemon juice

Extra virgin olive oil

Garnishes: finely minced red onion, chopped flat-leaf parsley,
    chopped fresh hot red pepper or dried hot pepper flakes

CLEAN THE ANCHOVIES as directed on page 31. Remove the backbone from each anchovy by grasping the end of the backbone closest to the head and lifting it out. It usually pulls away cleanly from the flesh, although sometimes it clings. If it does cling, gently work the backbone free with your fingers, damaging the flesh as little as possible. Separate the boneless anchovy into two fillets.

Layer the anchovy fillets, skin side down, in a 9-inch-square (23-centimeter-square) glass or ceramic dish, or an oval dish of comparable volume. Sprinkle each layer evenly with salt. Cover with vinegar and lemon juice, submerging them completely. Cover the dish with plastic wrap and refrigerate for 8 hours.

Drain the vinegar and lemon juice completely. Pat the anchovies dry with paper towels. Wash and dry the container. Return the anchovies to the clean container and add enough olive oil to submerge the fillets. Cover the dish with plastic wrap and refrigerate for at least 24 hours or up to 4 days.

To serve, arrange on serving plates and sprinkle with red onion, parsley, and hot pepper to taste.

SERVES 8 TO 10

To Clean Fresh Anchovies or Sardines

Holding the fish under cold running water, rub off the scales with your thumbnail, scraping from tail to head. By hand, snap off the head and pull down; most of the innards will come out with the head. Use your thumbnail or a small paring knife to slit the belly down to the tail. Remove any remaining innards and rinse the interior.

A Summer Antipasto Menu

Crispy Eggplant Meatballs (page 32)
Calabrian Rusks with Fresh Tomato and Garlic Topping (page 35)
Marinated Fresh Anchovies with Red Onion and Parsley (page 30)
Homemade Ricotta (page 144)

Polpette di Melanzane
CRISPY EGGPLANT MEATBALLS

These meatless "meatballs" are found in both Calabria and Sicily, but Sicilians would add currants and pine nuts. In parts of Calabria, cooks tuck a cube of Caciocavallo cheese inside each ball. Some cooks omit the fine breadcrumbs on the outside, but I like the contrast of crunchy coating and creamy interior. Eggplant *polpette* make a great appetizer for a stand-up party because they are bite-size and can be eaten with your fingers. They look exactly like meatballs, and when the budget is tight, Calabrian cooks will simmer them (without the breadcrumb coating) in tomato sauce (see Variation, page 33). They serve them as a second course, following pasta tossed with the tomato sauce.

SUGGESTED WINE: Fattoria San Francesco "Ronco dei Quattroventi," Cirò Rosso Classico, Calabria
A modern-styled, medium-bodied red wine with tomato, mint, and cranberry aromas similar to those in Pinot Noir.
ALTERNATE: Pinot Noir

---

1 large eggplant, about 1 pound (450 grams), unpeeled

Kosher salt

1 cup (80 grams) fresh breadcrumbs (page 127), or more if needed

¼ cup (25 grams) freshly grated pecorino cheese

2 tablespoons minced flat-leaf parsley

1 garlic clove, minced

Freshly ground black pepper

1 large egg, lightly beaten

⅓ cup (50 grams) fine dry breadcrumbs (page 127)

Extra virgin olive oil for frying

CUT THE EGGPLANT into 1-inch (2½-centimeter) to 1½-inch (4-centimeter) cubes. Bring 2 quarts (2 liters) of water and 1 tablespoon salt to a boil in a 4-quart (4-liter) pot over high heat and add the eggplant. Boil uncovered until the eggplant is soft, about 10 minutes. The cubes want to float, so you will need to push them down into the water repeatedly with a wooden spoon. Drain in a colander and let cool, then press on the eggplant with a wooden spoon to remove excess water. The eggplant should be as dry as possible. Very finely chop by hand.

In a bowl, combine the eggplant, fresh breadcrumbs, cheese, parsley, and garlic. Blend the ingredients gently with a fork, then season to taste with salt and pepper. Mix the egg in thoroughly. In a small skillet lightly coated with olive oil, fry a tablespoon of the mixture and taste for seasoning.

Working with a little of the mixture at a time, roll between your palms into small balls about 1 inch (2½ centimeters) in diameter and set them on a tray. If the mixture is too moist to roll easily, stir in a few more fresh breadcrumbs. Put the fine breadcrumbs in a small bowl, roll each ball in the crumbs to coat evenly, then set the coated balls aside on a clean tray.

Pour olive oil in a 10-inch (25-centimeter) skillet to a depth of ½ inch (12 millimeters). Don't skimp on the oil or the meatballs won't fry properly. Turn the heat to medium. When the oil begins to shimmer, put a test ball in the skillet; it should sizzle immediately. If not, let the oil heat a little longer. When the oil is ready, carefully place half the balls in the skillet. They should fit in a single layer without crowding.

Fry the balls, turning them gently with a spoon so as not to break them, until deeply browned all over, about 3 minutes total. With a slotted spoon, transfer the balls as they are done to a tray lined with paper towels. Repeat with the remaining balls. Let cool for about 10 minutes, then serve.

MAKES ABOUT THIRTY-TWO 1-INCH (2½-CENTIMETER) MEATBALLS

Variation

Make a double batch of Quick Tomato Sauce (page 53). Shape the balls but do not coat them with fine breadcrumbs. Fry them in olive oil as directed above, then simmer them, uncovered, in the sauce over medium heat for 10 minutes. Boil one pound (450 grams) of long or short pasta, such as spaghetti or penne, drain, and toss with about 1½ cups (355 milliliters) of the sauce and some freshly grated pecorino cheese.

Friselle (Calabrian rusk) with tomato, basil, and garlic topping

Friselle con Pomodoro Crudo
CALABRIAN RUSKS WITH FRESH TOMATO AND GARLIC TOPPING

Friselle, the long-keeping dry toasts, or rusks, that Calabrians make from bread dough, come to life when soaked in water and spread with a juicy topping. In my house, we consume endless *friselle* in summer, when I can blanket them with chopped fresh tomato and basil. I know of no more appealing warm-weather lunch. The garlicky tomato juices and olive oil seep into the *friselle*, which trap them like a sponge.

Friselle are rock hard and must be soaked just long enough to make them tender but not so soft that they fall apart. They must be served within a few minutes or they will continue to soften until they can no longer support the topping. My children love *friselle* as an after-school snack dressed only with fruity green olive oil, oregano, and salt, as described in the Variation below. Calabrians consider *friselle* to be finger food, eaten by breaking off one small chunk at a time. If you don't have *friselle* on hand, you can use this tomato topping on bruschetta. Alternatively, you can make Quick *Friselle* (page 130) using store-bought *ciabatta*, the flat Italian loaf.

SUGGESTED WINE: Terradora DiPaolo Fiano di Avellino, Campania
An oak-aged white wine with minerality and aromas of cantaloupe and apple.
ALTERNATE: dry Vouvray

---

1 pint (½ liter) cherry tomatoes, halved if small or quartered if large

8 to 10 fresh basil leaves, coarsely chopped

1 garlic clove, finely minced

1 tablespoon extra virgin olive oil

1 small fresh hot red pepper, minced, optional

¼ teaspoon kosher salt, or more to taste

2 Calabrian Rusks (page 128) *or* Quick Friselle (page 130)

IN A BOWL, combine the tomatoes, basil, garlic, olive oil, and red pepper, if using. Season with salt.

Put each rusk on a separate dinner plate and run under cold water until the top is well moistened and there is a pool of water on the bottom of the plates. Let the rusks bathe in the water until they are no longer hard, 30 to 60 seconds; they should be tender enough to eat without crunching, but not mushy. The bottom halves tend to need more soaking time than the top halves. Drain and top each rusk with some of the tomato mixture, dividing it evenly. Serve immediately.

SERVES 4 TO 6

Calabrian Rusks with Olive Oil, Oregano, and Garlic Variation

Soak the rusks as described in the recipe and drain. Immediately rub each rusk with the cut side of a halved garlic clove. Drizzle generously with extra virgin olive oil, then sprinkle with kosher salt and dried oregano, crumbling the herb between your fingers as you add it. All proportions are to taste. Serve immediately.

Pipi 'Mpajanati
CALABRIAN SWEET PEPPER FRITTERS

Every summer, Calabrians harvest some of the elongated sweet red peppers in their gardens and dry them for the winter months (page 293). Drying concentrates the peppers' flavor and allows them to last through the winter, so they can contribute their sweet intensity to cold-weather sauces and stews. Rehydrated to soften them, the peppers also turn up in the savory fritters known as *pipi 'mpajanati*, a specialty of my hometown of Verbicaro that roughly translates as "peppers wrapped in dough."

For *pipi 'mpajanati*, the yeast-risen batter completely encases a strip of the pliant pepper. You don't see the pepper until you bite into the hot, crisp fritter. In my favorite variation (see Variation, page 38), an anchovy fillet is tucked inside the pepper, so there's a second surprise.

In restaurants, you will find some of the other fritters that Calabrians enjoy. Sometimes called *frittelle*, they may contain anchovies alone or, in season, whole zucchini blossoms or thinly sliced raw artichokes. Along the coast, cooks will chop fresh seaweed and fold it into the batter to make a golden fritter with the saline taste of the sea. At La Tartana restaurant in Cirella, a beach town on the Tyrrhenian coast, the waiters bring every table a complimentary appetizer of *frittelle con alghe*, seaweed fritters, the perfect nibble to inaugurate a seafood meal.

SUGGESTED WINE: Cantine Farro Falanghina "Campi Flegrei," Campania
A lean, racy, flinty white wine with the scent of lemon verbena and Key lime.
ALTERNATE: Albariño

---

3 cups (435 grams) unbleached all-purpose flour

1 envelope (¼ ounce) or 2¼ teaspoons active dry yeast

2½ teaspoons kosher salt, plus more as needed

2 cups (500 milliliters) lukewarm water

10 Sun-Dried Sweet Peppers (page 293) *or* other large mild dried
    red peppers (see Resources, page 369)

1 tablespoon extra virgin olive oil, plus more for frying

2 garlic cloves

IN A LARGE BOWL, stir together the flour, yeast, and salt. Add the water and stir with your hand or a wooden spoon until the mixture is smooth and well blended. It will be moist, more like a batter than a dough. Cover the bowl with plastic wrap and set in a warm place. Let rise until doubled in volume and bubbly on top, about 1½ hours.

Cut the dried peppers in half and remove the seeds. Bring a pot of water to a boil. Add the peppers and cook for one minute to soften them. Drain and place in a bowl of cold water until cool, then drain again and squeeze them gently to remove excess water.

Heat the 1 tablespoon olive oil in a large skillet and add the whole garlic cloves. When the garlic is golden all over, add the peppers, season with salt, and sauté briefly so the peppers pick up the flavors of the garlic oil. Set aside.

To fry the fritters, set a 10-inch (25-centimeter) skillet over moderately high heat. Add enough olive oil to come ¼ inch (6 millimeters) up the side of the pan. When you think the oil is hot enough, test with a few drops of batter; the batter should sizzle on contact.

Uncover the batter and place a pepper directly on the batter's surface. Using a large spoon, scoop some batter over the pepper to enclose it in the batter. Then gently scoop the fully batter-coated pepper into the hot oil. Repeat until you fill the skillet with fritters, but do not overcrowd it.

Fry the fritters, turning them with a fork or slotted spoon, until they are golden on all sides, 3 to 4 minutes total. Transfer them as they are done to a paper towel–lined platter. Continue until you have used up the peppers and batter, adding more oil if needed to maintain a depth of ¼ inch (6 millimeters). Sprinkle the fritters with salt and serve hot.

MAKES ABOUT 20 FRITTERS

Anchovy-Stuffed Pepper Variation

You will need 20 anchovy fillets. After sautéing the peppers in olive oil, let them cool. Place one anchovy fillet on each pepper half; fold the pepper lengthwise over the anchovy. Coat with batter and fry as directed above.

Crostini di Pesce

WARM SEAFOOD CROSTINI

Italians use the term *pesce azzurro*—literally, "blue fish"—to describe fresh anchovies, sardines, and mackerel because of the blue tone of their skin. In Calabria, cooks use these three fish interchangeably in some recipes, although mackerel are bigger and have a stronger taste. This warm fish topping for toasts can be made with any of these three *pesci azzurri*, but I like it best with anchovies, which are the smallest and mildest. The boneless fillets cook through almost as soon as they hit the sauté pan. Then I shred them fine with olive oil and garlic and mound the resulting paste on slices of warm, garlic-rubbed baguette. My cooking students, who for the most part have used only tinned anchovies, are often surprised that fresh anchovies are so delicate.

Serve as a stand-up appetizer with a glass of white wine or rosé.

SUGGESTED WINE: Michele Calò "Mjere," Salento Rosso, Apulia
A light, easy-drinking red wine made largely from the Negroamaro grape, with black olive and cinnamon aromas and bright acidity.
ALTERNATE: French Grenache or Grenache-based blend

---

1 pound (450 grams) fresh anchovies or sardines

TOASTS

12 baguette slices, sliced on the diagonal about ½ inch
(12 millimeters) thick

2 tablespoons extra virgin olive oil

1 garlic clove, halved

TOPPING

3 tablespoons extra virgin olive oil

2 garlic cloves, minced

2 tablespoons minced flat-leaf parsley

¾ teaspoon kosher salt

1 teaspoon lemon juice, or more to taste

Ground hot red pepper

CLEAN THE ANCHOVIES or sardines according to the directions on page 31. Remove the backbone from each fish by grasping the end of the backbone closest to the head and lifting it out. It usually pulls away cleanly from the flesh, although sometimes it clings. If it does cling, gently work the backbone free with your fingers, damaging the flesh as little as possible. Separate the boneless fish into two fillets.

PREPARE THE TOASTS: Preheat the broiler and position a rack 3 to 4 inches (8 to 10 centimeters) from the element. Brush the baguette slices on both sides with the olive oil. Place on a baking sheet and broil, turning once, until the slices are just beginning to color around the edges, about one minute per side. Do not overtoast them or they will be too hard. Let cool for a couple of minutes, then rub one side of each toast with the cut clove of garlic.

PREPARE THE TOPPING: Heat 2 tablespoons of the olive oil in a 10-inch (25-centimeter) skillet over medium heat. Add the garlic and parsley and sauté briefly to release the garlic fragrance. Add the fish fillets and the salt and raise the heat to high. Cook briskly, stirring with a fork and mashing the fish until the flesh breaks up and becomes pastelike, about 2 minutes. Remove from the heat and stir in the remaining 1 tablespoon olive oil and the lemon juice. Season to taste with hot pepper and add more lemon juice if the dish needs a little more spark.

Divide the warm topping among the toasts, spreading it in an even layer. Serve immediately.

MAKES ONE DOZEN *CROSTINI*

A *Seafood Antipasto Menu*
Crostini with *Bottarga* Butter (page 41)
Fresh Tuna Preserved Under Oil (page 288)
Zucchini Preserved in Oil with Hot Peppers, Garlic, and Mint (page 286)

Tartine al Burro di Bottarga

CROSTINI WITH *BOTTARGA* BUTTER

A *bottarga* producer near the town of Pizzo gave me a small sheet of recipes when she sold me her product, and this simple idea was among them. Using a Microplane or cheese grater, I grate enough *bottarga*—pressed and dried tuna roe—to turn softened butter salmon pink and give it the taste of the sea. Spread on a slice of fresh baguette, it makes a quickly assembled accompaniment to a pre-dinner glass of Prosecco or a cocktail. You can double or triple the recipe and freeze the flavored butter for future use. *Bottarga* butter is delicious on grilled fish, on fresh pasta, or stirred into a seafood risotto.

SUGGESTED WINE: Statti Mantonico, Calabria
A white wine with aromas of nectarine and mango, with a crisp, dry finish and the richness of Viognier.
ALTERNATE: Arneis

4 tablespoons (½ stick) unsalted butter, softened

1 packed tablespoon (5 grams) finely grated *bottarga* (pressed and
   dried tuna roe, see page 42), plus more for garnish

12 baguette slices, sliced on the diagonal about ½ inch
   (12 millimeters) thick

IN A SMALL BOWL, mash the butter with a fork or the back of a spoon until smooth. Add the *bottarga* and blend it in thoroughly. Spread about 1 teaspoon of the seasoned butter evenly on each slice of bread. Top with a little additional grated *bottarga* and serve.

SERVES 6

Two Calabrian Caviars

Every May and June, the female bluefin tuna approach the Gulf of Saint Eufemia, on Calabria's Tyrrhenian coast, in search of warm, nutrient-rich water for their eggs. If fishermen catch them first, their two plump egg sacs will be quickly removed, destined to become one of Calabria's great seafood delicacies: *bottarga di tonno*. Rosa Fanfullo, who makes excellent *bottarga* and sells it from her modest roadside shop in Pizzo (see Resources, page 370), described her method to me.

The egg sacs, which can weigh several pounds each, are washed well to rid them of blood, then brined for a day. After removing them from the brine, Fanfullo arranges the egg sacs on a table in a single layer, covers them thickly with sea salt, and places a board on top. Then she repeats the layering, stacking egg sacs, salt, and boards several layers high. The boards press the sacs, helping flatten and firm them. After fifteen days, she unpacks the stacks, discards the used salt, and repeats the layering process.

The egg sacs remain in the salt for about another three weeks. Then she brushes them off and air dries them for eight to ten days. By that time, the *bottarga* will be as firm, compact, and dry as a cured sausage. In fact, some people jokingly refer to it as *soppressata Calabrese.* Each sac will have lost 50 to 80 percent of its weight. The color will be a rosy tan, the color of canned tuna, and the aroma and flavor that of the sea.

This *caviale*, or tuna caviar, is understandably costly and held in esteem. After all, only female tuna have ovaries, and they have only two. To serve, the *bottarga* is grated into fine crumbs or shaved with a knife or vegetable peeler. It is added to dishes at the last moment and never cooked, which would destroy its delicate, briny flavor. Thinly sliced *bottarga* may be dressed with olive oil, lemon juice, a sprinkle of parsley, and pinch of hot pepper and served with bread. It can be shaved over beans, tomato salad, seafood pasta, or a grilled steak—anywhere an anchovy-like burst of flavor would be welcome. Although you can buy *bottarga* already grated, you will experience much more of its heady aroma by buying a whole one and grating or shaving it yourself as needed.

Peel back just enough of the thin skin to grate or shave as much *bottarga* as you need. Rewrap leftover *bottarga* well in plastic wrap and refrigerate. It will keep for months.

In contrast to *bottarga*, the *caviale dei poveri* ("caviar of the poor") has nothing to do with fish eggs and is thus not caviar by anyone's definition. But like *bottarga*, it demonstrates the Calabrian ingenuity for preserving the sea's bounty under salt.

Called *sardella* on the Ionic coast and *rosamarina* on the Tyrrhenian side, this bold condiment is made by brining some of the tiniest fish in the sea— newborn anchovies and sardines—and then packing them in a paste of hot red pepper and salt. Some people add *pepe rosso* (Calabrian sweet paprika) and wild fennel seed. *Sardella* is ready to eat after one month but will last in the refrigerator for up to one year.

When ready to consume, *sardella* is a fiery, brick-red spread that Calabrians eat on crostini, add to a tomato sauce for pasta, or use as a filling for *pitta,* the Calabrian stuffed pizza. The ingredients cost little, and the curing method is simple. For the Calabrian peasant of times past, the pungent *sardella* provided an affordable way to break the monotony of the daily diet.

Sardella is a kitchen staple on Calabria's east coast, where it is also called *mustica*. Many people still make it at home or buy it in bulk from a local producer, and some restaurants make their own. At the Ristorante Max in Cirò Marina, north of Crotone, the *sardella* is housemade and the chef serves it in the traditional fashion, with sliced red onion and tomato wedges. The diner spreads some *sardella* on a piece of bread, then tops it with onion and tomato, an only-in-Calabria antipasto.

Shops all over Calabria sell *sardella*, sometimes labeled *caviale Calabrese* or *caviale del Sud* (caviar of the South). It makes a fine souvenir. Fortunately, Calabrians have acknowledged in recent years that the unregulated harvest of *neonate*, the baby fish used for *sardella*, harms the ocean ecosystem. As a result, they have severely restricted the fishing season, which lasts only from February to April.

On the left: Stacks of *soppressata Calabrese* (tuna *bottarga*), handmade by Rosa Fanfullo at her shop in Pizzo. Rosa's son, on the right, is trimming the *bottarga* for packaging.

Fusilli Calabresi (page 85) with tomato sauce (first course) and pork ribs (second course; page 88)

Pasta

For Calabrian women of my grandmother's generation, knowing how to make fresh pasta was not only a survival skill but a measure of marriageability. According to custom, a Calabrian girl was not ready to marry until she knew at least fifteen ways to transform flour and water into pasta. A housewife who had mastered that many shapes could serve pasta every day without her family finding the diet monotonous.

Although the transmission of technique from mother to daughter has largely succumbed to modernity—many Calabrian women work outside the home and buy their fresh pasta at the supermarket—Calabrians still hold their highest praise for handmade pasta. In practically every family, a grandmother or aunt retains some fresh pasta-making skills and is pressed into duty on Sundays and holidays.

Calabrian creativity with pasta has produced a repertoire of traditional shapes that are rarely seen outside of the region (page 48). Most of these shapes have multiple dialect names, depending on where they are made. Even for a native like me, untangling these names can be a dizzying task. Not only does one shape often have several names, but the same name can apply to different shapes.

One feature common to many Calabrian pasta doughs is the absence of egg. Calabrians traditionally make fresh pasta with only flour and water, so our noodles never have the golden hue or the silky texture of pasta from Northern Italy. Our pasta is pale, with a pure wheat taste and a firm, resilient texture. Most Calabrians think Northern Italians overcook their pasta because we are accustomed to a noodle with more bite.

I can only speculate about why Calabrians never embraced egg pasta. If you have no meat, as Calabrians often did not in the past, you view eggs as a valued protein. Omit eggs from the pasta dough and you can sell them or have them as a second course, in place of meat. Even Calabrians who keep chickens and have their own eggs for much of the year would not add them to pasta dough. When I make *pappardelle* the Northern Italian way, with eggs in the dough, my mother thinks the pasta tastes too rich. The high-protein hard wheat (*grano duro*) that Calabrians use for pasta doesn't require egg to produce a dough, so that may be another reason that Calabrians leave out the eggs.

Commercially dried pasta in boxes was expensive in Calabria when my parents were young. It had to come from Naples, where the manufacturers were. If you had a parcel of flat land, as my father did, it was cheaper to grow wheat than to buy boxed pasta. My mother still recalls the primitive equipment used for threshing on the farm. The freshly harvested wheat was deposited on a cleared slab of dirt. Then a mule or ox pulling a grinding stone crushed the wheat while workers turned the wheat constantly with pitchforks so the grain would fall to the bottom.

My mother shaping fresh gnocchi with a ridged paddle

When the wind was just right, they would lift up the threshed wheat with shovels and let the wind blow off the chaff, leaving the grain behind. Then my parents would leave some grain for the owner of the stone, in payment, and take home the remaining whole grain in sacks.

Once a month or so, they would load a couple of these sacks of wheat on a donkey and go to the mill in Verbicaro, returning home with sacks of flour for pasta and bread. At home, my mother would sift the flour through a pair of graduated sieves. The first and finer sieve yielded white flour. The second sieve, with a larger mesh, produced whole-wheat flour. The bran and coarse bits that didn't pass through the second sieve were reserved for our pig. Fortunately, our family was small. In her own childhood home, as one of six children, she would have to sieve thirty kilos (about 65 pounds) of flour every two weeks to keep the family in pasta and bread.

Today, Calabrians eat mostly packaged dried pasta, reserving the time-consuming homemade fresh pasta for Sunday lunch, religious holidays, and other special occasions. With few exceptions, this fresh pasta is paired with tomato sauce or *sugo*, a thick tomato sauce in which meat—typically pork, goat, chicken, or rabbit—is braised first. The meat is set aside for a second course; the flavor-enhanced sauce accompanies the pasta. Walk through the narrow streets of a Calabrian village late on a Sunday morning, and the scent of simmering *sugo* will greet you at every turn.

Pasta is a first course in Calabria, as it is elsewhere in Italy. Sometimes—when dining in a restaurant or celebrating a holiday—Calabrians might precede pasta with antipasto, but not usually. Pasta is also the largest course in terms of volume and, historically, the main source of calories. At my childhood table, my slender father would often eat a half-pound of pasta for dinner, followed by vegetables and a slice or two of prosciutto or other *salumi* (cured meats). Most Calabrians today would consider 100 grams (3 ounces) of pasta to be a reasonable serving.

For everyday meals, I use De Cecco pasta, imported from Italy. I believe this widely available brand offers the best quality for the price. It cooks through evenly— some lesser brands become mushy outside before they are fully cooked at the core— and it has a rough, not slick, exterior that encourages the sauce to cling. For unusual shapes, such as *cavatelli* and *strozzapreti*, I will splurge on Rustichella d'Abruzzo, an excellent artisanal pasta from Italy.

A FEW GUIDELINES ON COOKING AND SAUCING PASTA, FRESH OR DRIED

Use abundant water so the pasta has room to swim. For 1 pound (450 grams) of pasta, use at least 5 quarts (5 liters) of water. Bring the water to a rolling boil over high heat. Add ¼ cup kosher salt. This may seem like a shocking amount, but the water must be salty or the pasta will taste bland. Stir the pasta several times during the first few minutes to keep it from sticking to the bottom of the pot.

Pay no attention to the recommended cooking times on packaged pasta. The only way to determine if the pasta is done is to taste it. Check often and drain the pasta when it still has a touch of firmness at the core, a hint of resistance when you bite into it. If it is soft all the way through, it won't deliver the textural pleasure that is part of pasta's appeal. Pasta continues to cook during the time it takes to drain and sauce it, so drain it when it is still slightly underdone. Before draining, set aside about 1 cup of the hot pasta water to thin your sauce if necessary. Never rinse pasta or you will cool it off unnecessarily and wash away some of the salt.

At my house, I present fresh pasta according to the following ritual: First, I spread a small spoonful of sauce on a platter, just enough to coat it. Then I place the drained pasta on top, followed by a shower of grated pecorino cheese. The remaining sauce goes on top. With two large spoons, I divide the pasta among the diners, who toss pasta and sauce together in their own bowls. So when you are cooking for a Calabrian, always put the cheese on the pasta, not on the sauce. We believe the cheese adheres to the noodles better that way.

My family eats pasta so quickly that I don't bother to warm the platter or serving bowls, but you can do so if you are concerned about keeping the pasta hot. Lastly, don't drown the pasta in sauce. Use just enough to coat. You have used the right amount if there is little or no sauce left in your bowl when you have finished the pasta. Serve pasta in shallow bowls, not plates. It stays hotter that way, and long pasta is easier to swirl on a fork when served in a bowl.

In the pages that follow, you will find recipes for some of the signature Calabrian pasta shapes such as *cavatieddi* and *fusilli calabresi*, along with the full-bodied sauces that go with them, such as a roasted-tomato and breadcrumb sauce (page 57) and a rustic goat *sugo* (page 85). You will also find quickly-made weeknight pasta dishes, such as Spaghetti with a Creamy Potato and Pancetta Sauce (page 66), as well as an unusual couscous-like pasta from Calabria's Arbëresh community (page 60). Master a few of these much loved pasta dishes, and you will be an honorary Calabrian.

Calabrian Pasta: A Glossary of Shapes

Pasta does not respect regional boundaries, so many of the shapes Calabrians think of as theirs are found in neighboring regions as well. Calabrians also prepare some pasta shapes they have knowingly borrowed from the neighbors, such as the *orecchiette* of Puglia. So although it would be difficult to prove that some pasta shapes are of Calabrese origin while others are not, Calabrese home cooks do consider certain shapes to be part of their culinary heritage.

The following shapes, all made with flour and water only, are among the ones a young woman of my grandmother's generation might have been expected to know before she married. Some shapes have multiple names, with the familiar name depending on the region.

CANNARUOZZOLI
Smooth tubular pasta, similar to *ditali* but larger in diameter and longer; used in soups.

CANNELLONI
Rectangles of fresh pasta, typically rolled around a filling and baked. Similar to *schiaffettoni* but larger.

CAVATELLI, CAVATIEDDI
Shaped with two fingers held together, *cavatelli* are smooth on the outside. Sauced with beans, tomato sauce, or *ragù*.

COVATELLI CROTONESI
Shaped with one finger and a ridged paddle, *covatelli* are smaller than *cavatelli* and have a ridged exterior. Sauced with beans, tomato sauce, or *ragù*.

DROMËSAT, PASTA GRATTATA
Couscous-like pasta from the Arbëresh community, typically simmered in tomato sauce.

FUSILLI, MACCHERONI AL FERRETTO, FILEI, FILEJ, MPARRETTATI
A long noodle formed around a knitting needle, resembling thick spaghetti with a hole in the middle. *Filei* or *filej* are identical to *fusilli* but shorter. Served with a simple tomato sauce or a meat-flavored tomato sauce such as *sugo di capra* (goat sauce, page 85).

GNOCCHI, RASCKATIEDDI
Identical to *cavatelli* and sauced in the same ways but made with a potato-and-flour dough.

LAGANE LARGHE, TAGLIATELLE LARGHE OR MACCHERONI LARGHI
Wide ribbon pasta similar to pappardelle; served with meat-flavored tomato sauces, such as *sugo di costate di maiale* (pork-rib and tomato sauce, page 88).

continued on page 52

Homemade Calabrian pasta shapes: 1. *dromësat*, 2. *fusilli*, 3. *scilatelli*, 4. *gnocchi*, 5. *cavatelli*, 6. *laganieddi*, 7. *maccheroni larghi*, 8. *scorze di fagiolini*. (For complete glossary of shapes see pages 48–49 and 52.)

continued from page 49

LAGANIEDDI, LAGANI

Ribbon pasta, narrower and thicker than fettuccine; often used in brothy bean dishes such as *Lagani e Ceci* (Fresh Ribbon Pasta with Chick Peas, page 63).

RAVIOLONI

Stuffed pasta in large rounds; typically filled with cheese and sauced with tomato, as for *Ravioloni Calabresi* (Large Ravioli with Fresh Ricotta and *Soppressata*, page 80).

RICCI DI DONNA

"Lady's tresses": a spaghetti-length spiral made by coiling the dough around a knitting needle; sauced in the same ways as *fusilli*.

SCHIAFFETTONI

Small squares of fresh pasta, typically rolled around a meat filling and baked; similar to *cannelloni* but smaller. When dried, *schiaffettoni* are also known as *paccheri*.

SCILATELLI, FEDELINI, FILATIEDDI

Thick spaghetti made by elongating a rope of dough at the edge of a table so that the slowly lengthening rope slides off the work table and makes a single long coil on a tray below. The pasta breaks into shorter lengths as it cooks. Used with any meat or vegetable sauce.

SCORZE DI FAGIOLINI

"Bean-pod pasta" shaped with the three middle fingers of each hand; paired with tomato sauce or meat *ragù*.

TAGGHIULINI, TAGLIOLINI

Ribbon pasta similar to fettuccine; paired with any meat or vegetable sauce.

Sugo di Pomodoro
QUICK TOMATO SAUCE

This sauce is the foundation of Calabrian cooking. I make it several times a week, with fresh tomatoes in summer and early fall, and with home-canned tomatoes the rest of the year. It cooks only briefly, so it retains the bright, lively taste of ripe tomato and the tomatoes remain in soft but visible pieces. It is not intended to be a smooth puree.

Like most other Calabrians, I do not add onions, celery, carrot, oregano, sugar, or any other ingredients that might interfere with the direct, pure taste of tomato. My sauce is simple because the main ingredients are superb: sun-ripened tomatoes, heavy with flesh and juice, and extra virgin olive oil. I add a hint of fresh basil and the merest scent of garlic. Anyone with access to fragrant ripe tomatoes—from a home garden, a farmers' market, or a conscientious supermarket—can reproduce this sauce. And as long as you use a good brand of canned San Marzano tomatoes (see page 14 for guidance), you can achieve fine results as well.

On its own, this versatile sauce can be paired with any pasta shape, fresh or dried. It makes enough to sauce a pound of pasta. But it is also the starting point for countless other pasta sauces—with anchovies, fried eggplant, olives, 'nduja (page 199), canned tuna, or cooked beans, for example—and an ingredient in many other Calabrian dishes, such as Spicy Calabrian Rice with Tomato and Borlotti Beans (page 109) and My Mother's Pork Meatballs (page 209).

If you use fresh tomatoes, they should be fully red, aromatic, and as ripe as possible. If they are not quite ripe, leave them at room temperature for two or three days, until they develop more color and aroma and begin to soften.

3½ pounds (1½ kilograms) fresh tomatoes, peeled, seeded, and
    diced, *or* 1 quart (1 liter) Home-Canned Peeled Tomatoes
    (page 296) *or* one 28-ounce can Italian San Marzano tomatoes,
    with juice

3 tablespoons (45 milliliters) extra virgin olive oil

2 large garlic cloves, halved

5 fresh basil leaves

2 teaspoons kosher salt

1 small fresh or dried hot red pepper, halved, optional

IF YOU ARE USING Home-Canned Tomatoes or store-bought canned tomatoes, pour them into a bowl and break them up by hand, discarding any hard cores or bits of skin. I don't want a perfectly smooth sauce, so I don't process the tomatoes further. If you prefer a smooth sauce, pass the tomatoes (fresh or canned) through a food mill fitted with the medium disk, or puree them in a food processor or blender.

Heat the olive oil in a skillet over moderately high heat, add the garlic, and sauté until golden, about one minute. Add the tomatoes and their juices carefully. (They will splatter.) Tear the basil in half and add along with the salt. Add the hot pepper, if using. Simmer briskly, stirring occasionally, until you have a thick, chunky sauce. Fresh tomatoes and Home-Canned Tomatoes will take 10 to 15 minutes. Store-bought canned tomatoes will cook down more quickly, as they often contain tomato puree. Remove the garlic cloves before serving.

A small portion of the tomato harvest my garden produces every September

MAKES ABOUT 2½ CUPS

Spaghetti Aglio, Olio e Peperoncino in Tre Modi

SPAGHETTI WITH GARLIC, OLIVE OIL, AND HOT RED PEPPER, THREE WAYS

This is a favorite quick pasta preparation throughout Southern Italy, a dish to make when you are tired and hungry and in no mood to cook. Some people call it "midnight spaghetti" because it is the sort of uncomplicated and not-too-filling dish you crave late at night. Calabrian wedding feasts can last all day and well into the evening, but by 2 A.M., the guests will have a little appetite again and out will come the platters of *spaghetti aglio, olio e peperoncino*.

Every cook makes the dish slightly differently. Even within families, people disagree about how it should be made. My parents like it with enough *pepe rosso*, the mild Calabrian red pepper, to turn the pasta red. My cousin Alberto makes his version by browning a lot of halved garlic cloves in olive oil, then discarding the garlic and adding large pieces of dried hot red pepper. The peppers remain in the dish but aren't meant to be eaten. I use fresh hot red pepper in my rendition and add some chopped parsley for color.

On a few points, all Calabrian cooks agree: First, the pasta water needs extra salt because the sauce has none. Second, no cheese is ever served with this dish. And finally, if you burn the garlic, you may as well start over.

SUGGESTED WINE: Mastroberardino Lacryma Christi del Vesuvio Rosso, Campania
The hot peppers in this recipe call for a light-bodied red with minimal tannin; too much tannin would intensify the perception of heat in the dish.
ALTERNATE: Barbera d'Alba

Kosher salt

1 pound (450 grams) spaghetti

MY VERSION

6 tablespoons extra virgin olive oil

6 garlic cloves, minced

3 to 4 small fresh hot red peppers, such as cayenne or Thai, thinly sliced

2 tablespoons chopped flat-leaf parsley

MY PARENTS' VERSION

6 tablespoons extra virgin olive oil

6 garlic cloves, minced or thinly sliced

2 tablespoons Calabrian paprika (page 304) *or* Spanish sweet paprika

Ground hot red pepper

MY COUSIN ALBERTO'S VERSION

6 tablespoons extra virgin olive oil

8 large garlic cloves, halved

6 small dried hot red peppers, stems removed, halved lengthwise

---

BRING 5 QUARTS (5 liters) of water to a boil in an 8-quart (8-liter) pot over high heat. Add ⅓ cup (45 grams) kosher salt. Add the pasta and cook, stirring occasionally, until al dente, about 10 minutes. While the pasta cooks, prepare one of the sauces.

FOR MY VERSION: Heat the olive oil, garlic, and sliced fresh peppers in a 12-inch (30-centimeter) skillet over low heat. Cook just until the garlic releases its fragrance, about 2 minutes; do not allow the garlic to color. Stir in the parsley and remove from the heat.

FOR MY PARENTS' VERSION: Heat the olive oil in a 12-inch (30-centimeter) skillet over low heat. Add the garlic and cook gently until fragrant, about 2 minutes; do not let it color. Add the paprika and cook briefly just to release its fragrance; do not allow it to burn. Add the hot pepper to taste and remove from the heat.

FOR ALBERTO'S VERSION: Heat the olive oil and garlic in a 12-inch (30-centimeter) skillet over medium heat until the garlic is golden, about 4 minutes. Remove the garlic cloves with tongs and discard. Reduce the heat to low and add the dried peppers. Let warm in the oil for about 2 minutes, then remove from the heat.

Set aside 1 cup (250 milliliters) of the pasta water, then drain the pasta and add it to the skillet. Toss well, moistening with enough of the reserved pasta water to keep the pasta from clumping. Serve immediately.

SERVES 4

Cavatieddi con Pomodori Gratinati al Forno

PASTA "GNOCCHI" WITH ROASTED TOMATOES AND BREADCRUMBS

In summer, when my garden tomatoes are at their peak, I often cut them in half and bake them with a topping of olive oil and garlicky herbed breadcrumbs. One day I decided to toss those soft, juicy roasted tomatoes with homemade *cavatieddi*, or gnocchi-shaped pasta, and was more than pleased with the outcome. I now peel the tomatoes before roasting them, but even so, this sauce is easy and quick enough for busy weeknights. Reserve it for the couple of months in summer when you can get garden-ripe or farmers' market plum tomatoes that will melt into a creamy sauce. Underripe supermarket tomatoes won't soften properly in the oven.

SUGGESTED WINE: Librandi "Gravello," Val di Neto, Calabria
The deep, roasted flavors in the dish call for a wine with a little tannin, like this elegant, fruit-focused, medium-bodied red made with Gaglioppo and Cabernet Sauvignon.
ALTERNATE: St. Emilion or other Merlot-based Bordeaux

Homemade Fresh Pasta (recipe page 59) *or* 1 pound dried *cavatelli*,
    penne, or spaghetti

SAUCE

1½ pounds (675 grams) ripe plum (Roma type) tomatoes

⅔ cup Toasted Fresh Breadcrumbs (recipe page 59)

3 tablespoons minced flat-leaf parsley

2 teaspoons minced fresh oregano

2 large garlic cloves, minced

3 tablespoons freshly grated pecorino cheese

¼ cup plus 1 tablespoon extra virgin olive oil

Kosher salt and freshly ground black pepper

Ground hot red pepper, optional

TO SHAPE THE *cavatieddi* from homemade pasta, work with a little dough at a time and keep the rest covered with plastic wrap so it doesn't dry out. Cut off a piece of dough about the size of a cigar. Rolling with the palms of both hands, stretch the dough into a long rope about ¼ inch (6 millimeters) thick. Lay the rope on a work surface and cut into 1-inch (2½-centimeter) pieces. Hold the index and middle fingers of your dominant hand close together, then place those two fingertips on the long edge of one of the pieces, fingertips touching the work surface. Press down, then pull toward you while pressing, which will make the dough curl into a "C." It is important to press firmly and consistently so that the *cavatieddi* are evenly thin throughout. Repeat with the remaining dough. Transfer the *cavatieddi* as you make them to a tray lined with a clean kitchen towel or cotton cloth. The *cavatieddi* may be prepared up to 4 hours ahead and left uncovered at room temperature.

FOR THE SAUCE: Place a rack in the lowest position in your oven and preheat the oven to 450°F (225°F).

Fill a 4-quart (4-liter) pot with 2 quarts (2 liters) of water and bring to a boil. Prepare a large bowl of ice water. Immerse the tomatoes in the boiling water until you see the first sign of a split skin, 20 to 45 seconds, depending on ripeness. Remove the tomatoes immediately to the ice water. When cool, slip off the skins and remove the core. Cut lengthwise and scoop out the seeds with your fingers.

In a small bowl, combine the toasted breadcrumbs with the parsley, oregano, garlic, and pecorino. Mix with your hand to blend well.

Choose a baking dish large enough to hold the halved tomatoes in one layer without crowding and to accommodate the cooked pasta eventually. I use an oval dish that measures approximately 11 by 8 by 2 inches (28 by 20 by 5 centimeters). Coat the bottom of the dish with the 1 tablespoon of the olive oil. Arrange the tomato halves in the dish in a single layer, cut side up. Sprinkle with 2 teaspoons salt and several grinds of black pepper. Scatter the breadcrumb mixture over the tomatoes, dividing it evenly. Sprinkle with a little hot pepper, if using. Drizzle evenly with the remaining ¼ cup olive oil. Bake until the tomatoes are very soft and about to collapse, about 20 minutes. Remove from the oven and break them up a bit with a wooden spoon.

Bring 5 quarts (5 liters) of water to a boil in an 8-quart (8-liter) pot. Add ¼ cup (35 grams) kosher salt, then add the *cavatieddi* and cook, stirring occasionally, until they are no longer chewy but still firm to the tooth, 12 to 15 minutes.

Drain the pasta and transfer to the baking dish with the tomatoes. Stir well with a wooden spoon, breaking up more of the tomatoes as you stir until the sauce is creamy and coats the pasta nicely. Divide among bowls and serve at once. If you would like additional cheese, pass it separately.

SERVES 4 TO 6

Homemade Fresh Pasta

This eggless dough is the one my mother and I use for all our fresh pasta. The more often you make it, the more proficient you will become. Be sure to let the dough rest before rolling it to allow the flour to hydrate fully and the gluten to relax.

2 cups (280 grams) unbleached all-purpose flour

½ cup plus 1 tablespoon (135 milliliters) water, plus more if needed

PLACE THE FLOUR in a bowl, make a well in the center, and put the water in the well. Mix with one hand until you have a shaggy dough. Scrape the dough off your fingers and back into the bowl. Continue mixing and kneading with one hand until the dough cleans the sides of the bowl. Turn the dough out onto a work surface and knead with both hands until the dough is firm, smooth, and not sticky, about 10 minutes. The dough will be stiff and difficult to work at first, but resist the urge to add more water. If it fails to come together into a smooth dough after a few minutes of kneading, sprinkle with a few drops of water. Shape the dough into a ball, cover the surface closely with plastic wrap, and let rest for 30 minutes.

Note: You need a slightly moister dough for pasta shapes that require rolling the dough into a sheet. For *lagani* (page 63), *sagne chine* (page 77), *maccheroni larghi* (page 88), and *ravioloni* (page 80), you will probably need an additional 1 tablespoon water.

Toasted Fresh Breadcrumbs

The secret to making evenly browned breadcrumbs is to cook them in a skillet and stay on top of them, stirring without pause. You can also toast breadcrumbs in a moderate oven, but the minute you walk away, the breadcrumbs on the edges burn.

2 tablespoons extra virgin olive oil

¾ cup (55 grams) firmly packed fresh breadcrumbs (for homemade, see page 127)

WARM THE OLIVE OIL in a 10-inch (25-centimeter) skillet over medium heat. Add the breadcrumbs and stir to coat with oil. Cook, stirring constantly, until the breadcrumbs are evenly golden brown and crunchy, about 5 minutes.

MAKES ABOUT ⅔ CUP

Dromësat

HANDMADE ARBËRESH "COUSCOUS" WITH TOMATO SAUCE

The Arbëresh—Calabrians of Albanian descent—make an unusual pasta dish that I encountered for the first time as an adult, while researching Arbëresh recipes. Like North African couscous, made by rubbing semolina and water together until the dough forms fine pellets, *dromësat* requires neither a rolling pin nor a pasta machine. It is made with all-purpose flour sprinkled with just enough water to moisten it. Then the barely dampened flour is rubbed lightly between the palms to create fine, raggedy flakes that resemble wood shavings. These shreds of pasta are cooked briskly but briefly in boiling water flavored with tomato sauce until they swell, producing a thick, creamy, tomato-tinged soup. When I tasted *dromësat*—first at Kamastra in Civita, and again at La Capricciosa in Firmo, two fine restaurants in scenic Arbëresh villages—the dish reminded me of the rustic Tuscan *pappa al pomodoro*.

When I described *dromësat* to my mother, she said, "Ah, yes, *pasta grattata* (grated pasta)." Although she had never made it, she had seen other Calabrian cooks prepare it. Being non-Arbëresh, they had rechristened the dish with an Italian name.

SUGGESTED WINE: Pietratorcia "Scheria Rosso," Campania
From the island of Ischia, this medium-bodied, earthy red wine is a blend of Aglianico, Syrah, Guarnaccia (Grenache), and Piedirosso. It works nicely with the sweetness of tomato sauce, and its own aroma suggests cooked tomato.
ALTERNATE: Priorat or another Grenache-based wine

---

2 cups unbleached all-purpose flour

1½ cups (½ recipe) Quick Tomato Sauce (page 53)

2 teaspoons kosher salt

8 fresh basil leaves, torn into small pieces

Freshly grated ricotta salata or pecorino romano for garnish, optional

Ground hot red pepper, optional

ON A WORK SURFACE, spread the flour out to make a bed about ½ inch thick. Put 1 cup of water in a small bowl or measuring cup. You will use only about ⅓ cup, but it is easier to work with a larger amount.

Use the fingertips of one hand to sprinkle water over the flour while you mix with the other hand. Use a circular motion with your mixing hand, adding water just until all the flour is barely moistened and meal-like; you are not trying to make a cohesive dough. After you have added about ⅓ cup water, the moistened flour will begin to coalesce into fine, raggedy shreds or flakes and there will no longer be much loose, dry flour on the work surface.

Working with a little of the moistened flour at a time, rub the mixture briskly but gently between your palms, letting it fall from your palms in pieces that resemble wood shavings or coarsely grated cheese. If you rub too vigorously, the mixture will clump. Work your way through the mixture two or three times, until most of the flour has been incorporated into shreds. The pasta will be uneven—some fine shreds, some coarse—but there should not be any clumps.

Put the pasta in a fine sieve and shake to remove the unabsorbed flour. Do not try to moisten this flour and salvage it for *dromësat*; it will make gummy pasta. Spread the pasta on a clean kitchen towel or a baking sheet lined with parchment paper. Set aside.

In a 4-quart saucepan, combine the tomato sauce, salt, and 4½ cups water. Bring to a simmer over high heat. Add the *dromësat* a fistful at a time, letting it drip through your fingers gradually while stirring with a wooden spoon. Cook the *dromësat* at a vigorous boil, stirring continuously, for 3 minutes. The *dromësat* will hold their shape as the tomato broth thickens. Turn off the heat and stir in the basil. Taste and adjust the salt. Let cool for 5 minutes, then serve in bowls. Garnish each serving, if desired, with grated cheese and a sprinkle of hot pepper.

SERVES 4 TO 6

The Arbëresh in Calabria

Beginning in the early fifteenth century, immigrants from Albania—known then as Arbëria—settled in Calabria and other parts of Southern Italy and began to create their own communities. They came in waves over three centuries, but the earliest were soldiers who came to aid the Aragonese army. Rewarded with land, many stayed. More arrived in the mid to late 1400s, fleeing persecution by the Turks, an influx that surged after the death in 1468 of Albanian hero George Skanderbeg, who had led resistance to the Turks. They settled primarily in remote mountain villages and have managed, for more than five hundred years, to preserve a distinctive language, culture, and customs. Theirs is the language of pre-Ottoman Arbëria—not modern Albanian and not Italian, although it reflects some Italian influence.

Today, there are almost three dozen villages in Calabria that retain a significant Arbëresh (AR-ber-esh) presence. Most of these towns are in the province of Cosenza, although some are in Catanzaro and Crotone as well. Among the most prominent Arbëresh villages are Acquaformosa, Civita, Firmo, Frascineto, Lungro, San Basile, and Spezzano Albanese. In these villages, you may hear the Arbëresh language spoken and, if you are fortunate enough to be there on a holiday, to see people don traditional Arbëresh dress. The number of Arbëresh in Calabria is estimated at thirty thousand.

Over the centuries, Arbëresh cooking seems to have merged with Calabrian foodways, to the point that it is difficult to identify many dishes that are uniquely Arbëresh. Only two, both pasta dishes, come readily to the fore: *dromësat* (page 60), a sort of couscous made by rubbing flour and water between one's palms; and *shtridhëlat*, a homemade noodle resembling Calabrian *lagani* but made entirely by hand, with no rolling pin. Virtually all of the other dishes that turn up in Arbëresh restaurants and recipe collections have Calabrian equivalents.

Lagani e Ceci

FRESH RIBBON PASTA WITH CHICK PEAS

The ribbon-like, hand-cut noodles known as *lagani* in Calabria resemble fettuccine but are thicker and more rustic. In my hometown of Verbicaro, they are typically cooked with dried chick peas or with cranberry beans, either fresh or dried. Adding ground sweet pepper to the tomato sauce deepens the color and the flavor; we do it often when we make pasta with beans.

Rolling the dough by hand gives *lagani* a firm and slightly chewy texture that is part of their charm. You can roll the dough with a pasta machine and cut the noodles with the fettuccine cutter, but the texture won't be the same. To roll the dough by hand, a non-tapered, dowel-type rolling pin works best. You can make one easily from a 2-foot (60-centimeter) length of a 1¼-inch-diameter (3-centimeter-diameter) wooden closet rod.

This pasta is the first one I learned to make, at the age of nine. I still remember my mother scolding me for making the dough too wet. That meant I had to add more flour, which made too much dough, which was wasteful.

In my family, we don't put cheese on pasta with beans, but you can pass grated pecorino if you like.

SUGGESTED WINE: Argiolas "Korem," Isola dei Nuraghi, Sardinia
For a hefty dish with some depth, an intense, full-bodied red wine with both earthy and fruity qualities and aromas of Medjool date, sagebrush, and blueberry.
ALTERNATE: Zinfandel

LAGANI

Homemade Fresh Pasta (page 59) *or* 1 pound store-bought fresh
   fettuccine

Flour for dusting

¾ cup (150 grams) dried chick peas, soaked 12 hours in water to cover
   by several inches, *or* one 15-ounce (425-gram) can chick peas

Kosher salt

2 tablespoons extra virgin olive oil

1 large garlic clove, halved

2 cups (500 milliliters) Home-Canned Peeled Tomatoes (page
   296) or one 14-ounce (400-gram) can Italian San Marzano
   tomatoes, pureed in a blender

3 fresh basil leaves

1 tablespoon Calabrian paprika (page 304) *or* Spanish sweet paprika

Ground hot red pepper *or* hot red pepper flakes, optional

TO MAKE THE *LAGANI*: Dust the work surface lightly with flour. Flatten the ball of dough with your hands into a circle. With the rolling pin, roll the dough into a circle approximately ¼ inch (6 millimeters) thick. Roll from the center of the circle outward, giving the dough a quarter-turn after each roll to maintain the circle.

Now you will change your rolling technique. Lightly dust the surface of the dough with flour. Lift the edge of the dough closest to you and drape it tightly over the rolling pin, then roll the pin away from you so that about one-quarter of the dough is encircling the pin. Starting at the center of the pin, stretch the dough by rolling lightly with both palms and working outward. Continue to roll the dough around the rolling pin, stretching the dough out and away with your hands, along the length of the pin, as you roll. You do not need to put pressure on the pin. You are thinning the dough and increasing the circle's circumference by the stretching motion of your palms, not by pressure applied to the pin. When all the dough is rolled onto the pin, give the pin a quarter-turn and unfurl the dough. The circle should be larger than it was when you started. Dust the surface of the dough lightly with flour and repeat the rolling and stretching process until the circle is 16 to 18 inches (40 to 45 centimeters) in diameter and about ⅛ inch (3 millimeters) thick.

Dust the surface of the dough with flour. Cut the circle in half and keep one half covered with a kitchen towel while you work with the other half.

Working with one of the half-circles, uncut side toward you, lift the edge closest to you and fold 1½ inches (4 centimeters) of dough over. Continue folding the dough like a jelly roll until you have a long flat roll about 1½ inches (4 centimeters) wide.

With a large, sharp knife, cut the pasta roll into ¼-inch-wide (6-millimeter-wide) ribbons. Unfurl the ribbons and lay them on a clean, dry kitchen towel. You can cook the pasta immediately or let it rest, covered with another clean towel, for a few hours.

If using dried chick peas, drain and put them in a large pot with water to cover by 2 inches (5 centimeters). Bring to a simmer, skimming any foam. Adjust the heat to maintain a bare simmer and cook uncovered until the chick peas are tender, 45 minutes to 1½ hours, depending on age. Season to taste with salt about 10 minutes before they are done. Let the chick peas cool in the cooking liquid.

Heat the olive oil in a 10-inch (25-centimeter) skillet over moderate heat. Add the garlic and sauté until golden. Add the tomato puree carefully, as it may splatter. Tear the basil leaves in half and add to the skillet along with the paprika. Season to taste with salt and hot pepper, if using. Simmer briskly, stirring occasionally, until thick and saucelike, 10 to 15 minutes.

Bring 5 quarts (5 liters) of water to a boil in an 8-quart (8-liter) pot over high heat. Add ¼ cup (35 grams) kosher salt, then add the pasta and cook, stirring occasionally, until al dente, 7 minutes or more, depending on thickness. About one minute before the pasta is done, drain the chick peas (home-cooked or canned) and add them to the boiling pasta water to reheat them. Scoop out 2 cups (500 milliliters) of the pasta water and reserve. Drain the pasta and chick peas into a colander. Return to the warm pot over moderate heat. Add the tomato sauce and enough of the reserved water to make the mixture brothy, about 1½ cups (375 milliliters). Mix well and serve at once.

SERVES 4 TO 6

Summer Variation with Fresh Cranberry Beans

Shell 1 pound fresh cranberry beans. Put the shelled beans in a pot with cold water to cover. Bring to a boil over high heat and cook briskly until the beans are tender, 15 minutes or more, depending on their maturity. Season to taste with salt. Let them cool in the cooking liquid. Substitute for cooked chick peas.

Pasta e Patate "Santo Janni"

SPAGHETTI WITH A CREAMY POTATO AND PANCETTA SAUCE

The *agriturismo* Santo Janni is a mountain farm with guesthouse in the dense chestnut forests near San Pietro in Guarano, northeast of Cosenza. Most of the food the proprietors serve in their simple but comfortable dining room comes from ingredients they make or grow: prosciutto; ricotta and pecorino cheeses; homegrown eggplant; and sturdy homemade bread. *Pasta e patate* is a specialty of the house and quite unlike the version my mother makes. My mother's recipe calls for tomato and short pasta (such as ditali), and the potatoes remain in visible chunks. In the Santo Janni rendition, the potatoes are cooked with *guanciale* (cured pork jowl) until they are soft enough to mash, yielding a creamy, rich, and peppery sauce flavored with lots of ricotta salata. Pancetta can substitute for the hard-to-find *guanciale*.

SUGGESTED WINE: Casale della Ioria Cesanese del Piglio, Lazio
This medium- to full-bodied red wine from the hills outside of Rome resembles a wine from the Northern Rhône, with aromas of white pepper, bacon, and red plum jam.
ALTERNATE: Syrah

---

3 tablespoons extra virgin olive oil

2 ounces (55 grams) pancetta *or guanciale* (see Resources, page 368), minced

¾ pound (340 grams) russet potatoes, peeled and cut into ½-inch (12-millimeter) cubes

Kosher salt

½ pound (225 grams) spaghetti, broken in half lengthwise

⅓ cup (35 grams) finely grated ricotta salata, plus more for sprinkling

Freshly ground black pepper

IN A LARGE SKILLET, heat the olive oil and pancetta over medium heat, stirring until the pancetta renders its fat. Do not let it become brown or crisp. Add the potatoes and stir for about one minute to coat them with the fat, then add 2 cups (500 milliliters) water. Bring to a simmer and cook uncovered until the potatoes are soft enough to mash with a fork or potato masher, about 10 minutes. Mash them to a near-puree and set the skillet aside.

In a 4-quart (4-liter) pot, bring 3 quarts (3 liters) water and 2 tablespoons salt to a rolling boil over high heat. Add the spaghetti and cook until al dente.

Just before the pasta is done, return the skillet to medium heat. With tongs, lift the pasta out of the pot and transfer it, dripping wet, to the skillet. Reserve a cup of cooking water. Toss the pasta with the tongs, coating the pasta evenly with the creamy sauce. Add the ricotta salata and a generous amount of black pepper and toss again, thinning the sauce as needed with enough of the pasta water to make a creamy but not soupy dish. The sauce must cling to the pasta, but it should not seem starchy. Taste for seasoning; if the pancetta is salty, the dish may not need more salt. Serve at once, topping each portion with a little additional cheese.

SERVES 4

The town of Orsomarso, close to where my maternal grandparents had their farmhouse

Struncatura con Acciughe e Mollica
WHOLE-WHEAT LINGUINE WITH ANCHOVIES AND BREADCRUMBS

Struncatura is a type of rough, light-brown linguine rarely made in Calabria anymore, perhaps because it reminds people of hard times. Most Calabrians today don't know of it, and it is not a pasta I ate growing up. I first tasted it at Casa Janca, a rustic but charming *agriturismo* near Pizzo operated by Rita Callipo. According to Rita, the grain mills in Calabria used to give the wheat bran to the local peasants to feed their livestock, but the hungry peasants would try to make pasta with it. You can't make pasta with wheat bran alone—it won't hold together—so they added flour made from carob, which grows wild in Calabria. *Struncatura* is *contrabando* today, said Rita, sold only "under the counter." She had obtained the pasta for that evening's dinner through a friend.

I didn't understand how pasta could possibly be a prohibited food, so the following year, I returned to Casa Janca and asked Rita if she could set up an appointment for me to visit a *struncatura* producer and watch it being made. She looked skeptical. The first time she had tried to buy it, she told me, the experience was like buying illegal drugs. Rita and her friend drove to one location and then had to switch cars and go to another location where the pasta was handed over in an unmarked bag after the friend vouched for Rita's reliability.

The day after my request, Rita reported back to me on her telephone conversation with the producer. A meeting was not possible. So she prodded him for more information about where the pasta was made, how it was made, why it was contraband. *Troppe cose volete sapere*, he said to her, ominously. You ask too many questions.

Naturally, my curiosity was inflamed by this point, and I was not willing to let the matter drop. I planned a trip to Gioia Tauro, a small coastal town south of Pizzo where Rita had said she thought I stood the best chance of finding a *struncatura* producer. A few days later, standing on a street corner in Gioia Tauro on a busy Saturday morning, with shoppers racing past me, I turned to the middle-aged gentleman next to me and asked if he happened to know a shop where I might find *struncatura*. Not only did he know, but he insisted on taking me there.

We drove to a small, dimly lit market in town and he gestured toward the meat counter in the back. There, the clerk didn't hesitate when I asked for a kilo of *struncatura*. She reached into an unmarked box behind the counter and pulled out long strands of the dark dried pasta. But when I asked her where she got it, she said she didn't know. How was it made? She didn't know. I bought another kilo, but I got no further in deciphering the origins or composition of *struncatura*. The gentleman who had chauffeured me to the market told me that carob flour is considered animal feed in Calabria, unfit for human consumption. But as I learned at Casa Janca, and in experiments at home, *struncatura* rivals the best whole-wheat pasta.

The whole-wheat linguine manufactured by De Cecco has a pleasantly rough texture and nutty flavor similar to that of *struncatura*. Other brands I've tried are too slick. In the region of Reggio Calabria, where *struncatura* presumably originated, the traditional sauce is a simple one: garlic, hot peppers, and anchovies cooked slowly until the anchovies melt. Crisp toasted breadcrumbs are stirred in at the end to add some crunch. I leave some of the anchovies coarsely chopped so they don't dissolve completely and are perceptible in the sauce.

The same sauce, tossed with spaghetti, appears on Christmas Eve menus throughout Calabria. Made with whole-wheat linguine, a stand-in for *struncatura*, the dish has a wholesome and earthy quality that I love. Serve it as a first course before a seafood second course, such as Whole Salt-Baked Sea Bass (page 181) or Swordfish "Glutton's Style" with Tomato, Capers, and Olives (page 175).

SUGGESTED WINE: Luigi Vivacqua Cirò Rosso Riserva, Calabria
One of the best expressions of Cirò, this modern wine offers Bing cherry and pomegranate aromas and the vibrant fruit flavors and acidity desirable when partnering a dish with anchovies.
ALTERNATE: Nebbiolo

6 salt-cured anchovies (page 289) *or* 12 best-quality anchovy fillets
    in olive oil

Kosher salt

1 pound (450 grams) whole-wheat linguine

½ cup (125 milliliters) extra virgin olive oil

6 large garlic cloves, or more to taste, minced

1 to 2 small fresh hot red peppers, thinly sliced, *or* hot red pepper
    flakes to taste

2 tablespoons minced flat-leaf parsley

⅔ cup Toasted Fresh Breadcrumbs (page 59)

IF USING SALT-CURED ANCHOVIES, rinse them under cold water to remove the exterior salt. Pry them open along the back with your fingers and lift out the backbone to yield two fillets. Rinse the fillets again to remove any fine bones and pat dry on paper towels. If using anchovy fillets in olive oil, lift them out of the jar or can with a fork, leaving the oil behind.

Finely chop six of the anchovy fillets. Cut the remaining six fillets into 4 to 5 pieces each. Set aside.

Bring 5 quarts (5 liters) of water to a boil in an 8-quart (8-liter) pot over high heat. Add ¼ cup (35 grams) kosher salt and the pasta. Cook, stirring occasionally, until al dente, about 10 minutes.

While the pasta cooks, prepare the sauce. Put the olive oil, garlic, finely chopped anchovies, and hot peppers in a 12-inch (30-centimeter) skillet and cook over low heat, stirring, until the anchovies dissolve. Stir in the parsley and the remaining anchovies and turn off the heat.

When the pasta is almost done, set aside 1 cup (250 milliliters) of the pasta cooking water, then drain the pasta and transfer it to the skillet with the anchovy sauce. Toss quickly until all the strands are well coated. Add some of the reserved cooking water if the pasta seems dry. Set aside 2 tablespoons of the breadcrumbs, then add the remainder to the skillet and toss the pasta again. Divide the pasta among warm bowls and top each serving with a sprinkling of the reserved breadcrumbs. Serve right away.

SERVES 4

Spaghetti col Sugo di Baccalà
SPAGHETTI WITH SALT COD AND A SPICY TOMATO SAUCE

Calabrians prepare this dish on Christmas Eve and throughout the winter months. After simmering big chunks of salt cod in tomato sauce, which imparts a rich seafood flavor to the sauce, some cooks shred the fish into the sauce and toss it with pasta. That's what I've done here. Others, like my father, prefer to leave the cod chunks whole, lift them out of the sauce, and have them as a *secondo*, or second course. In that case, the first course would be spaghetti tossed with the fish-flavored sauce.

If you leave the salt cod in the pasta sauce, stay with fish for a second course. Consider a cool seafood salad, such as Marinated Octopus Salad with Olive Oil and Lemon (page 161). If you prefer a hot *secondo*, Whole Salt-Baked Sea Bass (page 181) would be a good choice. Follow the second course with a salad of winter greens or Cauliflower Salad (page 240). No cheese is served with this pasta. If you like, you can top it with Toasted Fresh Breadcrumbs (page 59).

SUGGESTED WINE: Palari "Rosso del Soprano," Sicily
Lighter red wines with zippy acidity are a good match for salt cod. This wine, a blend of indigenous red grapes, has a saline quality and aromas of cherry and ripe tomato that help to brighten this rich dish.
ALTERNATE: Côtes du Rhône

½ pound (225 grams) boneless, skinless salt cod

¼ cup (60 milliliters) extra virgin olive oil

2 large garlic cloves, halved

1 quart (1 liter) Home-Canned Peeled Tomatoes (page 296) *or* one
    28-ounce (800-gram) can Italian San Marzano tomatoes,
    broken up by hand, with juice

6 fresh basil leaves

Kosher salt

Ground hot red pepper *or* hot red pepper flakes

2 tablespoons chopped flat-leaf parsley

1 pound (450 grams) spaghetti or bucatini

IN THE REFRIGERATOR, soak the salt cod in water to cover for two to three days, changing the water once a day. Thick pieces will need longer than thin ones to rehydrate and shed their salt. Taste the cod after two days to see if it is still too salty. Take care not to oversoak or you will drain the cod of all flavor.

Heat the olive oil in a saucepan over moderate heat. Add the garlic and sauté until golden. Carefully add the tomatoes. Tear the basil leaves in half and add to the saucepan along with salt and hot pepper to taste. Simmer briskly, stirring occasionally, for about 10 minutes. Drain the salt cod and add to the saucepan. Simmer uncovered until the cod flakes easily, 15 to 20 minutes, turning the cod over in the sauce halfway through. Remove and discard the garlic cloves. Shred the cod in the sauce with a fork. Stir in the parsley, then taste and adjust the seasoning. Keep the sauce warm over low heat.

Bring 5 quarts (5 liters) of water to a boil in an 8-quart (8-liter) pot over high heat. Add ¼ cup (35 grams) kosher salt, then add the pasta and cook, stirring occasionally, until al dente, about 10 minutes. Set aside 1 cup (250 milliliters) of the pasta water, then drain the pasta into a colander and return it to the warm pot. Add the sauce and toss well, adding some of the reserved water if needed to thin the sauce. Serve immediately.

SERVES 4 TO 6

Paccheri con Pesce Spada e Pomodori di Pachino
LARGE PASTA TUBES WITH SWORDFISH AND CHERRY TOMATOES

Restaurants on Calabria's Tyrrhenian coast serve this dish throughout the summer, when the locally caught swordfish is plentiful and impeccably fresh. Some add capers and olives to the sauce. Others add fried eggplant or fried zucchini. I've had the sauce with fresh pasta, such as *filei* (page 48), but I particularly like it with *paccheri*, a Neapolitan pasta shape that Calabrians also enjoy. *Paccheri* are smooth, 2-inch-long (5-centimeter-long) pasta tubes, but unlike the tubular penne or rigatoni, *paccheri* collapse and become flat when cooked. I adore them with tomato sauce and seafood sauces and would like to see them more widely available in the United States (See Resources, page 369).

SUGGESTED WINE: Rosa del Golfo Salento Rosato, Apulia
A refreshing dry rosé primarily from the Negroamaro grape.
ALTERNATE: dry rosé

---

1 pound (450 grams) fresh swordfish in slices ½ inch thick
    (6 millimeters thick)

Kosher salt

1 pound (450 grams) dried *paccheri* (large pasta tubes, page 369) *or*
    rigatoni

¼ cup (2 fluid ounces/60 milliliters) extra virgin olive oil

4 garlic cloves, minced

1 small fresh hot red pepper, such as cayenne or Thai, chopped,
    optional

1 pound (450 grams) cherry tomatoes, halved

2 tablespoons chopped flat-leaf parsley

REMOVE THE SKIN from the swordfish, then cut the fish slices into ½-inch (12-millimeter) cubes.

Bring 5 quarts (5 liters) of water to a boil in an 8-quart (8-liter) pot over high heat. Add ¼ cup (35 grams) kosher salt and the pasta. While the pasta cooks, prepare the sauce.

Heat the olive oil in a 12-inch (30-centimeter) skillet over moderately high heat. When the oil is hot, add the cubed swordfish, garlic, and hot pepper. Cook, stirring constantly, until the swordfish is white all over and the garlic has released its fragrance, about 45 seconds.

Add the tomatoes and 1 tablespoon salt and cook, stirring, just long enough to soften the tomatoes and draw out some of their juices, about one minute. You don't want the tomatoes to collapse into a sauce. Stir in the parsley and remove from the heat.

When the pasta is al dente, drain and toss with the swordfish and tomato sauce, stirring until the pasta is well coated. Serve immediately.

SERVES 4 TO 6

Variation with Fresh Anchovies

Substitute 1½ pounds (675 grams) fresh anchovies, cleaned and filleted as directed on page 31, for the swordfish. Replace *paccheri* with spaghetti.

Fishermen pulling in their boat from the
Tyrrhenian Sea in Pizzo

Rigatoni alla Pastora
SHEPHERD'S-STYLE RIGATONI WITH RICOTTA AND SAUSAGE

This humble recipe uses the ingredients a Calabrian shepherd might have on hand: fresh, homemade ricotta and a little sausage. An even more austere version calls for ricotta only. I pass the ricotta through a sieve to make it creamier, although most Calabrian cooks don't. They simply beat the ricotta with a fork and thin it with hot pasta water. Be sure to use a ridged pasta shape, such as rigatoni or penne rigate, to hold the creamy sauce, and be generous with the black pepper.

SUGGESTED WINE: Salvatore Moletierri Aglianico "Cinque Querce," Irpinia, Campania
A rustic, medium-bodied red wine with a fragrance of black fruits, mint, and baking spices.
ALTERNATE: Syrah

¾ pound (350 grams) fresh sweet or hot Italian sausage *or* Fresh
    Homemade Fennel Sausage Calabrian Style (page 211)

2 tablespoons extra virgin olive oil

1 pound (450 grams) Homemade Ricotta (page 144) *or* store-bought
    whole-milk ricotta

Kosher salt and freshly ground black pepper

1 pound (450 grams) rigatoni *or* penne rigate

Freshly grated pecorino cheese, optional

Ground hot red pepper, optional

REMOVE THE SAUSAGE CASINGS. With a table knife, break the sausage up into small chunks about the size of an olive. Heat the olive oil in a 12-inch (30-centimeter) skillet over medium heat. Add the sausage and cook until browned all over, about 2 minutes. Keep warm.

Press the ricotta through a sieve into a large serving bowl. Add salt to taste and several grinds of black pepper.

Bring 5 quarts (5 liters) of water to a boil in an 8-quart (8-liter) pot over high heat. Add ¼ cup (35 grams) kosher salt, then add the pasta and cook, stirring occasionally, until al dente, about 10 minutes. Just before the pasta is done, whisk a few tablespoons of the hot pasta water into the ricotta to warm it and make it creamy and saucelike.

Set aside about ½ cup (125 millliliters) of the pasta cooking water, then drain the pasta. Add the pasta to the skillet with the sausage and toss over high heat just until hot throughout. Transfer the pasta and sausage to the bowl with the ricotta and mix well, adding some of the reserved pasta cooking water if needed to moisten the pasta. Add pecorino and hot pepper if desired. Serve immediately.

SERVES 6 TO 8

Ricotta draining in baskets

Sagne Chine

LASAGNE, CALABRIAN STYLE

Sagne chine is Calabria's lasagne, a neat pasta-wrapped "package" that doesn't reveal its delectable contents until it is sliced. It is admittedly a labor of love and not made routinely. In many families, *sagne chine* graces the table primarily on the day after Easter, known as *la Pasquetta* (page 79), when everyone heads to the countryside for a picnic. It holds well and is delicious at room temperature, so it is perfect for this occasion. I tend to reserve *sagne chine* for those important family events when we have many guests in the house and need to present the meal buffet style. When each of my two children was baptized, I made *sagne chine*.

The dish is made more or less the same way throughout Calabria, by layering squares of eggless pasta dough with tomato sauce, fresh peas, sliced mozzarella and—the time-consuming part—dozens upon dozens of marble-size meatballs. I am well aware that these tiny meatballs require some patience to make, but they are a signature of *sagne chine*. Enlist a friend or your children and you can shape all the meatballs in a pleasurable half hour.

Note that you can assemble and refrigerate the lasagne several hours before baking, or up to a day ahead.

SUGGESTED WINE: Roberto Ceraudo "Dattilo," Val di Neto, Calabria
A smooth, balanced red wine from the Gaglioppo grape, with cherry and mocha aromas and enough structure to handle the many layered flavors in this dish.
ALTERNATE: Sangiovese

Homemade Fresh Pasta (page 59), doubled, *or* 1 pound store-bought
    fresh egg pasta in sheets

Kosher salt

1 recipe My Mother's Pork Meatballs in Tomato Sauce (page 209),
    made with marble-size meatballs

1 pound (450 grams) small fresh peas *or* frozen petite peas

6 hard-boiled eggs, thinly sliced

1 pound (450 grams) whole-milk mozzarella cheese, not water-
    packed, in small dice

1¼ cups (125 grams) freshly grated pecorino cheese

CUT THE DOUGH into 6 or 8 equal pieces. Work with one piece at a time, keeping the others covered with a kitchen towel. Using a pasta machine, and beginning with the rollers on the widest setting, roll a piece of dough twice through each setting to thin it. Stop when the sheet of dough is about 1/16 inch (1½ millimeters) thick. Lay the sheet of dough on a work surface, uncovered, while you roll out the remaining pieces of dough. When you have rolled out all the dough, cut the sheets into 12-inch (30-centimeter) lengths.

Bring 5 quarts (5 liters) of water to a boil in an 8-quart (8-liter) pot over high heat. Add ¼ cup (35 grams) kosher salt. Working with two or three sheets at a time, parboil the pasta for about one minute. With tongs or a slotted spoon, transfer them to a bowl of ice water to stop the cooking. Lift them out of the ice water and let excess water drain off, then lay the pasta sheets on a kitchen towel without overlapping.

Prepare the Pork Meatballs in Tomato Sauce, but shape the meatballs about the size of a marble, using about ½ teaspoon of the pork mixture for each meatball. You should get about 240 meatballs. Simmer the meatballs in the tomato sauce for about 5 minutes, then set aside a generous 1 cup (250 milliliters) of tomato sauce. Add the peas to the meatballs and continue cooking until the peas are tender, thinning the sauce if necessary with a little water.

TO ASSEMBLE THE LASAGNE: Choose a baking dish or lasagne pan measuring about 12 by 9 by 3 inches (30 by 22 by 8 centimeters). The pan must be at least 3 inches (8 centimeters) deep to accommodate all the layers. Coat the bottom and sides of the pan with a little of the reserved tomato sauce. Line the bottom and sides with sheets of pasta, allowing the sheets to hang over the edge of the pan by about 4 inches all around. This overhanging pasta will be folded back over the top layer of filling. The pasta sheets should not overlap, but there should not be any gaps, either. Cut them to fit, as needed.

Top the pasta with one-fourth of the meatball mixture. Then make a layer of one-fourth of the eggs, one-fourth of the mozzarella, and ¼ cup of the pecorino. Without lining the sides of the pan again, repeat the layering process three more times, for a total of four layers of pasta, meatballs, eggs, mozzarella, and pecorino.

Put a final sheet of pasta on top to cover the center, then fold the overhanging pasta back over the lasagne to form a "package," making sure the filling is completely covered. It is okay if the pasta overlaps. Top with the rest of the reserved tomato sauce and sprinkle with the remaining pecorino cheese.

At this point, you can cover and refrigerate the unbaked lasagne for up to a day.

To bake, preheat the oven to 425°F (220°C). Bake the lasagne until it is puffed and bubbling, about 30 minutes (longer if it was refrigerated). Let rest for at least 30 minutes before serving or it will be difficult to cut. The dish can remain at room temperature for up to 2 hours.

SERVES 12

La Pasquetta: *A Holiday Country Picnic*

Natale chi toi, Pasca cu' ccu' voi.
Christmas with family, Easter with friends.

On the Monday after Easter, all Italy takes the day off. The occasion is *la Pasquetta*, ("little Easter"), which virtually everyone celebrates with a picnic in the country with friends. Many people call the holiday *la Scampagnata*—literally, a country outing.

In Calabria, most people bring a dish already prepared, typically something they made at home that morning, like *sagne chine* (Lasagne, Calabrian Style, page 77) or another baked pasta dish, or a wild asparagus and sausage frittata. Even if you had roast baby goat for Easter, you might prepare it again for *la Pasquetta*; it's the season, after all. Others will bring sausages for grilling outdoors, fresh fava beans, cheese, hard-cooked eggs, or homemade *salumi*.

The afternoon passes leisurely, starting with the feasting and ending with songs, stories, accordion playing, dancing, and outdoor games. This carefree day provides a respite from the duties of the holy week that precedes it.

Ravioloni Calabresi

LARGE RAVIOLI WITH FRESH RICOTTA AND *SOPPRESSATA*

These rustic, oversize ravioli are a specialty of my hometown of Verbicaro. Because they are so large—about 3½ inches (9 centimeters) in diameter—you don't need to prepare many; most people eat only two or three. The filling—ricotta, parsley, chopped *soppressata* (cured pork sausage), and pecorino cheese—rarely varies in Calabria, and the sauce is always either tomato or meat sauce. I had to come to the United States to learn that Italians make ravioli in other ways.

We roll the pasta dough by hand, but you can use a pasta machine. My mother gathers and re-rolls the dough trimmings so as not to waste a scrap. "People died of hunger," she reminds me, remembering the grim past of her region. "Calabrians don't throw anything away."

SUGGESTED WINE: Terre di Balbia "Balbium," Calabria
From the Magliocco grape, a richly fruity, rounded wine with a meaty, leathery character; a great food wine with restrained tannin.
ALTERNATE: Merlot

FILLING

2 cups (1 pound/450 grams) fresh ricotta, drained

4 ounces (115 grams) hot or mild *soppressata* (page 203) or *coppa* (page 199), skin removed and finely chopped

3 tablespoons freshly grated pecorino cheese, plus more for topping

2 tablespoons minced flat-leaf parsley

1 large egg

Kosher salt

Freshly ground black pepper

1½ recipes Homemade Fresh Pasta (page 59) *or* ¾ pound store-bought fresh egg pasta in sheets

1 recipe Quick Tomato Sauce (page 53) *or* pork-rib sauce (page 88)

FOR THE FILLING: In a large bowl, mix the ricotta with the *soppressata*, pecorino, parsley, egg, ¼ teaspoon salt, and pepper to taste.

TO ROLL OUT THE DOUGH BY HAND: Follow the instructions for rolling out *lagani* (page 64), but roll until the dough is about ⅟16 inch (1½ millimeters) thick.

Alternatively, roll the dough with a hand-cranked pasta machine into sheets ⅟16 inch (1½ millimeters) thick.

Using a 3½-inch (9-centimeter) round cutter, cut out as many circles as you can. Set half the circles aside, covering them with a kitchen towel so they don't dry out.

TO ASSEMBLE THE RAVIOLONI: Place 2 tablespoons filling in the center of the remaining circles. Top each with one of the reserved circles. Carefully press the edges of the top and bottom circles together. To seal the *ravioloni*, firmly press the edges all around with the tines of a fork held horizontally. Be careful not to pierce the dough. Arrange the *ravioloni* in a single layer on a tray lined with a kitchen towel. Cook the *ravioloni* within an hour, or refrigerate for up to 6 hours before cooking.

TO COOK THE RAVIOLONI: Bring 5 quarts (5 liters) of water to a boil in an 8-quart (8-liter) pot over high heat. Add ¼ cup (35 grams) kosher salt, then gently add the *ravioloni*. Cook until al dente, stirring from time to time with a wooden spoon, about 15 minutes.

Meanwhile, heat the tomato sauce. With a skimmer or slotted spoon, carefully lift the *ravioloni* out one at a time and place on a large serving platter. When they are all on the platter, sprinkle with pecorino cheese to taste, then spoon hot tomato sauce over all.

MAKES ABOUT 20 RAVIOLONI, TO SERVE 6 TO 8

Variation with Dried Pasta

You can bake stuffed *conchiglie* (large shells) with the same amount of filling and 1½ cups Quick Tomato Sauce. In a large pot of boiling salted water, boil 32 *conchiglie* (about 7 ounces/220 grams) until they are 2 to 3 minutes shy of al dente; drain. Stuff each shell with a heaped 1 tablespoon of filling. Spread ½ cup Quick Tomato Sauce on the bottom of a 9- by 13-inch (23- by 32-centimeter) baking dish. Top with the filled shells, placing them next to each other snugly. Top with 1 cup Quick Tomato Sauce and about 2 tablespoons grated pecorino cheese, or more if you like. Bake at 375°F (190°C) until piping hot, 25 to 30 minutes. Serves 5 to 6.

Scorze di Fagiolini con Ragù d'Agnello
"BEAN POD" PASTA WITH SPICY LAMB RAGÙ

My mother learned to make *scorze di fagiolini* ("bean pods") from our relatives from Basilicata, the region just north of Calabria, after they moved to our town. In that region, it is a typical pasta shape, so named because the lengths of dough look like empty bean pods. The same shape is also called *strascinati*, meaning "dragged," because you drag the dough with your fingertips to shape it.

The lamb *ragù* is not a Calabrian sauce but my adaptation of a meat sauce made all over Italy. I include the dish because it is a favorite of my daughter, Danielle, who typically requests it for her birthday dinner. Calabrians rarely use ground meat in a tomato sauce, preferring instead to simmer a large piece of meat, such as bone-in pork shoulder, in their tomato sauce and then serve the meat as a separate course.

As an alternative sauce for *scorze di fagiolini*, consider *sugo di costate di maiale* (pork-rib and tomato sauce, page 88).

SUGGESTED WINE: Criserà "Nerone di Calabria," Calabria Rosso, Calabria
This robust dish can use a big wine, like this jammy red with its aromas of violet, licorice, and black currant.
ALTERNATE: Montepulciano d'Abruzzo

Homemade Fresh Pasta (page 59) *or* 1 pound *strozzapreti* (see Resources, page 369), rigatoni, or penne

RAGÙ

2 tablespoons extra virgin olive oil, plus more if needed

1 pound (450 grams) boneless lamb shoulder *or* leg, all fat removed, cut into ⅓-inch (9-millimeter) dice

½ yellow onion, minced

1 large carrot, minced

1 large celery rib, minced

2 garlic cloves, minced

One 4-inch (10-centimeter) fresh rosemary sprig

Kosher salt and freshly ground black pepper

⅓ cup (80 milliliters) dry white wine

2 cups (500 milliliters) Home-Canned Peeled Tomatoes (page 296) *or* one 14-ounce (400-gram) can Italian San Marzano tomatoes, broken up by hand, with juice

1½ tablespoons Homemade Tomato Paste (page 299) *or* Italian tomato paste

Ground hot red pepper *or* hot red pepper flakes

½ cup (125 milliliters) chicken broth

Freshly grated ricotta salata *or* pecorino cheese

TO SHAPE THE *scorze di fagiolini*, work with a little dough at a time and keep the rest covered with a kitchen towel. Cut off a piece of dough about the size of a cigar. Rolling with the palms of both hands, stretch the dough into a long rope about ¼ inch (6 millimeters) to ⅜ inch (9 millimeters) thick. Cut the rope into 3½-inch-long (9-centimeter-long) pieces. Working with one piece at a time, hold the three middle fingers (index, middle, and ring fingers) of each hand next to each other. Place these six fingertips on top of the piece of dough, press down firmly, then pull the dough toward you to make it curl. The result should resemble an empty bean pod with the impressions from your fingertips marking where the bean seeds would have been. Repeat with the remaining dough, arranging the pasta on a clean kitchen towel. The pasta may be prepared up to 4 hours ahead and left uncovered.

FOR THE RAGÙ: Heat a 4- to 6-quart (4- to 6-liter) Dutch oven or other heavy-bottomed pot over moderately high heat. When the pot is hot, add the olive oil and swirl to coat. Add the lamb and cook until the meat is browned all over and sizzling, about 5 minutes. Transfer the lamb to a plate and set aside.

Add more oil to the pot if necessary, then add the onion, carrot, celery, garlic, and rosemary sprig to the pot and lower the heat to medium. Cook until the vegetables are softened and lightly browned, about 5 minutes. Return the lamb to the pot and season with salt and black pepper. Add the wine and bring to a boil. With a wooden spoon, scrape up any caramelized bits from the bottom of the pot. Simmer until the wine has almost completely evaporated. Stir in the tomatoes, tomato paste, and hot pepper. Simmer for 15 to 20 minutes to soften the tomato and develop the flavors, then stir in the broth. Cover and adjust the heat to maintain a gentle simmer. Cook until the meat is tender and the sauce is thick and flavorful, about 1½ hours. Remove the rosemary sprig and adjust the seasoning.

Bring 5 quarts (5 liters) of water to a boil in an 8-quart (8-liter) pot over high heat. Add the ¼ cup (35 grams) kosher salt, then add the *scorze di fagiolini* a handful at a time, stirring to prevent them from sticking. Cook until the pasta is al dente, 15 minutes or more, depending on how long the pasta has dried. Set aside 1 cup (250 milliliters) of the pasta water, then drain the pasta in a colander and return it to the warm pot over moderate heat. Add the *ragù* and cook the pasta and sauce together for about a minute, adding some of the reserved water to thin the sauce if needed. Remove from the heat and sprinkle with grated cheese to taste. Stir again and serve at once, passing a bowl of extra grated cheese at the table.

SERVES 4 TO 6

Fusilli Calabresi con Sugo di Capra
FRESH "KNITTING NEEDLE" PASTA WITH GOAT SAUCE

Fusilli are the signature pasta shape of Calabria, the first shape that every young girl learned at her mother's side in times past. Unlike the corkscrew-shaped pasta that many manufacturers call *fusilli*, Calabrian *fusilli* are hollow, spaghetti-length strands made by rolling the fresh dough around a knitting needle. In some parts of Calabria, they are known as *maccheroni al ferretto* or *filej* (prounounced fee-LAY), also spelled *filei*.

Women of my mother's generation are amazingly adept at the technique, having made *fusilli* for Sunday lunch for years on end. Regrettably, in many Calabrian households, the skill is not being passed down. My home is an exception. Although I am not as swift at shaping *fusilli* as my mother, my son is a whiz.

The most traditional sauce for *fusilli* is *sugo*, a tomato sauce infused with the flavor of braised meat, usually goat. You can make *sugo* with any cut that benefits from long, slow cooking, such as the shoulder of goat, lamb, or pork. When we kept chickens in Calabria, my mother would sometimes use an old hen or rooster. The sauce absorbs the flavor of the meat, but the meat itself is left behind in the pot when the pasta is sauced. It reappears as a second course, following the pasta and usually accompanied by fried potatoes.

Many Hispanic and Middle Eastern markets carry goat or can get it. It is a dark meat with a rich taste, and if you trim it well, the sauce will not be at all fatty. I like to add a couple of spoonfuls of my homemade tomato paste for added color and depth, but it's not essential.

You will need a No. 1 knitting needle to shape the pasta, or you can make a rod from the long side of a thick wire clothes hanger, snipped from the hanger with wire clippers. If you don't want to make homemade pasta, you can substitute dried pasta. Imported *filei Calabresi* (also called *maccheroni al ferretto*) are sporadically available in the United States and would be the closest substitute among dried pasta shapes. Another good choice with this sauce would be *strozzapreti* ("priest stranglers"). Rustichella d'Abruzzo makes an excellent version (see Resources, page 369). Despite their name, the familiar dried fusilli packaged by manufacturers such as De Cecco and Delverde do not resemble *fusilli Calabresi*.

SUGGESTED WINE: Odoardi "Vigna Garrone," Scavigna, Calabria
A smooth red wine with great depth of fruit but only moderate tannins, with aromas of dark chocolate, cardamom, and black cherry; one of Calabria's finest wines.
ALTERNATE: Rioja

1½ recipes Homemade Fresh Pasta (page 59) *or* 1 pound (450 grams) *filei Calabresi, strozzapreti,* rigatoni, penne, or bucatini

SAUCE

3 pounds (1½ kilograms) bone-in goat, preferably shoulder, trimmed of all visible fat

¼ cup (60 milliliters) extra virgin olive oil

5 garlic cloves, halved

Kosher salt

2 tablespoons Homemade Tomato Paste (page 299) *or* Italian tomato paste, optional

1 quart (1 liter) peeled, seeded, and diced fresh plum tomatoes *or* Home-Canned Peeled Tomatoes (page 296) *or* one 28-ounce (800-gram) can Italian San Marzano tomatoes, broken up by hand, with juice

8 to 10 fresh basil leaves, torn into smaller pieces

Ground hot red pepper, optional

Freshly grated pecorino or ricotta salata cheese

TO SHAPE THE *FUSILLI*: Work with a little dough at a time and keep the rest covered with a kitchen towel. Cut off a piece of dough about the size of a cigar and roll it into a rope about ⅜ inch (9 millimeters) thick. Cut the rope into 3- to 3½-inch-long (7½- to 9-centimeter-long) pieces. Working with one piece at a time, press a knitting needle into the center of the dough lengthwise. With the palms of both hands, begin rolling the dough around the needle, stretching it along the needle as you roll, until it is about 10 inches long. With one hand, quickly slide the pasta off the needle and place it on top of a kitchen towel until ready to cook. If the dough is properly made and you don't press too hard as you roll, the noodle will come off the needle without sticking. Repeat with the remaining dough. The *fusilli* may be prepared up to 4 hours ahead and left uncovered at room temperature.

FOR THE SAUCE: Ask the butcher to saw the goat meat into 12 approximately equal pieces. Heat a heavy 8-quart (8-liter) pot over high heat. Add the olive oil. When the oil is hot, add the meat and 6 of the garlic halves. Brown the meat on all sides, about 10 minutes. Remove and discard the browned garlic, then season the meat with 2 teaspoons salt. Stir in the tomato paste, if using, then add the diced tomatoes, basil, hot pepper to taste, if using, 2 teaspoons salt, and remaining 4 garlic halves. Cover and reduce the heat to maintain a gentle simmer. Cook until the meat is tender and beginning to fall off the bone, about 1½ hours. The sauce should be thick enough to coat the pasta nicely. If it is too thin, cook uncovered for the final few minutes to reduce it. If it is too thick, thin with a little water. Taste and adjust the seasoning. Keep warm.

TO COOK AND DRESS THE PASTA: Bring 5 quarts (5 liters) of water to a boil in an 8-quart (8-liter) pot over high heat. Add ¼ cup (35 grams) kosher salt, then add the pasta and cook, stirring occasionally, until al dente, 8 to 10 minutes. Drain and transfer the *fusilli* to a serving bowl or platter. Sprinkle the pasta with grated cheese, then add 1½ cups (375 milliliters) of sauce, leaving the goat meat behind. Toss the pasta and serve immediately. Serve the meat as a second course.

SERVES 6

My mom shaping *fusilli*: pressing a knitting needle into the pasta and stretching dough around the needle.

Maccheroni Larghi con Sugo di Costate di Maiale
WIDE NOODLES WITH PORK RIBS AND TOMATO

These *maccheroni larghi*, or wide handmade noodles, are common in my hometown of Verbicaro. Skilled home cooks like my mother roll the eggless dough by hand with a rolling pin, then cut it into wide strips with a knife. Thanks to the hand rolling and the lack of egg, the pasta has a firm, almost chewy texture.

In times past, the people of Verbicaro prepared this meaty pork-rib sauce primarily during *Carnevale*, the festive days before Lent. Most households would have recently killed their pig in the chill of winter and would have fresh pork ribs for the sauce.

The preparation provides two dishes in one. After the pork ribs become fork tender, they are set aside, to reappear as a second course with a little of the sauce spooned over them. The remainder of the savory, meat-flavored sauce dresses the fresh homemade pasta, served as a first course with a flurry of pecorino cheese. (Photograph on page 44.)

SUGGESTED WINE: Tenuta Viglione Primitivo, Gioia del Colle, Apulia
The pork ribs call for a wine with sweet fruit and not a lot of tannin, such as this spicy red.
ALTERNATE: Zinfandel

PORK-RIB SAUCE

2 pounds (900 grams) pork baby back ribs

2 tablespoons extra virgin olive oil

3 garlic cloves, halved

Kosher salt

2 pounds (900 grams) peeled, seeded, and diced fresh plum
    tomatoes, *or* 1 quart (1 liter) Home-Canned Peeled Tomatoes
    (page 296) *or* 28-ounce (800-gram) can Italian San Marzano
    tomatoes, broken up by hand, with juice

8 to 10 fresh basil leaves

Ground hot red pepper

Fresh Homemade Pasta (page 59) *or* 1 pound (450 grams) dried
    pasta, such as penne, rigatoni, or bucatini

Freshly grated pecorino cheese

FOR THE SAUCE: Cut between the ribs to make individual ribs. Heat a heavy 6-quart (6-liter) pot over medium heat and add the olive oil. When the oil is hot, add the ribs and the garlic. Season the meat with 1½ teaspoons salt and brown on all sides, about 15 minutes, letting it get crusty on each side before you turn it. Add the tomatoes, another 1½ teaspoons salt, and the basil, tearing the leaves in half as you add them. Cover and simmer gently until the meat begins to fall off the bone, 1½ to 2 hours. The sauce should be thick enough to coat the pasta nicely. If it seems too thin, cook uncovered for the final few minutes to reduce it. If it is too thick, thin with a little water. Season to taste with salt and hot pepper.

TO SHAPE THE *MACCHERONI*: Follow the instructions for rolling out *lagani* on page 64, until you have a circle of dough 16 to 18 inches (40 to 45 centimeters) in diameter. To cut the dough into *maccheroni larghi*, dust the surface of the circle with flour. Lift the edge closest to you and fold about 3 inches (8 centimeters) of dough over. Continue folding the dough like a jelly roll until you have a long flat roll about 3 inches (8 centimeters) wide.

With a large, sharp knife, cut the pasta roll into ¾-inch-wide (18-millimeter-wide) ribbons. Unfurl the ribbons and cut into 8-inch (20-centimeter) lengths. Lay on a clean, dry kitchen towel. You can cook the pasta immediately or let it rest, covered with another clean towel, for a few hours.

At serving time, reheat the sauce if necessary. Bring 5 quarts (5 liters) of water to a boil over high heat. Add ¼ cup (35 grams) kosher salt, then add the pasta and cook, stirring occasionally, until al dente, about 15 minutes.

Just before the pasta is done, set the ribs aside, leaving the warm sauce in the pot. Make a thin bed of tomato sauce on a platter. Drain the pasta and transfer it to the platter. Sprinkle with pecorino, then top with just enough sauce to coat the pasta. Serve immediately, tossing it with the sauce as you serve.

Return the ribs to the pot with the remaining sauce and reheat gently for a second course.

SERVES 4 TO 6

Rasckatieddi di Patate

POTATO GNOCCHI, CALABRIAN STYLE

In Southern Italy, we make gnocchi with just flour and potato, no egg. You might think they would be heavy, but they are light on the tongue. When I first tasted gnocchi in Italian-American restaurants, I thought they tasted like gummy mashed potatoes. Our gnocchi have a firmness to them, almost like pasta.

To produce the ridges characteristic of Calabrian gnocchi, you need a special wooden paddle. (See Resources, page 369.) You can shape gnocchi on a wooden cutting board, but they will lack the ridges that hold the sauce so nicely. Our dialect name for gnocchi, *rasckatieddi*, comes from *raschiare*, meaning to scrape. To make the nuggets of dough curl, you "scrape" them against the ridges of the gnocchi paddle.

Make the gnocchi no more than a couple of hours before you plan to cook them. You can also freeze them uncooked; when you are ready to eat them, boil without thawing.

Serve gnocchi with tomato sauce, as I've suggested here, or with *sugo di costate di maiale* (pork-rib sauce, page 88). Follow with a second course that doesn't contain tomato, such as Fresh Homemade Fennel Sausage (page 211).

SUGGESTED WINE: Terre di Balbia "Serra Monte Rosso," Calabria
A supple, full-bodied red wine from a blend of Magliocco, Gaglioppo, and Sangiovese grapes; it has enough fullness to complement the textural richness of the gnocchi and enough sweet fruit to manage the tomato sauce.
ALTERNATE: Chianti Classico

---

1 pound (450 grams) russet potatoes, unpeeled

Approximately 2¼ cups (11 ounces/315 grams) unbleached all-purpose flour, plus more for dusting

Kosher salt

½ recipe Quick Tomato Sauce (page 53) *or* Spicy Lamb *Ragù* (page 82)

Freshly grated pecorino cheese

PUT THE WHOLE POTATOES in a 4-quart (4-liter) pot and cover with cold water. Bring to a boil over high heat, then reduce the heat to a simmer and cook until the potatoes are tender when pierced, 30 to 40 minutes. Drain the potatoes and peel while hot, then let them cool completely. Pass them through a food mill fitted with the medium disk or a potato ricer. If you don't have either tool, you can mash the potatoes with a fork or potato masher until completely smooth. Don't use a food processor or you will have library paste.

Add 2 cups (280 grams) of the flour and mix thoroughly with your hands. Keep kneading, adding more flour until you have a smooth, firm, nonsticky dough. It should come together in just a couple of minutes.

Working with a little of the dough at a time, make a long rope about the thickness of your index finger. Dust with flour. Cut the rope into ¾-inch (2-centimeter) pieces. Dust again with flour.

Lightly flour a gnocchi paddle. Put a piece of dough on the paddle. Using the index and middle fingers of your dominant hand, press down on the dough, then pull toward you to make the dough curl into a "C." The dough is soft, so you don't need to press hard. As you shape them, transfer the pieces to a tray lined with a kitchen towel, keeping them in a single layer so they don't stick to each other. Repeat with the remaining dough, lightly flouring the gnocchi paddle as needed to keep the dough from sticking.

Bring 5 quarts (5 liters) of water to a boil in an 8-quart (8-liter) pot over high heat. Add ¼ cup (35 grams) kosher salt, then add the gnocchi and cook, stirring occasionally, until tender, 5 to 6 minutes.

While the gnocchi cook, warm the tomato sauce in a skillet. Drain the gnocchi. Put 2 tablespoons of the tomato sauce in a serving bowl and put the gnocchi on top. Sprinkle with cheese, then add the remaining sauce. Toss and serve immediately.

SERVES 4 TO 6

Chicken Soup with Ricotta Dumplings (page 96)

Minestre, Riso, Polenta
soup, rice, polenta

When a family meal in Calabria doesn't begin with pasta, it's a good bet that it will start with polenta, soup, or rice. With such sturdy, filling dishes, Calabrians historically have appeased the lion's share of their hunger, so that the smaller portion of meat or eggs to follow does not seem insufficient.

Reflecting the region's long lack of exposure to the rest of Italy, Calabria developed its own repertoire of these dishes. Other regions of Italy cook polenta, of course, but the Calabrian method is different. We prepare rice unlike Northern Italian cooks, and our soups have the rustic, artless, yet deeply satisfying character typical of dishes made by cooks challenged to create something from nothing.

Common to almost all of these recipes is the use of water instead of broth. Meat broth, or *brodo*, was a precious resource in Calabria in times past, reserved for sick people or fed to new mothers to restore their strength. Today, most Calabrians can afford to make *brodo*, but they don't want it in their rice or soup, believing that it masks the pure taste of the vegetables and other ingredients.

Polenta came to Calabria with the Spaniards, who introduced this remarkable grain from the New World. Corn thrived in Calabria, and people ate it because it was inexpensive, but it has never been as prized or valuable as wheat. To many of my parents' and grandparents' generation, corn symbolized hard times. It was what you ate to stretch your wheat supply.

The polenta preferred in Calabria is a fine grind, similar to what Americans know as cornmeal. After only fifteen minutes of cooking, it is silky and smooth, with no hint of graininess. When I have asked Calabrians knowledgeable about the regional gastronomy about this preference for fine polenta, they all speculate that it developed because the local mills were calibrated for wheat flour, the predominant grain. Curiously, the Veneto region, at the other end of the country, also uses fine cornmeal. In many other parts of Italy, polenta means coarse-ground cornmeal.

Calabrians also differ from their compatriots in stirring ingredients—usually vegetables—into polenta rather than spooning a sauce over it. For some recipes, the vegetable gets a head start in boiling salted water, then the polenta is added to the same pot and the two cook together.

These polenta dishes are from *la cucina casalinga*, the home cook's repertoire. You don't find them in restaurants as they are possibly considered too humble. My father grew corn for our pigs and chickens, so we ate polenta during the winter, but in general, it is not a dish that one would find at city tables or in Calabrian homes where corn isn't grown.

In poorer times, Calabrians could and did make soup with nothing but stale bread, water, salt, parsley, garlic, and olive oil. Fortunately, Calabrian cooks are no longer called on to work such miracles, but we have retained a taste for purity in our soups. We never use two herbs if one will do. We want to relish the essence of the main ingredient, usually a peak-season vegetable like green beans or fava beans. Too many other components would muddle the taste.

For the most part, Calabria soups fall into one of two categories: *minestra* or *zuppa*. People don't always agree on what differentiates a *minestra* from a *zuppa*, but my own experience suggests that *minestre* tend to be thicker and more substantial. *Zuppe* are typically more refined and brothy. The Calabrian *minestra*, which lies somewhere between a soup and a stew, is always vegetable based, dense, and chunky, with only a small amount of concentrated vegetable juices. *Minestra* often includes beans, potatoes, pasta, or even a slice of stale bread; a *minestra* is never dainty. I associate *minestra* with the peasant kitchen, while *zuppa* has more elegance.

Rice is not a big crop in Calabria, although some rice of the Carnaroli variety is grown on the piana di Sibari (plain of Sibari). Although Calabrians have come to know and enjoy risotto in recent decades, and to prepare it at home, the region's traditional recipes for rice do not follow the risotto method. The Calabrian approach is to boil the rice separately in salted water, then unite it for the final few minutes with beans or seasonal vegetables that have been cooked and seasoned separately. The result is *riso*, not *risotto*. The texture is soft and soothing, the flavors direct.

Riso typically showcases only one vegetable, not a melange. Common choices include escarole, cabbage, fava beans, peas, wild fennel greens, borlotti beans, tomato sauce, even potatoes. *Riso in bianco*, a notable exception, includes no vegetables at all unless you count garlic. This plain but aromatic porridge is what Calabrian mothers make for their sick children, simmering water, rice, olive oil, garlic, and a parsley sprig together until the rice is tender and creamy.

Like many Calabrians of my generation, I have come to love the creamy texture of Northern Italian risotto and have added the dish to my rice repertoire. Many Calabrian chefs have done so as well. Dining in the region's restaurants, I have sampled many sophisticated *risotti* made with local ingredients, such as wild mushrooms, or broccoli rabe and *bottarga*. I wanted to include at least one of these modern recipes—a risotto with fresh mussels (page 107)—because they reflect what Calabrians enjoy eating when they dine out today.

Polpette di Ricotta in Brodo
CHICKEN SOUP WITH RICOTTA DUMPLINGS

Another example of the Calabrian propensity to make "meatballs" out of almost any ingredient, these dumplings are featherlight and about the size of a large olive. Poach them in rich chicken broth to make a delicate first course. (Photograph on page 92.)

DUMPLINGS

1¼ cups (285 grams) Homemade Ricotta (page 144) *or* store-bought
    whole-milk ricotta

2 large eggs

½ cup (40 grams) fresh breadcrumbs

½ cup (50 grams) freshly grated pecorino cheese

2 tablespoons finely chopped flat-leaf parsley, plus more for garnish

Freshly ground black pepper

1 cup (5 ounces/140 grams) all-purpose flour for coating

2 quarts (2 liters) chicken broth, preferably homemade

PREPARE THE DUMPLINGS: If using store-bought ricotta, put it in a sieve set over a bowl for about 30 minutes to allow any excess moisture to drain. Homemade ricotta does not need additional draining.

In a bowl, combine the ricotta, eggs, breadcrumbs, pecorino, parsley, and several grinds of black pepper. Mix thoroughly with a fork. Refrigerate for 30 minutes to firm the mixture so the dumplings will be easier to shape.

Make a bed of flour on a dinner plate. For each dumpling, use 1 heaping teaspoon of the ricotta mixture and roll it between your palms into a ball about ¾ inch (18 millimeters) in diameter. Roll in flour to coat lightly, then arrange on a tray. You should be able to make sixty to sixty-five balls. You can make the balls up to 4 hours ahead. Refrigerate uncovered on the tray.

Bring the chicken broth to a boil in a 4-quart (4-liter) pot. Reduce the heat to a bare simmer and add the balls. Cook until they float to the surface, 2 to 3 minutes; do not allow the broth to boil or the dumplings may break apart. Divide among eight soup bowls and serve at once, garnishing with chopped parsley.

SERVES 8

Minestra di Fave e Cipolle
THICK FAVA BEAN AND SPRING ONION STEW

Fava beans and spring onions mature in Calabrian gardens at about the same time—in mid to late spring—so it is natural for cooks to combine them in the kitchen. My mother pairs the two vegetables in this *minestra*, more like a vegetable stew than a soup, seasoning it liberally with the sweet paprika we call *pepe rosso* (page 304). Modern Calabrians often use tomato to give their vegetable dishes color, but older recipes such as this one rely solely on *pepe rosso*.

When we lived in Calabria, and my parents preserved their homemade sausage under a layer of pork fat, my mother would sometimes reheat a chunk of sausage in this *minestra*. After the sausage had sufficiently flavored the beans, she would lift it out, and we would have the *minestra* as a first course with the sausage following. To replicate this flavor, you could pan-fry some thick slices of Fresh Homemade Fennel Sausage (page 211) or store-bought Italian sausage, then add them to the *minestra* during the final few minutes.

I serve this dish as a first course, followed by roast lamb, chicken, or pork. Leftovers thicken considerably as the beans absorb the juices, so I'll serve the remaining *minestra* on its second day as a *contorno*, or side dish. Note that the fava beans are shelled but not peeled for this soup. The peel keeps the beans intact, and most Italians like its faintly bitter flavor.

SUGGESTED WINE: Basilim "Sicone," Aglianico del Vulture, Basilicata
An elegant Aglianico on the lighter side, with vigorous acidity and aromas of plum, red currant, and clove.
ALTERNATE: Barbera d'Alba

---

8 pounds (3½ kilograms) fresh fava beans

1 pound (450 grams) spring onions, red or white, *or* green onions (scallions)

3 tablespoons extra virgin olive oil

Kosher salt

1½ tablespoons Calabrian paprika (page 304) *or* Spanish sweet paprika

Ground hot red pepper

SHELL THE FAVA BEANS but do not peel them. You should have about 3 pounds (1½ kilograms) of shelled beans.

If using spring onions, which have their leek-like stalks attached, halve the onions and stalks lengthwise, or quarter them lengthwise if they are large, then cut into pieces about 1 to 1½ inches (2½ to 4 centimeters) long. If using green onions, cut white and green parts crosswise into 1- to 1½-inch (2½- to 4-centimeter) pieces. You should have about 6 cups (1½ liters) of sliced onion.

Heat the olive oil in a large pot over moderately high heat. Add the onions and season with salt. Sauté until softened but not browned, about 5 minutes. Add the fava beans, the paprika, and hot pepper to taste. Add 4½ cups (1⅛ liters) water,

Fresh fava beans

which should just cover the beans. Bring to a boil and season again with salt. Boil briskly until the liquid is well reduced and the beans are tender, 30 to 35 minutes. Add more hot water if the beans threaten to cook dry. They should not be soupy, but there should be enough flavorful liquid to moisten them.

Serve hot or warm.

SERVES 6

Minestra di Fagiolini Verdi con Pomodoro
MIDSUMMER SOUP OF ROMANO BEANS, POTATOES, AND TOMATO

The preferred green bean in Calabria is a long, flat-podded pole bean similar to the Romano beans found in some seed catalogs. In the garden my father oversees in my California backyard, he uses scraps of salvaged wood or tree prunings—he buys nothing—to construct teepee-like trellises for the beans to clamber up. To my family's taste, no other green bean comes close to the intense, meaty flavor and creamy texture of these homegrown beans. You can find Romano beans, or Italian-style flat beans, at some farmers' markets in midsummer. They should be a rich green with no blemishes or bulges. If you can feel seeds developing inside, the beans are too mature. Snap them up during the brief period they're available and enjoy them in this brothy *minestra.*

As with all of our *minestre*, the vegetables here should be thoroughly cooked, the beans tender and even starting to split, and the potatoes beginning to break down so as to thicken the broth. I add the tomatoes near the end because their acidity would make the beans and potatoes soften more slowly. My mother likes to place broken *friselle* (page 128), Calabrian rusks, on the bottom of her bowl before she adds the soup to soak up the flavorful broth.

This quickly made soup concentrates all the flavors of my summer garden. I make it for lunch or serve it as a first course for dinner. A compatible second course would be Grilled Swordfish Rolls with Breadcrumb Stuffing (page 172) or any grilled meat.

SUGGESTED WINE: Librandi "Duca San Felice," Cirò Rosso Riserva, Calabria
A relatively light Cirò, this red wine has a tart cranberry character and would be appealing on a warm summer day.
ALTERNATE: Grenache

1½ pounds (675 grams) flat Italian-style green beans, such as Romano beans, ends trimmed

3 tablespoons extra virgin olive oil

½ pound (225 grams) Yukon Gold or russet potatoes, peeled and sliced ⅛ inch (3 millimeters) thick

3 large garlic cloves, halved

Kosher salt

1½ cups (375 milliliters) peeled, seeded, and diced ripe fresh tomato

Handful of fresh basil leaves, torn into smaller pieces

1 or 2 small fresh red or green hot peppers, such as serrano, halved lengthwise

2 Calabrian Rusks (page 128) or 4 to 6 slices of day-old bread, optional

IN A 6-QUART (6-liter) pot, put the whole beans, olive oil, and 4 cups (1 liter) water. The water should barely cover the beans; add more if needed. Bring to a boil over high heat and let boil briskly until the beans are beginning to soften but still have a bite, about 8 minutes.

Add the potatoes, garlic, and a generous pinch of salt. Boil until the potatoes are just tender, about 10 minutes, then add the tomatoes, basil, and hot peppers. Boil until the tomatoes have softened and the hot peppers have released their heat, about 5 minutes. Taste for salt, then let cool. Serve warm or at room temperature. For a heartier soup, divide the rusks or sliced day-old bread among the serving bowls and spoon the soup over.

SERVES 4 TO 6

My mother trimming Romano beans

Zuppa di Cipolla alla Casa Janca
RITA CALLIPO'S CREAMY RED ONION SOUP

Tropea, a picturesque beach town on the Tyrrhenian Sea, is famous for the sweet red onions grown nearby. Every souvenir shop in Tropea sells them, and you also find them in midsummer strung up and hanging from the beams at every roadside produce stand in the vicinity. Many Calabrians plant these red onions in their garden. They are so mild, they can be eaten raw—and usually are. The main growing area is actually south of Tropea, around Capo Vaticano and Ricadi, but the onions have taken the name of the more famous beach town.

My grandmother made a soup with the famous red onions of Tropea, as Calabrian cooks still do today, but I only vaguely recall it. So on one trip back to Calabria, I made it a mission to taste it again, but by the end of my stay, I still hadn't encountered it. On my last night, I checked in to Casa Janca, a rustic *agriturismo* near the fishing village of Pizzo, just northeast of Tropea. The proprietor, Rita Callipo, is a highly regarded cook. When I told Rita how disappointed I was to have missed the red onion soup of Tropea, she volunteered to make it for dinner. She purees part of the soup to give it more body, something I'm sure my grandmother didn't do but a refinement I have adopted. Through slow cooking, the onions become mellow and sweet; adding a little flour makes the finished soup creamy. Rita uses vegetable broth but I prefer to use water, as many Calabrian cooks do, to let the onion flavor shine through. For a more substantial dish, you can serve the soup over a thick slice of toasted bread.

To follow the soup, I might serve Swordfish in a Garlicky Broth (page 167) or Fresh Homemade Fennel Sausage (page 211) crisped on the grill.

The best onions for this soup are those identified in markets as "Sweet Italian." They may have an elongated torpedo shape, or they may be round and squat. Globe-shaped red onions tend to be less sweet, but they will work in this recipe.

SUGGESTED WINE: Librandi "Magno Megonio," Val di Neto, Calabria
A rich, velvety, rounded red wine from the Magliocco grape with a sweet cherry fragrance.
ALTERNATE: Merlot

3 pounds (1½ kilograms) sweet Italian red onions, halved and thinly
   sliced

⅓ cup (80 milliliters) extra virgin olive oil

1 tablespoon kosher salt, plus more as needed

2 tablespoons unbleached all-purpose flour

1½ quarts (1½ liters) water *or* vegetable broth, preferably
   homemade, plus more as needed

Freshly ground black pepper

6 tablespoons freshly grated pecorino cheese

PUT THE ONIONS, olive oil, and the 1 tablespoon salt in a 6- to 8-quart (6- to 8-liter) pot. Cook over moderately low heat, stirring occasionally, until the onions are very sweet and so soft that they have almost melted, and until any moisture they generate has evaporated, about an hour. Sprinkle in the flour and stir to blend it in. Cook for about 3 minutes to get rid of the raw flour taste. Add the water or vegetable broth, raise the heat to medium-high, and bring the soup to a boil. Lower the heat to maintain a gentle simmer and cook until the mixture is creamy and has a pleasing souplike consistency, about 30 minutes.

With a food mill fitted with the coarse plate, puree about half of the soup, then return the puree to the pot. Stir it in well and reheat over moderate heat. If the soup is thicker than you like, thin with water. Add several grinds of black pepper and adjust the salt.

Preheat the broiler and position a rack about 4 inches (10 centimeters) from the element. Divide the soup among six heatproof bowls. Sprinkle 1 tablespoon pecorino cheese on the surface of each bowl of soup. Working in batches if necessary, set each bowl under the broiler for a minute or two until the cheese has melted and browned lightly. Serve immediately.

SERVES 6

Vellutata di Ceci con Gamberi

CREAMY CHICK PEA SOUP WITH SHRIMP AND ANISE SEED

Located in the historic part of Rende, a university town near Cosenza, the restaurant Pantagruel specializes in seafood. This velvety soup, which chef Tonino Napoli garnished with the local black anise seed, was part of a parade of superb seafood dishes I enjoyed there. I have not been able to find black anise seed outside of Calabria—and it is even hard to find there—so I have substituted store-bought green anise seed. The flavors are comparable, although the black has a more licorice-like taste.

Follow the soup with Whole Salt-Baked Sea Bass (page 181) or Swordfish "Glutton's Style" with Tomato, Capers, and Olives (page 175).

SUGGESTED WINE: Romangia Società Cooperativa "Lamarina," Cannonau di Sardegna, Sardinia
A vibrant but light red wine—lighter than most Pinot Noir—from a cooperative on Sardinia's northwest coast.
ALTERNATE: Nebbiolo Langhe

½ pound (225 grams) dried chick peas, soaked 12 hours in water to cover by several inches

1 tablespoon kosher salt

SHRIMP STOCK

18 large unpeeled shrimp, about ¾ pound (340 grams)

2 flat-leaf parsley sprigs

2½ teaspoons kosher salt

3 tablespoons extra virgin olive oil

½ yellow onion, diced

1 large carrot, diced

1 celery rib, diced

1 garlic clove, minced

½ teaspoon anise seed, crushed medium-fine in a mortar

Ground hot red pepper

Creamy Chick Pea Soup with Shrimp

DRAIN THE SOAKED chick peas and put them in a 2-quart (2-liter) saucepan with 4 cups (1 liter) cold water. Bring to a simmer, skimming any foam. Adjust the heat to maintain a bare simmer and cook uncovered until the chick peas are soft, 45 minutes to 1½ hours, depending on age. Add the salt about 10 minutes before they are done. Let the chick peas cool in the cooking liquid. Strain and reserve the broth.

MAKE THE SHRIMP STOCK: Peel the shrimp, reserving the shells. Devein the shrimp by slitting them down the back and pulling out the thin dark vein. Rinse the shrimp, then put them in a bowl and refrigerate until you are ready to poach them.

Put the shrimp shells, parsley, and salt in a 4-quart (4-liter) saucepan with 2 quarts (2 liters) cold water. Bring to a simmer, skimming any foam. Adjust the heat to maintain a simmer and cook until the liquid has reduced by half, about 45 minutes. Strain, discarding the solids, and set the stock aside.

Heat the olive oil in a 4-quart (4-liter) saucepan over moderate heat. Add the onion, carrot, celery, and garlic. Sauté, stirring often, until the vegetables are soft but not colored, about 5 minutes. Add the drained chick peas and cook with the vegetables, stirring occasionally, for about 5 minutes. Add 3 cups of the shrimp stock. Bring to a simmer and simmer gently for 10 minutes to meld the flavors.

In a blender, puree the contents of the saucepan until completely smooth. Strain the puree through a fine sieve into a clean saucepan, pressing on the solids to extract as much flavor as possible. Using the reserved chick pea broth (1 cup of broth will probably be sufficient), thin the puree to a velvety consistency. Reheat the puree over moderate heat. Taste for salt.

While the soup is reheating, bring the remaining 1 cup shrimp stock to a simmer in a 10-inch skillet over high heat. Add the reserved shrimp and cook, turning once, until they turn white, 1 to 2 minutes. If the chick pea soup still seems a little thick, use this flavorful shrimp stock to thin it.

To serve, divide the hot soup among six bowls. Divide the shrimp among the bowls. Garnish each serving with a sprinkle of crushed anise seed and a dusting of hot pepper. Serve immediately.

SERVES 6

Risotto with Fresh Mussels

Risotto con le Cozze
RISOTTO WITH FRESH MUSSELS

Chefs at the beachfront restaurants on Calabria's Tyrrhenian coast make superb seafood risotto, having adopted that Northern Italian rice cooking technique. My favorite version uses mussels, with a little saffron and tomato to give the rice the deep coral color of lobster bisque. I'm not sure what gives this risotto its creamy richness; it tastes like it contains heaps of butter, yet it has none. I shell most of the steamed mussels before stirring them into the risotto but leave some in the shell for eye appeal.

You could make a dinner of this risotto, with a green salad after. For a more substantial meal, serve the risotto as a first course, followed by grilled swordfish steaks with the *salmoriglio* sauce on page 172.

SUGGESTED WINE: Ippolito 1845 "Liber Pater," Cirò Rosso Classico Superiore, Calabria
A lighter-bodied everyday red wine without significant tannin and with hints of mulberry and crabapple.
ALTERNATE: Côtes du Rhône or Chinon

---

2 pounds (900 grams) fresh mussels

5 tablespoons extra virgin olive oil

2 garlic cloves, halved

3 sprigs plus 2 tablespoons minced flat-leaf parsley

1 cup (250 milliliters) peeled, seeded, and diced fresh tomatoes,
    or Home-Canned Peeled Tomatoes (page 296), *or* canned San
    Marzano tomatoes, finely chopped

1 teaspoon kosher salt

1 small dried hot red pepper, optional

½ cup (125 milliliters) dry white wine

1 cup minced yellow onion

2 cups (400 grams) Italian Carnaroli or Arborio rice

Generous pinch of saffron threads

1 quart (1 liter) hot vegetable broth, preferably homemade

RINSE THE MUSSELS well in several changes of cold water. Discard any that are open or that fail to close when held under cold running water. With a food brush, scrub the mussel shells to remove any bits of sand or grit clinging to them and yank out the hairy beard between the shells.

Heat 2 tablespoons of the olive oil in a 12-inch (30-centimeter) skillet over medium-high heat. Add the garlic cloves and the parsley sprigs and sauté until the garlic begins to color. Add the tomatoes and the salt. Tear the hot red pepper in half, if using, and add it to the skillet. Simmer briskly for 1 to 2 minutes to soften the tomatoes and develop the flavor. Add the wine and the mussels. Cover and cook until the mussels open, about 2 minutes. Remove the skillet from the heat. With tongs, transfer the mussels to a bowl, leaving the tomato sauce behind in the skillet. Discard the garlic, parsley sprigs, and hot pepper, if using. Set aside two dozen mussels in their shells. Remove the remaining mussels from their shells and discard the shells.

In a 4-quart (4-liter) pot, warm the remaining 3 tablespoons olive oil over medium heat. Add the onion and sauté until softened, about 5 minutes. Add the rice and cook, stirring, until it is hot throughout, about 2 minutes. Add the tomato sauce from the skillet and the saffron, adjust the heat to maintain a steady simmer, and cook until the liquid has been absorbed, about 2 minutes.

Begin adding a ladleful of the hot broth about 1 cup/125 milliliters at a time, just enough to barely cover the rice. Adjust the heat so that the risotto bubbles steadily but not vigorously. Stir often until all the liquid has been absorbed, then add another ladleful of broth. It will take about 20 minutes for the rice to become al dente; the grains should be firm but not chalky at the core and the risotto should be creamy, neither soupy nor stiff. You may not need all the broth. Remove the risotto from the heat and stir in the minced parsley and the mussels, both shelled and unshelled. Taste for seasoning; the risotto will probably have sufficient salt. Serve immediately in bowls.

SERVES 6

Riso con Fagioli
SPICY CALABRIAN RICE WITH TOMATO AND BORLOTTI BEANS

Riso con fagioli should be pourable, not stiff, similar in texture to the *all'onda* (wavy) style of risotto favored in Venice. If you have tomato sauce on hand and any leftover cooked beans, you can make this dish effortlessly. I would serve it as a first course, followed by Pan-Fried Sausage with Broccoli Rabe (page 217) or any meat course that did not include tomato.

SUGGESTED WINE: Benanti "Rosso di Verzella," Etna Rosso, Sicily
With its vibrant red cherry, raspberry, and pomegranate nose, this light-bodied red from the Nerello Mascalese grape has a vivacity that brightens up this earthy dish.
ALTERNATE: Tempranillo

Quick Tomato Sauce (page 53; see below for adjustments)

1 small dried hot red pepper or ground hot red pepper

2 tablespoons chopped flat-leaf parsley

2 cups (375 grams) cooked cranberry (borlotti) beans, with some
    bean broth

2 tablespoons kosher salt, plus more as needed

2 cups (400 grams) Italian Carnaroli or Arborio rice

MAKE QUICK TOMATO SAUCE (page 53) with the following adjustments: Make the sauce in a 4-quart (4-liter) pot instead of a skillet. When you add the tomatoes to the pot, add 1 small dried hot red pepper or ground hot red pepper to taste. Replace the basil with 2 tablespoons chopped flat-leaf parsley.

When the tomato sauce is ready, drain the beans, reserving their broth, and stir the beans into the sauce. Keep warm over low heat.

In a 4-quart pot (4-liter), bring 2 quarts (2 liters) water and the 2 tablespoons salt to a boil over high heat. Add the rice and boil until the rice is al dente, no longer hard at the core but still firm, about 13 minutes. Drain and add the rice to the tomato sauce and beans. Bring to a simmer, stirring. Taste and adjust the salt. *Riso con fagioli* should be a little thinner than risotto—pourable, not stiff. Thin with reserved bean broth if necessary. Serve immediately.

SERVES 6

Polenta con Fagioli e Salsiccia

POLENTA WITH BEANS AND SAUSAGE

When I began to be interested in cooking, my mother would tell me about dishes that she remembered and loved from her childhood. This is one of them, although curiously, she never made it when I was growing up. Perhaps it is because, after marrying my father, she cooked to please him, and he preferred his polenta with cabbage. Listening to her describe traditional dishes like this one that she no longer prepared made me realize I had to write them down. If she didn't teach them to me, they would be lost in our family, and probably gradually lost in the region.

With such a robust dish, you don't need much to complete the meal. Follow with Cauliflower Salad (page 240), cooked mustard greens, or steamed asparagus.

A NOTE ABOUT POLENTA: In Calabria, polenta is made with fine cornmeal similar to the type used for American corn bread. It is identical to the white cornmeal that Venetians use for polenta, not the coarse cornmeal used in other parts of Italy. Consequently, our polenta cooks more quickly and has a smooth, soft, almost custard-like texture. Moretti's Bramata Bianca, a packaged white cornmeal from Italy (see Resources, page 369), produces excellent results. Albers Corn Meal, a supermarket brand, also works well.

SUGGESTED WINE: Planeta "Santa Cecilia," Sicily
This Nero d'Avola is relatively big in style, with the tannins and layered fruit that this hearty dish needs.
ALTERNATE: Zinfandel

½ pound (225 grams) dried cranberry (borlotti) beans (see Resources, page 369) *or* 3 cups drained canned borlotti beans

Kosher salt

2 tablespoons extra virgin olive oil

¾ pound (350 grams) hot Italian sausage links

2 cups (500 milliliters) Home-Canned Peeled Tomatoes (page 296) *or* one 14-ounce (400-gram) can Italian San Marzano tomatoes, pureed in a blender with the juice

Ground hot red pepper

2 cups (300 grams) fine white or yellow cornmeal (not coarse-ground polenta, see note above)

Polenta with Beans and Sausage

IF USING DRIED BEANS, soak the beans for at least 8 hours in water to cover generously. Drain and place in a large pot with fresh water to cover by 2 inches (5 centimeters). Bring to a simmer over moderate heat, skimming any foam. Adjust the heat to maintain a bare simmer and cook until the beans are tender, 45 minutes or more, depending on their age. Season with salt and let them cool in the liquid. You should have about 3 cups (750 milliliters) cooked beans. You can prepare the beans to this point a day or two ahead.

Heat the olive oil in a 6-quart (6-liter) pot over moderately high heat. Brown the sausages just until they are firm enough to slice, about 5 minutes. Set them aside to cool slightly, then cut into ¼-inch (6-millimeter) slices. Return the slices to the saucepan, in batches if necessary, and brown them until they are crusty on both sides. Lift them out with a slotted spoon and set aside.

Add the tomato puree to the saucepan. Season with salt and hot pepper to taste. Simmer briskly for about 5 minutes to develop the flavor, using a wooden spoon to scrape up any browned bits of meat on the bottom of the saucepan. Add 3 pints (1½ liters) water (you can substitute bean broth for some of the water) and bring to a boil.

Reduce the heat to low and add the cornmeal in a fine, steady stream, stirring constantly with a whisk so that no lumps form. When the mixture thickens, switch to a wooden spoon. Continue to cook, stirring constantly, until the polenta is thick, smooth, and creamy, with no graininess, about 15 minutes. Add small amounts of water if necessary to keep the polenta soft, not stiff. Drain the beans and stir them into the polenta. Cook for a couple of minutes more, then stir in the browned sausage. Taste for seasoning and serve at once.

SERVES 6 TO 8

Caciocavallo at a cheese store in La Sila

Pane, Pitte, Formaggi, Uova
bread, cheese, eggs

Crisci pasta, comu crischu Cristu nta fascia.
Grow, dough, as the Baby Jesus grew in his swaddling cloth.
(Calabrian baker's prayer)

Calabrians of my parents' generation do not know how to eat without bread. Thickly sliced, it appears at every meal, for sponging up the remnants of a pasta sauce or scooping up oil-preserved eggplant. Dense homemade bread, hard cheese, and *salumi* accompanied shepherds like my father when they left home before dawn to lead their sheep and goats on a day-long trek into the mountains. In less prosperous times in Calabria, bread was truly the staff of life, made with prayers and incantations and consumed with reverence. With divine assistance, the dough would surely rise; without it, who could say?

Rural Calabrian housewives like my mother and grandmothers were accustomed to making bread in quantity. A typical household with five or six children might devour four loaves of bread a day, especially if any of those children were growing young men doing farm chores. Consequently, every week or two, many housewives would devote an entire day to mixing, kneading, shaping, and baking several dozen loaves. In fact, the bread-making ritual began the day before baking, when the starter was made into a sponge with the addition of flour and water. Today, of course, this backbreaking practice is disappearing and most people, even in rural areas, buy their bread at a local bakery or market.

The Calabrian bread of every day (page 119) is a thickly crusted, dense loaf made from unbleached wheat flour and leavened with a starter. It can assume several different shapes, including rounds, long loaves, and rings. It is sturdy and faintly sour from the starter, with a tight crumb. In my mother's day, people made the loaves large—never smaller than 2 kilos (4½ pounds)—so they would stay fresh longer. Although the bread becomes progressively dryer, it remains edible for several days, unlike an airy baguette that becomes rock hard overnight. And even when it becomes too dry to eat, Calabrians don't mind. They consider dry bread as useful as fresh bread. If it is too hard to enjoy on its own, we put a thick slice in the bottom of our soup bowl and ladle beans or soup or braised vegetables over it.

When I was a child, my mother made a nourishing breakfast for me with stale bread and hot milk. She would pour the steaming milk over cubes of dry bread in a soup bowl, then dip the stem of a freshly cut fig leaf from our garden into the milk. The cut stem of a fig leaf exudes a chalk-white liquid that contains rennin, an enzyme that quickly coagulates milk. Within minutes, the milk in my bowl was a mass of warm, soft curds, and the bread had softened enough to eat. This comforting porridge was my mother's approximation of *ricotta 'mpanata*, warm ricotta and whey spooned over stale bread, which is the Calabrian shepherd's everyday breakfast. In the summer, when she and I would leave our village house and stay with my father at our farmhouse in the mountains, she would prepare the same dish with the hot whey and fluffy curds from the vat where my father made ricotta.

When bread gets really dry, after a week or so, Calabrians grate it for breadcrumbs (page 127). In my California home, leftover sliced bread from every meal goes into a deep drawer in the kitchen. When the stash is sufficiently large, I grate it into fine breadcrumbs and freeze them.

Two signature breads of Calabria merit particular attention, as they are uncommon. One is the *pitta*, a flatbread that is often stuffed, made in traditional homes on baking day. Before shaping the rounds, loaves, and rings that will sustain her family for the next week or two, a Calabrian home baker puts a little dough aside for a *pitta*, a treat for the children. Some of this reserved dough will be flattened into a rectangle or a round, spread with a filling, and sealed with a top layer of dough. Between batches of bread, the *pitta* is slipped into the oven. Unlike bread, which must cool completely, *pitta* is often served while still warm, a much anticipated snack and gratification for the labors of baking day.

That description fits my mother's *pitta*, which she makes in a large rectangle. Outside of her native region of Cosenza, *pitta* takes different shapes and may not even be stuffed. Some *pitte* are rolled around their filling like a jelly roll, then the two ends are brought together to make a ring. Some recipes call for kneading ingredients, such as grated cheese, chopped anchovies, or *ciccioli* (pork cracklings), into the dough, then flattening it and baking it like a focaccia. In Catanzaro, bakers make a large, plain, ring-shaped *pitta* for *morseddu* (page 194), the town's beloved innards sandwich. The ring is cut into smaller chunks, then split in half to make a slightly curved sandwich roll.

Most Calabrian bakeries and many takeout food shops make *pitte* of various types. Often they are baked in a heavy round pan similar to a cake pan, then cut into wedges for sale. Among the fillings you may encounter if you make a habit of sampling *pitta* around Calabria: tomato with anchovies; ricotta, Caciocavallo cheese, and hard-cooked eggs; the spicy fish spread known as *sardella* (page 42); or cooked greens. Harder to find commercially but still made in homes are the seasonal *pitta di Maju*, or May *pitta*, stuffed with elderflowers; and *pitta mijina* (page 140), a cornmeal flatbread topped with cracklings or anchovies.

Culinary historians believe that *pitta* is an ancient bread, its name derived from the Latin *picta*, meaning painted. The earliest *pitte* were probably decorated flat-breads made as religious offerings. Centuries later, in my own home, we eat *pitta* as a snack or simple lunch, or as a replacement for bread at dinner.

Another notable bread, the *frisella*, or *fresa*, is a rusk, or twice-baked bread, intended for long keeping. The baker makes a ring-shaped loaf resembling a large bagel, then halves it horizontally after the first baking. The two halves are dried out in a slow oven for several hours, then left in the turned-off oven overnight to dry thoroughly. *Friselle* keep indefinitely. Before they are eaten, they are softened in a little cold water, then drizzled with olive oil, oregano, garlic, and salt; or with olive oil and chopped tomato (page 35). Most bread bakeries sell *friselle* because they are a favorite Calabrian snack. They are a likely legacy of the Greeks, whose *paximathia*, or barley rusks, are prepared and served in the same way.

In the old Catholic churches in Calabria, where pagan and Catholic rituals converged, bread figures in several rites. On June 13, Saint Anthony's Day, Calabrians give thanks for the blessings they have received by baking small breads and giving them to poor people. On Holy Wednesday of the week before Easter, Calabrian women bring decorated baskets of sprouted wheat—*i lavurieddi*—to the church and set them on the altar, a rite probably linked to the ancient cult of Adonis, the god of nature in Greek mythology. On Holy Thursday, Calabrians gather at their church to re-enact the Last Supper, and the local women bake large *cudduredde*, ring-shaped loaves, to give to the apostles. With these devotions, Calabrians acknowledge the central role of bread in their past. Although people are far more prosperous today, most are only two or three generations removed from the days when having flour meant you were rich.

My parents grew their own wheat for bread and pasta, a durum wheat variety called "Senatore Cappelli." This variety was widely planted and greatly prized in Southern Italy until the 1960s, when it was largely replaced by higher-yielding varieties. It is now being reintroduced by some of the artisanal pasta producers, such as Latini. With a high protein content, the variety is what Americans call hard wheat and Italians call *grano duro*, and it is excellent for making bread and dried pasta because it develops strong gluten.

When she moved to California, my mother had to experiment with American flours to find one that would produce bread like she knew in Calabria. Over the years, she has made her bread (page 119) with many different brands and types of flour, with bread flour, bleached all-purpose flour, and unbleached all-purpose flour. In recent years, I, too, have joined in these experiments and have mastered her bread, a mother-to-daughter sharing of knowledge that I avoided for a long time, as I did not want to take over this task. In fact, her bread is simple to make, and although the rising time is long, the actual work time is not. It pleases me to know that we have kept this traditional bread alive, transferring it from one continent to another, and from one generation to the next.

Similarly, my mother has long tried to persuade me to put a chicken coop in my urban backyard so we can have the fresh eggs with deep-orange yolks that we had in Calabria. When she was growing up, every rural household had a chicken coop, and eggs contributed significant protein to the diet. Yet Calabrians of my parents' generation are frugal with eggs. Desserts that include eggs are prepared with the bare minimum because those eggs could make a family's supper.

Today, Calabrians can readily buy as many eggs as they desire, but the historical memories linger. In feudal times in this region, the nobles received the egg yolks and the servants got the whites. Some Calabrians still make a dish of beaten egg whites cooked in a skillet with sautéed green onions and hot pepper.

Calabrians don't typically eat eggs for breakfast, but they do eat them at lunch and dinner in a variety of savory frittatas: with fresh ricotta and onions (page 151); or broccoli rabe and sausage; or wild mushrooms. Calabrian frittatas may also include fava beans, sweet peppers, potatoes, or the wild hyacinth bulbs known as *lampascioni.* In rural homes, especially, frittatas appear often in the days after Easter to use up the eggs that have accumulated during the fast days of Lent. My mother recalls listening for the church bells on the morning of Holy Saturday, announcing that Lent was officially over. That was the signal for the local women to head for the kitchen and make a frittata with sausage.

Sliced hard-boiled eggs figure in several baked dishes, such as *sagne chine* (Lasagne, Calabrian-Style, page 77). When I was young, my mother would sometimes put a whole unshelled egg in the fireplace embers until the white was firm but the yolk was not. I would cut the top off and dip my bread into the soft, runny egg.

At Easter time, Calabrian home bakers make *buccellati* (also called *cuzzupe*), symbolic breads decorated with whole eggs, still in the shell. The eggs are nestled into the surface of the dough, held in place with criss-crossed strips of dough, and baked along with the bread. These decorative breads, symbol of Christ's resurrection, are given to children, with boys receiving a braided loaf and girls a loaf in the shape of a doll.

Like eggs from their own chickens, cheeses made from the milk of their own farm animals kept rural Calabrians nourished in earlier times. Today, cheese remains an everyday staple throughout Calabria, whether grated over pasta; layered with eggplant and tomatoes; packed in a farmer's lunch box; or served with *salumi* at the start of a restaurant meal. But when it comes to cheese, Calabrians are provincial, preferring their own cheese, or the one made by their neighbors, or possibly by someone in the next village. Most Calabrians know someone who makes cheese, and they will buy it by the wheel, usually direct from the maker.

A shepherd in Verbicaro

Cheesemaking in Calabria reflects the realities of this region's varied landscape. The province of Crotone, with its broad, flat, coastal pastures, is hospitable to sheep, and consequently, much of Calabria's best pecorino cheese comes from this area. Farmers with land on the hillsides will keep mostly goats and make goat ricotta and aged goat cheese. The high plateau of La Sila supports cattle husbandry and the production of cow's milk cheeses, such as Caciocavallo and Provola.

Some farmers keep mixed herds of goats and sheep, depending on the property they own, and they will often mix the milk for cheese. Thus, in Calabria, the name "pecorino" does not necessarily indicate a 100 percent sheep's milk cheese. Many Calabrian pecorinos include some goat's milk, with the proportion varying depending on the season. To a Calabrian, pecorino refers to a hard, piquant, and salty cheese intended for grating, regardless of the milk type. In a food shop, signage may indicate that the pecorino on offer is 100 percent sheep's milk. Otherwise, shoppers who have a preference for pure sheep's milk pecorino must inquire because a mixed-milk cheese is difficult to distinguish by eye.

Because my father kept mostly goats, our kitchen in Calabria was never without a wheel of aged pecorino made largely with goat's milk—a brittle, crystalline, salty cheese that produced a fine flurry when grated.

Cheese is rarely eaten as a separate course in Calabria. Instead, a few slices of local pecorino or Provola may appear on the antipasto platter in a restaurant, or at the end of the meal with honey, hot-pepper marmalade, or grape jam. In either case, the cheese may be moist and supple and as little as two weeks old, or a firmer, dryer, more concentrated cheese aged two months or more. When it becomes hard and sharp, after about six months of aging, pecorino is reserved for grating.

At the home table, where antipasto is rarely served, cheese often stands in for meat as a second course. It would not be uncommon at my parents' house to have pasta or soup to start, followed by sliced cheese, homemade bread, and a fresh or preserved vegetable, with seasonal fruit for dessert.

Pane Calabrese
MY FAMILY'S EVERYDAY BREAD

Bread has long had a sacred place on the Calabrian table, and until modern times, that bread was homemade. Commercial bakeries hardly existed in Calabria before World War II, so most families baked their own bread in their own wood-burning oven. Families were larger then—my mother was one of six children—and bread was on the table morning, noon, and night, so each family's needs were enormous. My mother recalls making 20 to 25 kilos of dough (about 50 pounds) at a time.

The bread-baking ritual in my grandmother's household was typical of the day. Because it was time consuming and costly to fire up the bread oven frequently, bread baking happened only every couple of weeks. Preparations began in the early morning, and baking went on all day to make enough to last until the next baking.

My grandmother had a *madia*, a large wooden trough with sloping sides for mixing the dough. The trough would be placed on a bench or on a row of chairs to position it at a comfortable height. The dough was so voluminous that two people would often work on it at once, bending over the trough and punching the dough as they worked their way from one end to the other. It could take an hour to knead so much dough to the proper consistency. Some housewives simply did not have the physique for this labor and would hire one of the strong local peasant women, who were paid in bread and other foods.

A loaf of bread I bought in the town of Camigliatello

Like most of her neighbors, my grandmother had practically no counter space in her modest kitchen, so she commandeered the bed for a bread-rising station. She would spread a big cloth over the bed, plop the mass of kneaded dough in the middle, and drape it in several blankets to keep it warm. When it had risen sufficiently, she would set her wooden pasta board on the bed next to the dough, cut the dough into smaller pieces, and shape each piece into a round, a ring, or a long

The breads my family and I make regularly (clockwise from upper left): *filone, cudduredda, panetta, friselle*

loaf. Then the loaves went back onto the cloth, snugly covered in blankets, for the second rise. Before covering them, she would make the sign of the cross over the loaves for good measure.

Long before shaping the dough, she would start the fire in her oven, using vine cuttings to kindle the olive and oak wood. When the wood had burned down to coals, she would sweep them out and load the first breads. Then she would bless the oven with the sign of the cross and repeat the home baker's prayer: *Alla gloria di San Martino, pane cotto e forno pieno* (Glory to Saint Martin, may the bread cook properly and fill the oven).

According to my mother, if you entered a friend's house and discovered that she was baking bread, you must immediately say, "*Dio ti benedica*" (God bless you). If your friend had bread in the oven, you couldn't leave her house until the bread emerged or you might somehow disrupt the operation of the oven or steal warmth from it. (It is not always easy to make sense of these customs.)

Every year, in preparation for Holy Thursday and Good Friday, my grand-mother and several other women would gather together to make giant ceremonial *cudduredde*, round loaves with a hole in the middle, like an enormous doughnut. On Holy Thursday, the locals would gather at the church for a staged re-creation of the Last Supper, with members of the congregation playing the roles of the disciples. Afterward, the outsize *cudduredde* would be presented to the priest and to the "disciples."

Calabrian bread is dense, substantial, and thick crusted—the aesthetic opposite of an airy baguette. In earlier times, when hunger was widespread, the bread had to fill bellies and to stay reasonably fresh until the next baking. Although Calabrians are more prosperous today, they have retained their taste for sturdy bread. And they continue to revere it, as bread is thought to represent the divine. I was taught as a child to kiss a piece of bread before eating it. If a piece fell on the floor, I was instructed to pick it up, blow on it to banish any dirt, and kiss it again. Wasting bread was considered a sin.

My mother has refined this recipe over the years to work with American flour. She has experimented with many brands of both bread flour and all-purpose flour. We are both convinced that bread flour makes no noticeable difference in the results, and because it is harder to find, I have written the recipe for unbleached all-purpose flour. Note that you need to start the bread sponge the night before baking, and if you do not have a starter, you will need to make one, a three-day process (page 125).

BREAD SPONGE

4 ounces (115 grams) Bread Starter (page 125), about ½ cup, at
   room temperature

1 cup (5 ounces/140 grams) unbleached all-purpose flour

½ cup (125 milliliters) warm water (105°F to 110°F/45°C)

DOUGH

3 pounds (1½ kilograms) unbleached all-purpose flour, plus more
   for dusting

2 tablespoons plus 2 teaspoons kosher salt

3¾ cups (900 milliliters) warm water (105°F to 110°F/45°C)

TO CREATE THE BREAD SPONGE: Put the starter in a 2-quart (2-liter) bowl and add the flour and water. Stir well with a wooden spoon. Cover the bowl with a plate or cloth. Wrap with towels or a blanket to keep it warm and leave in the warmest part of your kitchen overnight.

TO MAKE THE DOUGH THE FOLLOWING DAY: Put the flour in a large bowl, make a well in the center, and put the sponge in the well. Dissolve the salt in the warm water, stirring until the water becomes clear again. Add the salted water to the well gradually while mixing the water and sponge with your hand until blended. Begin incorporating the flour from the sides of the bowl, mixing with your hand until the dough begins to come together and clean the sides of the bowl. Switch to a kneading motion—my mother pounds the dough repeatedly and vigorously with her fist—and continue kneading or pounding until the dough is firm, smooth, and springy, 10 to 15 minutes. Although the dough may seem sticky at first, the flour will eventually absorb the moisture. Because the dough is so moist, I find it easier to manipulate in the bowl. If it is more comfortable for you, turn the dough out onto a work surface to knead it but try not to add any more flour.

FOR THE FIRST RISE: Shape the dough into a large ball and dust it lightly with flour. Place it in a large bowl and dust the top again with flour. Drape a clean kitchen towel over the bowl, then wrap the bowl in a thick blanket and set it in the warmest place in your kitchen. The objective is to provide an environment of about

80°F (27°C), which is warmer than most homes; the blanket wrap will help keep the dough warmer than the room temperature.

Let the dough rest until doubled in size, 2½ to 3 hours. It has risen enough when it develops "stretch marks" on the surface. If you're still unsure, cut into the dough with a paring knife and look for the pockets of gas that indicate that the dough has sufficiently fermented.

Note: If you are planning to make My Family's Everyday Bread again, now is the time to set aside a small amount of dough as your starter for next time. Place 4 ounces (115 grams) of dough in a bowl, cover the bowl with a lid or plate, and let stand at room temperature for one to two days to develop flavor. Then refrigerate in an airtight container.

TO SHAPE THE LOAVES: With a knife or bench scraper, divide the risen dough into three equal pieces. Flour the dough as needed to prevent sticking, but handle it gently; do not punch it down. (You can make one giant loaf, if you like, or two loaves instead of three, but these larger loaves tend to be bigger than most households can eat before the bread goes stale.)

You can shape the dough however you like, but the three shapes that my mother and I make most often are:

- *Panetta:* a round loaf. From this recipe, you can make three 6-inch-round (15-centimeter-round) *panette*. To shape a *panetta*, use your fingertips to grasp the edges of a piece of dough and draw them toward the center as if you were making a drawstring bag. Gently pinch them together, then turn the dough over so the pinched seam is down. Use your palms to finish shaping the dough into a neat round ball.

- *Filone:* an elongated loaf, thicker than a baguette, with tapered ends. From this recipe, you can make three *filoni,* each about 10 inches (25 centimeters) long. To shape a *filone,* use the palms of both hands to stretch each piece of dough as gently as possible into a log about 10 inches (25 centimeters) long and 5 inches (13 centimeters) wide.

- *Cudduredda:* a large doughnut or ring shape. With this shape, we make the Calabrian rusks called *friselle* (page 128). From this recipe, you can make three *cudduredde* or twelve *friselle.* To shape a *cudduredda,* form one of the three pieces of dough into a large round, as for a *panetta*. With your index finger and middle finger held together, punch a hole in the middle of the round, poking all the way through, as if making a bagel. Lift the dough with both hands and stretch it until the hole is about 2 inches (5 centimeters) in diameter. Repeat with the remaining two pieces of dough.

FOR THE SECOND RISE: Gently transfer the three shaped loaves to a lightly floured cloth, with folds of cloth between them to keep them from touching as they rise. Dust the tops of the loaves with flour and drape with another cloth. Cover with a blanket and let rise in the warmest place in your kitchen until doubled, about 2 hours.

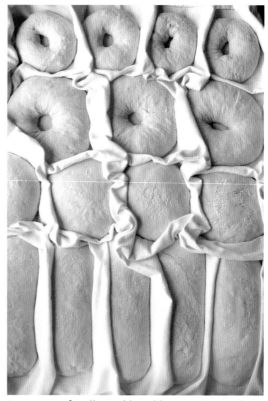

From top: *friselle, cudduredda, panetta,* and *filone* shaped for the second rise

TO BAKE THE LOAVES: You can bake the loaves directly on a rack lined with unglazed baking tiles (see Resources, page 368), the preferred method, or on parchment-lined baking sheets. Depending on the shape of your loaves and the size and number of your ovens, you may need to bake the bread in two shifts. It is better to bake in shifts than to try to bake on two racks in one oven. It won't hurt the loaves on the second shift to rise a little longer. If you do bake in shifts, be sure to return the oven temperature to the recommended starting temperature.

To bake directly on baking tiles, position a rack in the lower third of the oven and line it with baking tiles. Thirty minutes before baking, preheat the oven to 500°F (260°C). Just before you put the loaves in the oven, reduce the heat to 450°F (230°C). Gently transfer one of the loaves to a floured pizza peel and slide it off onto the hot tiles. If there is room, put a second loaf alongside. Bake until the bottom of each loaf is firm and deep gold, about 15 minutes, then reduce the oven temperature to 400°F (200°C) and continue baking until the loaves are well browned all over and hard on the top and bottom, 20 to 25 minutes longer. Cool completely on a rack before slicing.

To bake on baking sheets, line two baking sheets with parchment paper. Thirty minutes before baking, preheat the oven to 475°F (250°C). Just before baking, gently transfer the risen loaves to the prepared baking sheets—two loaves on one sheet, one on the other—disturbing the loaves as little as possible.

- *If using an electric oven*, put the baking sheet on the lowest rack and bake until the bottom of each loaf is firm and deep gold, 15 to 20 minutes. Transfer the baking sheet to a rack in the upper third of the oven, reduce the oven temperature to 400°F (200°C) and continue baking until the loaves are well browned all over and hard on the top and bottom, 25 to 30 minutes longer. Cool completely on a rack before slicing.

- *If using a gas oven*, put the baking sheet on a middle rack and bake until the bottom of each loaf is firm and deep gold, 15 to 20 minutes. Reduce the oven temperature to 400°F (200°C) and continue baking until the loaves are well browned all over and hard on the top and bottom, 25 to 30 minutes longer. Cool completely on a rack before slicing.

MAKES 3 LOAVES, ABOUT 1½ POUNDS (675 GRAMS) EACH

Whole-Wheat Variation

To make a whole-wheat version of this bread, substitute 1½ pounds (675 grams) whole-wheat flour for 1½ pounds (675 grams) unbleached all-purpose flour in the dough. Raise the volume of water in the dough to 4¼ cups (1 liter).

Bread Starter

My family's homemade bread contains no commercial yeast, only the airborne yeast and bacteria present in the starter my mother brought to California from Calabria in her purse. When she was growing up, starter was treated with great care and reverence. If your neighbor's starter had become sluggish from lack of use, you would give her a chunk of yours. Some neighbors shared a starter, passing it from house to house in accordance with each person's baking day. If you were taking a starter to a neighbor at night, you had to guard it from mishap by carrying the picture of a saint with you.

My mother has kept her current starter going for more than twenty years. With every batch of bread, she reserves about 4 ounces (115 grams) of dough as a starter for the next batch.

You can create your own starter with a little commercial yeast, but it takes three full days to get an actively growing population of the yeasts that will leaven the bread and the bacteria that will make it slightly sour.

Keep your starter refrigerated. Using it regularly will keep it vigorous. If you don't use it for three weeks, you will need to refresh it by giving the yeast and bacteria something to eat. To refresh the starter, stir in ½ cup (2½ ounces/70 grams) of unbleached all-purpose flour and ¼ cup (60 milliliters) warm water. Put the refreshed starter in a bowl covered with a plate or cloth, wrap it in towels or a blanket, and leave it in the warmest part of your kitchen for two days to reactivate it. Then refrigerate it in an airtight container.

TO CREATE A STARTER:

- *On Day One*, combine ½ cup (2½ ounces/70 grams) unbleached all-purpose flour and ¼ teaspoon active dry yeast in a 3- to 4-cup (750-milliliter to 1-liter) bowl. Stir with a fork to blend. Add ¼ cup (60 milliliters) of warm water (about 105°F/45°C) and mix with a fork or wooden spoon. The mixture will be stiff and a little difficult to stir but too moist to knead; blend as well as you can.

  Cover the bowl with a plate or cloth. Wrap with towels or a blanket to keep it warm and leave in the warmest part of your kitchen for 24 hours.

- *On Day Two*, divide the starter in half and discard one-half. Return the half you are keeping to the bowl and add ½ cup unbleached all-purpose flour and ¼ cup of warm water (about 105°F/45°C). Repeat the mixing and rising as for Day One.

- *On Day Three*, repeat the same procedure as for Day Two. After 24 hours, you can refrigerate the starter in an airtight container, or proceed with the creation of the Bread Sponge required for My Family's Everyday Bread (page 119).

MAKES ABOUT 12 OUNCES (340 GRAMS)

Breadcrumbs: A Useful End for Dry Loaves

In earlier times, every Calabrian household had a hand grater for reducing chunks of dry bread into a heap of crumbs. The drier the bread, the finer the crumbs. Today, virtually every Calabrian bakery sells *pangrattato* (literally, grated bread).

Breadcrumbs are used lavishly in the Calabrian kitchen. We dip cauliflower (page 266), fennel, and other vegetables in beaten egg and fine breadcrumbs to make crisp, golden fritters. We sprinkle toasted breadcrumbs for crunch on some pasta dishes, such as Whole-Wheat Linguine with Anchovies and Breadcrumbs (page 68). We use breadcrumbs for bulk in stuffings, as with Grilled Swordfish Rolls with Breadcrumb Stuffing (page 172). And we layer them with baked vegetables to absorb moisture, as for Potatoes Layered with Artichokes and Breadcrumbs (page 259). Consequently, I am never without a large bag of breadcrumbs in the freezer.

Most American loaves, even when stale, are not dense enough to grate, so I use the blender or food processor to make breadcrumbs. I prepare two types: fresh breadcrumbs from day-old bread; and fine dry breadcrumbs from bread that has become too hard to eat, typically after about a week. The fresh breadcrumbs are useful in stuffings and layered vegetable dishes and the dried breadcrumbs for coating vegetables or meatballs before frying.

TO MAKE FRESH BREADCRUMBS

Use a dense, day-old French or Italian country-style loaf containing only flour, water, yeast, and salt (no fat, sugar, honey, or herbs). Do not remove the crusts. Cut the bread into 1-inch cubes and process them in a blender, filling it no more than halfway, or in a food processor until they are as fine as possible. Freeze in a plastic freezer bag for up to a month. (See recipe for toasted breadcrumbs on page 59.)

TO MAKE FINE DRY BREADCRUMBS

Use a dense French or Italian country-style loaf containing only flour, water, yeast, and salt (no fat, sugar, honey, or herbs). Do not remove the crusts. Cut the bread into 1-inch cubes and leave them on a tray at room temperature for several days until they are rock hard. Process them in a blender, filling it no more than halfway, or in a food processor until fine. For the finest texture, sieve the processed crumbs and use only the fine crumbs. Reprocess and re-sieve the coarse crumbs. Freeze in a plastic freezer bag for up to a year.

Friselle
CALABRIAN RUSKS

Friselle, also called *frisedde* or *frese*, are round loaves of bread with a hole in the center, like an extra-large bagel. The bread is baked until done, then halved horizontally and re-baked at a low temperature until completely dry, golden brown, and crisp. *Friselle* are lightweight and last for months, so Calabrian shepherds and fishermen probably packed them when they were going away from home for long periods. *Friselle* must be reconstituted by being soaked briefly in water, just long enough to soften them but not so long that they crumble. Today, Calabrians typically eat them as a snack, topped with chopped fresh tomato, olive oil, garlic, and basil (page 35), or even more simply with garlic, olive oil, and dried oregano. Every Calabrian bakery sells them, since few people make them at home anymore. The packaged *friselle* I have sampled in this country are a disappointment—they're too small and the texture is too much like Melba toast—so I continue to make my own.

**My Family's Everyday Bread (page 119) *or* Whole-Wheat Variation
(page 125), prepared through the first rise**

AFTER THE FIRST RISE, shape the *friselle* as follows:

Divide the risen dough into 6 equal pieces. On a well-floured work surface, shape each piece of dough into a slightly flattened ball. With your index finger and middle finger held together, punch a hole in the middle of a ball, poking all the way through, as if making a bagel. Lift the dough with both hands and stretch it until the hole is about 2 inches (5 centimeters) in diameter and the whole ring is about 8 inches (20 centimeters) in diameter. Carefully transfer the ring to a floured cloth. Repeat with the remaining dough. Cover the rings with a kitchen towel and a blanket and let rise in the warmest place in your kitchen for 2 hours.

Shaping the *friselle* (or *cudduredda*) after the first rise

Stretching the *friselle* (or *cudduredda*) dough to create a hole in the center

TO BAKE THE FRISELLE: Preheat the oven to 475°F (250°C). Line a baking sheet with parchment paper and transfer two *friselle* to the baking sheet. As you place them on the baking sheet, stretch them to restore the hole to a 2-inch (5-centimeter) diameter and flatten them slightly with the palm of your hand. You don't want them to puff in the oven like bread. Bake one sheet at a time unless you have multiple ovens. Between batches, return the oven temperature to 475°F (250°C).

- *If using an electric oven*, bake the *friselle* on the lowest rack until the bottoms are firm and deep gold, about 15 minutes. Transfer the baking sheet to a rack in the upper third of the oven, reduce the oven temperature to 400°F (200°C) and continue baking until the *friselle* are golden all over, about 15 minutes longer. Cool completely on a rack. Repeat with the remaining *friselle*.

- *If using a gas oven*, bake the *friselle* on a middle rack for 15 minutes, then reduce the oven temperature to 400°F (200°C) and continue baking until the *friselle* are golden all over, about 15 minutes longer. Cool completely on a rack. Repeat with the remaining *friselle*.

FOR THE SECOND BAKING: Reduce the oven temperature to 300°F (150°C). Using a serrated knife, slice the cooled *friselle* in half horizontally. Place the split *friselle* on unlined baking sheets, cut side up. Using racks in the upper third and lower third of the oven, bake two sheets at a time until the *friselle* are lightly colored, 1 to 1½ hours, switching the position of the baking sheets halfway through. Now reduce the oven temperature to 175°F to 200°F (80°C to 95°C) and continue baking until the *friselle* are dry to the touch, about 2 hours more. Turn off the oven and leave the *friselle* in the oven overnight. Store in paper bags or in an airtight container. If properly dried, they will keep for months.

YIELD: 12 RUSKS

Quick Friselle Variation

Choose a sturdy, chewy, relatively flat Italian loaf such as *ciabatta*. Cut the loaf in half horizontally and bake as described in "For the second baking," above.

Pitta con Verdura
STUFFED PIZZA WITH CHARD AND DILL

Borage and dill grew wild around my hometown of Verbicaro in spring, so local cooks would gather these aromatic herbs to fill a *pitta*, the Calabrian version of stuffed pizza. If they couldn't find borage, they would use chard from their garden. You don't often see fresh dill in Italian recipes, but it is traditional in this one.

Curiously, the greens are not cooked first. They are chopped and mixed with scallions or spring onions and wilted with salt, as if for sauerkraut. The 30-minute salting draws out moisture so that the filling won't be soggy. Let the *pitta* cool before slicing so the crusty bread will absorb the flavorful juices from the greens. If you cut it too soon—a big temptation—the juices will run out.

Although *pitta* is traditionally made with a chunk of bread dough, I usually make mine with a pizza dough that contains yeast and olive oil. The pizza dough is easier to make in small quantity than My Family's Everyday Bread (page 119), so I can make *pitta* more often.

SUGGESTED WINE: Conti Zecca "Nero," Salento Rosso, Apulia
A rich, earth-driven Negroamaro to complement the earthiness of chard.
ALTERNATE: Chianti Classico

DOUGH FOR *PITTA* AND PIZZA

4¼ cups (1 pound 4 ounces/600 grams) unbleached all-purpose
   flour, plus more as needed

1 tablespoon plus 1 teaspoon kosher salt

1½ cups (375 milliliters) warm water (105°F to 110° F/45°C)

1 teaspoon active dry yeast

3 tablespoons extra virgin olive oil, plus more oil for coating
   the bowl

FILLING

1 bunch (about 1 pound/450 grams) Swiss chard, leaves separated
    from ribs

1 bunch scallions

3 tablespoons kosher salt

3 tablespoons minced fresh dill

1 tablespoon Calabrian paprika (page 304) *or* Spanish sweet paprika

¼ to ½ teaspoon ground hot red pepper *or* hot red pepper flakes

2½ tablespoons extra virgin olive oil

FOR THE DOUGH: Put the flour and salt in a large bowl and stir to distribute the salt well. Put the warm water in a small bowl and sprinkle the yeast over it. Let stand for 2 minutes to soften, then whisk with a fork to blend. Make a well in the center of the flour and put the dissolved yeast and the olive oil in the well. Begin incorporating flour from the sides with one hand. When you have incorporated all the flour and the dough cleans the sides of the bowl, which should only take about a minute, switch to a one-handed kneading motion, securing the bowl with the other hand. The dough will be moist and a little sticky at this point but resist adding additional flour. By kneading it in the bowl instead of on a work surface, you should be able to avoid adding flour. When the dough is no longer sticky, after about 5 minutes, turn it out onto a work surface. Knead with both hands until the dough is smooth and soft, about 5 minutes longer, dusting with flour only as needed to prevent sticking.

FOR THE FIRST RISE: Transfer the dough to a clean bowl lightly coated with olive oil and turn the dough to coat it with the oil. Cover the bowl tightly with plastic wrap. Let rise in the warmest place in your kitchen until it doubles in volume, 1½ to 2 hours.

FOR THE SECOND RISE: Turn the dough out onto a lightly floured surface and shape it into a ball. Dust the ball lightly with flour and place it on a clean kitchen towel. Cover loosely with another clean kitchen towel. Let rise again in the warmest place in your kitchen until it doubles in volume, about 1½ hours.

Top left: Stretching dough in the pan for the *pitta*'s bottom layer. Top right: Sealing the *pitta* with the top layer of dough. Bottom: *Pitta* stuffed with Swiss chard, dill, and scallions just out of the oven.

FOR THE FILLING: If the chard ribs are more than 1 inch (2½ centimeters) wide, halve them lengthwise, then cut crosswise into ¼-inch (6-millimeter) pieces. Cut the leaves lengthwise into 2-inch-wide (5-centimeter-wide) ribbons, then stack the ribbons and cut crosswise into about ½-inch (12-millimeter) pieces. Leaving the scallions whole, slit the white part in half lengthwise, or quarter lengthwise if large, then cut the scallions—white and green parts—crosswise into ¾-inch (18-millimeter) pieces. In a large bowl, combine the chard ribs and leaves, the scallions, and the salt. Toss well with your hands to distribute the salt evenly. Let stand for at least 30 minutes to wilt the greens, or up to an hour.

Drain the greens to remove accumulated liquid, then rinse them repeatedly to remove excess salt. Taste to make sure they are no longer too salty. Working in batches, squeeze the greens between your hands to remove all excess liquid, then transfer them to a bowl. Add the dill, paprika, hot pepper to taste, and olive oil and mix well with your hands.

Preheat the oven to 475°F (250°C). Lightly oil a heavy 12- by 18-inch (30- by 43-centimeter) baking sheet. Place the risen dough on the baking sheet and gently press and pat it until it covers the baking sheet and is evenly thick everywhere.

With a short side of the baking sheet nearest you, cover the bottom half of the dough with the filling, spreading the filling evenly but leaving a 1-inch (2½-centimeter) border. Lift the exposed half of the dough over the filling to enclose it and press the edges together to seal. You should have a rectangle approximately 8½ by 12 inches (22 by 30 centimeters). If you feel an air bubble under the surface, pierce the dough in one or two places with a skewer and press to vent the air.

Bake for 20 minutes, then rotate the pan in the oven and lower the oven temperature to 400°F (200°C). Continue baking until the *pitta* is golden brown on top and bottom, about 10 minutes longer. Transfer to a rack and let cool for at least an hour before slicing.

MAKES ONE *PITTA*, TO SERVE 6

Pizza con Tonno e Bottarga di Pizzo
TUNA AND RED ONION PIZZA WITH *BOTTARGA*

The pizzerias throughout Calabria make *pizza con tonno*, with local oil-packed tuna and the region's famous sweet red onions. My cousin Alberto, who has a wood-burning oven at his home in Santa Maria del Cedro, near Scalea, considers it his specialty. I've embellished Alberto's recipe a bit, brushing the flattened pizza dough with garlicky oil before topping it, and adding a flurry of grated *bottarga* when the pizza comes out of the oven. You can omit the *bottarga*, but I like its salty ocean flavor with the tuna. Capers would be another good addition. This style of pizza, with no tomato sauce, is known as *pizza bianca* (white pizza) in Italy.

Pizza dough freezes so successfully that I always make a large batch. This recipe makes enough dough for four 8-inch (20-centimeter) pizzas or three 12-inch (30-centimeter) pizzas. The tuna and red onion topping is sufficient for two 8-inch (20-centimeter) pizzas. To freeze the remaining two balls, flatten them into disks after the second rise, wrap each disk tightly in plastic wrap, then place each one in a plastic freezer storage bag and freeze. To use, thaw the disks at room temperature, then stretch them, add toppings, and bake.

SUGGESTED WINE: Contini "'Inu," Cannonau di Sardegna Riserva, Sardinia
This medium-bodied, fruit-forward red wine has a scent of stewed tomato and red currant and comes from the province of Oristano, where bottarga *is produced.*
ALTERNATE: dry rosé or Priorat

Dough for *Pitta* and Pizza (page 131), prepared through the first
    rise

TOPPING

7-ounce (200-gram) tin or jar of tuna packed in olive oil

1 large red onion, ends removed, quartered, and very thinly sliced

½ teaspoon kosher salt

3 tablespoons extra virgin olive oil

2 garlic cloves, finely minced

1 tablespoon chopped flat-leaf parsley

Bottarga (page 42)

TURN THE RISEN DOUGH out onto a lightly floured surface and divide into 4 equal pieces. Roll each piece into a ball, dust the balls lightly with flour, and place them on a kitchen towel lightly dusted with flour. Cover loosely with plastic wrap and let rise again in a warm place until doubled, about 1½ hours. Now you will have two extra balls, which you can freeze or bake with another topping. You will work with only two balls for this recipe.

Line the bottom rack of your oven with unglazed quarry tiles or a pizza stone. Preheat the oven to 550°F (290°C) or to the highest setting for 30 minutes.

FOR THE TOPPING: Drain the tuna of its oil and set aside, reserving 2 tablespoons oil in a small bowl. In another bowl, put the sliced red onions, the salt, and the reserved oil. Toss well with your hands and set aside.

In a small skillet, combine the olive oil, garlic, and parsley. Warm briefly over low heat, just until the garlic begins to give off its fragrance. Set aside.

TO ASSEMBLE THE PIZZA: With your hand, flatten one ball of dough on a work surface, pressing it into a circle. Pick the dough up with both hands and stretch it into an 8-inch (20-centimeter) round, keeping it as evenly thin as possible. Set the round of dough on a floured pizza peel. Brush with half of the garlic-parsley oil. Top with half of the onions, scattering them evenly, then with half of the tuna, breaking up any chunks into small pieces. Transfer the pizza to the preheated tiles or stone and bake until the dough is well browned and crisp on the edges and bottom, about 6 minutes. Remove from the oven and grate *bottarga* over the surface with a fine grater, such as a Microplane, using as much as you like. Cut into wedges and serve immediately.

Repeat with the second ball of dough and the remaining topping.

MAKES TWO 8-INCH (20-CENTIMETER) PIZZAS

Pizza con Zucchine e Fiori di Zucchine
PIZZA WITH GRILLED ZUCCHINI AND STUFFED ZUCCHINI BLOSSOMS

Many Calabrian pizza restaurants offer a *pizza all'ortolana* ("pizza from the garden"), topped with grilled zucchini, eggplant, and peppers. My garden produces so many pretty zucchini blossoms that I wanted to create a pizza that would show them off, too. The zucchini plant produces two types of blossoms: male and female. The female flower yields the fruit. The male, after fertilization duty, serves no purpose. Those are the ones to pick for stuffing. They have long stems, while the female flowers have the zucchini attached. Pick the blossoms in the early morning, while they are open. If you are purchasing the blossoms at a farmers' market or retail shop, buy the perkiest ones you can find, male or female. If you are not using the blossoms right away, put them in a plastic bag, inflate with air, close tightly, and refrigerate.

SUGGESTED WINE: COS "Pithos," Cerasuolo di Vittoria, Sicily
A light, vibrant red with a cranberry scent.
ALTERNATE: Pinot Noir

Dough for *Pitta* and Pizza (page 131), prepared through the first
    rise

TOPPING

½ pound (225 grams) zucchini, each about 5 inches (13 centimeters) long

½ teaspoon kosher salt

2 tablespoons extra virgin olive oil

10 large zucchini blossoms

3 ounces (85 grams) fresh goat cheese, divided into 10 pieces

5 anchovy fillets, cut in half crosswise

GARLIC-PARSLEY OIL

3 tablespoons extra virgin olive oil

2 garlic cloves, finely minced

1 tablespoon chopped flat-leaf parsley

3 ounces (85 grams) fresh whole-milk mozzarella, sliced thin and
    torn into smaller pieces

⅔ cup grated aged Asiago cheese

1 ounce (30 grams) fresh goat cheese

Pizza with Grilled Zucchini and Stuffed Zucchini Blossoms about to go into the oven.
The zucchini blossoms thrive in my garden in July.

TURN THE RISEN DOUGH out onto a lightly floured surface and divide into 3 equal pieces. Roll each piece into a ball, dust the balls lightly with flour, and place them on a kitchen towel lightly dusted with flour. Cover loosely with plastic wrap and let rise again in a warm place until doubled, about 1½ hours. Now you will have two extra balls, which you can freeze or bake with another topping.

Line the bottom rack of your oven with unglazed quarry tiles or a pizza stone. Preheat the oven to 550°F (290°C) or to the highest setting for 30 minutes.

FOR THE TOPPING: Preheat a gas grill to high, or prepare a hot charcoal fire. Cut the zucchini lengthwise into slices about ³⁄₁₆ inch (5 millimeters) thick. Salt the slices and brush with the olive oil on both sides. Grill, turning once, until tender, about 2 minutes per side. Avoid washing the zucchini blossoms, which would wilt them, but do inspect them carefully for bugs and brush off any dirt. With your fingers, remove the stamens—the threadlike particles—inside each blossom. Tuck a nugget of goat cheese and a piece of anchovy in each blossom.

In a small skillet, combine the ingredients for the garlic-parsley oil. Warm briefly over low heat, just until the garlic begins to give off its fragrance. Set aside.

TO ASSEMBLE THE PIZZA: With your hand, flatten the one ball of dough on a work surface, pressing it into a circle. Pick the dough up with both hands and stretch it into a 12-inch (30-centimeter) round, keeping it as evenly thin as possible. Set the round of dough on a generously floured pizza peel. Brush with half of the garlic-parsley oil. Top with the mozzarella and Asiago cheeses. Arrange the zucchini slices on the pizza like spokes on a wheel. Place the stuffed blossoms between the slices. Brush the blossoms and zucchini with the remaining garlic-parsley oil. Crumble the goat cheese on top.

Transfer the pizza to the preheated tiles or stone and bake until the dough is well browned and crisp on the edges and bottom, about 6 minutes. Cut into wedges and serve immediately.

MAKES ONE 12-INCH (30-CENTIMETER) PIZZA

Pitta Mijina

CORNMEAL FLATBREAD COOKED ON A CABBAGE LEAF

My grandmother would make cornbread in her wood oven occasionally in winter as a way of stretching her wheat supply. Before she swept the coals out and swabbed the oven floor in preparation for baking, she would make *pitta*, or flatbread, on the oven's brick floor with some of the cornmeal dough. No one had baking sheets in those days, so she would spread the moist *pitta* dough on a large, flattened outer leaf of cabbage. She would dimple the flattened dough vigorously with her fingertips in several places, then bake it quickly in the fiercely hot oven. When it emerged, crisp and golden, she would drizzle it generously with olive oil, which would pool in the dimples, and sprinkle it with sweet and hot red pepper and bits of anchovy or pork cracklings. My mother and her siblings would be standing by for this hot-from-the-oven snack.

Although my mother had often told me about *pitta mijina*, she never made it after we moved to California because she didn't think our ovens were hot enough. But one of the first dishes she tried after I installed an outdoor wood-burning oven was *pitta mijina*. As we discovered, a little wheat flour lightens the texture and yields a dough that produces good results in a conventional indoor oven. Unless you grow Savoy cabbage, as we do, you will probably not have access to the jumbo outer leaves, which are usually trimmed before the cabbage comes to market. Parchment paper makes a fine substitute.

Pitta mijina should be eaten while hot, like American cornbread. If you want to omit the anchovies, salt the surface of the *pitta* when it comes out of the oven. Serve as a light lunch with a salad or in thin wedges as an appetizer.

SUGGESTED WINE: Paolo Petrilli "Agramante," Cacc'e mmitte di Lucera, Apulia
This simple, rustic wine has some Sangiovese in the blend and the scent of tomato, cranberry, and orange zest.
ALTERNATE: Grenache

---

2 cups (10 ounces/280 grams) fine white or yellow cornmeal

2 teaspoons kosher salt

1¾ cups (425 milliliters) boiling water

¼ cup (60 milliliters) warm water (105°F to 110°F/45°C)

2 teaspoons active dry yeast

1 cup (5 ounces/140 grams) unbleached all-purpose flour

1 large outer leaf of Savoy cabbage, at least 12 inches (30 centimeters) in diameter, left at room temperature for one day to wilt, optional

1 garlic clove, halved

Ground hot red pepper

Calabrian paprika (page 304) *or* Spanish sweet paprika

3 tablespoons extra virgin olive oil

6 anchovy fillets, or to taste

IN A LARGE BOWL, stir the cornmeal and salt to blend. Add the boiling water and stir until the cornmeal is thoroughly moistened. Set aside until cool.

Put the warm water in a small bowl. Sprinkle the yeast over the water and let stand for 2 minutes to soften. Whisk with a fork until the yeast dissolves.

Add the flour and the dissolved yeast to the cornmeal. Mix with your hand until the ingredients come together into a well blended but sticky dough. Cover the bowl tightly with plastic wrap and let rise until the dough has doubled, about 1½ hours.

Line the lowest oven rack with baking tiles or a baking stone. Preheat the oven to its highest setting, at least 525°F (275°C) if possible.

On a pizza peel or rimless baking sheet, place the flattened cabbage leaf, if using, or place a sheet of parchment paper about 12 inches (30 centimeters) square. Dust the parchment lightly with flour. The cabbage leaf does not need flour.

Turn the dough out onto the cabbage leaf or parchment paper and prod it with moistened fingertips into a flat 10-inch (25-centimeter) circle. With one moistened fingertip, make about 2 dozen evenly spaced dimples in the dough, poking almost but not all the way through.

Slide the *pitta* onto the preheated tiles or baking stone and bake until golden brown and firm on both top and bottom, about 15 minutes. Use the pizza peel or rimless baking sheet to transfer the *pitta* to a work surface; do not turn off the oven. Peel off the cabbage leaf or parchment paper. Rub the surface of the *pitta* all over with the cut side of the garlic halves. Sprinkle generously with hot pepper to taste and paprika, then drizzle with olive oil. Tear the anchovy fillets into ¼-inch (6-millimeter) pieces and sprinkle them evenly over the surface.

Return the *pitta* to the oven until it is again piping hot, about 3 minutes. Cut into wedges and serve immediately.

MAKES ONE 10-INCH (25-CENTIMETER) *PITTA*, TO SERVE 8 TO 10 AS AN APPETIZER

Pizza Fritta
FRIED PIZZA WITH A TOMATO TOPPING

Whenever my grandmother made bread, she made a small fried flatbread for my mom as a snack. After removing a fistful of the risen bread dough, she would fashion a flattened round, then fry it in a skillet to make a small, plain *pizzella*. After we moved to California, my mother befriended an immigrant from Naples who said she also made fried pizzas from her bread dough and topped them with tomato sauce. Ever since, when my mother makes bread, she sets aside a little of the dough to make *pizza fritta* with a tomato topping. My two children devour it. They have also discovered the *pizza fritta* with a similar tomato topping sold at the beach in Scalea, on Calabria's west coast, where we vacation every other summer. A vendor strolls among the sunbathers with an insulated container hung around his neck, peddling irresistible fried pizzas made by his wife.

If you don't want to make bread, you can make *pizza fritta* with pizza dough. It works just as well. However, if you are making Everyday Bread (page 119) and want to make *pizza fritta* with some of that dough, set aside one-third of the bread dough after the first rise. Proceed as described below for the pizza dough after its first rise.

SUGGESTED WINE: Tenuta La Lumia "Don Totò," Sicily
A medium-bodied red wine from Nero d'Avola grapes, with aromas of black plum, juniper berrries, and chocolate-covered cherries.
ALTERNATE: Rioja

Dough for *Pitta* and Pizza (page 131), prepared through the first rise

5 to 6 tablespoons extra virgin olive oil for frying, or more if needed

Quick Tomato Sauce (page 53)

TURN THE RISEN DOUGH out onto a work surface and divide into 2 equal pieces. Shape each piece into a ball and put each in a lightly oiled bowl; turn the dough to coat with the oil. Cover each bowl tightly with plastic wrap. Let rise until doubled, about 1½ hours.

Heat a 12-inch (30-centimeter) skillet over moderately high heat. Add 3 tablespoons of the olive oil and swirl to coat. While the oil heats, transfer one ball of dough to a work surface and punch it down. Pick it up with both hands and stretch it into a circle as you would stretch dough for pizza, making a round just large enough to cover the bottom of the skillet. Lay the round of dough back down on your work surface and make sure it is of even thickness. Carefully place the round in the hot oil and immediately make nine or ten slits in the dough with the tip of a soup spoon, piercing all the way through. The slits keep the pizza from puffing excessively.

Cook, adjusting the heat as necessary, until the bottom is richly browned, 2 to 4 minutes. As the pizza cooks, use two soup spoons to rotate the pizza clockwise in the skillet so the bottom browns evenly. Turn with tongs and cook the second side, again rotating it frequently with the two spoons to ensure even browning. When the second side is well browned, in 2 to 4 minutes, transfer the fried pizza to a serving platter.

Add enough additional oil to the skillet to make 3 tablespoons. Repeat the stretching and frying with the second round of dough.

Reheat the tomato sauce if necessary. Divide the hot sauce between the two pizzas, spreading it evenly over the surface. Cut into wedges and serve immediately.

MAKES TWO 12-INCH (30-CENTIMETER) PIZZAS

Ricotta Fresca

HOMEMADE RICOTTA

This recipe most closely duplicates the creamy texture and rich taste of the ricotta I grew up with, the ricotta my father made daily. In Southern Italy, ricotta is a by-product of pecorino cheese production. Dairy farmers like my father would reheat the whey drained from the pecorino, often with some fresh milk added, to coagulate the remaining bits of nutritious protein in the whey. ("Ricotta" means "recooked.") Whatever ricotta my father didn't sell fresh, on the day it was made, he would salt and age to make ricotta salata. These cheeses would be stored on a rack suspended from the ceiling beams, directly over the hearth, and they would dry and become lightly smoked as they aged. *Ricotta affumicata* (smoked ricotta) is still a Calabrian specialty, delicious grated on pasta or eaten as a table cheese.

Fresh, warm ricotta on crusty bread is a favorite Calabrian breakfast or snack. My children love it with honey on top, or for dessert with bits of bittersweet chocolate and sugar. Most people no longer have the luxury of tasting warm ricotta, however, because production has become industrialized. With this recipe, you can have that experience in your own kitchen.

In Calabria, fresh ricotta is often sold in the perforated plastic basket it drained in. At home, you invert the basket, revealing a cheese with an attractive shape that's easy to slice. Ricotta made on the farm is sometimes packed and sold in small, tubular baskets hand woven from a sturdy dried grass called *giunco* (*Juncus depauperatus*). The baskets hold about 2 cups (450 grams), but they are always generously mounded on top, so they look almost like ice cream cones.

When my father was young, in the days before plastic wrap, cheesemakers would lay wild fern leaves on top of the molded ricotta, criss-crossing them to cover it, and then tie the leaves in place

Fresh ricotta wrapped in wild fern leaves

with a strip of *giunco*. At serving time, you removed the fern leaves, twisted the tubular basket as if you were wringing out a towel, and the ricotta emerged in a log shape. Although the *giunco* baskets aren't available here (and are disappearing in Calabria), the plastic draining baskets are not hard to find. (See Resources, page 368). They aren't essential—you can drain ricotta in a sieve—but they give your ricotta a more professional appearance.

When my mother and I initially developed this recipe, we were trying to duplicate the richness of sheep's milk ricotta. That's why we enriched the milk with a little cream. Although I frowned on the idea for a long time, I finally made the ricotta with low-fat (2 percent) milk only and was surprised by the good results. The low-fat ricotta is light on the tongue, without the richness of the full-fat version, but still better than anything you can buy. If you are calorie- or fat-conscious, you can successfully make this ricotta with a gallon of low-fat milk and omit the cream.

Rennet loses strength over time. Replace liquid animal rennet that is older than one year; replace liquid vegetable rennet after six to nine months.

---

1 gallon (4 liters) whole milk

¾ cup (180 milliliters) heavy cream

2 teaspoons kosher salt

1 teaspoon liquid vegetable or animal rennet (see Resources, page 368)

Two 2½-cup (600-milliliter) ricotta draining baskets (see Resources, page 368) *or* a fine sieve with a 6-cup (1½-liter) capacity

---

PUT THE MILK and cream in a heavy-bottomed pot and stir to mix well. Warm the mixture over moderate heat. Remove from the heat as soon as the milk begins to foam and climb toward the top of the pot. The temperature of the milk will be 200°F to 210°F (95°C to 100°C).

Pour the milk into another pot to leave behind any scorched milk adhering to the bottom of the pot. Add the salt and stir to dissolve it.

Let the milk cool to 100°F (38°C), which takes about an hour. (You can speed this process considerably by placing the pot in a bath of ice water.) Skim any foam

Top: Bringing the whey to a boil to make ricotta. Bottom left: Scooping up fresh ricotta curds. Bottom right: Spooning ricotta into draining baskets.

or skin that forms on top of the milk as it cools. In a small bowl, mix the rennet with ¼ cup (60 millimeters) cold water, then stir the diluted rennet into the pot. Let stand undisturbed until the milk has visibly thickened, about 10 minutes.

With a wooden spoon, cut a large "cross" in the milk. Stir quickly with a wooden spoon for 15 to 20 seconds to break up the coagulated milk. Using a perforated metal skimmer immersed in the milk, slowly and gently stir in one direction—so slowly that it takes about 20 seconds to make one revolution. You will see the milk begin to separate into curds and whey. Continue the slow, gentle stirring with the skimmer, moving the curds toward the center of the pot, until you have gathered a big pile of curds with whey surrounding them. (The whey may be dotted with bits of curd.) This process can take up to 5 minutes.

Slowly and gently pour off the whey, either directly into the sink or, if you want to catch every stray curd, into a cheesecloth-lined colander. Disturbing the curds as little as possible, fill the ricotta draining baskets or the fine sieve spoonful by spoonful, mounding the curd in the baskets if necessary.

If using ricotta draining baskets, set them in shallow plastic containers or on a tray to drain. If using a sieve, set it over a bowl to drain. Let stand at room temperature until the whey stops dripping from the baskets or sieve, about 2 hours, emptying the drained whey several times. The ricotta can be used immediately or refrigerated for later use. If the ricotta is in baskets, nestle the baskets in another container to catch any dripping whey, and cover the top with plastic wrap. To use, remove the plastic and invert the basket onto a plate. If the ricotta is in a sieve, invert the ricotta into a plastic container, cover, and refrigerate. The ricotta is best used within 2 to 3 days.

MAKES 4 TO 5 CUPS, ABOUT 2 POUNDS (900 GRAMS)

Traditional Cheeses of Calabria

Calabria produces a large volume of cheese, although not a vast variety. The cow's milk cheeses are practically all of the *pasta filata* type, made from curd cooked in hot water until it is capable of being stretched and pulled into the desired shape. *Pasta filata* cheeses, like Caciocavallo and Provola, have an elastic texture and become harder and drier as they age. (See photograph of cheeses on page 154.)

BUTIRRO: This unusual cow's milk cheese typically resembles a small Caciocavallo with its pear shape and topknot. The exterior is the same *pasta filata* used for Caciocavallo, but inside is a surprise: a large knob of butter. Initially, Butirro was the shepherd's way of preserving his butter. Today, Calabrians slice it thinly and eat it with bread as part of an antipasto platter.

CACIOCAVALLO SILANO: This cheese is Calabria's only DOP (*denominazione di origine protetta*), or name-protected cheese, which means that it can only be made in certain regions by tightly defined methods. The permitted regions include, in addition to Calabria, the neighboring regions of Campania, Basilicata, Puglia, and Molise. But the "Silano" in the cheese's name suggests that it originated in La Sila, the high mountain plateau in central Calabria where dairy cattle are raised. The texture ranges from semisoft to semifirm, depending on age. The flavor is relatively subdued with young cheese, similar to an Asiago or mild Provolone, and becomes piquant with extended maturation. When a recipe calls for grated Caciocavallo and I can't find it, I substitute equal parts grated Asiago and mild Provolone. Calabrians eat Caciocavallo as a table cheese, especially when it is relatively young, and slice or grate it for cooking.

PECORINO CROTONESE: Made in the province of Crotone and in parts of Cosenza and Catanzaro, Pecorino Crotonese is one of Calabria's most esteemed cheeses. Aged anywhere from two months to a year, it becomes more nutty and complex as it matures. It is not protected by a DOP, so producers are not restricted in how they make it. Some use all sheep's milk; others add some proportion of goat's milk. Wheels typically weigh 4½ to 5 pounds (about 2 kilos) and have a semifirm to firm golden interior. Pecorino Crotonese is enjoyed as a table cheese when young or semimature; wheels that are fully mature and hard are used for grating. Currently, Sardinia produces and exports a great deal of so-called Pecorino Crotonese, which the Calabrians consider inferior to the cheese made in Crotone.

PECORINO DEL MONTE PORO: A sheep's milk cheese from the province of Vibo Valentia, Pecorino del Monte Poro may also contain some goat's milk. It is moist and mellow when young, but age makes it harder, saltier, and more peppery. Younger wheels are eaten as a table cheese, with *salumi*, sun-dried tomatoes, and other vegetables preserved under oil; mature wheels are used for grating.

PROVOLA: This pasta *filata* cheese is made with cow's milk according to a recipe similar to that used for Caciocavallo. The cheeses are usually shaped like a thick log that tapers at one end, and the size varies. Provola is aged anywhere from a few days to a couple of months, becoming firmer and more pronounced in taste with age. Calabrians eat it as a table cheese and slice or grate it for cooking. Provolone, despite the similar name, is a more piquant cheese.

RICOTTA: The whey drained from pecorino curds is never thrown away in Calabria. Instead, it is reheated, usually with a little milk added, to make ricotta. In a traditional ricotta operation, the whey or milk-enriched whey and some salt will be heated almost to boiling, which causes curds to coalesce on the surface. These fluffy curds are scooped off and into waiting perforated molds. Within an hour, they have drained sufficiently to send to market. Ricotta this fresh is warm, moist, milky, and sweet, with delicate curds that dissolve on your tongue.

Ricotta in Calabria may be made with sheep's, goat's, or cow's milk, or a mixture of sheep's and goat's milk, depending on the animal husbandry in the region. My personal preference is for ricotta made with sheep's milk, which is higher in fat than goat's or cow's milk and produces a particularly rich and creamy ricotta with a distinctive animal-like scent. It is most prevalent in the zones where sheep are raised, such as in the Crotone area.

It is increasingly hard to find Calabrian shepherds who operate as my father did, maintaining a small herd of goats and sheep and making pecorino and ricotta for the local market. Few shepherds have the resources to build a cheesemaking facility that meets the European Union's hygiene standards, so most sell their milk to larger dairies now. Yet Calabrians in search of natural, handmade foods still know where to find these cheesemaking shepherds, and know they must get there by mid-morning to stand a chance of securing some fresh ricotta. When my family vacations in Calabria in summer, we phone ahead to reserve our ricotta. We pick it up in the morning and enjoy it warm for lunch. Ricotta is always best the day it is made, especially if it has not been refrigerated. If it is two or three days old, we use it in cooking.

Most Calabrian kitchens are never without ricotta. It is spread on toast with honey for breakfast, made into meatballs, added to frittatas, and used in numerous pasta dishes, vegetable and *pitta* stuffings, and holiday desserts.

Ricotta salata: Ricotta intended for longer keeping is salted on the outside and air dried for at least a week or two, often much longer. The more it is aged, the dryer and saltier it becomes. In Calabria, *ricotta salata* is a rindless cheese, usually in the shape of a small log. Unless it is quite young, it is used primarily as a grating cheese for pasta and is especially compatible with summer vegetables such as tomato, eggplant, zucchini, and peppers.

Ricotta affumicata: On the Ionian side, *ricotta affumicata* (smoked ricotta, see Resources, page 368) largely takes the place of *ricotta salata.* In the most traditional farmstead operations, the fresh ricotta is unmolded as soon as it can hold its shape, then salted, put on mats, and kept for about three days in an area where it is infused with wood smoke. There might be a small smokehouse on the premises or, in more rudimentary settings, the ricotta is suspended near the fireplace that heats the milk vat. *Ricotta affumicata* is grated over pasta dishes and is particularly tasty with lamb *ragù* (page 82).

Ricotta salata   *Ricotta affumicata*

Frittata di Ricotta
FRITTATA WITH FRESH RICOTTA

If you take care not to overcook it, this frittata will be moist and as light as air. If you have leftovers, make a frittata sandwich. My mother prepared them all the time for my father when he worked on our farm in Calabria. She would sandwich a piece of frittata between slices of homemade bread and pack it to go.

Many Calabrians add sausage to this frittata. If you would like to try that variation, remove a sweet or hot Italian sausage link from its casing, brown the crumbled sausage, and add it to the onion before adding the beaten egg to the skillet.

SUGGESTED WINE: Terre di Pantelleria "Cinque Denti," Pantelleria Bianco, Sicily
A dry wine from the Zibibbo grape (also known as Muscat of Alexandria), with the fragrance of jasmine and orange blossom and a crisp finish.
ALTERNATE: dry Riesling

---

1 cup (8 ounces/225 grams) Homemade Ricotta (page 144) *or* store-bought whole-milk ricotta

6 large eggs, lightly beaten

¼ cup (25 grams) freshly grated pecorino cheese

2 tablespoons finely chopped flat-leaf parsley

1 teaspoon kosher salt

Freshly ground black pepper

3 tablespoons extra virgin olive oil

1 large yellow onion, halved and thinly sliced

PREHEAT THE OVEN to 400°F (200°C) and position a rack in the middle of the oven.

If using store-bought ricotta, put it in a sieve set over a bowl for about 30 minutes to allow any excess moisture to drain. Homemade ricotta does not need additional draining.

In a large bowl, combine the eggs, ricotta, pecorino, parsley, ½ teaspoon of the salt, and several grinds of pepper. Mix with a fork until well blended.

Heat the olive oil in a 10-inch (25-centimeter) nonstick skillet over medium heat. Add the onion and remaining ½ teaspoon salt. Sauté until the onion is softened and translucent, about 5 minutes; do not let it brown.

Add the egg mixture to the skillet and distribute it evenly. Cook without stirring until the frittata begins to firm and the bottom is golden brown, 6 to 7 minutes. Lift the edges with a rubber spatula to check the bottom for doneness, and lower the heat if necessary to keep the bottom from overbrowning. The surface will still be slightly moist.

Transfer the skillet to the middle rack of the oven and bake until the top of the frittata is firm, golden, and puffy, about 10 minutes. If you're not sure that it is fully cooked, make a small slit on the surface with a paring knife to see whether the interior is set or still runny and needs to cook a bit more.

Slide the frittata onto a cutting board. Serve hot, warm, or at room temperature. Cut into wedges to serve.

SERVES 4 TO 6

On the left: Pecorino curds just after being placed in the basket and before being pressed down. On the right: Two hours later, pecorino before being salted.

Making Rennet the Old Way

Like cheesemakers for centuries before him, my father made his own rennet, the ingredient that helps turn milk into curds. This natural coagulant, from the enzyme chymosin, abounds in the stomachs of young, milk-fed animals such as baby goats and lambs. The process may sound pitiless to some because the young animal must be sacrificed, but it is a routine part of traditional farm life in Calabria.

On my father's farm in the mountains above Verbicaro, goats were born in late winter, when there was little fresh grass to eat. Consequently, the mothers' milk production was low. If a doe gave birth to twins, she would not have enough milk for both. My father would sacrifice one twin when it was between one and three weeks old, the time of maximum rennin production.

He would harvest the stomach and inflate it using a hollow reed or a length of tubular pasta to channel the air from his mouth. Then he would tie the inflated stomach shut, hang this curious vessel by the chimney, and wait for its contents to dry. A few weeks later, he would add some fresh milk to the contents, which by then resembled dry cottage cheese. The enzyme would coagulate the fresh milk, producing more curds, and when they dried down sufficiently, he would slit open the stomach and scrape out the paste-like contents. After salting the paste heavily, he would store it in a sealed container, ready to do its part when he resumed cheesemaking in the spring.

An olive-size nugget of this rennet was sufficient to coagulate 20 quarts (20 liters) of milk. My father would wrap the nugget in a cloth and steep it in water to make an extract, then add the extract to the fresh goat's milk.

Baby goat stomachs hanging to dry to use as rennet for making ricotta

Traditional Calabrian cheeses (clockwise from top left): 1. fresh ricotta in a woven basket; 2. fresh Caciocavallo; 3. Pecorino; 4. *Ricotta salata*; 5. Butirro sliced in half lengthwise with the butter inside, the way Calabrians preserved butter in the days before refrigeration (For complete glossary of cheeses, see pages 148–50.)

Uova Strapazzate con Peperoni
SCRAMBLED EGGS WITH SWEET PEPPERS

My mother used to prepare these savory scrambled eggs for the laborers who helped her and my father on their farm near Verbicaro. Farm work started early, and by mid-morning, everyone needed some sustenance. This quickly made dish and a little wine would keep the crew going until lunch. In the spring, she might substitute wild asparagus for the peppers; in winter, she would use her own dried sweet peppers (page 293).

My mother still makes *uova strapazzate* often, especially for lunch or as a meat-less second course. In my house, it's usually a brunch dish. *Strappare* means to tear or beat up, so *uova strapazzate* is an evocative name for eggs "beaten up" with fried peppers. The juicy peppers infuse the eggs with their sweetness.

SUGGESTED WINE: Casa d'Ambra "Tenuta Frassitelli," Ischia, Campania
A rich, dry, aromatic white from the Biancolella grape, with aromas of pear, apricot, and slate.
ALTERNATE: Alsatian Pinot Gris

---

2 pounds (900 grams) long sweet Italian peppers, red or green, *or*
    2 pounds (900 grams) red bell peppers

½ cup (125 milliliters) extra virgin olive oil

Kosher salt

8 large eggs

CORE THE PEPPERS, halve them, and remove the white ribs and seeds. Cut the peppers into roughly 2-inch (5-centimeter) squares.

Heat the olive oil in a 12-inch (30-centimeter) nonstick skillet over high heat, then add the peppers. Season with 1 tablespoon salt and stir to coat the peppers with oil. Fry briskly, stirring frequently to prevent scorching, until the peppers are soft, about 10 minutes. You can fry the peppers a few hours ahead. Reheat them before you add the eggs.

Beat the eggs with 1½ teaspoons salt. Add the eggs to the peppers and cook over high heat, stirring constantly with a wooden spoon, until the eggs are just done, about 2 minutes. Serve immediately.

SERVES 6

Fishermen in Pizzo cleaning their nets after a day on the sea

Pesce
seafood

Si non ci fussi carni e stoccu
'u nostru visu sarrìa smortu.

If not for meat and stockfish, our faces would be pale indeed.

Calabria boasts the longest coastline of any region in Italy, so one might
expect that Calabrians eat a lot of fresh seafood. In fact, the relationship between
Calabrians, the sea, and the food it provides is suprisingly complex, influenced by
the region's topography, history, and long isolation.

Tuna and swordfish—the most prized of the region's catch—have been fished
commercially off Calabria's Tyrrhenian coast since Phoenician times. According to
Aristotle, the Phoenicians knew how to preserve tuna in jars, a precursor of the
canned tuna industry important to the Calabrian economy today. Several centuries
later, the Arabs perfected the *tonnara*, the clever method of catching tuna with
elaborate net traps that persisted in Calabria until the mid-twentieth century (page
179). The Arabs were using the system in Sicilian waters as early as A.D. 1000.

Probably because of this generous sea, Calabria's early settlers clustered along
its coasts. The Greeks established major settlements on the Ionian waterfront—
most notably, Sibari, Locri, and Crotone, which were stars in the Magna Graecia
crown. But after the fall of the Roman empire, life near the water became more
perilous, subject to upheaval from a constant stream of invaders and pirates. Pizzo,
situated on a point on the Gulf of Saint Eufemia, on the west coast, was pillaged
many times.

In the ensuing centuries, Calabrians abandoned the coasts in large numbers,
moving onto the hillsides and into the mountains for safety. But as they established
their hilltop settlements and cut down forests to clear land for farming, they unwit-
tingly contributed to making the coastland even less hospitable. On the Ionian side,
land that had been healthy and farmable during Greek times became gradually more

Left: (*top*) striped sea bream (*mormora*); (*middle*) John Dory (*pesce San Pietro*); (*bottom*) red mullet (*triglie*). Right: pearly razorfish (*pesce topo*). These fish were brought in by fishermen from the Tyrrhenian Sea and sold the same day at a fish auction in Vibo Valentia. Locals cook these varieties of small fish whole, on the bone, fried or grilled with fresh tomatoes and herbs.

marshy and malarial, due in part to erosion from the mountainsides that disrupted river flows and created swamps in the plains. Over the centuries, the Ionian coast was slowly transformed into marshy wetlands, and malaria routinely cut short the lives of its inhabitants. This deadly disease, which some Calabrians erroneously associated with the sea, was not eradicated in the region until about 1950.

Even today, there is little commercial fishing along the Ionian coast. The wetlands have gradually been reclaimed for farming and viticulture, but no major harbor supports a fishing fleet. Local fishermen working from small boats supply the local markets, but the demand is not huge, as there are few major towns on this coast. Instead, the region's commercial fishing centers around Reggio Calabria, Scilla, and Bagnara for swordfish, and around the Tyrrhenian port of Pizzo for bluefin tuna.

With the completion in 1894 of the railroad connecting Calabria to Rome, and the construction of highways and better roads in Calabria in the decades that followed, many people began to leave the hills and establish small towns along the coasts. The rapid commercial development of the Tyrrhenian coastline from about 1970 on brought restaurants, condominiums, and tourist facilities that have helped sustain the fishing industry.

Today, Calabrians who live along the coast, especially on the Tyrrhenian side, enjoy a wealth of Mediterranean seafood. Fish markets offer the hefty fresh tuna and swordfish in season, sliced to order, and locals line up early to get first dibs on these just-caught fish before they are snapped up, usually by noon. Calabrians also adore anchovies, sardines, and mackerel—the so-called *pesci azzurri*, or blue fish, named for the color of their skin. Octopus, squid, cuttlefish, mussels, clams, scallops, and shrimp beckon shoppers, as do fin fish such as mullet, grouper, hake, bream, and sea bass. A great delicacy, served in the coastal restaurants, are the *neonate* (page 42), or tiny newborn sardines and anchovies, typically coated with a flour-and-egg batter and deep-fried.

Calabrians celebrate their fishermen and the local catch at a variety of annual *sagre*, most of them held in midsummer when many tourists are around. There is a *sagra* for tuna at Pizzo, for swordfish at Bagnara Calabra, for blue fish at Cirò Marina, and for fish of all kinds at Soverato. At a *sagra*, you can sample the featured food prepared in many different ways by local cooks and participate in the general merriment.

But travel inland from the coast, and not even very far, and fresh seafood becomes much more limited. Were it not for the Catholic Church and its ban on meat consumption on Fridays, mountain-dwelling Calabrians would have little familiarity with fish at all. As it is, they are passionate about dried cod (*stoccafisso*) and salt cod (*baccalà*; page 186), among the only fish that made it into the mountains in the days before the roads improved. Even now that they have better access to fresh fish, they remain loyal to preserved cod and have not lost their enthusiasm for it. On Christmas Eve menus throughout Calabria (page 188), *stoccafisso* and *baccalà* are the stars, appearing in multiple dishes, in multiple guises.

Being small and easy to transport, anchovies and sardines did travel a short distance inland from the coast. My mother recalls the vendors who would come two to three times a week to our hilltown of Verbicaro in summer, peddling these popular fish. The town crier, provided with a megaphone, would announce to the residents that the fresh anchovies had arrived, and housewives like my mother would come out to buy them. The fresh anchovies would then be dipped in flour and fried (page 164); or butterflied and layered with breadcrumbs and pecorino and baked (page 165); or cooked with spaghetti and cherry tomatoes. If the anchovies were plentiful and the price was right, my mother and her neighbors would buy kilos and preserve them under salt (page 42). The same peddlers brought fresh seaweed, which some people believed was good for their health. My mother boiled it and made me eat it, and I detested it. Only as an adult, dining in the seafood restaurants of Diamante, where it is often dipped in a yeast batter and fried, did I rediscover seaweed with pleasure.

Calabrians, like most Italians, prefer their fish on the bone. Swordfish and tuna are virtually the only fish that are sliced into steaks in Calabrian markets. Although seafood carpaccio is fashionable in the tourist restaurants of Diamante, Scalea, and Tropea, many Calabrians would never consider eating raw fish or even rare tuna. The historical memory of seafood as vaguely dangerous still persists, especially among older people. Consequently, most people prefer their seafood well cooked.

If you have a local source for fresh fish and shellfish, you can re-create the seafood dishes Calabrians love, from Swordfish "Glutton's Style" with Tomato, Capers, and Olives (page 175) to a dramatic Whole Salt-Baked Sea Bass (page 181), which never fails to impress.

Insalata di Polipo
MARINATED OCTOPUS SALAD WITH OLIVE OIL AND LEMON

Fresh octopus is a summer mainstay in Calabria's coastal restaurants and markets. Few people would consider cooking a frozen one out of season; Calabrians eat this tentacled denizen of the Mediterranean enthusiastically, but only when fresh. Because it is so prized, most cooks treat octopus simply. In one typical preparation, it is boiled in salted water to tenderize it, then grilled to give the flesh a charred edge. Alternatively, as I describe here, the octopus is boiled, cooled, sliced, and served as a salad with the most basic of dressings: just olive oil, lemon juice, minced garlic, and parsley. Some cooks add boiled and sliced potatoes to this salad. Either way, octopus is rarely mixed with other seafood or with celery, onion, tomato, or other ingredients typical of seafood salads. Calabrians don't want to mask its briny flavor and pleasantly chewy texture by over-embellishing it.

Octopus is rarely available fresh in the United States, but the frozen product is a more than adequate substitute. You need reasonably large octopus for this recipe—at least 2 pounds (900 grams) each—so the tentacles will be thick enough to make meaty chunks when sliced. The baby octopus available in some markets is too small.

Many people hesitate to cook octopus because they fear it will be tough. If cooked slowly for a long time, it will become tender, although you want to stop the cooking while it still has some "chew." Every culture that enjoys octopus has a different theory on how to tenderize it. Some people slap it repeatedly against a hard surface before cooking it. In the Sicilian beach town of Mondello, near my husband's home, the street vendors dip the octopus into a cauldron of boiling water three times before cooking it, a process they claim makes it tender. I have always done the same, and I can't be sure it makes a difference because I would never *not* do it.

Octopus salad is an appetizer in Calabrian restaurants. At home, we tend to eat it as a room-temperature second course, after a first course of pasta with clams or Risotto with Fresh Mussels (page 107).

SUGGESTED WINE: Pietracupa Greco di Tufo, Campania
A white wine with some richness and robust acidity to stand up to the meaty octopus and the lemon notes in the dish.
ALTERNATE: dry rosé

Marinated Octopus Salad with Olive Oil and Lemon

2 fresh or frozen octopus, about 2 pounds (900 grams) each

Kosher salt

¼ cup plus 2 tablespoons extra virgin olive oil

3 tablespoons lemon juice

2 tablespoons minced flat-leaf parsley

2 large garlic cloves, finely minced

IF THE OCTOPUS is fresh, ask the fishmonger to clean it for you by removing all viscera from the head sac. If the octopus is frozen, it will have been cleaned before freezing. Thaw it slowly in the refrigerator.

Bring 4 quarts (4 liters) water to a boil in an 8-quart (8-liter) pot over high heat. Add 3 tablespoons salt. Working with one octopus at a time, pierce the head with a meat fork and dip the whole creature, tentacles first, into the boiling water. Hold it in the water for about 5 seconds, then lift it out. Repeat the dipping two times. This procedure is said to tenderize the octopus, and it causes the tentacles to curl attractively.

When both of the octopus have been dipped three times, return them both to the boiling water. Partially cover the pot and adjust the heat to maintain a gentle simmer. Cook until the octopus are tender when pierced with a knife, about one hour. If you aren't sure, cut off a small piece from a tentacle and taste it. It should offer a little resistance to the tooth, but it shouldn't be chewy. When the octopus are done, cover the pot, remove from the heat, and let them cool completely in the water.

At this point, if you do not like the gelatinous dark skin or the tiny suction cups on the tentacles, you can easily rub them off with your fingers. Italians tend to leave these parts intact. Cut the tentacles on the diagonal into 1-inch (2½-centimeter) pieces. Cut the head into ½-inch-wide (12-millimeter-wide) slices.

Put the sliced octopus in a bowl and add the olive oil, lemon juice, parsley, garlic, and 1½ teaspoons salt. Stir well. Let marinate at room temperature for one hour, then taste, adjust the seasoning, and serve. If you like, you can marinate the octopus up to 2 days before serving. Keep it refrigerated, but remove from the refrigerator about 30 minutes before serving to take the chill off.

SERVES 6

Alici Fritte

FRIED FRESH ANCHOVIES

For me, a plate of crisp fried anchovies is as hard to resist as French fries. When the fish are small, we eat them in one bite; the bones are soft and not even noticeable. For bigger anchovies—say, longer than four inches (ten centimeters)—we sometimes remove the backbone before frying them, as for Marinated Fresh Anchovies with Red Onion and Parsley (page 30). In restaurants, Calabrians often eat fried anchovies as an antipasto. In homes, where antipasto is rarely served, the fried fish are a second course, after pasta.

SUGGESTED WINE: La Sibilla Falanghina, Campi Flegrei, Campania
With its grapefruit and lemon zest aromas and strong mineral notes, this crisp white wine brightens fried fish like a squeeze of lemon.
ALTERNATE: Sauvignon Blanc

---

1 pound (450 grams) fresh anchovies

Kosher salt

Extra virgin olive oil for frying

Unbleached all-purpose flour

CLEAN THE ANCHOVIES as directed on page 31. Sprinkle them generously with salt. Heat ¼ inch (6 millimeters) of olive oil in a skillet over moderate heat. Make a bed of flour on a plate.

When the oil reaches 375°F (190°C), hot enough to sizzle an anchovy on contact, toss a few of the anchovies in the flour, coating them all over. Transfer them to a platter, shaking off excess flour. Add them to the hot oil, taking care not to crowd the pan. Fry until crisp and golden, about 2 minutes, then transfer to a paper towel–lined plate. Continue flouring and frying the anchovies in batches. Sprinkle with salt and serve hot.

SERVES 6

Tortiera d'Alici
BAKED FRESH ANCHOVIES WITH BREADCRUMBS

A *tortiera* is like a savory cake—in this case, a layer cake of fresh anchovies and breadcrumbs. Drizzled with olive oil and baked until the fish have melded with the garlicky crumbs, the *tortiera* can be sliced into neat squares. My mother never puts tomato in her *tortiera*, but I enjoyed it that way at Dattilo, a picturesque olive- and grape-growing *agriturismo* (a farm that welcomes overnight guests) near the village of Strongoli, north of Crotone, so I am including the tomatoes as an option. For Dattilo's refined restaurant, the chef makes the *tortiera* in individual casseroles, something you could try if you have small baking dishes.

I would serve the *tortiera* with a green salad or fresh vegetable, and precede it with pasta with a seafood or vegetable sauce.

SUGGESTED WINE: Di Giovanna Grecanico, Sicily
A white wine with the racy acidity that anchovies need, as well as some plush stone-fruit aromas to complement the richness of the baked breadcrumbs.
ALTERNATE: Verdicchio

---

2 pounds (900 grams) fresh anchovies or sardines

1½ cups (120 grams) firmly packed fresh breadcrumbs (page 127)

¾ cup (75 grams) freshly grated pecorino cheese

¼ cup minced flat-leaf parsley

3 garlic cloves, finely minced

Ground hot red pepper, optional

6 tablespoons extra virgin olive oil

Kosher salt

6 large bay leaves, halved

1 cup (250 milliliters) peeled, seeded and chopped fresh tomato,
    optional

CLEAN THE ANCHOVIES as directed on page 31. Remove the backbone from each anchovy by grasping the end of the backbone closest to the head and lifting it out. It usually pulls away cleanly from the flesh, although sometimes it clings. If it does cling, gently work the backbone free with your fingers, damaging the flesh as little as possible. Keep the tail intact. Lay the boneless anchovies open "butterfly" style.

In a bowl, combine the breadcrumbs, cheese, parsley, and garlic. Sprinkle with ground hot pepper, if desired. Mix well.

Preheat the oven to 400°F (200°C).

Choose a baking dish with a 6-cup (1½-liter) capacity, such as an 8-inch (20-centimeter) square or an oval of comparable surface area. The dish should have relatively high sides to accommodate the layers of anchovies and breadcrumbs. Using 1 tablespoon of the oil, coat the bottom of the baking dish. Make a thin layer of breadcrumbs, just enough to coat the bottom of the dish.

Top with a layer of butterflied anchovies, skin side down, arranging them snugly and even overlapping them a little. Salt the anchovies, then drizzle with 1 tablespoon oil. Top with a layer of breadcrumbs and 4 bay leaf halves. Repeat the layering—anchovies, salt, oil, breadcrumbs, bay leaves—two more times. For the final (fourth) layer, arrange the last of the anchovies on top of the breadcrumbs. Season with salt and drizzle with oil. Top with chopped tomato, if using. Scatter the last of the breadcrumbs over the surface; you should still have enough to make a thin but solid covering. Drizzle with the remaining 2 tablespoons olive oil.

Bake until the surface is browned, the anchovies are sizzling, and their flesh is white and flaky, about 20 minutes. Let rest for at least 15 minutes so the *tortiera* can settle before being cut into serving portions. It's even good at room temperature.

SERVES 6

Variation
Sarde Ripiene (Stuffed Baked Sardines)

Clean and butterfly 2 pounds sardines as for the *tortiera* (page 31). Arrange half of the boneless butterflied sardines skin side down in an oiled baking dish large enough to hold them in one layer. Sprinkle with salt. Top with the breadcrumb mixture, dividing it evenly and pressing it into an even layer. Top each sardine with another sardine, skin side up. Drizzle with 1 tablespoon olive oil. Bake until the fish are sizzling hot and the flesh is white and flakes easily when prodded with a fork, 12 to 15 minutes. Let cool for 30 minutes before serving. Divide the sardines among serving plates, drizzle each portion with a little extra virgin olive oil, and accompany with lemon wedges.

Pesce Spada alla Bagnarese
SWORDFISH IN A GARLICKY BROTH, BAGNARA STYLE

Bagnara Calabra—Bagnara for short—is the center of Calabria's swordfish fishery, occupying a sliver of Tyrrhenian coast between mountains and sea. From April to July, these giant migratory fish travel along the Costa Viola, between Bagnara and Scilla, on their way to the Strait of Messina. For more than forty years, the town of Bagnara has staged an annual swordfish festival the second weekend in July to honor the local specialty. Thousands of people from all over Italy descend on the town to enjoy fresh swordfish with pasta, or grilled, or steamed by this unusual method common in Bagnara.

You will need a baking dish or lidded casserole just large enough to hold the fish in one layer and a larger flameproof baking dish or roasting pan that can hold the smaller dish in a bath of simmering water. The thin steaks steam quickly in their own juice, producing an aromatic broth with the mingled flavors of parsley, capers, and garlic. Serve with crusty Italian bread to soak up the tasty broth.

American fishmongers slice swordfish too thickly, in my opinion. In Italy, it is always sliced more thinly, so it cooks quickly and remains juicy and tender. If you can only find thick steaks, halve them horizontally with a long, sharp knife. This dish is so delicate and simple that fresh, not frozen, swordfish is a must.

You can double the recipe to serve four people, but make sure you have a baking dish large enough to hold all four steaks in one layer, and a deep flameproof roasting pan large enough to hold the baking dish. *Struncatura* (page 68) or another seafood pasta would be an appropriate first course.

SUGGESTED WINE: Pasetti Zarache, Trebbiano d'Abruzzo, Abruzzo
A lean, dry white wine from the Trebbiano grape with enough body to stand up to meaty swordfish.
ALTERNATE: Dry Chenin Blanc

Swordfish in a Garlicky Broth, Bagnara Style

2 skinless fresh swordfish steaks, about ⅜ inch (9 millimeters) thick
and 5 to 6 ounces (160 grams) each

Kosher salt and freshly ground black pepper

1 tablespoon extra virgin olive oil, plus more for garnish

1 large garlic clove, very thinly sliced

1 tablespoon capers, preferably salt-packed, rinsed

1 tablespoon chopped flat-leaf parsley

1 tablespoon fresh lemon juice

SEASON THE SWORDFISH on both sides with salt and pepper. Using the 1 tablespoon olive oil, coat a baking dish just large enough to hold the swordfish. Put the swordfish in the baking dish and scatter the garlic around it. Sprinkle the surface of the fish with capers and parsley. Spoon the lemon juice and 1 tablespoon water over the fish. Cover the baking dish tightly with a lid or aluminum foil.

Choose a large roasting pan or other deep pan that can take stovetop heat and accommodate the baking dish. Set the pan on a burner and put the baking dish in it. In a separate pan or teakettle, bring several cups of water to a boil for pouring into the roasting pan. Turn the heat to high under the roasting pan and add enough boiling water to come halfway up the sides of the baking dish. After the water returns to a boil, cook the fish for 8 minutes. Uncover and check for doneness; the fish should be cooked through but still moist and surrounded with flavorful juices. Taste the juices and add more salt if necessary.

Serve the swordfish in shallow bowls, spooning the garlicky broth over the fish. Drizzle each portion with additional extra virgin olive oil.

SERVES 2

Fish auction in Vibo Valentia. The man on the left is holding up a dogfish (*palombo*); coiled up in boxes are scabbard fish (*spatola*).

La Sagra: When Calabrians Celebrate Food

As befits people who have long depended on farming and fishing, Calabrians take great pride in their local foodstuffs. Every food specialty of the region, it seems, has its own festival, or *sagra*, in which people gather to show their appreciation for the featured food by consumi ng it in every possible way.

Most *sagre* are held on weekends, when people have more time for revelry, and many occur in summer when tourists can swell the crowd. But a dedicated food lover could probably find a *sagra* somewhere in Calabria every weekend of the year.

There is a *sagra* for *'nduja* (spicy pork spread); for *pesce azzurro* ("blue fish" such as mackerel, anchovies, and sardines); for smoked ricotta; for the red onions of Tropea; for chestnuts; eggplant; sausage; strawberries; bread; chick peas; wild mushrooms; homemade pasta. And the list goes on.

A *sagra* can be as modest as a few oilcloth-covered folding tables set up in the village square, with local men and women preparing the food for their fellow towns-people. I stumbled on a tripe *sagra* in Torre Melissa, on the Ionian coast, one spring that was no more elaborate than that. Local men dished up bowls of thick tripe stew with chunks of bread; a local winery donated the red wine; and children cavorted to taped folk music as their parents ate and socialized.

But *sagre* can also be major tourist events that enrich the coffers of a town and its merchants. The preeminent Calabrian *sagra*, with the biggest reputation, is surely the five-day *festival del peperoncino*, or hot-pepper festival, in Diamante the first week in September. The gathering draws thousands of people from all over Italy and beyond, who come to indulge in all manner of spicy food, sample every conceivable hot pepper condiment, and enjoy the festival's music, films, and pepper-eating competition.

As far as I can tell, no entity maintains a master calendar of *sagre* in Calabria. But many towns have Web sites that list major *sagre* in the vicinity. If a *sagra* is scheduled while you are visiting a town, you will know it from the proliferation of banners and fliers.

Braciole di Pesce Spada alla Griglia
GRILLED SWORDFISH ROLLS WITH BREADCRUMB STUFFING

Sliced thin and pounded to flatten them further, swordfish steaks can be rolled around a savory filling, just like pork *braciole* (page 197). The Calabrian filling is simple: breadcrumbs, grated pecorino, parsley, and capers. (My Sicilian mother-in-law adds pine nuts and currants.) You can grill the rolls over charcoal, as described here; bake them in the oven, or cook them in a ridged grill pan. They are finished with a light sauce of olive oil, lemon juice, garlic, and herbs known throughout Southern Italy as *salmoriglio*. The *braciole* are as enjoyable at room temperature as they are hot, which makes them a good choice for a buffet.

To make it easier to cut the swordfish into uniformly thin slices, partially freeze the fish for an hour or so first.

SUGGESTED WINE: Passopisciaro Passopisciaro, Sicily
The oily breadcrumbs and baked flavors make a red wine possible here. This wine, from Nerello Mascalese grapes, has bright cherry, dried cranberry, and orange peel aromas and lively acidity.
ALTERNATE: Pinot Noir in a light style

SALMORIGLIO

½ cup (125 milliliters) extra virgin olive oil

⅓ cup (80 milliliters) lemon juice

1 garlic clove, minced

1 tablespoon finely chopped fresh oregano

1 tablespoon finely chopped flat-leaf parsley

1½ teaspoons kosher salt

1 small fresh hot red pepper, thinly sliced, optional

2 pounds (900 grams) fresh swordfish, in one piece

Kosher salt and freshly ground black pepper

FILLING

½ cup (40 grams) fresh breadcrumbs

¼ cup (25 grams) freshly grated pecorino cheese

2 tablespoons minced flat-leaf parsley

1 tablespoon finely minced capers

1 garlic clove, minced

1 tablespoon extra virgin olive oil

MAKE THE *SALMORIGLIO* first, as it needs to rest. Whisk all the ingredients together in a bowl. Set aside for at least 30 minutes.

Put the swordfish on your work surface, skin side down. Cut it into twelve thin slices, or steaks. (If the swordfish is large in diameter, you may find it easier to cut six slices and then cut them in half after pounding them.) Cut the skin away from each steak. One at a time, cover each steak with plastic wrap and pound lightly with a meat mallet to make it even thinner. Season both sides of each steak with salt and pepper and arrange on a tray.

MAKE THE FILLING: Combine all the ingredients in a small bowl. Mix with your hands to blend.

Sprinkle about 1 tablespoon of the filling on each steak, spreading it evenly but stopping short of the edge. Roll the swordfish around the filling like a jelly roll. Secure with toothpicks.

Prepare a medium-hot charcoal fire.

Set aside ¾ cup (180 milliliters) of the *salmoriglio*. Brush the swordfish rolls with the remaining ¼ cup (60 millimeters). Set the swordfish rolls on the grill rack directly over the coals and grill, turning once, until done throughout, about 5 minutes total. Transfer to a platter, remove the toothpicks, and spoon some of the reserved *salmoriglio* over each roll.

SERVES 6

Variation

Substitute the stuffed but uncooked swordfish rolls for the swordfish steaks in Swordfish "Glutton's Style" with Tomato, Capers, and Olives (page 175).

Hunting Swordfish on the Costa Viola

From the end of April through June, the scenic fishing town of Scilla, near the Strait of Messina, is preoccupied with an ancient ritual: the annual swordfish hunt. If you visit the town during that period, you may catch a glimpse of the specialized swordfish boats in action; at the least, you will see these peculiar vessels docked in the port.

Called *passarelle*, these unusual boats are based on a centuries-old design that takes advantage of the swordfishes' coupling habits. The Costa Viola, between Bagnara Calabra and Scilla, is one of their preferred mating grounds once the water warms in late spring. The male, which is considerably smaller, will court the female. After mating, the pair remain faithful. The male swims in front of his mate but never leaves her. Fishermen know that if they can catch the female first, the male will stay with her through the fight, not abandoning her even as she dies and thus setting himself up to be next.

The *passarella* measures 22 meters (22 yards long), with an even longer, narrow gangplank that extends from the prow and a watchtower 26 meters (26 yards) high. When the watchman spots a pair of swordfish, he alerts the crew, and the *lanciatore*, or harpoonist, walks out on the gangplank to position himself for the strike. Ideally, the helmsman maneuvers the boat to put the *lanciatore* at just the right angle to spear the female between the dorsal fin and the back of the head.

These enormous fish put up a fierce fight, struggling to pull away from the harpoon. The battle can last for hours before the fish gives up, leaving the male to mourn his loss. Conversely, if he is caught first, the female shows no such loyalty and flees the scene quickly.

In modern times, fishermen abandoned the *passarella* in favor of fishing with nets, which gave them an even greater advantage over their prey. But overfishing ensued, and today net fishing is restricted in favor of the traditional *passarella*.

Every year in mid-July, the town of Bagnara Calabra holds a swordfish *sagra*, or festival, to honor the fishermen. Local cooks sear swordfish steaks on huge grills in the town's main *piazza* and prepare other specialties, such as swordfish *involtini* (swordfish rolls stuffed with breadcrumbs) and pasta with swordfish sauce. Before the festivities get under way, a mass is held in the local church to honor fishermen lost at sea, and a laurel wreath is tossed into the sea to commemorate them.

Pesce Spada alla Ghiotta

SWORDFISH "GLUTTON'S STYLE" WITH TOMATO, CAPERS, AND OLIVES

This preparation is popular in restaurants along Calabria's Tyrrhenian coast, where the swordfish are caught. In towns such as Scilla, Bagnara Calabra, and Pizzo, you are likely to find it on the menu in summer. Thin swordfish steaks are first seared, then briefly simmered in a quick pan sauce of fresh tomatoes, capers, and olives. Some people do not sear the swordfish first, but I think that step gives the sauce more depth. In winter, Calabrians prepare stockfish (page 186) *alla ghiotta*, substituting canned tomatoes for the fresh ones.

Swordfish steaks vary considerably in diameter, depending on the size of the fish. If your market has large swordfish, you may need to buy only three slices, each ⅜ inch (9 millimeters) thick, to have enough fish for six people. In that case, cut these large slices in half to make six ⅜-inch-thick (9-millimeter-thick) slices of an appropriate serving size.

I buy unpitted olives for this dish and pit them myself; the pit helps preserve the olive's texture and flavor.

SUGGESTED WINE: Marco De Bartoli Grappoli del Grillo, Sicily
A rich, rounded, elegant white wine with tropical aromas, vinified in French oak.
ALTERNATE: white Rhône

---

1 cup (150 grams) large unpitted green olives, such as Sicilian or
    Cerignola olives

⅓ cup (65 grams) salt-packed capers

6 swordfish steaks, about 5 ounces each (140 grams) and ⅜-inch
    (9 millimeters) thick, skin removed

1 teaspoon kosher salt

Freshly ground black pepper

Unbleached all-purpose flour

¼ cup (60 milliliters) extra virgin olive oil

1 large yellow onion, ends removed, halved, and thinly sliced from
    stem to root end

2 cups (500 milliliters) peeled, seeded, and diced fresh tomatoes

2 tablespoons chopped flat-leaf parsley

WITH A SMALL KNIFE, slice the olive flesh away from the pit. Set the pitted olives aside. Rinse the capers well; if they are still very salty, soak them in cold water for 15 minutes. Lift them out of the water and chop coarsely if they are large; leave whole if small.

Season the swordfish on both sides with the salt and several grinds of black pepper. Make a bed of flour on a plate and lightly coat the swordfish on both sides, shaking off any excess.

Heat the olive oil in a 14-inch (35-centimeter) skillet over high heat. (If you don't have such a large skillet, use a 10- or 12-inch (25- or 30-centimeter) skillet and fry the swordfish in batches.) When the oil is shimmering, add the swordfish and cook briefly until the surface is lightly colored on both sides, about 45 seconds per side. The fish should still be slightly underdone—not white throughout. It will finish cooking in the sauce. Transfer to a platter, leaving any oil behind in the skillet.

Add the onions to the skillet, reduce the heat to medium-high, and cook, stirring, until they soften, about 3 minutes. Add the tomatoes, olives, and capers and cook, stirring, until the tomatoes soften and release some of their juices, about 3 minutes. Reduce the heat to medium-low, stir in the parsley, and taste for salt. Return the swordfish to the skillet, burying the steaks in the sauce. If they don't fit in one layer, that's okay; just spoon the sauce over them. Reheat gently, then transfer the fish and sauce to a platter and serve. Although I typically serve this dish hot, it is equally delicious warm or at room temperature.

SERVES 6

Tonno alla Menta

FRESH TUNA PIZZO STYLE WITH WINE VINEGAR, GARLIC, AND MINT

Until modern times brought good roads and refrigerated trucks to Calabria, most of the tuna and swordfish caught along the region's Tyrrhenian coast never made it into the interior. These hefty fish were simply too large to transport far, so they were consumed in the towns around Pizzo, the main tuna fishing village.

On one of my visits to Pizzo, a *gelataio* (ice cream producer) there related a curious bit of local history. He told me that, in the days before refrigeration, Pizzo had a trading relationship with Serra San Bruno, a mountain town southeast of Pizzo. Strong men from the Pizzo area would carry the fresh 200-pound bluefin tunas caught locally all the way to Serra San Bruno on their shoulders, a distance of roughly twenty miles. There, they would trade the fish for ice, which they would bring back down to Pizzo for use in fruit ices and ice cream.

This method of preparing fresh tuna is common to the area around Pizzo. The fish is sliced into thin steaks, lightly floured, and quickly seared in olive oil. Then a dressing of olive oil, wine vinegar, garlic, and mint is whisked up in the still-warm skillet and poured over the steaks. The tuna rests at room temperature for an hour or so, absorbing the moisture of the dressing and its mint and garlic fragrance. Served at room temperature, the fish is juicy and vibrant in flavor, with a refreshing vinegar tang. I serve it as a second course in summer, after a seafood or vegetable pasta, such as Large Pasta Tubes with Swordfish and Cherry Tomatoes (page 73).

I have always known that Calabrians never waste any part of a creature they have killed for the table. But I got a fresh reminder of this resourcefulness when I stopped for lunch at the restaurant Medusa in Pizzo and the proprietor proudly announced that he had some fresh *lattume*. I had only heard of this delicacy—the sperm sac of male tuna—but never tried it. The chef prepared it *alla menta*, by the same method I've described below for tuna steaks. Its firm texture reminded me of swordfish; its flavor was clearly of the sea but mild. If you are traveling in Calabria in summer, *lattume alla menta* is a treat not to be missed.

SUGGESTED WINE: Capichera Vermentino di Gallura, Sardinia
Richer than most Vermentino, this white wine hints of marzipan and tangerine peel and has enough acidity to handle the vinegar in the dish.
ALTERNATE: Fiano di Avellino

1½ pounds (675 grams) fresh red-meat tuna, such as yellowfin (ahi), skin removed

Kosher salt and freshly ground black pepper

¼ cup unbleached all-purpose flour

About 10 tablespoons extra virgin olive oil

2 garlic cloves, thinly sliced

6 tablespoons white wine vinegar

10 to 12 fresh mint leaves, plus 4 to 6 more for garnish

SLICE THE TUNA into ⅜-inch-thick (9-millimeter-thick) slices. Season the fish steaks on both sides with salt and several grinds of black pepper.

Make a bed of flour on a plate and lightly coat the tuna on both sides, shaking off the excess.

Heat 2 tablespoons of the olive oil in a 12-inch (30-centimeter) skillet over medium-high heat. When the oil shimmers, add as many tuna slices as you can fit comfortably in one layer. Fry for 30 seconds, then turn the slices with an offset spatula and fry on the second side for 30 seconds. Transfer the tuna to a platter large enough to accommodate all the slices in a single layer. Add enough additional oil to the skillet to bring the volume of oil back to 2 tablespoons, then fry the remaining tuna for 30 seconds per side, transferring it to the platter when done.

Remove the skillet from the heat and add 6 tablespoons olive oil. Immediately add the sliced garlic and let it sizzle in the retained heat of the skillet. When it stops sizzling, add the vinegar, 1 teaspoon salt, and the mint leaves, tearing them into small pieces. Whisk to blend, then pour this warm vinaigrette over the fried tuna. Let marinate at least until the tuna cools to room temperature, about 30 minutes. It will be even tastier if allowed to marinate for a couple of hours at room temperature, basted occasionally with the marinade. Alternatively, you can refrigerate the tuna for up to 2 days, but bring it to room temperature before serving. Just before serving, tear 4 to 6 more mint leaves over the tuna steaks.

SERVES 4 TO 6

La Tonnara: *Man Versus Tuna*

In an annual migration as dependable as sunrise, bluefin tuna (*Thunnus thynnus*) head for the Gulf of Saint Eufemia on Calabria's west coast every summer. They descend from Sardinia beginning as early as April to deposit their eggs in the warm water of the gulf, near Pizzo, then turn west toward Sicily. Consequently, Calabrians have long joked that they get the best tuna and Sicilians get the rest.

The bluefin tuna, known as *tonno rosso* (red tuna) in Italian, is prized among connoisseurs. Its flesh is firm, meaty, and beet red. The fatty belly meat, or *ventresca*, is particularly sought after and priced accordingly.

Today, Calabrians fish for tuna with sonar and other sophisticated modern equipment, but until the 1960s, they trapped these large fish with an elaborate and ancient system of nets known as *la tonnara*. According to most historical accounts, the Arabs introduced *la tonnara* to Sicily around A.D. 1000. The method spread to Calabria, and for many centuries, the annual *tonnara* provided jobs for fishermen around Pizzo and excitement for the locals.

La tonnara consisted of a complex series of net traps that ensnared the tuna and funneled them gradually into a final chamber known as *la camera della morte* (the death chamber). On a calm, windless day in April, the fishermen would drop the nets and begin their wait. The *tonnara* stretched for miles, with several boats monitoring and maintaining it, each boat having a defined task.

The final boat, or captain's boat, was responsible for lifting the death chamber. When it was full, the captain would raise a flag to notify the other boats. Alerted by the flag, locals would gather along the seashore to watch the struggle between man and fish. Before killing their prey with harpoons, the fishermen sang a mournful ritual chant—"*U Leva Leva*"—asking the tuna's forgiveness for what was about to happen.

The fishermen on the kill boat faced considerable danger, as these enormous tuna, weighing as much as 500 pounds (225 kilos), often put up a fierce fight. Men would occasionally lose a hand or a limb due to the flailing fish and sharp gaffs. Rita Callipo, whose family owns a large cannery near Pizzo, remembers being frightened by the *tonnara* as a child. The sea would turn black with tuna, recalls Callipo, then red with blood.

The church bells would ring to announce a successful catch, and the largest fish would be taken to the priest. In a good year, this scene would be repeated many times between April and July, with the best fishing in May and June. In October, the bluefin would return to the gulf on their way back to Sardinia, but by then, they were tired and not as desirable, as their quality had declined.

By the mid-twentieth century, the Japanese, great fans of bluefin, had begun coming to the area with their modern boats and catching most of the tuna before the fish reached the *tonnara*. The Calabrian fishermen, to save their livelihood, had to abandon this centuries-old ritual and embrace modern fishing technology. Pizzo saw its last *tonnara* in 1963.

Branzino Sotto Sale

WHOLE SALT-BAKED SEA BASS

Roasting a whole fish buried in salt is a cooking method common all over Southern Italy. Surprisingly, the cooked fish isn't excessively salty but it is exceptionally moist, much more so than baked or grilled fish. The thick salt coat seals the fish during cooking so none of its juices can escape. Mixed with egg whites and water, the salt forms a hard crust in the oven, like pottery, which you will need a mallet or hammer to crack. Because you can't see the fish to judge its doneness, you must carefully measure its thickness before you pack it in salt to determine how long to bake it. I find that 15 minutes per inch (2½ centimeters), measured at the thickest part—about 40 minutes for a fish that is 2½ inches (6 centimeters) thick—is a reliable guide. If you are unsure about your oven, you might want to make this dish once for family to test the timing before you make it for guests.

Any whole fish can be baked this way. If you can't find sea bass or striped bass, you can use red snapper or salmon. You can serve the fish simply with lemon wedges and a drizzle of good olive oil, but I usually make *salmoriglio*, a whisked dressing of olive oil, lemon juice, garlic, and fresh herbs, to spoon over the fish before serving or to pass at the table. Accompany the fish with boiled potatoes or a seasonal green vegetable such as wilted chard or roasted asparagus.

For this recipe, please use only Diamond Crystal kosher salt. Morton kosher salt, another popular supermarket brand, is made by a different process, so the crystals have a different shape and are less absorbent.

SUGGESTED WINE: Tasca d'Almerita Le Rose di Regaleali, Sicily
A *refreshing summertime wine with red-fruit aromas and plenty of acidity and juiciness.*
ALTERNATE: any dry rosé

Salmoriglio (page 172)

1 whole fresh sea bass or striped bass, weighing about 3 pounds
    (1½ kilograms), cleaned and scaled

3 to 4 sprigs each of fresh thyme, oregano, and flat-leaf parsley

½ lemon, thinly sliced

2 garlic cloves, sliced

2 teaspoons extra virgin olive oil

3 pounds (1½ kilograms) Diamond Crystal kosher salt

4 large egg whites

Striped bass prepared for baking under salt   Packing fish in a mixture of salt and egg white

PREPARE THE *SALMORIGLIO* and set aside for at least 30 minutes to allow the flavors to marry, but no more than 2 hours ahead or the herbs will darken and lose their fresh taste.

Preheat the oven to 425°F (215°F).

With a ruler, measure the thickness of the fish at the thickest part to determine the necessary cooking time (15 minutes per inch/2½ centimeters). With kitchen scissors, clip off all the fish fins and clip the tail to 1 inch (2½ centimeters) so the fins and tail don't poke out of the salt. Stuff the cavity of the fish with the herb sprigs, lemon slices, and garlic. Coat the outside of the fish with the olive oil.

In a large bowl, combine the salt with the egg whites and 1 cup (250 milliliters) water. Mix with your hands until the salt feels like wet sand.

Line a rimmed baking sheet with a sheet of parchment paper. (This step will make cleanup easier.) Make a ½-inch-thick (12-millimeter-thick) bed of salt a little larger than the fish. Pat the salt into an even layer. Place the fish on the salt bed and cover with the remaining salt, patting the salt in place so it adheres and completely seals the fish. No part of the fish should remain exposed.

Bake for the predetermined amount of time, approximately 40 minutes for a 3-pound (1½-kilogram) fish.

Remove the fish from the oven. Using a small hammer or meat mallet, crack the hard salt crust. It will lift off in large chunks. Remove as much salt as you can from the top surface of the fish. Use a pastry brush to remove any salt that clings to the skin. With a fork, carefully peel back the skin to reveal the top fillet. Remove the top fillet—it will lift easily off the bone—and transfer to individual plates or a serving platter. Now you can easily lift out the skeleton with the head attached, leaving the bottom fillet still on the salt bed. With a fork or spatula, lift the bottom fillet off the skin and transfer to individual plates or a serving platter. Spoon the *salmoriglio* over the fish, or pass separately.

SERVES 4

Baccalà alla Verbicarese

SALT COD WITH SWEET RED PEPPERS AND POTATOES

One of several fish dishes served on Christmas Eve in my hometown of Verbicaro, *baccalà alla Verbicarese* reflects the local fondness for salt cod. On some families' tables, *stoccafisso* (stockfish, or air-dried cod, page 186) would take its place. The Calabrian talent for transforming humble ingredients is manifest here as plumped cod, potatoes, tomatoes, and dried sweet peppers fuse into a savory stew. If you can't find the dried peppers, slice and sauté two fresh red bell peppers separately and add them near the end of the cooking time.

Don't serve this dish piping hot. Let it rest for a bit to allow the flavors to settle. It's tasty warm or even at room temperature.

SUGGESTED WINE: Rosa del Golfo "Quarantale," Salento, Campania
A medium-intensity red wine, made largely from Negroamaro, with juicy fruit that echoes the sweetness of the peppers.
ALTERNATE: Nero d'Avola

---

1 pound (450 grams) salt cod (page 186), cut into 6 equal pieces

2 pounds (900 grams) Yukon Gold potatoes

3 tablespoons extra virgin olive oil

1 tablespoon plus 1 teaspoon kosher salt

3 garlic cloves, halved

1 small fresh hot red pepper, halved lengthwise, optional

6 Sun-Dried Sweet Peppers (page 293), each torn into 4 to 5 pieces, seeds removed, *or* 2 fresh red bell peppers (see recipe introduction)

1 cup (250 milliliters) Home-Canned Peeled Tomatoes (page 296) *or* canned Italian San Marzano tomatoes, broken up by hand

---

TO SOAK SALT COD: Place the pieces of salt cod in a large bowl and cover with cold water. Let soak at room temperature, changing the water twice a day until the cod has rehydrated and is no longer too salty, 2 to 3 days, depending on the thickness of the pieces. To determine if the cod has soaked long enough, taste a small amount from the thickest part of each piece. If it seems appropriately salty to your taste, it is ready to drain. The thin pieces need less soaking time than thicker ones;

remove the thin pieces as they are ready, pat dry, and refrigerate in a covered container while you continue soaking the thicker pieces. When all the cod is sufficiently soaked, drain it. If you don't want to proceed with the recipe immediately, you can refrigerate the soaked and drained cod for 2 to 3 days.

Peel the potatoes and cut into 1½-inch (4-centimeter) pieces. The exact size doesn't matter as long as they are of comparable size so they cook evenly. Place in an 8-quart (8-liter) pot with 5 cups (1¼ liters) water, the oil, and the salt. Add more water if necessary to cover the potatoes completely. Bring to a boil over high heat, then adjust the heat to maintain a low rolling boil.

Boil the potatoes for 5 minutes, then add the garlic and hot pepper, if using. Boil for 5 minutes longer, then test the potatoes for doneness; they should be easily pierced with a fork. If not, continue cooking until they are tender. Add the salt cod and adjust the heat so the mixture simmers gently. Cook for 5 minutes, then add the sweet peppers and tomatoes. Stir gently to distribute them, then continue simmering until the peppers are tender and the broth is flavorful and reduced to about one-third of the original water volume, about 10 minutes. Do not stir during this time to avoid breaking up the cod or potatoes.

Taste for salt and adjust if needed. Divide the cod, potatoes, peppers, and broth among individual soup bowls.

SERVES 6

Baccalà *and Stoccafisso: Preserved Cod Two Ways*

It is curious that Calabrians, blessed with a long coastline, have such a passion for preserved fish from far away. But *baccalà* (salt cod) and *stoccafisso*, also called *pescestocco* (air-dried cod, or stockfish), from the Nordic countries are among most Calabrians' favorite seafoods. *Baccalà* is preferred in the Cosenza region, *stoccafisso* in Reggio Calabria, but both are highly regarded and essential on Christmas Eve.

Centuries ago, Calabrians got their salt cod and stockfish from Naples, where Nordic ships would stop and exchange preserved fish for other goods. People in the mountains had no access to fresh fish, so the salted and dried fish filled a need, especially for the religious, who observed many meatless days.

The fish must be soaked for a couple of days, with several changes of water, to rid it of its salt and soften the flesh. Then it may be prepared in numerous ways. *Baccalà* is often simply floured and fried, but it may be also prepared *alla ghiotta* (in tomato sauce with olives and capers); simmered in tomato sauce with peppers, either fresh or dried; made into meatballs; grilled; poached and served as a salad with boiled potatoes; or cooked with tomato for a pasta sauce.

Unlike *baccalà*, *stoccafisso* is not salted. It is much harder than *baccalà* and takes eight days of soaking to reconstitute, preferably in cold running water. The village of Mammola, in the province of Reggio Calabria, has built its reputation on *lo stocco*, as the dried cod is often called, claiming that the town's mineral-rich springwater is ideal for rehydrating the fish. The local restaurants specialize in preparing it, and local stores sell it already rehydrated and ready for cooking.

Reconstituting stockfish at home is a smelly business. Most people do not have a basin large enough to hold the whole fish nor the means to keep it under running water for eight days. I have tried rehydrating it in standing water, changing the water frequently, but it still smells. Consequently, my preference is to prepare *baccalà* at home and to reserve the pleasure of eating *stoccafisso* for my visits to Calabria.

Hidden in every stockfish is a delicacy much appreciated in Calabria: the *ventricelli* (or *ventricieddi*), an internal organ that Calabrians reconstitute in water and typically braise in tomato sauce with sweet and hot peppers and potatoes. Despite many queries, I have not been able to confirm the anatomical name in English for *ventricelli*, but I believe it is the cod's swim bladder. Cooking renders it gelatinous, akin to jellyfish or braised beef tendon. It does not have a lot of flavor of its own, but, like tripe, it absorbs other flavors, and its texture is appealing.

Insalata di Baccalà con Patate
SALT COD AND POTATO SALAD WITH RED ONION AND CAPERS

This winter salad is on many Calabrian Christmas Eve tables. Some cooks add dried oregano or roasted red peppers, and it's common to dress it with a great deal of extra virgin olive oil, more than I have specified here. In my family, this dish would be served after a seafood main course or seafood pasta.

SUGGESTED WINE: Feudi di San Gregorio Fiano di Avellino, Campania
A modern expression of the Fiano grape, with aromas of lemon curd and almonds, enough acidity to balance the salt cod's richness, and more creaminess than Fiano typically exhibits.
ALTERNATE: white Burgundy

---

1 pound (450 grams) salt cod, cut into 6 equal pieces

1 pound (450 grams) Yukon Gold potatoes, unpeeled

½ large red onion, thinly sliced

2 tablespoons salted capers, rinsed, left whole if small or coarsely chopped if large

2 tablespoons chopped flat-leaf parsley

⅓ cup (80 milliliters) extra virgin olive oil

¼ cup (60 milliliters) lemon juice

2 garlic cloves, finely minced

2½ teaspoons kosher salt

SOAK AND DRAIN the salt cod as directed on page 184. In a 4-quart (4-liter) pot, bring cod and 1½ quarts (1½ liters) water to a boil. Lower the heat and simmer until the fish flakes when prodded with a fork, about 10 minutes. Drain and let cool.

Put the potatoes and 1½ quarts (1½ liters) water in a 4-quart (4-liter) pot. Bring to a simmer and cook until the potatoes are tender when pierced with a fork, about 20 minutes, depending on size. Drain and peel. Cool the peeled potatoes completely, then slice ⅜ inch (9 millimeters) thick.

Soak the onion in cold water for 5 minutes to remove any sharpness. Drain.

Flake the cod and put in a serving bowl. Add the potatoes, onions, capers, and parsley. In a small bowl, whisk together the olive oil, lemon juice, garlic, and salt. Pour over the salad, toss gently, taste for seasoning, and serve.

SERVES 6

Il Cenone: *A Calabrian Christmas Eve Feast*

Literally "the big meal," *il cenone* is the highlight of a Calabrian Christmas Eve. In traditional families like my own, the menu always revolves around seafood and includes thirteen dishes—one for Jesus and each disciple. *Baccalà* (salt cod) takes center stage and may appear in two or three different guises, but it wouldn't be *il cenone* without it. In southern Calabria, especially in the Reggio Calabria region, *stoccafisso* (dried cod) often replaces *baccalà,* but the recipes are otherwise the same.

Pasta con mollica—spaghetti with anchovies and breadcrumbs—may seem like a humble dish to have on Christmas Eve, but many Calabrian families serve it. It reminds them of more difficult times, when anchovies were the only seafood their ancestors could afford. Despite being more prosperous today, many Calabrians have not lost their enthusiasm for this frugal dish.

At my house, preparations begin a couple of days ahead, with the soaking of the *baccalà.* On the morning of Christmas Eve, I go to my favorite seafood market as soon as it opens to get the best available fish and shellfish. My mother begins frying the *cannariculi* (page 316) at her house; they don't suffer from being made a few hours ahead. In the afternoon, she will fry the *grispelle* (page 324), and as soon as they are done, she and my father come to my house and our family goes together to Mass.

When we return in the early evening, the meal gets under way, around a dining table extended to accommodate in-laws, cousins, and a few close friends. The slowly unfolding feast lasts at least three hours, followed by games and more conversation until midnight.

My menu changes a little from year to year, although all the desserts and some savory dishes, like *grispelle,* are fixtures. Other possibilities at my table include fried squid; fried salt cod; spaghetti with clams, mussels, or swordfish; and salt cod braised with tomato and dried red peppers. Sometimes, reflecting my years in California, I make spaghetti with Dungeness crab.

Il Cenone (Christmas Eve Feast)

Grispelle

Warm Christmas Doughnuts

Tartine al Burro di Bottarga

Crostini with Bottarga Butter

Pipi 'Mpajanati

Calabrian Sweet Pepper Fritters

Spaghetti col Sugo di Baccalà

Spaghetti with Salt Cod and Tomato

Branzino Sotto Sale

Whole Salt-Baked Sea Bass

Pesce Spada alla Ghiotta

Swordfish "Glutton's Style" with Tomato, Capers, and Olives

Insalata di Mare

Mixed Seafood Salad

Insalata di Baccalà con Patate

Salt Cod and Potato Salad with Red Onion and Capers

Insalata di Cavolfiore

Cauliflower Salad

Chinule

Sweet Christmas Ravioli with Chestnut Filling

Cannariculi

Fried Ridged Pastry with Honey Glaze

Panettone

Frutta e Dolci

Clementines, panicelli (page 330), crocette (page 336),
hazelnuts and walnuts, roasted chestnuts, and torrone

My cousin's pig in Calabria, being fattened up

Carne
meat

Pork is the undisputed king among meats in Calabria. His Majesty the Pig, as this invaluable animal is affectionately known, has saved many Calabrians, for many generations, from hunger and want. In my grandparents' day, if your family had a pig, you were considered well off because you had the wherewithal to eat for a year.

From one 350-pound pig, a family could make prosciutto and pancetta; many pounds of fresh sausages, *capocolli*, *soppressate*, and other cured *salumi*; and dozens of *braciole* (stuffed pork rolls) that could be safely stored for months under rendered pork fat. The pig also provided a year's worth of cooking fat, supplemented by olive oil; and plenty of fresh meat to enjoy in the first few weeks following the January slaughter.

My parents and rural families like ours would purchase a young pig, one to two months old, in September and raise it for fifteen to sixteen months. For the first year or so, our pig subsisted largely on grasses, wild chicories, cabbage leaves, fallen fruit, and whatever else my mother could scavenge from our property. Any kitchen scraps such as potato peels, the scrapings off our plates, and unusable leftovers went to his majesty, of course. Even pasta water, which had some nourishing starch, would be saved for the pig. In a frugal Calabrian home, you do not waste a calorie.

By the following August, the fattening regimen moved into high gear and my mother began treating the pig like the royalty he was. Every evening, after our dinner, my mother would cook for the pig, preparing a nutritious gruel using pasta water or potato water, and adding ripe or dried figs, potatoes, winter squash, cornmeal, acorns, and wheat bran. From an early age, I was taught how to make the pig's meal. By January, when the weather had turned cold enough to provide natural refrigeration, the pig would have reached an acceptable slaughter weight and would meet its end.

Farm families like ours always had meat for the table because we raised our own animals. Even so, meat played a relatively minor role in our everyday meals, secondary to pasta, beans, bread, cheese, and vegetables. People in the towns ate even less meat than we did, as they had to buy it. For them, meat might only appear on Sundays and holidays and even then in modest portions. Today, fortunately, Calabrians' fortunes have improved, and they no longer consider meat a luxury reserved for special occasions.

Like other rural people, we were never without a brood of chickens, usually a dozen or so. Ours roamed freely during the day, fattening up on grubs and gleaning fallen grains after the wheat harvest. In winter, my mother cooked hot cornmeal porridge for them to keep them warm and well fed. Because we had mountain property, my father also raised goats, which are nimble enough to thrive on steep hillsides. Those who had farms in the foothills or the flatlands, such as the area around Crotone, would keep sheep, which were better adapted to that landscape.

Consequently, goat and lamb were and still are widely eaten in Calabria. And throughout the region, people reserve a special place on the table for milk-fed goat (*capretto*) and milk-fed lamb (*agnellino*), young animals slaughtered before they are weaned, at just a few weeks old. Their meat is pale, mild, and unbelievably succulent, and few Calabrians are without one or the other on their Easter table. The cooking method is always exceedingly simple, so as not to obscure the fine flavor of the meat. Some cooks spit-roast their baby goat or lamb over a wood fire. Others cut the carcass into serving-size pieces and roast the meat in the oven with olive oil, rosemary, white wine, and garlic (page 224). Roast potatoes basted with the pan juices are the unvarying accompaniment.

Americans tend to be squeamish about eating such young creatures, but when you are raised with farm animals, as I was, you are more pragmatic. The females earn their keep by giving milk. The males are eaten within the family or sold to neighbors for meat. Whether slaughtered young, at their most tender and sweet, or later, when they will be tougher and stronger in taste, the creatures' fate is not in doubt.

When they have lamb or goat from a more mature animal, Calabrian cooks will typically braise it until it becomes fork-tender. They may simmer it on the bone in tomato sauce, or as *braciole*, stuffed boneless cutlets. Alternatively, they might grind the meat and mix it with breadcrumbs and pecorino to make meatballs, similarly braised in tomato sauce. In all three cases, the preparation yields two courses: a garlicky, meat-flavored sauce to toss with pasta for a first course, and a second course of the meat itself, cloaked with a little of the remaining sauce.

Calabrians have few traditional recipes for beef. Apart from the high plateau of La Sila, where dairy cattle thrive on the cool mountain air and lush pasture, Calabria's rocky landscape and hot climate are not conducive to cattle. As a result, beef has always been expensive in Calabrian markets and people have never developed much of a taste for it. My parents had never eaten a thick, American-style steak until they came to the United States in their early forties. Even today, what Calabrian restaurants call *bistecca* (beefsteak) is likely to be tough, pitifully thin, and not very tasty. Some home cooks do make *braciole* with beef on occasion, or grilled beef cutlets, but pork is the meat of choice.

Calabrian chicken recipes are simple and few. I suspect this is because the many Calabrians who kept chickens in times past, such as my parents, did so primarily for the eggs. After a couple of years, when the hens had reached the end of their useful life as layers, they were too tough for anything but braising. *Pollo col sugo*, chicken braised in tomato sauce, sometimes with fresh or dried sweet peppers or mushrooms, remains an everyday family meal, with the flavorful sauce served first on pasta, and the chicken following as a second course. *Pollo fritto*, or fried chicken Calabrian style, is simply cut into pieces, seasoned with dried oregano, and fried in a heavy pan filmed with olive oil. But it is far more succulent than that brief description suggests. Cooked slowly and turned frequently, the bird pan-roasts to a deep golden brown, so it more closely resembles a juicy roast chicken than batter-coated American-style fried chicken. Thick potato wedges shallow-fried in olive oil are the traditional accompaniment. Another common preparation is *pollo alla Calabrese* (page 218), chicken baked with potatoes, tomatoes, oregano, and hot red pepper.

Calabrians seem a little more inspired by rabbit, which many people in small towns and rural areas still raise themselves. My cousins in Santa Maria del Cedro, near Scalea, keep rabbits in a backyard hutch because they just don't believe factory-raised rabbits have a comparable flavor. My parents raise eight or nine rabbits at a time in their Oakland backyard, pampering them like others do their pets. I save pea shells, carrot peels, and the outer leaves of cauliflower for them, and my mother routinely asks vendors at the farmers' market for their wilted lettuce or carrot tops. When she spots a vacant lot overrun with sow thistle or wild fennel, she will pick some for her precious rabbits. And when it's hot, she and my father rig up fans to keep them cool. To my chagrin, my parents refuse to leave their house for more than two days for fear that no one else will provide such good care. When the rabbits are about six months old, my father dispatches them humanely and my mother cleans them. Usually, I receive one or two to cook for my family.

In the Calabrian kitchen, rabbit is typically braised with sweet peppers, fresh or dried (page 222); or prepared *in agrodolce*, in a sweet and sour sauce with red wine, wine vinegar, sugar, raisins, and bay leaf. Or it may simply be cut up and baked with tomatoes and potatoes in the same manner as chicken, or braised in tomato sauce to make a *sugo*, or meat sauce for pasta.

Calabrian techniques for cooking tough cuts occasionally depart from methods used in other Italian kitchens. Elsewhere, recipes often call for browning meat, then braising it in a covered pot in a small amount of liquid. We typically do the reverse, simmering meat in a generous quantity of salted water, sometimes with olive oil, until the meat is tender and the water has almost evaporated, leaving just enough concentrated pan juices to coat the meat. Calabrians use this procedure with rabbit, with *braciole* of pork skin, and with old stewing hens. *Soffritto*, an offal dish beloved by rural Calabrians, is often made this way. The innards—heart, lungs, liver, spleen, kidneys—are chopped and simmered in salted water until it evaporates, then fried in olive oil with onion, sometimes with tomato added. If you are skeptical about this unorthodox method, you will be persuaded by the intense, heightened taste of Spicy Braised Rabbit with Sweet Peppers and Oregano (page 222) and Pork Skin Rolls Braised in Tomato Sauce (page 204).

Typical of people who are frugal by habit, Calabrians appreciate innards and know how to prepare them. My grandmother would wrap pieces of pork liver in caul fat, a lacy membrane that surrounds the pig's internal organs. Then she would skewer the meat alternately with bay leaves and sear it on the grill. Tripe is a great favorite, too, simmered in tomato sauce with sweet peppers (page 230), potatoes, or beans. In the Catanzaro area, a delicious, if vanishing, specialty is *morseddu*, formerly a street food and now served in just a handful of tradition-minded trattorias, such as U Tamarru in Catanzaro. For *morseddu*, a mixture of innards, or sometimes just tripe alone, is braised in tomato sauce with garlic, onion, oregano, and a great deal of hot red pepper. The fiery stew is spooned inside a chunk of soft bread cut from a large ring to make a messy but memorable sandwich.

On the following pages, you will find recipes for Calabrian meat dishes that largely come from the farmhouse tradition. I have favored recipes that differ from those found in other regions of Italy, such as Calabria's *Vrasciole alla Verbicarese*

(Stuffed Pork Rolls in Tomato Sauce Verbicaro Style, page 197), which do not have the breadcrumb filling typical in other parts of Southern Italy; and the tender *polpette alla Verbicarese* (Pork Meatballs in Tomato Sauce, page 209), which are made with pork only. I have included some recipes that I have seen nowhere else, such as the luscious *braciole di cotenne* (Pork Skin Rolls Braised in Tomato Sauce, page 204) and Catanzaro's sumptuous *Tiella d'Agnello* (Baked Lamb Shoulder with Artichokes, Peas, and Breadcrumbs, page 227). Also here are recipes for the roast baby goat with which Calabrians celebrate Easter (*capretto arrostito con patate*, page 224), and some family favorites, such as *pollo alla Calabrese* (Baked Chicken with Potatoes, Tomatoes, and Hot Pepper, page 218) and *salsiccia alla Calabrese* (Fresh Homemade Fennel Sausage Calabrian Style, page 211).

Browned *vrasciole* (browned pork rolls before adding tomatoes)

Vrasciole alla Verbicarese
STUFFED PORK ROLLS IN TOMATO SAUCE VERBICARO STYLE

This recipe from my hometown of Verbicaro is an example of *la cucina povera* (peasant cooking), a dish that makes ingenious use of meager resources. The filling for the cutlets (*vrasciole* in the local dialect; *braciole* in Italian) consists of nothing more than minced pork fat, parsley, and garlic. Today, Southern Italians stuff *braciole* with breadcrumbs, cheese, pine nuts, currants, hard-cooked egg, and the like, but no version is more delicious than this simple one. The rolls are browned, then simmered with tomatoes to produce a meaty sauce enriched with the melting pork fat and the aromas of parsley and garlic. A dish for Sundays and holidays, it is two courses in one: Calabrians typically toss some of the sauce with homemade *fusilli* (page 85) for a first course, then have the *braciole* as a second course.

I can still hear the sound of my grandmother's knife as she minced the pork fat by hand. She would be at it for half an hour because, with six children, she cooked nothing in small quantities. You can put the pork fat through a meat grinder, or mince it by hand, using the flat side of your chef's knife to mash it to a paste.

SUGGESTED WINE: Vestini Campagnano Pallagrello Nero, Campania
A red wine with blueberry and chocolate notes and generous tannin, fruit, and acidity for a dish that calls for a substantial wine.
ALTERNATE: Montepulciano d'Abruzzo

3 pounds (1½ kilograms) boneless pork butt (shoulder),
    trimmed of external fat

Kosher salt

¼ pound (115 grams) pork back fat, finely ground or minced to
    a paste by hand

2½ tablespoons finely chopped flat-leaf parsley

2 garlic cloves, finely minced, plus 2 whole garlic cloves

Freshly ground black pepper

Kitchen twine

Extra virgin olive oil

2 quarts (2 liters) peeled, seeded, and diced ripe tomatoes *or*
    two 28-ounce (800-gram) cans Italian San Marzano
    tomatoes, broken up by hand

5 fresh basil leaves, torn into smaller pieces

CUT THE PORK into scaloppine-like slices about 5 by 3 inches (13 by 8 centimeters) and ¼ inch (6 millimeters) thick. They don't have to be perfect rectangles. The 3 pounds (1½ kilograms) meat should yield about 12 slices. Working with one slice at a time, put the meat between two sheets of plastic wrap and pound with a meat mallet to flatten the pork to about ⅛ inch (3 millimeters) thick and to enlarge the surface area. When all the slices have been pounded, sprinkle both sides with salt.

FOR THE STUFFING: Combine the pork fat with the parsley and garlic. Season with ¾ teaspoon salt and pepper to taste. Mix until smooth and creamy.

Top each piece of pork with 2 teaspoons of the stuffing. Spread the stuffing evenly but stop short of the edges. Working from the shorter side, roll the slices tightly like a jelly roll. Using a 12-inch (30-centimeter) length of kitchen twine, tie each roll by looping the twine around the roll, working from one end of the roll to the other, and then back again. Tie the ends of the twine together.

Choose a 6-quart (6-liter) heavy pot or Dutch oven large enough to hold all the *braciole* snugly in one layer. Set the pot over moderately high heat and add enough olive oil to coat the bottom. When the oil is hot, add the *braciole* and brown the rolls on all sides, about 5 minutes total. A nice crust should develop on the bottom of the pan. Add the 2 whole garlic cloves and sauté briefly to release their fragrance, then add the tomatoes and basil. With a wooden spoon, scrape up all the crusty browned bits on the bottom of the pan. Season with salt and simmer gently, uncovered, until the sauce thickens and the meat is fork tender, 1 to 1½ hours.

Remove the *braciole* from the sauce and cut away the string. Return them to the sauce and keep warm over low heat. Reserving some sauce to coat the *braciole*, use the remaining sauce to coat 1 pound (450 grams) of pasta for a first course (see recipe introduction), then serve the *braciole* as a second course.

MAKES 12 *BRACIOLE*, TO SERVE 6 TO 8

Calabria's Prized Salumi

Amaru chi lu puorcu nun s'ammazza, a li travi sui nun mpica sazizza.
He who doesn't kill a pig will have no sausage hanging from the rafters.

Cured meats, known by the generic name *salumi*, comprise a significant part of the Calabrian diet. For rural families in times past, the *salumi* in the cellar were insurance against hardship, as reassuring as money in the bank. One elderly *salumi* producer near Reggio di Calabria told me that people used to bequeath a cured sausage to each of their pallbearers, a sign of how greatly people prized their homemade sausage.

Because of USDA regulations, Calabrian meat products are not exported to the United States. Consequently, when you visit Calabria, you should go out of your way to try them. The following *salumi* are the ones you are most likely to encounter in homes, restaurants, and food shops:

CAPOCOLLO: Made with whole (not ground) pieces of meat from the neck and loin, *capocollo* is braced with strips of bamboo on either side to keep it hanging straight while it cures. It is air dried, then sliced thin and enjoyed as a cold cut or chopped for stuffings. The *coppa* available in Italian delis in the United States is made in a similar fashion.

GUANCIALE: To make *guanciale*, pork jowls are buried in salt for about a week, then air dried for about two months. The flavor is similar to pancetta, but *guanciale* has proportionately more fat. It may be sliced thin for sandwiches or antipasto, like prosciutto, or chopped and fried to add meaty flavor to sauces, soups, or cooked greens. A few American artisan *salumi* producers are now making *guanciale*.

LARDO: The pig's thick, firm back fat is salted, then air dried to make *lardo*. Calabrians slice *lardo* thinly and enjoy it on warm toast as an antipasto. It has a pearly appearance, like the fat on prosciutto.

'NDUJA: This fiery, smoked pork spread is unique to Calabria. 'Nduja (in-DOO-jah or in-DOO-yah) is prepared with fatty parts of the pig selected to ensure a finished fat content of 40 to 50 percent. The meat and fat are ground, seasoned with salt, mild red pepper, and a generous quantity of hot red pepper, and worked until the mixture is creamy, spreadable, and uniformly red. It is then stuffed into a natural hog casing, smoked for seven to ten days, and then air dried.

continued on page 203

Salumi hanging at a market in Pizzo

Calabrian salumi: 1. dried, cured Calabrian sausage, 2. pancetta, flat style, 3. *guanciale*, 4. *lardo*, 5. *sopressata*, 6. *capocollo*, 7. *'nduja*. (For complete glossary of salumi, see pages 199 and 203.)

'Nduja di Spilinga inside the casing (background) and spread on bread (foreground)

continued from page 199

The town of Spilinga in the Vibo Valentia region is famous for 'nduja, and most commercial production takes place in that area. Calabrians spread 'nduja on bread or toast for an antipasto or as a sandwich condiment, or add a spoonful to tomato sauce or pasta-and-bean soup for a meaty and fiery taste. It also appears as a filling for *pitta* and a topping for pizza.

PANCETTA: Unlike most American pancetta, Calabrian pancetta is fully cured and can be eaten without cooking. It is the whole pork belly—the same cut used for bacon—cured under salt, then air dried. Some Calabrians also give it a coating of sweet or hot red pepper. It is cured flat, not rolled as it typically is in the United States. You can slice it thin for an antipasto platter or a sandwich, or chop it to flavor braised cabbage (page 267) or pasta with potatoes (page 66). La Quercia, an Iowa producer of artisan cured meats, makes a flat (unrolled) and fully cured pancetta that resembles the Calabrian product (see Resources, page 368).

PROSCIUTTO: Calabrian prosciutto is sliced thin and served as part of an antipasto assortment or in a sandwich. It resembles *prosciutto di Parma*, with a similar silky texture, although the taste is perhaps not as sweet. You will find the best Calabrian prosciutto in the mountain areas, such as La Sila and the Parco del Pollino, where there is a long history of prosciutto production.

SALSICCIA CALABRESE: Made in spicy (*piccante*) and mild (*dolce*) styles, these dry, cured sausages are prepared primarily with ground pork shoulder and flavored with salt, wild fennel seed, and mild or hot red pepper or both. The casing used is from the narrowest section of the pork intestine, so the cured sausages are about one inch in diameter.

SOPPRESSATA: Traditionally made with pork loin and fat chopped more coarsely than the meat for *salsiccia*, *soppressata* can be mild or spicy. The casing used is bigger in diameter than the one used for *salsiccia*, and the traditional recipe calls for pressing the sausage under weights to flatten it (hence the name). *Soppressata* needs about one month to cure. It is sliced thin for antipasto or chopped for use in stuffings.

SPALLA: The pig's shoulder is cured in the same way as the hind leg, or prosciutto. Cured *spalla* is leaner than prosciutto, without its marbling and rich flavor.

Braciole di Cotenne

PORK SKIN ROLLS BRAISED IN TOMATO SAUCE

With the floppy skin from a pig's back, all traces of fat removed, Calabrians stuff and roll *braciole* identical to the ones they make with pork shoulder (page 197). *Cotenne*, the pork skin, is never discarded; it's a prized ingredient, not only in this dish but in beans as well. One well-known Bay Area chef tells me that he slips *cotenne* into many recipes unannounced. He thinks that customers would shy away from a dish if they knew it contained pork skin, yet they always ask what made the food so delicious.

We buy *cotenne* in Oakland's Chinatown, and you would be amused to see my Italian father try to communicate with the Chinese butcher about the cuts that he wants from the pig. They both point to their own body parts, nodding or shaking their heads in what looks like a comic dance.

If the pork skin you purchase still has fat attached, you will need to trim it or ask the butcher to do it. You should be left with a thin sheet of skin only. Reserve the fat for the filling, a paste of finely minced fat, garlic, and parsley. As the rolls simmer with crushed tomatoes, a luscious sauce emerges, enriched and seasoned with the *braciole* and their filling. If you want to have enough sauce for both the *braciole* and a pasta course, double the quantity of tomatoes, basil, and hot red pepper.

SUGGESTED WINE: I Favati "Cretarossa," Aglianico D'Irpinia, Campania
A medium-full red wine with cherry-like fruit that works well with the sweetness of pork and tomato.
ALTERNATE: Grenache

1 sheet of pork skin, about 12 by 16 inches (30 by 40 centimeters)
    and ⅛ inch (3 millimeters) thick, all fat removed

Kosher salt

¼ pound (115 grams) pork fat, finely ground or minced to a paste
    by hand

2½ tablespoons finely chopped flat-leaf parsley

2 garlic cloves, finely minced

Freshly ground black pepper

Kitchen twine

1 quart (1 liter) Home-Canned Peeled Tomatoes (page 296) *or* one
    28-ounce (800-gram) can Italian San Marzano tomatoes,
    broken up by hand

4 to 5 fresh basil leaves, torn in half

1 small dried hot red pepper, broken in half, *or* ground hot red
    pepper

WITH A KNIFE, cut the pork skin into twelve 4-inch (10-centimeter) squares. Season the inside of each piece with salt.

FOR THE STUFFING: Combine the pork fat with the parsley and garlic. Season with ¾ teaspoon salt and pepper to taste. Mix until smooth and creamy.

Top each piece of pork skin with 2 teaspoons of the stuffing. Spread the stuffing evenly but stop short of the edges. Roll the pork skin tightly like a jelly roll and tie with kitchen twine.

Put the *braciole* in a saucepan. Add water to cover by 2 inches (5 centimeters) and a generous pinch of salt. Bring to a boil over high heat, then adjust the heat to maintain a brisk simmer. Cook uncovered until the *braciole* are tender, 45 minutes to 1 hour, and the water has almost completely evaporated. Test one for tenderness by cutting a thin slice off the end. If it's still a little chewy, add additional hot water and continue simmering until the *braciole* are tender and the water has all but evaporated.

Add the tomatoes, the basil, and hot pepper to taste. Simmer briskly until the sauce is thick and flavorful, 15 to 20 minutes. With tongs, lift the braciole onto a cutting board and remove the strings. Transfer the braciole to a serving platter and top with the sauce.

SERVES 6

From One Hog, Food for a Year

Cu si marita sta contentu 'nu jiournu, cu 'mmazza 'u puorco cuntentu n'annu.
Get married and you'll be happy for a day. Kill a pig and you'll be content all year.

When I was growing up in Calabria, my family raised and butchered one pig a year, as did most of our neighbors. The three to four days devoted to this ritual—to butchering, salting, and sausage making—were a much anticipated time of the year, involving friends and neighbors in both the work and the festivities, and concluding with a sense of accomplishment. Although each family had its own particular customs, my family's procedures were typical.

After months of fattening the family pig with table scraps and grain, butchering day would arrive. The date for the hog's demise depended largely on the weather and on the availability of friends and neighbors, as my parents needed at least three to four helpers. The sacrifice was typically planned for sometime in January because it was imperative to have cured sausages ready by Carnevale, usually in February. My father would wait until he anticipated several days of clear, cold weather. Like others, we relied on "nature's refrigeration" to prevent spoilage.

Beginning before dawn, my father and his helpers would tie the pig's legs together and tie his mouth shut so he couldn't bite. My mother would position a bucket in the appropriate spot, and after my father's quick, practiced incision just below the neck, the blood would flow into the bucket. My mother would add some halved oranges to perfume the blood, and then she or I would stir the blood with a wooden spoon or a thick piece of reed to prevent coagulation and to collect the impurities, which would cling to the stirrer. The scented blood would later be mixed with sugar, chocolate, breadcrumbs, raisins, cloves, and cinnamon and stuffed into the largest part of the intestine to make *sanguinaccio*, a sweet blood sausage.

The next task was to remove the pig's hair, which took about an hour. Scalding the pig with boiling water made it easier to shave off the hairs with sharp knives. The thick, stiff bristles down the center of the back were pulled out by hand and sold to the local shoe repairman. He would use them as a leader for his thread when stitching leather. The pig's side hairs were discarded, but in earlier times, they were gathered and sold for paint brushes and clothes brushes.

Next, the pig's hind legs were spread and strapped to a rod suspended from a beam or tree branch. From this upside-down creature, my father would cut out the belly in one piece—the part that would later be salt cured for pancetta—and expose the internal organs, which were quickly removed and cleaned. The women would wash the intestines in the river's current with great care; these well-rinsed membranes, of varying diameter, would become sausage casings. Meanwhile, the men would carefully cleave the pig further, from rump to neck, although not completely in half.

The butterflied carcass, still hanging, needed to dry overnight, so it was an opportune time to clean up and prepare lunch, a thank-you for all the helpers. The menu was never in question. The customary lunch on the day a hog is butchered is *soffritto*, a savory stew of coarsely chopped heart, lungs, liver, and kidneys—the most perishable parts of the pig—simmered over a wood fire with garlic, olive oil, oregano, and hot red pepper. For a Calabrian with rural roots, there is no finer dish. Fried potatoes always accompany it. Before the *soffritto*, my mother would serve handmade pasta with a pork-rib and tomato sauce (page 88).

The next morning, the men would cut the carcass in half and begin breaking down the halves into the appropriate pieces. There was nothing ad hoc about this process; every square inch of the pig had a predetermined use.

The two hind legs would be removed and salted for prosciutto. One of the shoulders would also be salted and cured in the same way as prosciutto, although it was smaller and would be ready sooner. The other shoulder would be ground for sausage.

Meat from the neck and part of the back was set aside for *capocollo*. The loin was reserved for *soppressata*. The prime back fat would be salt cured like pancetta, to make *lardo*. The jowls would be removed whole and packed in salt to make *guanciale*. The ears, snout, feet, tongue, and remaining head meat would become *gelatina*, similar to head cheese. My mother made the *gelatina*, simmering these gelatinous cuts until soft in salted water with bay leaf and garlic. Then she would add a generous amount of wine vinegar, and the meat and tangy broth would be divided among several containers. When cool, the broth would solidify into jelly.

Also on the first day, the men would remove the hog's bladder and wash it carefully. Then they would blow into it to inflate it like a balloon and hang it up to dry. Once it dried, they would put a funnel in it and fill it with melted pork fat. This natural vessel would be hung from the rafters until the fat was needed for some use in cooking. My mother says that the fat stored this way really did taste better than pork fat stored in the conventional way, in earthenware crocks.

Along with the shoulder, any usable trimmings of meat and fat would be collected for sausage. This meat would be ground and put in a big wooden trough, then seasoned with salt, wild fennel seed, and hot red pepper, and mixed well. A small amount would be cooked and tasted for seasoning. When everyone was convinced it was properly spiced, the mixture was left to cure overnight. The following morning, it would be stuffed into the casings.

After grinding the meat for sausage, the women would coarsely chop the loin for *soppressata*, salt it, and let it rest overnight. On the third day, the sausage and *soppressata* fillings would be laboriously hand-stuffed into their casings and hung in front of the fireplace to be exposed to smoke from the chimney.

While the women chopped meat, my father would salt the cuts that required curing. In a large wooden vat, he made layers separated by salt: first the prosciutto; then the shoulder; then the back fat for *lardo*; and finally the pancetta and *guanciale*, or pork jowl.

In a large copper cauldron set on a tripod in our fireplace, all the chunks of fat and fatty trimmings not needed for sausage would be rendered slowly with water until all the water had evaporated. As a test, my mother would throw a little hot fat on the coals in the fireplace; if it hissed and steamed, there was still water remaining. The melted fat would be poured off into earthenware crocks, while the small crisp meaty bits, or cracklings, called *ciccioli*, were skimmed off and stored separately. Over the next few weeks, *ciccioli* would be kneaded into flatbreads or scattered over hot *pitta mijina* (page 140), stirred into cooked winter greens such as broccoli rabe, or sprinkled on fried eggs.

Any leftover cuts that had no other destination were set aside for *frittoli*, the Calabrian version of *confit*. These scraps, meaty ribs, and fatty chunks would be salted for two weeks in the wooden vat along with the other meats, then rinsed and cooked slowly in a large cauldron, gradually rendering their fat. Near the end of the cooking time, chunks of the now two-week-old sausage would be added. Then the meats and sausage would be packed in a glazed clay pot and covered with the cooking fat, which had turned red from the hot pepper in the sausage. Stored in a cool, dark cellar, the *frittoli* would last for months. When my mother needed a piece of cured meat or sausage to flavor cabbage or beans, she would dig down in the *frittoli* pot for some treasure.

Any scraps of fat that couldn't be melted for *strutto* (lard) would be turned into big chunks of soap by heating the fat with water, flour, and potassium purchased at the farm supply store. By the end of the annual ritual, every ounce of the pig had been accounted for.

Polpette alla Verbicarese
MY MOTHER'S PORK MEATBALLS IN TOMATO SAUCE

The meatballs I grew up with are made entirely with pork, which is still the custom among many Calabrians. In my grandparents' day, rural people made meatballs only when they had fresh pork, for a few days following the butchering of a pig. My mother has remained true to this traditional all-pork recipe, adding neither onion nor garlic but a little pecorino cheese and parsley for flavor. The meatballs have a particularly sweet taste because we grind our pork fresh, using pork butt (shoulder) trimmed of most of the fat. If you choose to grind your own meat, use the fine plate on the grinder. Often I double this recipe and put half the fried meatballs in the freezer unsauced. Then, when I am pressed for time, I can reheat them in tomato sauce for a quick dinner.

I'm not sure where the idea of tossing meatballs with pasta came from. It is not Italian. We toss spaghetti, penne, or homemade *fusilli* (page 85) with some of the flavorful sauce from the meatballs and serve that as a first course. The meatballs themselves follow as a second course.

SUGGESTED WINE: Masseria Felicia "Ariapetrina," Falerno del Massico, Campania
A dark red from a blend of Piedirosso and Aglianico grapes, this medium-full wine has a rich blackberry character, austere tannins, and abundant acidity.
ALTERNATE: Dolcetto

MEATBALLS

1½ pounds (675 grams) ground pork

1 large egg

¾ cup (115 grams) fine dry breadcrumbs (page 127)

¼ cup finely chopped flat-leaf parsley

¼ cup (25 grams) freshly grated pecorino cheese

1 teaspoon kosher salt

½ teaspoon freshly ground black pepper

Extra virgin olive oil for frying

7 cups (1¾ liters) Quick Tomato Sauce (page 53)

FOR THE MEATBALLS: In a large bowl, combine the ground pork, egg, bread-crumbs, parsley, cheese, salt, and pepper. Mix thoroughly with your hands. Add ⅓ cup (80 milliliters) water and mix well. Fry 1 tablespoon of the mixture in a nonstick skillet and taste for seasoning.

With moistened hands, shape the mixture into 1½-inch (4-centimeter) meatballs.

Put ½ inch (12 millimeters) of olive oil in a large skillet and turn the heat to medium-high. When the oil is hot, carefully add the meatballs in a single layer, in batches if necessary. Brown the meatballs well all over, turning them carefully with a spoon so as not to break them. Transfer them to a tray as they are done.

Put the tomato sauce in a large skillet that can hold all the meatballs. Add the meatballs and simmer briskly uncovered, turning them occasionally in the sauce, until the meatballs are fully cooked and the sauce is flavorful, about 10 minutes. Taste the sauce for salt.

Reserving some sauce to coat the meatballs, use the remaining sauce to coat 1 pound (450 grams) of pasta for a first course, then serve the meatballs as a second course.

MAKES ABOUT 3 DOZEN MEATBALLS, TO SERVE 6

Homemade prosciutto and Calabrian sausage
curing in my father's basement in Oakland

Salsiccia Calabrese
FRESH HOMEMADE FENNEL SAUSAGE CALABRIAN STYLE

Calabria's traditional fresh pork sausage is liberally seasoned with ground sweet pepper and hot red pepper and laced with wild fennel seeds. My parents and I still gather wild fennel seed in California—the plant is ubiquitous—but store-bought fennel seed works in the recipe as well. In Calabria, my parents made mountains of sausage whenever my father killed a hog. I remember my mother filling sausage casings by hand for hours, pushing the stuffing through a funnel with her thumb. (Today, thank goodness, we have sausage stuffers.) What we didn't eat fresh in the first few days, my father would preserve by one of two methods. Some he would air dry. The remainder would be partially air dried, then cooked in lard and stored under the cooled lard for long keeping.

You need at least 25 percent fat to make a juicy, flavorful sausage. With less fat, your sausage will be dry. Most pork today is too lean and well trimmed to make a successful sausage without additional fat. I use boneless pork butt (shoulder) purchased from a Chinese market and ask the butcher to leave on the surface fat. Sometimes I buy additional fatty trimmings just as insurance. After you grind the pork butt, use your eye to estimate whether the ground meat contains about 25 percent fat. If it doesn't, grind the fatty trimmings, too. Alternatively, use a sharp knife to trim the pork butt, separating the fat from the lean. Then weigh them to make sure you have at least 25 percent fat. If you don't have a meat grinder, ask the butcher to grind the meat for you.

Salt-packed hog casings are available by mail order and from some meat markets in ethnic neighborhoods. They come in several different diameters. You may have to buy a lot, but they keep indefinitely in the refrigerator if covered with salt.

The amount of ground hot red pepper in this recipe makes a spicy sausage that is true to Calabrian taste. You can use more or less hot pepper, as you like. But the signature flavor of Calabrian sausage is the sweet ground pepper (*pepe rosso*). My grandmother would say you haven't used enough of the *pepe rosso* if your hands aren't red after mixing.

Note that you don't have to make links with this sausage mixture. If you prefer, you can shape it by hand into patties, then wrap and freeze them. Use in any recipe that calls for bulk sausage.

Fresh Homemade Fennel Sausage Calabrian Style (*salsiccia Calabrese*)

SUGGESTED WINE: Odoardi "Polpicello," Scavigna, Calabria
Gaglioppo is the principal grape in this red wine, yielding a big wine with layers of plum and chocolate flavor but not a huge amount of tannin.
ALTERNATE: "Super Tuscan" blend of Sangiovese and Cabernet Sauvignon

5 feet of salt-packed hog sausage casings, 1¼ to 1½ inches (3 to 4 centimeters) in diameter (see Resources, page 368)

3 pounds (1½ kilograms) fresh boneless pork butt with surface fat (see recipe introduction)

¼ cup (30 grams) Calabrian paprika (page 304) *or* Spanish sweet paprika

2 tablespoons kosher salt

1 tablespoon wild fennel seed (see Resources, page 370) or store-bought fennel seed

2 teaspoons ground hot red pepper

Meat grinder with coarse grinding plate and sausage-stuffing attachment

Kitchen twine

RINSE THE CASINGS of their external salt, then flush the interior of the casings by running cold water through them repeatedly, like water through a hose. To keep them from becoming tangled after they are rinsed, keep them submerged in a bowl of water until you are ready to use them.

Trim the pork, removing any bits of bone, cartilage, or bloody bits. Slice the pork into 1-inch-wide (2½-centimeter-wide) strips so that it will be easier to feed through the meat grinder.

Fit the meat grinder with the coarse grinding plate. Grind the meat directly into a large bowl. Add the paprika, salt, fennel seed, and hot pepper. Mix thoroughly with your hands for several minutes so that the meat, fat, and seasonings are uniformly blended.

Mount the sausage-stuffing attachment on your meat grinder, stand mixer, or sausage-stuffing machine. Moisten the tubular attachment with water to make it easier to slip on the casing. Put one end of the casing over the tube, then gradually work all the casing onto the tube. Do not tie this end off yet.

Begin funneling the sausage mixture through the feed tube so that it fills the tube. As the meat emerges, it will be preceded by an air bubble. (That's why you left the end open.) Tie off the casing, then continue stuffing the casing. The process works best and most efficiently if one person feeds the machine with the sausage mixture while another person holds the gradually lengthening sausage, making sure that the casing fills evenly and fully and coiling the sausage on a plate as you go. The finished coil should be plump, but if you overfill it, the casing may burst.

This amount of stuffing should make a coil about 4½ feet (1½ meters) long. If your casing is not long enough to contain all the stuffing, use a partial piece from another casing. When you have used all the meat, tie the other end of the casing.

FOR LINKS: Typically, in Calabria, fresh sausages are made in one large coil, like a big snake. To prepare multiple links instead, pinch the coil about 6 inches (15 centimeters) from one end and twist four to five times at that point to make a link. Continue to pinch the sausage in that spot while pinching with your other hand 6 inches (15 centimeters) farther along the coil and twisting there to make a second link. You can now release the first pinch point as you have secured that twist. Continue to pinch and twist the coil every 6 inches (15 centimeters), keeping the previous twist from unwinding by pinching it until you have completed the next. With this method, you avoid untwisting one link while you twist the next. You should end up with nine links. With kitchen twine, tie off the ends of the links, then cut between the ties to separate the links before cooking.

Sausages may be grilled, pan-fried, or baked. You can judge doneness by touch—cooked sausages will be firm—or, if you are unsure, with an instant-read thermometer. When the internal temperature reaches 150°F (65°C) on a meat thermometer, they are done.

TO GRILL, prepare a moderate charcoal fire or preheat a gas grill to medium. If cooking one large coil, skewer it to make it easy to turn. Grill the coil or individual links, turning once or more, until browned and fully cooked, about 15 minutes.

TO PAN-FRY, place individual links in a skillet with enough water to come halfway up the sides of the pan. Simmer over medium heat, turning the sausages occasionally, until the water almost completely evaporates, 12 to 15 minutes. Lower the heat, add a drizzle of oil to the pan, and brown the sausages.

TO BAKE, preheat the oven to 400°F (200°C). Place the sausage coil or individual links on an oiled baking sheet and bake until fully cooked, 15 to 20 minutes, turning halfway through.

MAKES 9 LINKS, EACH ABOUT ⅓ POUND (150 GRAMS)

Harvesting Wild Fennel

It's fortunate that my immigrant parents settled in Northern California, where wild fennel thrives. The small aromatic seeds from this plant give Calabrian sausage its characteristic taste and season both the green and ripe olives we cure in the fall. Wild fennel seeds contribute an essential licorice-like flavor to the pickled eggplants and pickled mushrooms we preserve under oil. And the feathery, dill-like greens, harvested in spring, are a prized addition to pasta sauces and soups. I don't know what we would have done if my parents had immigrated to the East Coast.

Wild fennel (*Foeniculum vulgare*) abounds along country lanes and in abandoned lots in Northern California, where it has naturalized. My mother has her "spots," where traffic passes infrequently and she knows the plants will be unpolluted.

Unlike cultivated fennel, which is grown for its fleshy bulb, the wild fennel bulb is flat, undeveloped, and of no culinary use. But in spring, when the lacy fronds are fresh and their stems tender, many Calabrians harvest and cook them. I use wild fennel greens in a traditional pasta sauce with sausage and in *pasta con le sarde* (pasta with sardines and wild fennel), a dish from my Sicilian husband's side of the family.

By midsummer, the stems have lengthened and toughened and developed a flowering head—actually, a collection of many small flower clusters, each one attached to a short, thin stem. Once the yellow pollen falls, each cluster is filled with small green seeds. Over the next few weeks, these green seeds develop some white striping. Then they grow larger and harder and darken to brown, the final stage. My mother prefers the seeds at the striped stage, which is usually about mid-August. With scissors, she clips the flower heads, leaving an inch or two of sturdy stem attached.

At home, she washes the flower heads repeatedly in very hot water, sloshing them in the water, then lifting them out and changing the water until they no longer release any insects or dirt. At this fresh stage, I use the small seed clusters in Pickled Eggplant Preserved in Oil with Hot Peppers, Wild Fennel, and Garlic (page 281), picking the clusters off their tender stems. But most of the harvest is destined for further drying.

My mother lays the heads out on a brown paper grocery bag, indoors but away from direct sunlight, and lets them air dry for two to three weeks. At that point, the flower clusters on the end of each thin stem will be brittle and some seeds will fall out at the touch. By hand, she painstakingly picks out all the seeds, leaving any stemmy debris behind. Then she packs these precious seeds in an airtight glass jar for our family's use over the following year.

Wild fennel seed from Calabria is now available in jars, for those who don't live in Northern California or don't want to undertake the labor-intensive process of harvesting it. See Resources (page 370).

Vruocculi ca' Savuzuizza
PAN-FRIED SAUSAGE WITH BROCCOLI RABE

In winter, when broccoli rabe thrives in Calabrian gardens, this dish is a dinner staple. I always slice the pan-fried sausage and mix it with the greens to flavor them, but you can leave the sausage whole. I simmer it in water before browning it, but you can use any cooking method, such as grilling, that you prefer.

SUGGESTED WINE: Tormaresca Masseria Maime, Salento, Apulia
From the Antinori family's Puglia property comes this red wine, a Negroamaro on the fuller side with aromas of Mission fig and oregano.
ALTERNATE: Tempranillo

---

2 bunches broccoli rabe, about 1 pound (450 grams) each

⅓ cup (80 milliliters) extra virgin olive oil, plus more for frying

6 garlic cloves, halved

1 small dried hot red pepper *or* hot red pepper flakes

Kosher salt

4 links Fresh Homemade Fennel Sausage Calabrian Style (page 211),
    each about ⅓ pound (150 grams), *or* store-bought hot Italian
    sausage links

TO TRIM THE broccoli rabe, remove large, tough stems, then slit smaller stems so they cook quickly. Cut the broccoli rabe crosswise into 2 or 3 pieces.

Bring a large pot of water to a boil. Add the broccoli rabe and boil until tender, about 2 minutes. Drain, chill under cold running water, then drain well.

Heat the olive oil in a large skillet over moderate heat. Add the garlic, and hot pepper to taste, and sauté until the garlic is golden. Add the broccoli rabe and toss to coat with the seasonings. Season with salt and cook until hot and infused with the seasonings, about 5 minutes.

Place the sausages in a large skillet with enough water to come halfway up the sides of the pan. Simmer, turning the sausages occasionally, until the water almost completely evaporates, 12 to 15 minutes. Lower the heat, add a drizzle of oil, and cook until the sausages brown, about 2 minutes.

Slice the sausages on the diagonal as thick as you like. Combine with the broccoli rabe in the skillet and cook until hot. Taste for salt. Serve hot.

SERVES 4

Pollo alla Calabrese

BAKED CHICKEN WITH POTATOES, TOMATOES, AND HOT PEPPER

This simple, home-style recipe is prepared in Calabria with chicken and rabbit. The meat juices infuse the potatoes, and in the end, both meat and vegetables are cloaked in a savory glaze. The use of oregano and hot red pepper is the Calabrian signature. I prefer to make the dish with chicken legs and thighs because they take about as long to cook as the potatoes do. You can use a whole cut-up chicken or just bone-in breasts, but you will need to remove the breasts when they are done. They cook faster than the potatoes. My cooking students tell me that this dish has become their "comfort food," a nutritious dinner that takes almost no time to prepare.

SUGGESTED WINE: Mastroberardino "Radici," Taurasi, Campania
A medium-full red wine with Bing cherry and wild blackberry aromas, good acidity, and moderate tannin.
ALTERNATE: Cabernet Sauvignon

---

3 pounds (1½ kilograms) bone-in chicken legs and thighs, trimmed
of all visible fat

3½ teaspoons kosher salt

Freshly ground black pepper

1½ pounds (675 grams) Yukon Gold potatoes, peeled or unpeeled,
cut into 2-inch (5-centimeter) chunks

¾ pound (340 grams) ripe tomatoes, cored and cut into 1-inch
(2½-centimeter) chunks

1 large yellow onion, halved and cut into ½-inch-thick
(12-millimeter-thick) slices

3 garlic cloves, halved

3 tablespoons chopped fresh oregano *or* 1 tablespoon dried oregano

¼ cup (60 milliliters) extra virgin olive oil

Ground hot red pepper

PREHEAT THE OVEN to 450°F (230°C) and position a rack on the lowest level. Season the chicken all over with 2 teaspoons of the salt and several grinds of black pepper.

Put the potatoes, tomatoes, onion, and garlic in a baking dish large enough to hold the chicken in one layer. (A 9- by 13-inch/23- by 33-centimeter glass or ceramic baking dish works well.) Sprinkle the vegetables with the remaining 1½ teaspoons salt. Place the chicken in the baking dish, add the oregano (crumbling the dried oregano, if using, between your fingers as you add it), and drizzle with the oil. With your hands, toss the chicken and vegetables to coat them thoroughly with the seasonings. Then remake the bed of vegetables, arranging the chicken on top, skin side up. Sprinkle the chicken with hot pepper to taste.

Place the baking dish in the oven on the bottom rack and bake until the skin is crisp and golden, 30 to 45 minutes. Turn the chicken pieces over and continue baking until the chicken juices run clear, the potatoes are tender, and most of the pan juices have been absorbed, 20 to 30 minutes. Serve immediately, spooning the remaining pan juices over the chicken.

SERVES 4 TO 6

Pollo con Melanzane

BRAISED CHICKEN WITH EGGPLANT, TOMATOES, AND PANCETTA

I have found versions of this recipe in many Calabrian cookbooks, with fried peppers sometimes replacing the fried eggplant. In its rustic spirit and informality, it resembles chicken *cacciatore*, with tomatoes and mushrooms, which Calabrians also make. The pancetta and white wine are my contribution, added to give the sauce a little more depth. I fry the sliced eggplant separately, then fold it into the dish when the chicken is almost done so the eggplant doesn't overcook and collapse. In the end, both chicken and eggplant are cloaked in a spicy tomato glaze. Save this dish for late summer, when eggplants are plump, firm, and shiny, with bright green tops.

Most Calabrian cooks would make this dish with a whole chicken, cut into serving pieces. I prefer to use all thighs because they cook in the same time and the meat is always moist. You can use mixed chicken parts if you prefer, or even all breasts, but you will have to adjust the braising time. Breasts will cook faster than thighs.

SUGGESTED WINE: Marisa Cuomo Furore, Costa d'Amalfi, Campania
An elegant, full-bodied red with impressive structure, this wine—a blend of Aglianico and Piedirosso—has ripe aromas of black currant and leather along with firm tannins and acidity.
ALTERNATE: Brunello or Barolo

---

1 pound (450 grams) globe eggplants *or* slender Italian eggplants
    (page 234)

Kosher salt

Olive oil for frying

8 bone-in chicken thighs, all visible fat removed

Freshly ground black pepper

3 tablespoons extra virgin olive oil

2 ounces (60 grams) pancetta, chopped

3 garlic cloves, halved

1 cup (250 milliliters) dry white wine

2 cups (500 milliliters) peeled, seeded, and diced ripe tomatoes

1 small fresh hot red pepper, such as cayenne or Thai, halved
    lengthwise, optional

3 tablespoons chopped flat-leaf parsley

CUT THE EGGPLANTS into large chunks, about 1 inch (2½ centimeters) thick and 2 inches (5 centimeters) long. If you are using a globe eggplant, you can quarter it lengthwise, then cut crosswise into 1 inch (2½ centimeter) pieces. If you are using the smaller Italian eggplant, you may only need to halve it lengthwise, then cut crosswise into 1-inch (2½-centimeter) pieces. If the pieces are too small, they will fall apart when cooked.

Sprinkle the eggplant all over with 1 teaspoon kosher salt. Heat enough olive oil in a 10-inch (25-centimeter) skillet to come ½ inch (12 millimeters) up the side of the pan, about 2 cups (500 milliliters) oil.

Pat the eggplant dry with paper towels. When the oil is hot enough to sizzle the edge of a piece of eggplant, fry the eggplant in batches until golden all over, 2½ to 3 minutes total. Do not crowd the pan. With a slotted spoon, transfer the cooked eggplant to a plate lined with paper towels.

Season the chicken thighs all over with 2 teaspoons salt and several grinds of black pepper. Heat a 12-inch (30-centimeter) deep skillet or Dutch oven over high heat. Add the extra virgin olive oil, the pancetta, and the garlic and sauté until the garlic is golden, about 1 minute. Add the chicken thighs skin side down. Sauté without moving them until the skin side is browned and releases easily from the pan, about 5 minutes. Turn and brown the second side, lowering the heat if necessary to prevent burning, about 5 minutes.

Transfer the chicken with tongs to a plate and pour off the accumulated fat, leaving the garlic and pancetta in the pan. Return the chicken to the pan and add the wine. Simmer until all the wine has evaporated.

Add the tomatoes and hot pepper, if using. Taste and add more salt if desired. Simmer steadily, uncovered, until the chicken thighs are fully cooked (their juices will be clear, not pink) and the tomatoes have collapsed into a sauce, about 10 minutes. Add the fried eggplant and stir gently to coat the eggplant pieces with sauce without breaking them up. Continue simmering until the tomato sauce is reduced to a glaze, about 2 minutes. Stir in the parsley and serve.

SERVES 4

Coniglio con Peperoni

SPICY BRAISED RABBIT WITH SWEET PEPPERS AND OREGANO

In late summer, when the long Italian peppers have turned from green to poppy-red, I harvest some to braise with rabbit. These intensely sweet, thin-skinned peppers resemble the "Corno di Toro" variety sold at farmers' markets, but bell peppers are more widely available, so I have substituted them here. In winter, I use the same sweet Italian pepper but in its dried state, as described in the Variation below.

Although many recipes for rabbit call for browning it first, my mother and I prefer to simmer the rabbit pieces in salted water with olive oil until they are tender and the juices reduce to an intense, concentrated broth. Then we add tomato, sweet peppers, oregano, paprika, and garlic and simmer until the flavors meld. Rabbit is delicate in taste, and we don't want the caramelized note that browning introduces.

SUGGESTED WINE: Cantine Lento "Federico II," Calabria
A medium-bodied Cabernet Sauvignon is well suited to rabbit's delicate flavor.
ALTERNATE: Chianti Classico

One fresh or frozen rabbit, 2½ to 3 pounds (1 to 1½ kilograms),
    thawed if frozen

4 tablespoons extra virgin olive oil

Kosher salt

3 red bell peppers, halved, seeded, and cut into ¾-inch-wide
    (18-millimeter-wide) strips

2 garlic cloves, halved

1 tablespoon dried oregano

½ cup (125 milliliters) peeled, seeded, and diced ripe tomato, *or*
    chopped Home-Canned Peeled Tomatoes (page 296), or canned
    Italian San Marzano tomatoes, broken up by hand

1 teaspoon Calabrian paprika (page 304) *or* Spanish sweet paprika

Ground hot red pepper *or* hot red pepper flakes

1 tablespoon Homemade Sweet Pepper Paste (page 301), optional

ASK YOUR BUTCHER to cut the rabbit in half lengthwise, then into 4 to 6 pieces per half, depending on size. From each half, you will get a hind leg (separated into

My father feeding his rabbits

leg and thigh if large), a loin section, a rib section (halved if large), and a foreleg.

Put the rabbit pieces in a nonreactive 12-inch (30-centimeter) straight-sided skillet, 4-quart (4-liter) sauté pan, or other heavy, wide-bottomed pot with 2½- to 3-inch (6- to 8- centimeter) sides. Add just enough water to cover the rabbit. Bring to a boil over moderate heat, skimming any foam. Add 2 tablespoons of the olive oil and 1 tablespoon salt. Adjust the heat to maintain a steady simmer. Cook uncovered, turning the rabbit pieces occasionally, until the meat is tender when probed with a fork, about an hour. You should have about ¼ inch (6 millimeters) of liquid remaining in the bottom of the skillet. If you have more, simmer until the liquid reduces. If you have less, add water to bring the liquid to the required depth.

While the rabbit cooks, heat the remaining 2 tablespoons oil in a large skillet over moderate heat. Add the bell peppers and cook, stirring almost constantly, until they have just begun to soften, about 10 minutes. Season with salt and set aside.

Add the garlic and oregano to the rabbit. Simmer for 5 minutes, uncovered, then add the peppers and their oil, the tomato, the paprika, the hot pepper to taste and the Homemade Sweet Pepper Paste, if using. Taste the broth for salt. Simmer, stirring often, until the tomatoes have softened and the sauce has reduced to a glaze that just coats the rabbit, about 5 minutes.

SERVES 4 TO 6

Variation with Sun-Dried Sweet Peppers

Omit the red bell peppers and the paprika. Remove the stem and seeds from 12 Sun-Dried Sweet Peppers (page 293), then tear each pepper into quarters. Simmer the rabbit with all 4 tablespoons of the olive oil. Add the sun-dried peppers when you add the tomato and hot pepper.

Capretto Arrostito con Patate
ROAST BABY GOAT WITH POTATOES

Many of the baby goats and lambs born in late winter in Calabria are destined for the Easter table. When they are less than two months old and have still not had anything to eat but mother's milk, they will be sacrificed for this longstanding Calabrian tradition. Roast *capretto* (baby goat) is eaten with reverence and great enthusiasm. The meat is pale, delicate, sweet, and succulent beyond words.

People accustomed to eating medium-rare lamb or beef may be surprised at how long Calabrians cook baby goat, but the meat from milk-fed animals has a more appealing texture and taste when fully cooked. In most homes, the preparation never varies. Some people spit-roast their *capretto*, basting it as it turns with olive oil, white wine, rosemary, and garlic. Others cut it into manageable pieces and roast it—in a wood-fired oven, preferably—with the same mixture of oil, wine, rosemary, and garlic. The meat is too subtle to withstand bolder seasonings and too prized to treat in any but the simplest way. Many cooks will put raw potatoes in the roasting pan with the meat, adding them partway through, but potatoes prepared that way always taste steamed to me. I prefer to roast them separately so they get crackling crisp, then combine them with the meat and its juices just before serving.

I am well aware of how difficult it is to find baby goat or lamb in many communities. Every year, my family struggles to find a source so we can maintain this tradition, and we are often disappointed. To a Calabrian, a *capretto* worthy of the Easter table will weigh only 12 to 15 pounds (5½ to 7 kilograms) before slaughter, and perhaps 7 pounds (3¼ kilograms) cleaned. We occasionally locate a willing farmer, but my father usually has to do the slaughtering and butchering himself.

Middle Eastern and Hispanic markets are your best bet for finding baby goat or lamb, although you will have to order it well ahead. Be sure to specify that you want meat from a milk-fed animal; once goats and lambs begin eating grass, the meat loses that sweet, milky delicacy. You can apply this same method of roasting to shoulder chops from a more mature goat or lamb (see the Variation with Lamb Shoulder, below), but the meat will have a stronger flavor and will release more fat.

Braised peas, asparagus, artichokes, and other spring vegetables are good companions for roasted *capretto*.

SUGGESTED WINE: Paternoster "Don Anselmo," Aglianico del Vulture, Basilicata
This muscular red wine is a traditionally styled Aglianico, with plenty of tannin and acidity—a classic match for the goat raised in the Vulture area.
ALTERNATE: Cabernet Sauvignon

MEAT

7 pounds (3¼ kilograms) bone-in milk-fed baby goat *or* baby lamb, sawed by the butcher into 16 to 18 pieces

2½ teaspoons kosher salt

Freshly ground black pepper

5 garlic cloves, lightly smashed

Leaves from two 6-inch (15-centimeter) fresh rosemary sprigs

¼ cup extra virgin olive oil

1 cup (250 milliliters) dry white wine

POTATOES

2½ pounds (1 to 1¼ kilograms) Yukon Gold potatoes

¼ cup extra virgin olive oil

6 garlic cloves, lightly smashed

Leaves from two 6-inch (15-centimeter) fresh rosemary sprigs

2 teaspoons kosher salt

Freshly ground black pepper

FOR THE MEAT: Preheat the oven to 450°F (225°C). Position a rack in the upper third of the oven and another rack in the bottom third.

Remove any visible clumps of fat on the meat. Put the meat in a roasting pan large enough to hold it snugly in a single layer. Sprinkle each piece on all sides with salt and pepper. Scatter the garlic and rosemary leaves around the roasting pan. Add the olive oil and toss with your hands to coat the meat evenly. Cover the roasting pan tightly with aluminum foil.

Roast on the lower oven rack for an hour, then remove the foil cover and turn the pieces of meat over with tongs. They will have thrown off some juice and will not be brown yet. Add the wine and move the roasting pan to the upper rack to make room for the potatoes. Continue roasting uncovered until the meat is fork tender, lightly browned, and beginning to pull away from the bones, about 45 minutes longer. Turn the meat over partway through to keep it moist. If the pan juices are reducing too quickly, add a little water. You want to have about 1½ cups (350 milliliters) of reduced pan juices remaining when the meat is done, just enough to cloak both meat and potatoes.

FOR THE POTATOES: Peel the potatoes and cut them in half lengthwise, then in wedges about 1 inch (2½ centimeters) wide at the widest part. The exact size is not important as long as they are roughly the same size so they cook evenly. Put them in a 9- by 13-inch (23- by 33-centimeter) nonstick baking dish or other oven-safe nonstick pan large enough to hold the potatoes in a single layer. Add the olive oil, garlic, rosemary leaves, salt, and several grinds of black pepper. Toss with your hands to coat the potatoes evenly, then arrange them in the baking dish with one cut side down. (Do not season the potatoes too far ahead of time or they will throw off moisture and will not brown properly.)

Roast them on the lower rack of the oven for 20 minutes, then turn the potatoes with a metal spatula so the other cut side of each wedge is down. Continue roasting until the potatoes are crusty and tender when pierced, 15 to 20 minutes longer.

Remove the meat and the potatoes from the oven. Add the potatoes to the roasting pan with the meat and stir gently to moisten them with meat juices. Serve immediately.

SERVES 6

Variation with Lamb Shoulder

Purchase 4 pounds (1¾ kilograms) shoulder blade lamb chops, ½ to ¾ inch (12 to 19 millimeters) thick. (Lamb shoulder from a mature animal is meatier than baby goat or lamb, so you need fewer pounds to serve the same number of people.) Trim excess fat, then cut each chop in half lengthwise. Season as directed for baby goat but reduce the salt to 2 teaspoons and the rosemary to one 8-inch (20-centimeter) sprig. Roast as directed for baby goat. The lamb shoulder will release more fat than baby goat, so you will need to degrease the pan juices before adding the roast potatoes. To degrease, transfer the lamb to a platter and tent with foil to keep it warm. Pour the pan juices into a clear measuring cup and let them settle for about 5 minutes. Spoon off the fat that rises to the top. Return the degreased pan juices to the roasting pan along with the meat. Add the potatoes and stir gently to moisten them with meat juices. Serve immediately. Serves 6.

Tiella d'Agnello

BAKED LAMB SHOULDER WITH ARTICHOKES, PEAS, AND BREADCRUMBS

Made with baby goat or lamb, this dish is the centerpiece of the Easter table in the Catanzaro region. I first tasted it in a Catanzaro restaurant, U Tamarru, where the kitchen also added potatoes. The meat, still on the bone, is oven braised with artichokes and peas until tender, then blanketed thickly with a breadcrumb topping and baked further until the crumbs turn crisp. I have substituted lamb shoulder chops, which are easier to find than baby goat or lamb and more succulent than rib or loin chops. A *tiella* is any pot used for oven baking, made of any material, but if you have a large terra cotta casserole, this recipe would put it to good use.

SUGGESTED WINE: Fattoria La Valentina "Binomio," Montepulciano d'Abruzzo, Abruzzo
A full-bodied, velvety-smooth red wine with blackberry aromas and rich tannins.
ALTERNATE: Caberbert Sauvignon or Merlot

3 pounds (1½ kilograms) shoulder blade lamb chops, trimmed of excess fat

1½ teaspoons kosher salt

Freshly ground black pepper

4 garlic cloves, lightly smashed

1 tablespoon coarsely chopped fresh oregano

3 tablespoons extra virgin olive oil

1 lemon

1 pound (450 grams) small artichokes, about 2 ounces (60 grams) each

1 cup (250 milliliters) dry white wine

PEAS

2 tablespoons extra virgin olive oil

1 yellow onion, coarsely chopped

2 cups (500 milliliters) fresh peas *or* frozen petite peas (no need to thaw)

1 teaspoon kosher salt

1 cup (80 grams) firmly packed fresh breadcrumbs (page 127)

½ cup (50 grams) grated pecorino cheese

3 tablespoons finely chopped flat-leaf parsley

2 garlic cloves, minced

PREHEAT THE OVEN to 450°F (225°C).

Cut the lamb chops in half lengthwise to make more attractive serving pieces. Season the meat on both sides with salt and pepper. Put the chops in an 11- by 13-inch (28- by 33-centimeter) roasting pan or other pan large enough to hold the meat, artichokes, and peas snugly. Add the garlic cloves, oregano, and olive oil. Rub the oil all over the meat with your hands. Cover the pan tightly with aluminum foil and bake for 45 minutes.

Fill a bowl with cold water and add the juice of the lemon. To prepare the artichokes, pull off and discard the tough green outer leaves until you reach the pale, tender leaves. Remove the artichoke stem and trim the base to remove all trace of green, then cut off the top ½ inch (12 millimeters) of the artichoke. Cut each artichoke in half lengthwise. Immediately put the halves in the lemon water to prevent browning.

Remove the roasting pan from the oven, uncover, and add the wine. Drain the artichokes and add them to the roasting pan, scattering them around the lamb and coating them with pan juices. Replace the foil cover and return the roasting pan to the oven for 20 minutes.

PREPARE THE PEAS: Heat the olive oil in a 10-inch (25-centimeter) skillet over moderate heat. Add the onion and sauté until softened, about 5 minutes. Add the peas and salt. Cook, stirring, for about 2 minutes to infuse the peas with onion flavor. Set aside.

PREPARE THE TOPPING: Combine all the ingredients in a small bowl and blend well.

Remove the roasting pan from the oven and discard the foil cover. Pour off all the pan juices into a clear measuring cup. Let the juices settle for 5 minutes, then spoon off the fat that rises to the top. Set aside 1 cup of the degreased pan juices but return the remaining juices to the pan. Add the peas and onions to the pan and gently stir them in.

Sprinkle the topping over the lamb and vegetables, coating them evenly. Pour the reserved pan juices over the topping, moistening it evenly. Return the roasting pan to the oven until the topping is browned and crusty, about 20 minutes. Serve immediately.

SERVES 4

Trippa con Peperoni

TRIPE WITH TOMATOES AND SWEET PEPPERS

My mother makes this dish often in late summer when the garden almost over-whelms us with ripe tomatoes and peppers. It is my father's favorite tripe preparation. Like a sponge, the tripe soaks up the intense, sun-sweetened taste of the vegetables he has nurtured for the past few months, capturing the flavor of the last weeks of summer. The peppers and tomatoes are both cooked separately from the long-simmered tripe, then merged with it for the final few moments.

These days, tripe is thoroughly cleaned and partially cooked before it reaches the retail counter. That's the good news. The bad news is that many processors clean tripe with a bleaching agent that imparts an objectionable aroma. The longer the tripe sits, the stronger the bleach aroma gets. Seek out a market with high turnover, such as a Mexican market, and look for tripe that's beige or ivory, not bone white.

SUGGESTED WINE: Li Veli Pezzo Morgana, Salice Salentino, Apulia
A single-vineyard red wine from Negroamaro with an aroma of black plum.
ALTERNATE: Tempranillo

2 pounds (900 grams) honeycomb tripe, fresh or frozen and
   thawed, fat removed

4 large bell peppers of mixed colors, preferably red, yellow,
   and orange

4 tablespoons extra virgin olive oil

Kosher salt

3 large garlic cloves, halved

2 cups (500 milliliters) peeled, seeded, and diced ripe tomatoes

Ground hot red pepper

BRING A LARGE pot of salted water to a boil over high heat. Cut the tripe into 5 or 6 pieces that will fit comfortably in the pot and add them to the pot. Skim any foam that collects on the surface as the water returns to a boil. Cover and adjust the heat to maintain a simmer. Cook until the tripe is very tender and no longer chewy, 2 to 3 hours or more, adding more hot water if necessary to keep the tripe well submerged. Drain and let cool, then cut into 1- to 1½-inch (2½- to 4-centimeter) squares. Set aside.

Halve the bell peppers and remove the ribs, seeds, and core. Cut them into ½-inch-wide (12-millimeter-wide) strips. If the peppers are very long, cut the strips in half.

Heat 3 tablespoons of the olive oil in a large skillet over moderately high heat. Add the bell peppers, season with salt, and cook, stirring often, until they are softened. Remove the peppers and set aside.

In the same skillet, warm the remaining 1 tablespoon olive oil over moderately high heat. Add the garlic and sauté until lightly browned. Add the tomatoes and a pinch of salt. Cook briefly just to soften the tomatoes. Add the tripe and cook for about 5 minutes to infuse the tripe with the tomato flavor. Add the bell peppers and a generous dash of hot pepper to taste and simmer briefly to blend the flavors. Serve hot.

SERVES 6

Whole Fried Sweet Peppers with Anchovies (page 241)

Verdure
vegetables

Whenever Calabrians have a square meter of bare ground, they plant a garden. The typical Calabrian *orto*, or home garden, is a bountiful jungle of eggplant, peppers, potatoes, red onions, green beans, tomatoes, and zucchini in summer. Hard-shelled squash and borlotti beans overtake the *orto* in fall. In winter, location permitting, Calabrians grow Savoy cabbage, escarole, and broccoli rabe. Spring is peak season for homegrown fava beans, peas, and artichokes.

Of all the regions of Italy, Calabria may well claim the diet richest in vegetables. Far more than meat or fish, vegetables dominate our meals. Our soups celebrate vegetables, from the silky red onion soup of Tropea (page 101) to the rustic green bean and tomato *minestra* (page 99), or thick soup, that my mother makes when my father hauls in armloads of beans. Most Calabrian pasta dishes—at least those served on weekdays, not Sundays—showcase a single seasonal vegetable, whether it's eggplant in summer or artichokes in spring.

The second course in a family meal always includes at least one *contorno*, or side dish, of vegetables, and sometimes two or three. The vegetables may be fresh from the garden or, in winter, pulled from the family's stash of preserves, such as Sun-Dried Zucchini with Calabrian Paprika (page 248). A vegetable dish with vinegar, such as the eggplant, green tomatoes, or other vegetables that Calabrians preserve under oil, would appear afterward, as a palate-cleansing salad. In difficult times, Calabrians who had nothing else always had homegrown vegetables, and they have retained the habit of centering their meals around them.

Among the many vegetables appreciated in Calabria, the tomato heads the list. It is probably safe to say that tomatoes in some form appear on the table at least once a day—and not just in summer. In winter and spring, Calabrian home cooks turn to the whole canned tomatoes, sun-dried tomatoes, and tomato paste that they preserved in summer and fall. Tomatoes, either canned or fresh, bind many of our vegetable stews and provide texture and backbone to every *sugo*, the pasta sauce we make with braised meats. We stuff tomatoes—with breadcrumbs, rice, or ricotta; we use them as toppings for pizza and fillings for *pitta* (Calabrian stuffed pizza); and we preserve them in their green state as a spicy pickle or a sweet jam.

In their gardens, most Calabrians grow the esteemed San Marzano tomato, an elongated, thick-walled variety suitable for canning as *pelati* (whole peeled tomatoes) and for sun drying. For sauce, Calabrians want their tomatoes fully ripe, but for salad, we like them firm and still slightly green. If they are red all over, they will be too soft for our taste.

The eggplant is second only to the tomato in Calabrians' affections. The Arabs introduced eggplant to neighboring Sicily, and it easily made the leap to Calabria, where it thrives in the region's long, hot summers. Southern Italians embraced it long before the North did, and today, even the most indifferent Calabrian home cook knows at least a dozen ways to prepare it. The famous Eggplant *Parmigiana* (page 252), despite its name, has nothing to do with Parma, the northern city. It is indisputably a creation of the South, with both Calabria and Sicily claiming credit. In the province of Reggio Calabria, eggplant dishes can resemble those prepared in Sicily, with pine nuts, currants, sugar, and vinegar.

The most common Calabrian eggplant is long and slender with a deep purple skin and few or no seeds, similar to the variety identified as "Italian eggplant" in many American markets. The "Violetta Lunga" and "Gitana" varieties available from some seed sources (see Resources, page 370) resemble the eggplant in Calabrian gardens. They have creamy flesh and are never bitter, unlike the large, seedy globe eggplant. The skin is tender, and Calabrians rarely remove it. Nor do most Calabrian cooks salt eggplant before cooking it to extract bitterness. As long as the stem end is firm and green, the skin taut and shiny, and the flesh devoid of seeds, the eggplant will not taste bitter.

The sweet peppers used in Calabria also bear mentioning, as they differ from the familiar bell peppers in the American marketplace. The sweet pepper found in home gardens and markets in Calabria is 9 to 12 inches (23 to 30 centimeters) long, tapered, and slender, with relatively thin walls. The "Sweet Italian" and "Marconi" sweet peppers available from some seed sources (see Resources, page 370) come closest to the pepper my father and other Calabrians grow.

Calabrians enjoy sweet peppers in their green (unripe) stage and also when they begin to ripen to red. These green or half-ripe peppers are stuffed with ground meat or breadcrumbs and pecorino and baked; or pan-fried (sometimes with an anchovy inside, see page 38) and added to frittatas and scrambled eggs (page 155); or grilled over a wood fire, then peeled and seasoned with olive oil and garlic; or tossed with pasta, with or without tomato sauce; or braised with other summer vegetables, such as eggplant, potatoes, zucchini, and tomato, in stews like *ciambotta* (page 244). In the Cosentino region, especially, gardeners plant extra peppers to string up and sun dry (page 293) for winter dishes, like Spicy Braised Rabbit with Sweet Peppers and Oregano (page 222). Some of these dried sweet peppers will be ground for *pepe rosso*, the mild, paprika-like seasoning employed liberally in the Cosentino area.

It might surprise people to learn that Calabrians eat sweet potatoes, a vegetable rarely associated with the Italian table. We call them *patate Americane* and use them primarily in the dough for *grispelle* (Warm Christmas Doughnuts, page 324), or we roast them whole in the hot ashes of a wood fire.

Asparagus and mushrooms are among the gifts of the earth that Calabrians treasure most, but in traditional kitchens, only the wild ones are considered worth cooking. In spring, we gather the delicate, pencil-thin, wild asparagus spears in sunny, grassy, uncultivated spots. With luck, we have them on the Easter table in a frittata or in a pasta or rice dish. Most often, wild asparagus is tossed with pasta or added to a frittata. I have not included recipes for wild asparagus because it is hard to come by in the United States. Similarly, Calabrians don't cook with cultivated mushrooms; they prefer wild mushrooms, for which they forage avidly in fall and spring.

This chapter includes recipes for the simple salads I make from produce my father grows, such as the winter Cauliflower Salad (page 240) with anchovies and olives, and an Eggplant Salad with Garlic, Mint, and Hot Peppers (page 237) that benefits from being made ahead. He also grows flat Italian-style green beans that I boil and dress with olive oil, red wine vinegar, and garlic—a summer replacement for a green salad at my house. But you don't need a garden to make any of these dishes. Even a supermarket can provide firm Yukon Gold potatoes for Potatoes Layered with Artichokes and Breadcrumbs (page 259) or sweet red onions for the Cooked Red Onion Salad with Oregano (page 238). These vigorously seasoned vegetable dishes are central to the Calabrian way of eating.

Eggplant Salad with Garlic, Mint, and Hot Peppers

Melanzane all'Insalata
EGGPLANT SALAD WITH GARLIC, MINT, AND HOT PEPPERS

For this dish, we use small Italian eggplant weighing only about 3 ounces (90 grams) each, kept intact at the stem end but sliced to allow the marinade to penetrate. If you can't find them, look for the elongated Japanese eggplant. The longer the eggplant marinates, the better.

3 pounds (1½ kilograms) small Italian eggplants (about 15)

3 tablespoons kosher salt

MARINADE

⅔ cup (160 milliliters) red wine vinegar

⅓ cup (80 milliliters) extra virgin olive oil

4 garlic cloves, sliced crosswise

3 small fresh hot red peppers, or to taste, sliced crosswise

¼ cup chopped fresh mint leaves

2 teaspoons kosher salt, or more to taste

LEAVING THE CAP and stem intact to hold the eggplant together, make four to six lengthwise slices, depending on size.

Place the eggplants in a large pot and add enough water to cover them. Bring the water to a boil over high heat, then add the salt. Boil until the eggplants are tender but not mushy, 3 to 5 minutes or longer. Push them down frequently with a wooden spoon to keep them submerged. As they are cooked, lift them out carefully and arrange them on a rack or in a colander, not overlapping, to dry for one hour.

Transfer the eggplant to a deep baking dish large enough to hold them snugly in one layer. Whisk together the vinegar, oil, garlic, hot peppers, mint, and salt. Pour over the eggplant. Baste with the dressing to make sure the seasonings are evenly distributed. Taste for salt.

Cover and marinate at room temperature for 24 hours before serving. For longer storage, refrigerate; refrigerated eggplants will keep up to 2 weeks. Bring to room temperature and taste before serving.

SERVES 6

Insalata di Cipolla Rossa
COOKED RED ONION SALAD WITH OREGANO

Sweet red onions are among the most anticipated summer crops in Calabria. Some of the onions are elongated, like the ones known as torpedo onions in the United States. Others are rounded but squat, similar to the onions often identified in American markets as "sweet Italian." The latter type is what I use for this salad because they most closely resemble what I remember my grandmother using. She would cut the peeled onions into wedges and boil them until they had lost their raw crunch but still had some firmness. After they cooled, she would dress them with olive oil, a generous splash of homemade wine vinegar, and dried oregano or, on occasion, chopped fresh mint. The vinegar gives the onions a gorgeous amethyst color.

In Calabria, these tangy onions are not a condiment, as they might be in the United States, but a refreshing summer salad. I serve them that way at my house, although I think they would also be a delicious accompaniment to a hamburger or a sandwich, in place of pickles. In recent years, I have also occasionally made this salad with oven-roasted onions. Roasting intensifies the onions' sweetness, and their texture is similar to the boiled onions if you take care not to roast them too long. I like the salad both ways, so I have included the roasted variation here. The boiled-onion salad will hold up for several days in the refrigerator, the roasted-onion salad not as long.

---

2 pounds (900 grams) Sweet Italian red onions

Kosher salt

3 tablespoons extra virgin olive oil

2 tablespoons plus 1 teaspoon red wine vinegar, or more to taste

2 teaspoons dried oregano

Freshly ground black pepper

CUT OFF THE ends of the onions, then peel and halve them. Cut each half into wedges that are about ¾ to 1 inch (18 to 25 millimeters) at the widest part. Break the wedges apart by hand into the individual onion layers.

Put 2 quarts (2 liters) of water and 2 tablespoons salt in a 4-quart (4-liter) pot. Bring to a boil over high heat and add the onions. After the water returns to a boil, cook for 2 minutes, then drain. Let cool completely.

In a small bowl, combine the olive oil and vinegar. Add the oregano, crushing it between your fingers as you add it to release its fragrance. Add 2 teaspoons salt and several grinds of black pepper. Whisk to blend. Pour the dressing over the onions and toss well. Taste and adjust with more vinegar or salt if needed. You can serve the onions immediately, but the flavor will only improve if they are dressed several hours before serving.

SERVES 6

Roasted-Onion Variation

Preheat the oven to 425°F (215°C). Rub each unpeeled onion with one teaspoon extra virgin olive oil, then wrap each onion individually in aluminum foil. Put the onions in a baking dish to catch any drips. Roast until the onions have some give when squeezed, about 1 hour for a ¾ pound (340 gram) onion. Remember that the onions will continue to cook as they cool, and you don't want them to be mushy. Cool to room temperature in the foil. Unwrap the onions, then peel away the skin and cut off the top and bottom ends. Halve the onions, then slice into wedges that are ¾ to 1 inch (18 to 25 millimeters) at the widest part. Dress as described above.

A bunch of red onions in Tropea

Insalata di Cavolfiore
CAULIFLOWER SALAD

In winter, I make cooked salads not only with the crunchy escarole my father grows but also with cauliflower, broccoli rabe, potatoes, or the wild chicory that my parents sometimes gather in abandoned fields. All of these salads follow roughly the same format. The vegetable is boiled until tender, drained well, and then dressed to taste with fruity olive oil, kosher salt, freshly ground black pepper, and a liberal dose of strong wine vinegar. The result is a refreshing, palate-invigorating dish.

My parents dress their cauliflower salad with only olive oil and vinegar. I add anchovies and black olives, as is common in parts of Calabria, especially for Christmas Eve. You can make this salad several hours in advance and keep it at room temperature.

Large head cauliflower, about 2 pounds (900 grams)

Kosher salt

¼ cup (60 milliliters) extra virgin olive oil

2 tablespoons white wine vinegar, or more to taste

4 anchovy fillets, coarsely chopped

4 or 5 dry-cured black olives, pitted and quartered

Freshly ground black pepper

SEPARATE THE CAULIFLOWER into florets, discarding the cauliflower's thick core. If the florets are large, cut them in half. They should all be about the same size so they will cook evenly.

Bring 5 quarts (5 liters) of water to a boil in an 8-quart (8-liter) pot. Add ¼ cup (35 grams) kosher salt and the cauliflower and let boil until tender but not mushy, 3 minutes or so. To avoid breaking up the florets, lift them out of the water with a strainer or slotted spoon and place them in a colander to cool.

Gently put the cooled florets in a serving bowl and add the olive oil, vinegar, anchovies, and olives. Season with salt and pepper and toss well. Cauliflower takes a great deal of seasoning so don't be afraid to add more oil, vinegar, salt, or pepper until it is just right. Marinate for at least 15 minutes before serving.

SERVES 6

Peperoni Fritti con Acciughe
WHOLE FRIED SWEET PEPPERS WITH ANCHOVIES

It is worth seeking out elongated sweet Italian peppers for this recipe instead of bell peppers. Look for them in farmers' markets and specialty produce stores beginning in late July. They have thin skins that don't need peeling and relatively thin walls, so they soften quickly when pan-fried. The anchovy fillet tucked inside softens, too, seasoning the pepper flesh with its saltiness. You can cook the peppers several hours before serving and keep them at room temperature.

We eat *peperoni fritti* as a side dish, but they're appropriate as part of an antipasto course and delicious tucked between two slices of crusty bread for a sandwich. Don't leave the stove while the peppers are frying or you could burn them beyond recovery. You really have to baby them. (Photograph on page 232)

8 long sweet Italian-style peppers, red, green, or a combination

8 flat anchovy fillets

Extra virgin olive oil

Kosher salt

WITH A PARING KNIFE, cut out the stem and core of each pepper, leaving the seeds and ribs inside. Insert one anchovy fillet into the cavity of each pepper.

Put ¼ inch (6 millimeters) olive oil in a 12-inch (30-centimeter) skillet. Add the peppers in a single layer. It's okay if they fit snugly. Turn the heat to moderately high. Cover and cook until the peppers are blistered on all sides, about 10 minutes, turning every 2 to 3 minutes. To minimize splattering, remove the pan from the heat before you uncover it to turn the peppers. Keep a close eye on the peppers to prevent burning.

Transfer the peppers to a serving platter and sprinkle them lightly with salt, keeping in mind that the anchovies are salty. Drizzle with a little oil from the pan. Serve at room temperature.

SERVES 4

An Oakland Orto: My Father's Astonishing Garden

U crupu ad acqua fadi mirachili di santi.
Manure and water make saints' miracles.

No one walking past my home, with its formal columned façade, could imagine that behind it is a landscape out of rural Calabria. Fig, apple, peach, nectarine, persimmon, loquat, and citrus trees jostle for sun and space with raised beds and terraces. Kiwi vines clamber over a trellis, while containers filled with basil, hot peppers, and strawberries consume most of the patio. By midsummer, I can hardly move between the terraces, so thickly are they planted with tomatoes, eggplants, sweet peppers, beans, and onions.

I cannot take credit for this astonishingly prolific patch of ground. My father, often assisted by my mother, does all the work of planting and maintaining this garden, as well as another plot at their own home nearby. As a result, my family is almost self-sufficient when it comes to fruits, vegetables, and herbs; I buy very little.

When my parents first came to California as immigrants in 1974, they were grateful for the opportunity that America represented but distressed by the food they found. Why could Americans not grow a decent piece of fruit? they wondered. Where were the slender, elongated eggplants; long, sweet green frying peppers; and fleshy San Marzano tomatoes that they required for their meals?

Fortunately, they had brought some seeds with them, and gradually they located other Calabrian immigrants who had managed over the years to bring in seeds and seedlings from the old country. They gave my father cuttings from their fruit trees and seeds for the familiar vegetable varieties. Many years later, when my parents began returning to Calabria for vacation, they collected more seeds for the varieties they missed, like the tiny, fiery *diavoletti* hot peppers that Calabrians grow in pots on their balconies. Our *noce pesca gialla* (thin-skinned yellow nectarine) grew from a cutting that my father obtained in Calabria and stuck inside an apple to keep it moist during the trip back.

With the resourcefulness of the Calabrian farmer he once was, my father gardens with almost no purchased inputs. We get goat and rabbit manure, our only soil amendments, free from a local farmer. My father digs most of it into the soil in the spring before planting but reserves some for making manure tea, an infusion that he and my mother feed to new seedlings as a sort of booster shot. He mulches with grass clippings and leaves; stakes the peas with fruit-tree prunings; and ties his tomato vines to their trellis with strips of rags.

Although I am not a gardener, I am in awe of my father's skill. My soil, once life-less, is dark and fluffy now. Every flower on his tomato plants sets fruit. Everything grows bigger in his care; even the mint leaves are enormous. He waters by hand in the evenings; when I installed a labor-saving drip system, he took it out because it wasn't moistening the entire root zone.

As much as I appreciate his work and the bounty he produces, I wouldn't mind having a few ornamental flowers here and there. But my practical father, recalling harder times, will not stand for it. "You can't eat flowers," he says.

My father harvesting tomatoes in my garden

Ciambotta

SOUTHERN ITALY'S SUMMER VEGETABLE STEW

Ciambotta is the ratatouille of Southern Italy. You will find it on tables from Naples southward, and of course every region claims that it's theirs. No two versions are identical because cooks always add more of the summer vegetables they like and less or none of the ones they don't. At my house, my mother and I fry all the vegetables separately because they have different cooking times, then we unite them in a spicy tomato sauce for the final few minutes. *Ciambotta* always tastes best at room temperature, when the flavors have had a chance to marry. Serve with grilled swordfish, sausage, or other grilled meats.

1 pound (450 grams) slender, dark-skinned Italian eggplants

1 pound (450 grams) zucchini

4 large red, yellow, or orange bell peppers, or a combination, in
    1- to 1½-inch (2½- to 4-centimeter) squares

1 pound (450 grams) Yukon Gold potatoes

1 large yellow onion

Extra virgin olive oil for frying

Kosher salt

2 garlic cloves, minced

1½ pounds (675 grams) fresh tomatoes, peeled, seeded, and diced

Handful of fresh basil leaves

Ground hot red pepper

REMOVE THE EGGPLANT stems, then quarter lengthwise and cut into ½-inch-wide (12-millimeter-wide) chunks. Cut the zucchini the same way. Halve the peppers and remove the ribs and seeds, then cut into 1-inch (2½-centimeter) squares. Peel the potatoes and onion and cut into pieces about the same size as the eggplant.

Heat ½ inch (12 millimeters) of oil in a 12-inch (30-centimeter) nonstick skillet over moderate heat. Toss the eggplant with salt. When the oil is hot, fry the eggplant in three batches until golden. When each batch is done, remove it to a large tray with a slotted spoon.

Pour off and reserve the oil from the skillet. Return 3 tablespoons of the oil to the skillet and return to moderate heat. When the oil is hot, add the peppers, season with salt, and fry until they are tender. Transfer them to the tray with a slotted spoon.

Add 1 tablespoon of reserved oil to the skillet and raise the heat to high. Add the zucchini and season with salt. Fry until nicely browned and tender, then transfer to the tray with a slotted spoon.

Add any remaining reserved oil to the skillet along with ¼ cup (60 milliliters) of fresh oil. Reduce the heat to moderate. Add the potatoes and season with salt. Fry until well browned, crusty, and tender, then transfer to the tray with a slotted spoon.

Raise the heat to moderately high, add the onion and garlic, and sauté briefly to soften. Add the tomato and basil leaves, tearing them in half as you add them. Cook briskly, stirring, until the tomatoes soften, then return all the fried vegetables to the skillet. Season with hot pepper to taste and taste for salt, then simmer the *ciambotta* for about 5 minutes to blend the flavors. Let rest for at least 30 minutes before serving.

SERVES 8

Zucchine Ripiene con Ricotta

BAKED RICOTTA-STUFFED ZUCCHINI

Calabrian cooks often make stuffed zucchini, but the filling is usually based on meat or breadcrumbs. I created this recipe when I needed a vegetable to serve at a class I taught on homemade ricotta. The filling—a blend of breadcrumbs, zucchini flesh, and ricotta—is moist and delicate, and it browns attractively on top. I like to use the short, plump, pale-green zucchini that I find at farmers' markets in early summer to midsummer. They are young enough not to have seeds but big enough to offer room for a stuffing. Any type of summer squash will work, even round types, and an assortment of shapes would be pretty on a platter.

Served hot, warm, or at room temperature, these baked stuffed zucchini make a good summer side dish for any grilled or roasted meat, such as Roast Baby Goat with Potatoes (page 224). You could also serve them with a tomato sauce as the centerpiece of a vegetarian meal.

If you are using store-bought ricotta, drain the ricotta in a sieve for thirty minutes if the cheese has any standing whey. Otherwise, your filling will be too wet.

6 small, tender zucchini, about 6 inches (15 centimeters) long

Extra virgin olive oil

1 small yellow onion, finely chopped

2 garlic cloves, minced

6 tablespoons fresh breadcrumbs (page 127)

3 tablespoons minced flat-leaf parsley

1 cup (225 grams) Homemade Ricotta (page 144) *or* store-bought
    ricotta, drained

3 tablespoons freshly grated pecorino cheese

1 large egg, lightly beaten

Kosher salt and freshly ground black pepper

PREHEAT THE OVEN to 400°F (200°C).

Cut the zucchini in half lengthwise. With a teaspoon or melon baller, scoop out the pulp, leaving a shell. Be careful not to tear the sides or bottom. Finely chop the pulp.

Heat 3 tablespoons of olive oil in a skillet over medium heat. When the oil is hot, add the onion and garlic. Sauté until the onion is soft and translucent, about 5 minutes. Add the zucchini pulp and cook until tender. Add the breadcrumbs and cook, stirring, for 2 to 3 minutes to blend the flavors.

Remove from the heat and add the parsley, ricotta, 2 tablespoons of the pecorino, and the egg. Mix well and add salt and pepper to taste.

Lightly salt the interior of the zucchini shells and fill them with the stuffing. Place the twelve filled shells on an oiled 12- by 17-inch (30- by 43-centimeter) baking sheet. Top each with a sprinkle of the remaining pecorino cheese and drizzle with 2 tablespoons olive oil.

Bake for 20 minutes. The top of the filling should be golden brown. If not, place the baking dish under a broiler briefly to complete the browning. Serve hot or at room temperature.

YIELDS 12 ZUCCHINI HALVES, TO SERVE 6 PEOPLE

Zucchini Seccati al Sole con Pepe Rosso
SUN-DRIED ZUCCHINI WITH CALABRIAN PAPRIKA

My parents and grandparents dried summer zucchini to have more variety on their table in winter, but we maintain the tradition today in California because we are attached to the taste. Drying this mild squash concentrates its flavor, and when the zucchini are reconstituted by the following method, they taste almost like oyster mushrooms. After boiling them briefly and squeezing them dry, I sauté them in olive oil with garlic and both sweet and hot red pepper. Calabrian families serve them this way as a side dish, but as I've learned from my cooking classes, my students love the warm, spicy zucchini spooned on top of sliced bread, *crostini* style. Sometimes, Calabrian cooks will simmer some chopped fresh tomato with sun-dried zucchini prepared this way to create a pasta sauce.

¼ pound (110 grams) Sun-Dried Zucchini (page 291), about 4 cups

⅓ cup (80 milliliters) extra virgin olive oil

3 garlic cloves, halved

2½ teaspoons kosher salt, or more to taste

1½ teaspoons Calabrian paprika (page 304) *or* Spanish sweet
   paprika

Ground hot red pepper

FILL A 4-QUART (4-liter) pot with 2½ quarts (2½ liters) water and bring to a boil over high heat. Rinse the dried zucchini by immersing them in a large bowl of warm water while the water in the pot heats.

Drain the zucchini and add to the boiling water. Boil until the zucchini are tender but not mushy, 5 to 15 minutes. Timing will vary depending on the original size of the zucchini, how thickly they were sliced, and how long the zucchini have been dried. Stop the cooking as soon as you can pierce the zucchini skin easily with your thumbnail.

Drain the zucchini in a colander, return it to the empty pot, and cover with cold water. Set aside until cool. You can leave the zucchini in the water for up to 2 hours before proceeding.

Drain the zucchini. Working in batches, squeeze the zucchini between your hands to remove as much excess water as possible.

Heat the olive oil in a 10-inch (25-centimeter) skillet over medium heat. Add the garlic cloves and sauté until they turn golden, then add the zucchini and sauté for about 2 minutes to coat it with the oil and infuse it with the garlic flavor. Add the salt, the Calabrian paprika, and the hot pepper to taste. Cook, stirring with a wooden spoon, for about 15 minutes to allow the zucchini to absorb the seasonings. Serve warm or at room temperature.

SERVES 4 TO 6

Pomodori Invernali: *Calabria's Winter Tomatoes*

With more than fifty tomato plants between my own and my father's garden, my family ought to be tired of tomatoes by mid-autumn, when the plants begin to decline. But we are not. Years ago, my father brought from Italy seeds for our beloved *pomodori invernali*, or winter tomatoes, so named because they last well into the new year if properly handled.

These tomatoes are larger than a cherry tomato but smaller than a San Marzano. They have a tough skin, meaty pulp, and a pronounced point at the blossom end. They grow in thick, heavy clusters, like grapes. The closest named variety I have found to what we grow is "Principe Borghese" (see Resources, page 370).

As the *pomodori invernali* begin to change color but before they turn fully red, beginning in late summer, my father harvests them. My mother ties the clusters together like a *ristra* of hot peppers. In Italy, people hang the harvested clusters outside, in a cool, dry, shaded area, such as under a balcony. In my California home, we keep ours indoors, in a cool, well-ventilated basement. Then we ignore them for a couple of months.

By early December, the tomato vines outdoors have usually succumbed and my father has pulled them up. Perfect timing: the *pomodori invernali* are looking ripe. Throughout December and well into January, I have these full-flavored tomatoes for my pasta sauces and salads, extending the fresh season well beyond what others think possible.

Parmigiana di Zucchine

BAKED ZUCCHINI LAYERED WITH TOMATO, MOZZARELLA,
AND PARMIGIANO-REGGIANO

Eggplant *parmigiana* is made throughout Italy, but I have never seen a zucchini version outside of Calabria. In place of fried eggplant, Calabrian cooks will often substitute fried zucchini made with long, wide slices from the large squash that lurk in every Calabrian garden. The zucchini are layered with tomato sauce, sliced mozzarella or sharp Caciocavallo cheese, and grated Parmigiano-Reggiano, then baked until the layers coalesce into a thick, savory cake that holds together when sliced. Calabrians rarely use Parmigiano-Reggiano—they prefer pecorino—but they do use it here and in eggplant *parmigiana* in accordance with the dish's name. Some cooks embellish their version with layers of sliced hard-boiled egg or ham, but I prefer this simpler way. Don't be put off by the amount of oil used to fry the zucchini; the vegetable absorbs very little of it.

Serve *parmigiana di zucchine* as a side dish with roasted or grilled poultry, red meat, or fish.

---

3 pounds (1½ kilograms) large zucchini, at least 5 inches (13 centimeters) long and 1½ inches (4 centimeters) in diameter

1 tablespoon kosher salt, plus more as needed

1 cup (250 milliliters) extra virgin olive oil

2 cups (500 milliliters) Quick Tomato Sauce (page 53)

½ cup (50 grams) freshly grated Parmigiano-Reggiano cheese

6 large fresh basil leaves

8 ounces (225 grams) fresh mozzarella or Caciocavallo cheese, thinly sliced

Freshly ground black pepper

SLICE THE ZUCCHINI lengthwise about ⅜ inch (9 millimeters) thick. Layer the slices in a colander, sprinkling the layers with 1 tablespoon salt to draw out moisture. Let drain for 15 minutes, then rinse under cold water and pat thoroughly dry with paper towels.

Heat the olive oil in a 10-inch (25-centimeter) nonstick skillet over high heat. When the oil is hot enough to sizzle when you dip in a piece of zucchini, add a few slices of zucchini—don't crowd the pan—and fry until soft and lightly colored on both sides, about 2 minutes total. With tongs, transfer the cooked zucchini to a plate lined with paper towels. Continue until you have fried all the zucchini.

Preheat the oven to 400°F (200°C).

Spread ⅓ cup (80 milliliters) tomato sauce on the bottom of a 9- by 9-inch (23- by 23-centimeter) baking dish, just enough to coat it lightly. Make a layer of zucchini slices placed side by side; it is okay if they overlap slightly. Top with another ⅓ cup (80 milliliters) tomato sauce, 2 tablespoons of Parmigiano, two leaves of basil torn in small pieces, and one-third of the mozzarella or Caciocavallo. Repeat the layering of zucchini, tomato sauce, Parmigiano, basil, and mozzarella or Caciocavallo two more times. Finish with a final layer of zucchini slices, the remainder of the tomato sauce, and the remaining 2 tablespoons of Parmigiano.

Bake until bubbling and browned on top, about 30 minutes. If the dish is hot throughout but the surface is not browned sufficiently, broil briefly to color it. Let rest for at least 15 minutes to allow it to settle before cutting into squares. The dish is also good at room temperature.

SERVES 8

Parmigiana di Melanzane

EGGPLANT *PARMIGIANA* WITH FRESH RICOTTA

The traditional Calabrian method for making *parmigiana di melanzane* produces a dish so rich I can't eat it. The usual recipe calls for frying the eggplant, then layering it with tomato sauce, sliced hard-boiled eggs, sliced *soppressata*, and a small mountain of grated Caciocavallo and Parmigiano-Reggiano cheese. But at the restaurant La Rondinella in Scalea, I had a much lighter version that I loved and have adopted. The cooks there omit the eggs and sausage and replace the Caciocavallo with fresh ricotta. I'm sure they fry the eggplant, but I have taken to baking or grilling mine because it conserves a lot of oil and makes the dish lighter still.

Despite the association with Parmigiano-Reggiano, a cheese from Northern Italy, *parmigiana di melanzane* has southern roots. To my palate, a salty aged pecorino tastes better with eggplant and tomatoes than the nutty Parmigiano-Reggiano, but either type of grating cheese will work.

Serve eggplant Parmigiana as a *contorno* (side dish) with any simply roasted or grilled meat, such as grilled Fresh Homemade Fennel Sausage Calabrian Style (page 211). Alternatively, serve it as a meatless lunch or dinner with a salad.

---

3 Italian eggplants, about 1 pound (450 grams) each

Kosher salt

¼ cup (60 milliliters) extra virgin olive oil

Quick Tomato Sauce (page 53)

½ cup (50 grams) freshly grated pecorino or Parmigiano-Reggiano
  cheese

2 cups (450 grams) whole-milk ricotta

PREHEAT THE OVEN to 400°F (200°C).

Slice the eggplants crosswise into rounds about ⅜ inch (9 millimeters) thick. Salt the rounds on both sides, using a total of 2 teaspoons salt. Brush both sides with olive oil.

Arrange the eggplant slices on two nonstick baking sheets or two aluminum baking sheets lined with parchment. Place them in the oven on two racks and bake for 10 minutes. Turn the slices over with tongs and switch the position of the baking sheets. Continue baking until the slices are lightly browned and tender, about 10 minutes longer. Set aside to cool.

Choose a 2- to 2½-quart (2- to 2½-liter) baking dish at least 2½ inches (6 centimeters) deep. Put ¼ cup (60 milliliters) of tomato sauce on the bottom, spreading it to make a thin film. Add a layer of eggplant slices, using one-fourth of the total. They should fit snugly but not overlap; cut them to fit if necessary. Top the eggplants with ½ cup (125 milliliters) tomato sauce, spreading it evenly, then with 2 tablespoons pecorino. Top with ⅔ cup (150 grams) ricotta in small, evenly spaced dollops. Repeat this layering—eggplant, tomato sauce, pecorino, ricotta—two more times. Top with a final layer of eggplants and the remaining tomato sauce, spreading it evenly. Sprinkle the final 2 tablespoons of pecorino on top. Bake until the contents are bubbling hot, about 30 minutes. Let rest for at least 30 minutes before serving to allow the layers to settle and the flavors to merge. The dish is best when barely warm.

SERVES 6 TO 8

Funghi con Pomodoro
SAUTÉED MUSHROOMS WITH GARLIC AND TOMATOES

My family rarely cooks cultivated mushrooms from the supermarket; we prefer the wild mushrooms my dad gathers. Raised in Calabria, a forager's paradise, he mastered the secrets of mushrooms at an early age—where to look for them and when; which ones are edible and which are not. When I was growing up, many rural Calabrians knew how to harvest the woods' bounty.

I recall visiting my aunt's mother at her farmhouse near Verbicaro once in the fall when I was ten or twelve. There was nothing in the house for lunch, so she set off for the woods and I followed her. In no time, she had gathered the most astounding heap of porcini I had ever seen. I helped clean them, and she sautéed them with oil and garlic, a feast I can still taste.

The forests of the high Sila plateau are especially renowned among foragers (see page 256), but even in the Pollino National Park around my father's farm, the porcini, chanterelles, and oyster mushrooms were plentiful from September until Christmas. Although we live in the urban San Francisco Bay Area now, my father still manages to find the mushrooms. I sauté them with garlic, hot peppers, and tomatoes, and we eat them as a side dish with grilled sausage or other grilled meat. You could also toss these well-seasoned mushrooms with tagliatelle or stir them into risotto. Sometimes my mother adds sweet green peppers, fried separately.

2 pounds (900 grams) fresh wild mushrooms, such as porcini or
    chanterelles, *or* cultivated oyster mushrooms

3 tablespoons extra virgin olive oil

3 large garlic cloves, halved

1 tablespoon kosher salt

1 or 2 small dried hot red peppers

1½ cups (350 milliliters) peeled, seeded, and diced ripe tomatoes *or*
    1 pint cherry tomatoes, quartered or halved

2 tablespoons minced flat-leaf parsley

USE A MUSHROOM BRUSH or old toothbrush to remove all traces of dirt from the mushrooms. If necessary, use a damp paper towel to remove dirt that the brush can't dislodge. With a small knife, trim the stem ends of the mushrooms, removing any tough parts. If you are using porcini, separate the caps from the stems. Slice the caps ¼ inch (5 millimeters) thick. Slice the stems ¼ inch (6 millimeters) thick, halving them lengthwise first if they are large. Chanterelles and oyster mushrooms are usually tender enough to tear lengthwise into ¼-inch-thick (6-millimeter-thick) pieces; the exact size is not important as long as they are roughly the same size.

Warm the olive oil and the garlic in a 12- to 14-inch (30- to 35-centimeter) non-stick skillet over high heat. When the garlic begins to color, add the mushrooms. Season with salt and add the hot peppers, tearing each into 2 or 3 pieces. Refrain from stirring the mushrooms until steam begins rising from the sides of the skillet. You want to sear the mushrooms; if you stir too soon, they will release a lot of liquid. Cook the mushrooms briskly until they soften, all their liquid evaporates, and they begin to sizzle and brown, 10 to 12 minutes.

Add the tomatoes and cook, stirring, until they collapse, about 5 minutes. Stir in the parsley. Taste and adjust the seasoning and serve hot.

SERVES 6

Wild Things: The Calabrian Knack for Foraging

In more difficult times, Calabrians foraged for wild foods out of necessity. Today, they do it for pleasure, for the thrill of the hunt, and out of passion for the taste of these seasonal treasures. For many, it simply seems criminal to waste what nature provides for the taking.

My own parents embarrassed me greatly when, as new immigrants to California, they would stop by the side of the road because they had spotted chicory or mushrooms. I was a teenager then, fearful of others' disapproval. Today I join them in gathering wild fennel and all manner of wild greens in spring, participating in a ritual as old as civilization.

AMONG THE SOUGHT-AFTER WILD FOODS IN CALABRIA:

Asparagi, or asparagus, grow wild in Calabria in spring, the pencil-thin spears usually emerging just in time for Easter. Their flavor is more intense than that of the cultivated type. A wild asparagus frittata is a much anticipated dish prepared for Easter or *la Pasquetta*, the day-after-Easter picnic in the country (page 79).

Wild asparagus at Vibo Valentia's farmers' market in Calabria

Camomilla, or chamomile, is thought to cure stomachaches and to help one fall asleep. My mother harvests it in June, shearing the plant at ground level. She lets the cut stems dry for about a month, then folds them into small packets and ties each packet with a string. One packet steeped in boiling water for a few minutes makes a fragrant and soothing tea.

Cicoria (chicory), *boragine* (borage), *ortiche* (stinging nettles), and *crespino* (sow thistle) are perhaps the most popular of the many nutritious wild greens that Calabrians eat with relish. These greens abound in early spring, and my mother cannot pass a parcel of bare ground at that time of year without scanning it for these edibles. Non-Calabrians would be amazed at how much nourishing food she can extract from what looks like a weed patch. Wild greens are always cleaned with great care (my mother's rule is three changes of water) and boiled until soft; purslane and watercress are among the few eaten raw. Typically, the cooked greens are dressed with olive oil, sliced garlic, and lemon juice and served as a salad, but they also appear in pasta, soups, and *pitte* (stuffed flatbreads, page 115), and are often braised with borlotti beans. Among my favorite preparations is a thick soup of borage or chicory and potatoes. Long before nutritionists had any notion of vitamins, Calabrians knew that these edible wild greens had great health benefits.

Finocchio selvatico, or wild fennel, is a signature taste in the Calabrian kitchen. Practically every Calabrian knows what it looks like, how to harvest it, and how to use it. Unlike cultivated fennel, wild fennel is valued for its feathery fronds and aromatic seeds, not for its bulb, which is relatively puny. In April and May, we pick the tender fronds and boil them for use in pasta and *minestre*, our thick vegetable soups. In summer, the plant flowers and forms a seed with a powerful anise scent. We harvest the seed for use in sausage (page 211), liqueur, and many kinds of cookies and pastries. Calabrese sausage would not taste right without wild fennel seed. Highly prized and much rarer is the black anise seed, a smaller seed with a pungent licorice aroma. It grows in La Sila and is used in cookies made in that region.

Fragoline, the tiny woodland strawberries that the French call *fraises des bois*, grow profusely in La Sila and other high-elevation areas. In the chestnut forests, they make a thick ground cover, and people gather them in early summer to make liqueurs and *rosolio*, a sweet infusion of fruit in alcohol. When my mother was a youngster, she and her siblings would pick them and sell them for pocket money. Today, on the road from Basilicata to Calabria, the *stradale* 505, mountain people still sell trays of fragrant *fragoline* from the side of the road.

Fresh strawberries for sale in May at a farmers' market in Pizzo, Calabria

Funghi, or wild mushrooms, hold no secrets for Calabrians, who know where and when to hunt for each type. For the most part, Calabrians do not buy cultivated mushrooms. They cook only with the wild fungi that lurk in the woods. The mountainous region of La Sila is famous for mushrooms, especially porcini. Experts say it may be the most bountiful mushroom region in Italy. The many food shops on the main street in Camigliatello Silano, a charming vacation town in the Sila Grande, are filled with magnificent dried porcini in gift packages at carriage-trade prices, along with lesser-quality specimens at a more affordable price. It's common knowledge in Calabria that most of the dried porcini in the fancy shops in Milan come from Calabria.

Lampascioni are the bulbs of a wild blue hyacinth (*Muscari comosum*). They resemble shallots, but with a bitter flavor that is not to everyone's taste. In Calabria and neighboring Puglia, *lampascioni* are considered a delicacy, and as with truffles, people are secretive about where they find them. The peak season is May. In the kitchen, they are typically treated like onions. My mother sliced and fried them for frittata, but they can also be boiled in vinegar, then preserved in olive oil, or they can be grilled.

Oregano grows so prolifically on Calabrian hillsides that few cooks would consider buying the cultivated variety. Those who don't forage for the wild herb and dry it themselves, as many people do, will buy it from foragers at the local farmers' market. Every market has vendors selling big bundles of dried wild oregano tied with string, and the fragrance is incomparable.

Sambuco, or European elderberry (*Sambucus nigra*), is known in Calabrian dialect as *u màju*, the May plant, because its delicate white blossoms appear then. Calabrians have, historically, found many therapeutic uses for the flowers, leaves, and roots of *sambuco*. The short list of maladies that it purportedly cures include headaches, nosebleeds, earaches, kidney stones, diarrhea, coughs, sore throats, and the common cold. The flowers and berries also have culinary uses. The fragrant blossoms are used in *pitte* (Calabrian stuffed pizza) and in *frittelle*, or fritters. The berries are made into marmalade.

But it's not just wild foods that attract the eye of a Calabrian forager. Any fruit or vegetable going to waste is cause for alarm. In Northern California, where my parents live now, my mother is constantly shaking her head over the fruits and nuts that homeowners fail to harvest. She will not hesitate to ask a stranger if she can pick his or her olives or oranges if it looks like no one has plans for the crop. She's not trying to save money, but from her early years of hardship and now many years of habit, she simply can't bear to see good food left to rot.

Tortiera di Patate e Carciofi
POTATOES LAYERED WITH ARTICHOKES AND BREADCRUMBS

In this traditional side dish, thinly sliced artichokes and potatoes are layered with well-seasoned breadcrumbs and baked until the vegetables are tender and the breadcrumbs crusty. The vegetables settle into a "cake" that you can slice neatly and serve with lamb, pork, chicken, or practically any meat. Calabrians prepare many vegetables by this method, including tomatoes, mushrooms, and zucchini—alone or in combination. I sometimes treat fennel this way, too, although the fennel, if sliced thinly, does not need to be cooked first.

Take care to make the potato slices equally thin so they will cook evenly. A mandoline or other vegetable slicer makes this job easier.

---

2 pounds (900 grams) Yukon Gold potatoes, peeled and sliced
⅛ inch (3 millimeters) thick

Juice of 1 lemon, plus 1 lemon half

10 small artichokes, 2 to 3 ounces (60 to 90 grams) each

8 tablespoons extra virgin olive oil

Kosher salt

Freshly ground black pepper

1 cup (80 grams) firmly packed fresh breadcrumbs (page 127)

½ cup (50 grams) grated pecorino cheese

3 tablespoons finely chopped flat-leaf parsley

2 garlic cloves, minced

PUT THE POTATO SLICES in a bowl with cold water to cover.

Fill another bowl with cold water and add the juice of the lemon. To prepare the artichokes, pull off and discard the tough green outer leaves until you reach the pale, tender leaves. Remove each artichoke stem and trim the base to remove all trace of green, then cut off the top ½ inch (12 millimeters) of the artichoke. Rub the artichoke all over with the lemon half. Cut each artichoke in half and slice lengthwise ¼ inch (6 millimeters) thick. Immediately put the sliced artichokes in the lemon water to prevent browning.

Heat 2 tablespoons of the olive oil in a 10-inch (25-centimeter) skillet over moderate heat. Drain the artichokes and add them to the skillet along with ½ cup (125

Potatoes Layered with Artichokes
and Breadcrumbs

milliliters) water and 1 teaspoon salt. Cook uncovered, stirring occasionally, until the water has evaporated and the artichokes are tender, about 10 minutes. Season the artichokes with salt and pepper.

Preheat the oven to 400°F (200°C).

In a bowl, combine the breadcrumbs, cheese, parsley, and garlic. Mix well.

Lightly oil the bottom and sides of a 9- by 13-inch (23- by 33-centimeter) baking dish. Without draining the potatoes, use your hands to lift out about one-third of the slices and arrange them in the bottom of the baking dish, overlapping them slightly. (The water clinging to them will generate steam as they bake.) Season with ½ teaspoon salt and several grinds of pepper. Sprinkle the potatoes evenly with ¼ cup of the breadcrumb mixture. Drizzle with 1 tablespoon oil. Top the potatoes and crumbs with one-half of the artichokes, spreading them evenly. Sprinkle the artichokes with ¼ cup of the breadcrumb mixture and 1 tablespoon oil. Repeat this layering process once more, ending with a top layer of potatoes, salt, and pepper, the remaining breadcrumb mixture, and a final drizzle of 2 tablespoons oil.

Cover with aluminum foil and bake for 30 minutes. Uncover and continue baking until the potatoes are fully cooked and the top is golden brown, about 20 minutes longer. If necessary, broil the surface briefly to brown it. Let rest for at least 10 minutes before serving. The *tortiera* is as good warm as it is hot.

SERVES 6 TO 8

Patate Fritte con Peperoni
CRISP-FRIED POTATOES AND SWEET PEPPERS

Many restaurants in Calabria serve *patate fritte*, fried potatoes, with grilled or roasted meats. The potatoes are cut into wedges and browned in olive oil until crusty. They are good, but not as good as my mother's. She slices the potatoes into rounds, then fries them crisp in oil that she has previously used to fry sweet peppers. The slices clump, which I love because you end up with clusters of potatoes that are crisp outside and creamy within. She returns the peppers to the skillet at the end and fries them with the potatoes briefly to fuse the flavors.

I typically serve this dish as an accompaniment to poultry, lamb, or pork. But in my childhood home in remote Verbicaro, it was often part of a largely meatless dinner. Unlike Americans, who tend to plan their dinners around animal protein, my family often did not have fresh meat for dinner. We would have pasta or soup, followed by a couple of vegetables dishes such as this one. My mother might assemble a platter of cold cuts or sliced prosciutto for my father, but she and I would be content with garden vegetables.

---

1 pound (450 grams) long sweet Italian peppers or bell peppers,
    preferably mixed colors

½ cup (125 milliliters) extra virgin olive oil

2 garlic cloves, halved

1 small fresh hot red pepper, such as cayenne or Thai, halved,
    optional

Kosher salt

2 pounds (900 grams) small russet potatoes, peeled and
    thinly sliced

CORE THE SWEET PEPPERS, halve them, and remove the white ribs and seeds. If using bell peppers, cut them into ¾-inch-wide (18-millimeter-wide) strips. If using long Italian peppers, cut them in half crosswise before cutting into ¾-inch-wide (18-millimeter-wide) strips.

Heat the olive oil in a 12-inch (30-centimeter) nonstick skillet over high heat. When the oil is hot, add the sweet peppers, the garlic, and the hot pepper, if using. Stir to coat with oil and fry, stirring constantly to prevent burning, until the peppers are soft, 8 to 10 minutes. Season with 2 teaspoons salt and transfer the peppers to a plate with a slotted spoon, leaving the oil behind.

Add the sliced potatoes to the skillet. Season with 2 teaspoons salt. Cook over high heat, turning the potatoes often with a wooden spoon so they brown evenly on both sides. Some slices will clump; don't try to separate them. The potatoes should be tender inside and crisp and golden on the outside in about 10 minutes.

Return the peppers to the skillet. Cook, stirring constantly, for about 2 minutes to allow the flavors to blend. Taste and adjust salt if needed. Transfer the potatoes and peppers to a serving platter with a slotted spoon, leaving excess oil behind. Serve immediately.

SERVES 4 TO 6

Zucca Gialla con la Menta
BUTTERNUT SQUASH MARINATED WITH GARLIC AND MINT

This mint-and-vinegar marinade appears throughout Southern Italy, with fried zucchini or grilled eggplant in summer and, in colder months, with hard-shelled squash similar to butternut. In Calabria, cooks layer the sliced and fried squash with red wine vinegar, mint, and garlic, then let the dish rest for several hours, until the seasonings have fused and mellowed. The squash becomes silky in texture and nuanced in taste, its natural sweetness balanced by vinegar and brightened with mint. Many Calabrians, myself included, don't eat the garlic, but we consider it essential for flavor.

My Sicilian mother-in-law makes a similar dish, but it includes sugar and thus has more of a sweet-and-sour taste. In Campania, most cooks omit the sugar but heat the vinegar, garlic, and mint before pouring it over the squash to make *zucca* (winter squash) or *zucchine a scapece*.

In traditional Calabrian homes, *zucca gialla con la menta* would be served as a side dish, but restaurants in the region often serve it as an antipasto these days, with olives and cured meats. Although you need a lot of olive oil to fry the squash properly, the vegetable absorbs very little of it, and you can reuse the oil for frying.

---

2 pounds (900 grams) butternut squash

1 cup (250 milliliters) extra virgin olive oil

Kosher salt and freshly ground black pepper

⅓ cup (80 milliliters) red wine vinegar

¼ cup fresh mint leaves, torn into smaller pieces

4 garlic cloves, very thinly sliced crosswise

CUT OFF THE stem end of the butternut squash, then peel the squash with a vegetable peeler or a knife. You may find it easier to peel if you first cut it crosswise where the slender neck swells into a bulbous base. Cut the peeled squash in half lengthwise and scrape out the seeds. Slice each piece into ³⁄₁₆-inch-thick (4½-millimeter-thick) slices crosswise. You will get half-moons from the neck portion and half-rings from the base, where the seed cavity is.

Choose a serving dish or deep platter that will allow you to make three layers of squash once it's fried. An oval gratin dish about 8 inches (20 centimeters) wide and 13 inches (33 centimeters) long is perfect.

Heat the oil in a 12-inch (30-centimeter) skillet over high heat. Fry the sliced squash in batches, turning once with tongs, until the slices develop golden-brown markings on each side, 2 to 3 minutes total. As they are done, transfer them to the serving dish or platter. When you have a layer that covers the bottom of the dish, season it with salt and pepper, sprinkle it with wine vinegar, and scatter the mint and garlic evenly, using about one-third of each ingredient. Continue frying, layering, and seasoning the squash until you have used all the squash and the seasonings.

Let the squash marinate at room temperature for at least 4 hours before serving, or refrigerate it overnight and serve it the following day, bringing it to room temperature before serving.

SERVES 4 TO 6

Cavolfiore Impanato
FRIED CAULIFLOWER

We eat these crisp, crusty florets as a *contorno* (side dish) in winter. You can use the same method on baby artichokes or zucchini, although you wouldn't need to precook them, as you do the cauliflower.

Large head cauliflower, about 2 pounds (900 grams)

Kosher salt

3 large eggs

Freshly ground black pepper

1½ cups (225 grams) fine dry breadcrumbs, homemade (page 127)
    or unseasoned store-bought

⅓ cup (35 grams) freshly grated pecorino or Parmigiano-Reggiano
    cheese

Extra virgin olive oil for frying

SEPARATE THE CAULIFLOWER into large florets about 2 inches (5 centimeters) across the top. Bring a large pot of water to a boil. Add 3 tablespoons salt and the cauliflower. Cook until the florets are tender, about 3 minutes after the water returns to a boil. Drain and cool.

In a shallow bowl, beat the eggs with a generous pinch of salt and several grinds of pepper. In another shallow bowl, mix the breadcrumbs with the cheese.

Working with one floret at a time, dip it in the beaten egg, making sure the exterior is well coated. Lift it out with a fork, letting the excess egg drain off. Then dredge the floret in the breadcrumbs, patting the breadcrumbs in place. Set the floret on a tray and continue until all the florets are coated.

Put ½ inch (12 millimeters) of olive oil in a 10-inch (25-centimeter) skillet and heat over moderately high heat. When the oil reaches 375°F (190°C), add as many florets as will fit loosely in a single layer. Don't crowd the pan. Leave the florets undisturbed until they form a nice golden crust, then turn them with two spoons and fry the other side, about 3 minutes total. Transfer to a tray lined with paper towels and continue until all the florets are fried. Serve hot.

SERVES 4 TO 6

Cavolo Cappuccio con Pepe Nero
BRAISED CABBAGE WITH PANCETTA AND BLACK PEPPER

The enormous heads of Savoy cabbage that my father nurtures in my urban California backyard are ready for harvest by January. One of my favorite ways to prepare this winter vegetable is the simplest: blanched, then braised with pork fat and finished with a tongue-tingling amount of black pepper. My grandmother made this dish, but she used homemade *guanciale* (cured pork jowls) and *lardo* (cured pork fat) in her cabbage. Both of those products are hard to come by in the United States, so I have substituted olive oil and pancetta.

Serve Braised Cabbage with Pancetta and Black Pepper as a side dish for pork, rabbit, sausages, duck, or game.

---

1 head Savoy cabbage, about 1½ pounds (675 grams)

2 tablespoons extra virgin olive oil

3 ounces (90 grams) pancetta, sliced as thick as bacon, then chopped

2 garlic cloves, halved

½ teaspoon kosher salt, or more as needed

Freshly ground black pepper

HALVE AND CORE the cabbage, then separate each half into leaves. Cut away the thick central ribs. Stack the leaves a few at a time and cut into 1-inch-wide (2½-centimeter-wide) strips.

Bring 4 quarts (4 liters) of water to a boil in an 8-quart (8-liter) pot. Add the cabbage and cook until tender but not soft, about 3 minutes after the water returns to a boil. Set aside 1 cup (250 milliliters) of the cooking water, then drain.

Heat a 12-inch (30-centimeter) skillet over medium-high heat. Add the olive oil and pancetta and cook, stirring with a wooden spoon, until the pancetta softens and gives off some fat; do not let it brown or become crisp. Add the garlic and sauté for about 1 minute to release its fragrance. Add the cabbage, the salt, and the reserved cooking water. Stir well, then reduce the heat. Simmer until all the liquid evaporates and the cabbage starts to glaze a bit, about 10 minutes. Season generously with black pepper and taste for salt. Serve immediately.

SERVES 4

Jars of *'nduja* (page 199), packed without the casing for sale abroad

La Dispensa Calabrese

the Calabrian pantry
sweet and savory preserves, pickles, marmalades,
jams, pastes, and liqueurs

In the days before refrigeration, a well-stocked pantry carried many Calabrian families through hard times. Especially in the rugged mountains, where winters could be severe, people long ago learned to preserve the summer and autumn *abbondanza* for months when nature was not so generous. I remember climbing the ladder to the attic pantry in my own childhood home with anticipation, knowing that delicacies lurked in the darkness at the top of the stairs. There, in a space barely high enough for me to stand, were earthenware crocks filled with pickled eggplants and mushrooms, hanging strands of dried peppers and drying grapes, and a treasure trove of chewy, home-dried figs.

Today, of course, Calabrians can buy sun-dried tomatoes, dried figs, jams, and marinated eggplant in jars. Outside of rural areas, the centuries-old preserving techniques are being abandoned because people no longer need to put food away to survive and don't have the drying and storage space in urban apartments.

Despite my own fast-paced life, my mother and I continue these annual rituals in California. We don't preserve food out of necessity but for the satisfaction of using everything we grow and because so many of these preserves are unavailable otherwise. Like many Calabrians, my family has come to love the concentrated taste of our sun-dried sweet peppers and zucchini and our oil-preserved eggplant and mushrooms as much as we love the fresh produce they came from. It is hugely gratifying in winter to go to my kitchen pantry and open a jar of home-cured olives and another of oil-preserved zucchini and have, with sliced bread, an instant antipasto. These preserves capture fruits and vegetables at the pinnacle of flavor, with that heightened taste that produce acquires when it reaches full ripeness.

If you don't have a garden, you can find the best that nature offers at a local farmers' market. There you can hand-select sugary figs or green tomatoes for preserving and know your finished product will be all natural and preservative free. In a weekend, you can put up enough canned plum tomatoes for a year of pasta sauce. You will save money, eat better, and possibly have enough of your own handiwork to share with friends.

Calabrians employ a wide variety of techniques when they preserve food. They cure ripe olives and fresh fish (anchovies, sardines, and bottarga) with dry salt. They sun dry fruits (peaches, nectarines, grapes, figs) and vegetables (zucchini, tomatoes, eggplant, peppers, mushrooms). They preserve many fresh vegetables in vinegar and olive oil (see page 280), with a few fennel seeds or fresh mint and hot peppers. They turn citrus fruits into marmalade and candied peel. They infuse raspberries, rose petals, and other fruits, flowers, and herbs in grain alcohol to make fragrant liqueurs. And, of course, they turn His Majesty the Pig into a year's worth of cured meats and sausages. The pig's fat was used to preserve *braciole* (stuffed pork rolls) and sausages, which would last for months in a crock under a thick blanket of lard.

On back roads in rural Calabria and in small villages, you can still see the trays of fruits and vegetables set out to dry in midsummer. My mother remembers making drying trays from a strong local reed (*Arundo donax*). She would halve the long rods lengthwise, dry them in the sun for a couple of days, then weave the strips into trays for drying figs and Zibibbo grapes. The local *ginestra*, or Scotch broom, was also woven lattice-style into mats for sun drying. These resourceful Calabrians never bought anything they could possibly make with available materials.

Sun-dried vegetables appeared on the winter table in many guises. My mother often made a sort of winter *ciambotta*, or vegetable stew, with potatoes and dried eggplant, peppers, and zucchini. (Our summer *ciambotta*, made with fresh vegetables, is on page 244). She would reconstitute the three dried vegetables in water, then fry them together in olive oil with garlic. The potatoes would be fried separately to keep them crisp, then combined with the softened and seasoned dried vegetables and a generous sprinkle of *pepe rosso* (Calabrian paprika) to give the color that tomatoes provide in summer.

My parents also dried tree fruits like peaches and nectarines, although not in halves. Instead, we pared each fruit into one long strip of skin and flesh, working around the circumference of the fruit as if paring an apple. The ribbon of moist fruit would be coiled loosely around a bamboo rod perched horizontally on supports, so the fruit would dry in a coil.

Sugar was expensive in Calabria until after World War II, so it made more sense in earlier times to dry one's fruit than to preserve it as jam. Many households did make fig preserves, as the fully ripe figs didn't require a lot of sugar. But for the most part, families reserved their sugar for coffee and for holiday baking. For everyday sweetening, Calabrians used honey or *mosto cotto*, the dark, syrupy, cooked-down juice from wine grapes. They also used to make a sort of honey out of figs by cooking them and then draining the syrup through a cloth. The collected juices, known as *miele di fichi* (fig honey), were used for sweetening desserts.

Old Calabrian homes often had an underground storage space where the earthenware crocks filled with *sott'oli* (vegetables preserved under oil) and with meats under lard were kept. Homemade prosciutto might hang from beams in these dark, cool rooms, while bottles filled with peeled tomatoes or tomato puree lined shelves. In my childhood home, the sausages were hung from beams in the kitchen, absorbing smoke from the fireplace. The *lardo* (cured pork jowl) also hung from a rafter, with half of an eggshell suspended underneath it to catch any drips. I am amazed, looking back, at the ingenuity that allowed these people to live on little more than what their patch of earth provided.

In this chapter, I have gathered recipes for the preserved foods my family makes every year. Some of them, like Home-Canned Peeled Tomatoes (page 296) and Homemade Tomato Paste (page 299), have commercial equivalents, but I believe the homemade version is vastly superior. Others, such as Sun-Dried Zucchini (page 291), simply can't be purchased. You will find recipes for Fresh Fig Jam (page 277) and Green Tomato Jam (page 275), sparkling enhancements for weekday toast or weekend biscuits. I have included a quintet of *sott'oli* (foods preserved under olive oil), made with eggplants (page 281), mushrooms (page 283), zucchini (page 286), green tomatoes (page 279) and fresh tuna (page 288). Any one of these preserves, accompanied by bread, can make a quick lunch or launch a dinner party. Served together, they make a grand antipasto. You will also discover in this chapter some of the pantry ingredients that give Calabrian stews, ragùs, and sauces their savory backbone, such as Salt-Cured Anchovies (page 289) and Homemade Sweet Pepper Paste, as well as two homemade seasonings—Ground Hot Red Pepper (page 303) and Calabrian Sweet Paprika (page 304)—that my

Green tomatoes preserved by my mother and me from our gardens in Oakland

family can't cook without. With these addictive seasonings in your own pantry, you can reproduce the scent of Calabria in the simplest tomato sauce.

The Year in Preserves

For rural Calabrian women of my mother's generation, the year unfolded in a predictable progression of preserving tasks. If you were the wife of a *contadino* (farmer), as my mother was, stocking the pantry with sun-dried, pickled, salted, jellied, canned, or otherwise preserved foods was part of the labor you contributed to the household. On a typical Calabrian farmstead in the 1950s, when my parents were starting married life, the preserving schedule might look like this:

JANUARY AND FEBRUARY The family pig is slaughtered and made into sausages, *capicolli*, prosciutto, pancetta, *lardo*, *braciole*, and other pork products intended for long keeping (see page 206). With the citrus harvest, women make marmalade and liqueurs.

MARCH In the cooler areas, artichokes are ready for packing under oil. This is also the month for making *rosamarina* or *sardella* (page 42), the spicy fish preserve.

MAY Fresh anchovy and sardine season begins. Time to pack them under salt (page 289).

JUNE The bluefin tuna catch begins, providing the raw material for Fresh Tuna Preserved Under Oil (page 288). At higher elevations, *fragoline* (woodland strawberries) ripen and are harvested for liqueur and *rosolio* (page 307).

JULY The zucchini are flourishing in the garden. The biggest ones are sun-dried.

AUGUST A month of nonstop preserving of tomatoes, peppers, and eggplant.

SEPTEMBER Both figs and grapes are heavy with sugar and ready for sun drying. The shell beans are plump in their pods and have dried on the vine; time to shell them.

OCTOBER AND NOVEMBER The woods abound in fresh porcini. Any mushrooms not eaten fresh will be sliced and dried. Green olives may be harvested and cured with water (page 24).

DECEMBER Olives left on the tree have matured and turned black and are ready for salt curing (page 27).

Master Directions for Water-Bath Processing

The following method is the one my mother and I have used for years to process jars of peeled tomatoes and fruit preserves. The water-bath processing creates a vacuum seal that allows us to store these jarred foods safely for months in a cool, dark place.

EQUIPMENT NEEDED

Water-bath canner with a rack insert (available at most hardware stores) *or* a deep stockpot with lid

Clean kitchen towels

Jar lifter or long-handled tongs

Clean half-pint, pint, or quart canning jars, such as Mason jars

New canning lids

Screwbands (may be new or used)

CLEANLINESS IS EXTREMELY important when canning. Make sure that your produce is well washed; that your jars have been washed in hot, soapy water and rinsed in scalding water; and that canning lids, tongs, and towels are clean, too. Keep cleaned jars upside-down on a clean towel until ready to use.

Fill jars to ½ inch (12 millimeters) below the rim with the peeled tomatoes or hot jam, prepared according to recipe directions. The headspace allows for expansion when the jars are processed and for a vacuum to form when the jars are cooled.

Clean the jar rims with a damp paper towel. Add the lids and screwbands, tightening the screwbands firmly.

If using a water-bath canner, place the filled jars on the wire rack insert and lower them into the canner.

If you don't have a water-bath canner, choose a pot just large enough to accommodate the jars in a single layer and tall enough to allow for 1 to 2 inches (2½ to 5 centimeters) of water above the jars, plus enough room for the water to boil without sloshing over the rim. Put a folded kitchen towel on the bottom of the pot to prevent the jars from touching the bottom, which might cause them to break during the vigorous boiling. Put the filled jars in the pot and place another folded kitchen towel across the top to prevent the jars from rattling during processing.

Fill the pot or canner with warm water, covering the jars by 1 to 2 inches (2½ to 5 centimeters). Cover the pot or canner. Bring to a boil over high heat, then adjust the heat to maintain a steady boil and process for the time recommended in each recipe, starting from the time the boiling began. Keep the water boiling continuously and add more boiling water if necessary to keep the jars submerged.

Turn off the heat and leave the jars in the pot or canner until the water is cool enough to remove them. With a jar lifter or long-handled tongs, transfer the jars to a rack or a countertop covered with a clean kitchen towel. Allow the jars to cool thoroughly. You will hear a popping sound as they seal.

When the jars are completely cool, make sure each has sealed properly by pressing on the lid. It should not pop back and forth as you press and release it. (Sometimes the jar will seal when you press the lid to test it.) You may remove the screwbands, but it's not necessary. Jars that have not sealed should be refrigerated and used promptly. Label the sealed jars with the processing date and store in a cool, dark place.

Marmellata di Pomodori Verdi

GREEN TOMATO JAM

This chunky jam stumps many tasters, who sometimes deduce from the sea-green hue and sweet-tart flavor that the dominant fruit is kiwi. Calabrians often make jam with their green tomatoes, the ones that lose the race to ripen before cold weather sets in. Simmered with sugar, the tomatoes melt into a thick preserve with a crystalline sheen and an apple-like acidity. If you aren't a gardener, ask growers at your local farmers' market for green tomatoes. They should be green and firm, with no sign of red blush. Spread this lemony jam on breakfast toast, serve alongside young pecorino cheese, or use as a filling for a *crostata* (lattice-topped tart, page 346). Green tomatoes contain a lot of pectin, so the jam will stiffen as it cools.

5 pounds (2¼ kilograms) firm green (unripe) tomatoes

3½ cups (700 grams) sugar

Grated zest (yellow part only) of 2 lemons

⅔ cup (160 milliliters) lemon juice

CORE THE TOMATOES, halve them, and dig out the seeds with a table knife. Cut the tomatoes into ¾-inch (18-millimeter) cubes.

Put a small plate in the freezer to chill. You will use it later to test doneness.

Place the tomatoes in a heavy 6-quart (6-liter) pot with the sugar, lemon zest, and lemon juice. Stir well, then bring to a boil over moderate heat. Reduce the heat to maintain a slow simmer and continue cooking until the tomatoes become translucent and the syrupy liquid thickens considerably, about 40 minutes, stirring occasionally to prevent the jam from sticking. When the temperature reaches 215°F (102°C) on a candy thermometer, remove the chilled plate from the freezer and spoon a little jam onto it.

Return the plate to the freezer until the jam is cold. If the jam is still too runny, continue cooking it. Otherwise, remove the pot from the heat.

Fill and process jars according to the Master Directions for Water-Bath Processing (page 273). Process half-pint (250-milliliter) or pint (500-milliliter) jars for 15 minutes.

MAKES 2 PINTS (1 LITER)

Fresh Fig Jam with figs from my garden in Oakland

Marmellata di Fichi

FRESH FIG JAM

Leafy fig trees blanket the warm coastal plains and foothills of Calabria, providing the fruit for one of the region's best-known exports (page 336). Wild fig trees are as ubiquitous as weeds, sprouting miraculously from patches of untended ground. The abandoned lot in the old quarter of Verbicaro where my childhood home once stood is now overgrown with wild fig, thriving on neglect. The fruit of the wild fig is not tasty, but any Calabrian with land will have a cultivated tree or two—or many more. There are dozens of varieties, such as the green-skinned and golden-fleshed Kadota, known in Calabria as the *fico dottato*, and a green-skinned fig with red flesh known in Verbicaro as *fico del paradiso*. I can't resist any of them. When I visit my parents' summer home in Santa Maria del Cedro, near Verbicaro, I take long morning walks along the country roads, and no ripe fig within reach is safe.

Most fig trees produce two crops a year: an early-summer crop that forms on year-old branches, and a late-summer to early-fall crop that develops on new wood. Because ripe figs are so fragile, many farmers pick and ship them to distant markets firm and underripe. Consequently, farmers' markets are the best source for tree-ripened figs, which are soft to the touch, often starting to split on the surface, and sometimes showing a drop of syrupy juice at the blossom end.

My fresh fig preserves have an amber hue and a bright background note of lemon. Enjoy them on breakfast toast, or use them as the filling for an Italian *crostata* (lattice-topped tart). You can double this recipe, although you will need a larger pot.

2 pounds (900 grams) ripe, green-skinned figs, such as Kadota

2 cups (400 grams) sugar

Grated zest (yellow part only) of 1 lemon

¼ cup (60 milliliters) fresh lemon juice

PUT A SMALL plate in the freezer to chill. You will use it later to confirm whether the jam has thickened sufficiently.

Remove the fig stems and quarter the fruit. In a 3- or 4-quart (3- or 4-liter) stainless saucepan, combine the figs, sugar, lemon zest, and lemon juice. Stir until well mixed. Bring to a simmer over high heat, skimming any foam. Reduce the heat to medium and simmer, stirring occasionally, for 15 minutes to soften the figs.

Pass the mixture through a food mill fitted with a large-holed disk. Return the puree to the saucepan and simmer over medium-low heat, stirring often, and monitoring the temperature with a candy thermometer. When the temperature reaches 215°F (102°C), remove the chilled plate from the freezer and spoon a little jam onto it.

Return the plate to the freezer for a few moments until the preserve is cold. If the preserve is still too runny, continue cooking it. If it has the consistency you like, remove the pot from the heat.

Fill and process the jars according to the Master Directions for Water-Bath Processing (page 273). Process half-pint (250-milliliter) or pint (500-milliliter) jars for 15 minutes.

MAKES 3 CUPS (750 MILLILITERS)

Pomodori Verdi Sott'Olio
GREEN TOMATOES PRESERVED IN OIL

These pickled green tomatoes would be sublime on a hamburger or as a relish for leftover grilled lamb, but that's not how most Calabrians eat them. Traditionally in Calabria they are a *contorno*, or side dish, offered with the meat course as an American cook might serve a salad. They are mellow, not fermented or sharply sour like American pickles, and they have a slightly chewy texture, like rehydrated dried mushrooms. Pull them out of your pantry to add a personal touch to a store-bought roast chicken, or add them to an antipasto platter, with assorted *salumi*.

5 pounds (2¼ kilograms) green (unripe) tomatoes

½ cup (70 grams) kosher salt

6 cups (1½ liters) white wine vinegar

¼ cup chopped fresh mint

5 garlic cloves, sliced crosswise

4 small fresh hot red peppers, such as cayenne or Thai, or to taste,
    sliced crosswise

Extra virgin olive oil for topping jars

CUT THE TOMATOES into ¼-inch-thick (6-millimeter-thick) slices. Make layers of tomatoes and salt in a nonreactive colander. Top them with a heavy weight. (A pot smaller than the colander, filled with water, works well.) Let stand for 24 hours to draw out the juices.

In a heavy 8-quart (8-liter) pot, combine the vinegar and 3 cups (750 milliliters) water and bring to a boil over high heat. Add the tomato slices, pushing them down into the liquid with a wooden spoon. Return to a boil and cook until the tomatoes are tender, not mushy, about 1 minute. Don't overcook the tomatoes or they will fall apart.

Drain the tomatoes and place in a large colander. Top them with a heavy weight to squeeze out the liquid. Let the tomato slices drain under the weight for 15 minutes or until cool enough to handle.

Lay several clean kitchen towels on a table covered with thick cardboard. Arrange the tomato slices on the towels, spreading the tomatoes apart. Let dry at room temperature for 24 to 48 hours. They should look dry but still feel a little damp.

Place a layer of the tomato slices in a wide-mouth 1-quart canning jar or in each of two 1-pint canning jars. Sprinkle with some of the mint, garlic, and hot peppers, and drizzle with olive oil. Repeat the layering until you have used all the tomatoes, pressing gently on the layers as you make them. When you have made the final layer, top with enough oil to submerge the tomatoes completely.

Cover and refrigerate for at least 2 weeks before sampling to give the tomatoes time to absorb the seasonings. Bring them out of the refrigerator about an hour before serving to allow the oil to liquefy. Return leftover tomatoes to the refrigerator, topping with oil so they remain completely submerged. If kept submerged in olive oil and refrigerated, the tomatoes will last for up to 6 months.

MAKES ABOUT 1 QUART (1 LITER)

A Note About Calabrian Sott'Oli (*Foods Preserved Under Oil*)

Calabrians have been preserving vegetables, such as eggplant and zucchini, under oil for centuries. The vegetables are heavily salted, boiled in straight wine vinegar, then covered completely with oil. If this method of preservation were not safe, it probably would have been abandoned a long time ago. Nevertheless, this is not a typical American method of preservation, and the USDA does not address it in its considerable literature on home food preservation. Nor will representatives of the USDA comment now on the safety of the *sott'oli* method. Many of these recipes contain garlic, and the USDA discourages keeping garlic under oil, even after refrigeration and in a low-pH environment.

Most Calabrian families, including my own, keep their *sott'olio* vegetables in a cool pantry with a weight on top to keep the vegetables submerged in oil, but refrigerating them provides an additional measure of safety and I recommend it.

Melanzane Sott'Olio

PICKLED EGGPLANT PRESERVED IN OIL WITH HOT PEPPERS,
WILD FENNEL, AND GARLIC

It's simply impossible to eat during the summer months all the eggplant that the typical Calabrian home gardener produces. But a good share of that harvest is not intended to be eaten fresh; we grow it to preserve for the winter months, when vegetable options are fewer. At least in my family, the goal was to preserve enough eggplant—either by drying it (page 292) or packing it under oil—to last for at least six months, until the spring garden began producing fresh vegetables.

Eggplant preserved *sott'olio*—under oil—requires three important steps. The sliced eggplant is salted first to draw out moisture. Then it is cooked in vinegar to help preserve it. Finally it is layered with seasonings—at my house, sliced hot peppers, sliced garlic, and clusters of the aromatic seed pods of wild fennel—then packed under oil to keep air from spoiling it.

The ideal container for *melanzane sott'olio* is a wide-mouthed earthenware crock. A wide-mouthed French canning jar is another option. With a wide opening, you can pack the container and retrieve the contents more easily.

Melanzane sott'olio was my favorite winter snack as a child. I would fetch the earthenware crock from the pantry and spoon the spicy pickled eggplant, dripping with golden olive oil, on bread. In traditional Calabrian homes, it is a winter *contorno*, or side dish, although modern restaurants throughout the region serve it as part of their *antipasti*.

5 pounds (2¼ kilograms) long, slender Italian-style *or* Asian
    eggplants

½ cup (70 grams) kosher salt

2½ quarts (2½ liters) white or red wine vinegar

¼ cup fresh wild fennel seed clusters (page 215), firmly packed, *or*
    chopped fresh mint

12 garlic cloves, sliced thinly crosswise

5 small fresh hot red peppers, such as cayenne or Thai, or to taste,
    sliced crosswise

1 cup (250 milliliters) extra virgin olive oil, plus more for topping
    jars

REMOVE THE STEM ends of the eggplants. Slice the eggplants lengthwise into ¼-inch (6-millimeter) slices. Layer the slices in a large bowl, sprinkling each layer with salt and using the full ½ cup (70 grams) salt. Let stand for 6 hours. With your hands, flip the eggplant layers in the bowl so that the top layer is on the bottom. Let stand for another 6 hours. Drain the eggplants and, with your hands, gently squeeze them in batches to remove excess water.

Put the vinegar in a heavy 8-quart (8-liter) pot and bring to a boil over high heat. Add the eggplants and return to a boil. Cook until the eggplants are tender but not mushy, 2 to 3 minutes, prodding the slices gently with a wooden spoon to keep them submerged.

Drain the eggplants and place in a large colander. Top with a weight, such as a heavy pot filled with water, and let drain until cool enough to handle, about 30 minutes.

Cover a table or work surface with thick cardboard and a clean kitchen towel or two, enough to accommodate the eggplant slices in one layer. Arrange the slices side by side on the towel and let dry until no longer damp but still pliable, 24 hours or more.

Choose an earthenware crock with a 2-quart (2-liter) capacity or a wide-bottomed and wide-mouthed jar of comparable volume. The crock or jar must be wide enough for the eggplant to lie flat and deep enough to hold all the eggplant slices plus enough olive oil to submerge them. Place two layers of the eggplant slices in the bottom of the crock or jar. Sprinkle with some of the fennel seeds, garlic, and hot peppers and drizzle with a little olive oil. Continue this layering process until you have used all the eggplants, fennel seeds, garlic, and hot peppers. Press firmly on the eggplant layers as you add them to remove any air pockets. When you have made the final layer, top with enough oil to submerge the eggplant completely.

Cover and refrigerate for at least 2 weeks before sampling to give the eggplants time to absorb the seasonings. Remove from the refrigerator about an hour before serving to allow the oil to liquefy. Return any leftover eggplants to the refrigerator, topping with oil so the eggplants remain completely submerged. If kept submerged in olive oil and refrigerated, they will last for up to 6 months.

MAKES ABOUT 1 QUART (1 LITER)

Funghi Sott'Olio

MUSHROOMS PRESERVED IN OIL WITH HOT PEPPERS, WILD FENNEL, AND GARLIC

My father's fall forays to undeveloped secret pockets of the thoroughly developed San Francisco Bay Area always produce an edible return. He can find mushrooms in the shadows of highways, it seems. While he has to look harder for them here than he did in the woods around our home in Calabria, we never lack for wild mushrooms to preserve under olive oil. After a few weeks of curing, when they have absorbed the fragrance of wild fennel and garlic, we spoon the sliced mushrooms and their flavorful oil onto homemade bread for an antipasto, or serve them as a winter salad. Usually I don't wash mushrooms—I brush them clean—but because these will eventually be simmered in vinegar, I save some time by cleaning them quickly in water.

5 pounds (2¼ kilograms) wild or cultivated oyster mushrooms

½ cup (70 grams) kosher salt

2 quarts (2 liters) white wine vinegar

1 cup (250 milliliters) extra virgin olive oil, plus more for topping jars

1½ teaspoons wild or cultivated fennel seeds

8 garlic cloves, sliced crosswise

5 small fresh hot red peppers, such as cayenne or Thai, or to taste, sliced crosswise

WITH A SMALL KNIFE, trim the stem ends of the mushrooms, removing any tough parts. Tear the mushrooms lengthwise into strips about ½ inch (12 millimeters) wide; the exact size is not important as long as the strips are roughly the same size.

Place the mushrooms in a bowl filled with cold water and gently agitate them with your hands to dislodge any dirt. Lift them out, leaving the dirty water behind. If the mushrooms are particularly dirty, you may need to wash them a second time in fresh water.

The preserved foods my family makes every year (clockwise from top): cracked green olives; ground hot peppers in oil; preserved wild mushrooms; tomato *conserva*; tuna packed in oil; preserved eggplant; preserved tomatoes

Put the washed and drained mushrooms in a bowl and toss with the salt. Let stand for an hour. They will give off a lot of liquid. Drain the mushrooms and gently squeeze them to remove excess water.

Put the vinegar in an 8-quart (8-liter) pot and bring to a boil over high heat. Add the mushrooms and return to a boil, then boil until the skin on the mushroom caps is no longer leathery and you can pierce it easily with a fingernail, about 5 minutes. Drain the mushrooms and put them in a large colander. Top them with a heavy weight to squeeze out the liquid. A heavy pot smaller than the colander, filled with water, works well. Let the mushrooms drain under the weight for 15 minutes.

Lay several clean kitchen towels on a table covered with thick cardboard. Arrange the mushroom slices on the towels, spreading the slices apart. Let them air dry until they are no longer damp but still pliable, about 24 hours. Don't let them dry too long or they will become leathery.

Put the mushrooms in a bowl and toss with the olive oil, fennel seed, garlic, and hot peppers. Taste for salt, then let marinate at room temperature for 1 to 2 days.

Divide the mushrooms and their seasonings between two 1-pint (½-liter) glass jars. Pack them tightly, pushing down with a fork or spoon to remove any air gaps. Top with enough olive oil to submerge the mushrooms completely. Cover and refrigerate for at least 2 weeks before sampling to give the mushrooms time to absorb the seasonings.

Remove from the refrigerator about an hour before serving to allow the oil to liquefy. Return any leftover mushrooms to the refrigerator, topping with oil so the mushrooms remain completely submerged. If kept submerged in olive oil and refrigerated, the mushrooms will last for up to 6 months.

MAKES ABOUT 2 PINTS (1 LITER)

Zucchine Sott'Olio

ZUCCHINI PRESERVED IN OIL WITH HOT PEPPERS, GARLIC, AND MINT

My mother and I make 100 pounds (45 kilograms) or more of these preserved zucchini every summer. My cooking students love them, and I have convinced them that giant zucchini are fit for something other than the compost pile. For preserving, we like the zucchini to weigh 2 to 3 pounds (900 grams to 1½ kilograms) each so they are firm enough to support the marinade without breaking down. If you can't find such hefty zucchini at your local supermarket, ask at a farmers' market. Every grower has zucchini that have surpassed market size.

Preserved zucchini have a springy, slightly chewy texture that may remind you of rehydrated porcini. Like sponges, they soak up the vivid flavors of peppers, garlic, and mint. I often spoon them over small slices of Italian bread for an appetizer. You could also accompany with sliced *salumi* and olives for an easy mixed antipasto, or serve them as a sandwich complement, in place of a dill pickle.

5 pounds (2¼ kilograms) large zucchini, preferably 2 to 3 pounds (900 grams to 1.4 kilograms) each

½ cup (70 grams) kosher salt

3 cups (750 milliliters) white wine vinegar

¼ cup chopped fresh mint

5 garlic cloves, sliced crosswise

3 or 4 small fresh hot red peppers, or to taste, sliced crosswise

½ cup (125 milliliters) extra virgin olive oil, plus more for topping

CUT THE ZUCCHINI crosswise into 3-inch (8-centimeter) pieces. Cut each piece in half lengthwise, then cut out all the seeds and spongy pulp from the center. Slice each section crosswise ³⁄₁₆ inch (4½ millimeters) thick. (A mandoline or other manual vegetable slicer is helpful for this.)

Make layers of sliced zucchini and salt in a large bowl, then toss well. Macerate for 12 hours to draw the water out of the zucchini. Drain the zucchini, then squeeze a handful at a time to remove excess water.

Place the zucchini in a heavy nonreactive pot and add the vinegar and 1 cup (250 milliliters) water. The liquid should barely cover the zucchini.

Bring to a boil over high heat. Stir to redistribute the zucchini, then reduce the heat to medium and cook until the zucchini slices are cooked through but still whole, about 5 minutes. Do not allow them to break apart. Smaller zucchini will take less time.

Drain the zucchini and put them in a large colander. Top them with a heavy weight, such as a pot filled with water, to squeeze out the liquid. Let the zucchini drain under the weight for 15 minutes.

Lay several clean kitchen towels on a table covered with cardboard. Arrange the zucchini slices on the towels, spreading the slices apart. Let dry at room temperature until they feel a little leathery and are no longer damp, 24 to 48 hours. They will shrivel considerably.

Place the zucchini in a bowl and toss with the mint, garlic, hot peppers, and the ½ cup (125 milliliters) olive oil. Taste for salt and let the mixture marinate at room temperature for a day.

Transfer the zucchini to a 1-pint (½-liter) glass jar. Pack them in tightly, pushing them down with a fork or spoon to remove any air gaps. Top with olive oil so they are completely submerged. Cover and refrigerate for at least 2 weeks before sampling to give the zucchini time to absorb the seasonings.

Bring them out of the refrigerator about an hour before you plan to serve them to allow the oil to liquefy. Return any leftover zucchini to the refrigerator, topping with oil so the zucchini remain completely submerged. If kept submerged in olive oil and refrigerated, the zucchini will last for up to 6 months.

MAKES ABOUT 1 PINT (½ LITER)

Tonno Sott'Olio
FRESH TUNA PRESERVED UNDER OIL

High-quality tuna packed in oil is the pride of the Calabrian pantry. Calabrians who live near the Tyrrhenian coast and have access to superb local tuna in summer often preserve their own. Home-canned tuna is rich and creamy, with big, meaty chunks that you find only in the best commercial brands. It could hardly be easier to can your own, although to produce a safe product, you must have a pressure cooker, and you must follow the recommended cooking times and temperatures precisely. It is also important to start with the freshest possible fish.

Wait at least a month before opening your jars. Refrigerate jars after opening. Unopened jars will last at least a year and, according to the experts at Callipo, Calabria's most esteemed tuna processor, the flavor improves with age. Use *tonno sott'olio* in salads with boiled potatoes, green beans, and tomatoes; in pasta with fresh tomato; on pizza (page 135); or as part of an antipasto platter.

---

2 pounds (900 grams) fresh albacore or yellowfin (ahi) tuna steaks,
    1½ inches (4 centimeters) thick

⅔ cup (95 grams) kosher salt

Extra virgin olive oil for topping jars

PLACE 3 QUARTS (3 liters) water in a 6-quart (6-liter) pot and bring to a boil over high heat. Add the tuna and the salt. The water should cover the steaks.

Return the water to a boil, then reduce the heat to maintain a simmer. Cook for 2 hours, then measure the internal temperature of the tuna with an instant-read thermometer. It should read at least 165°F (75°C). Remove the fish from the water and set it on a clean kitchen towel or paper towels to absorb moisture. Place the fish in a sealed container and refrigerate overnight to firm and dry the meat.

The following day, cut away any discolored flesh or bloodline. Cut the meat into pieces that will fit in pint or half-pint canning jars. Fill the clean jars, pressing the fish in place to make a solid pack. Top the jars with olive oil, leaving 1 inch (2½ centimeters) of headspace. Cover the jars with new lids and rings, then process in a pressure cooker, following the manufacturer's directions, for 100 minutes at 10 psi. Let the jars cool, then store in a pantry or other cool place.

MAKES 2 PINTS OR 4 HALF-PINTS (1 LITER)

Alici Sotto Sale
SALT-CURED ANCHOVIES

Salted anchovies are a cornerstone of the Calabrian kitchen, and in my grandmother's day, almost every home had a big earthenware crock of them. When fresh anchovies were running—in May, June, and July—vendors would transport them on foot from the fishing boats in Scalea to the rural people who lived away from the coast. Today, many people have given up curing their own anchovies and instead buy them at the market. The cured fish are packed in salt in big bins, so customers can buy as few or as many as they need.

My mother always cured her own anchovies in Calabria, and she and I continue the annual ritual in California. Once a year, in late spring or early summer, we order several pounds of the tiny silvery fish from my local fish vendor and spend the better part of a morning cleaning them and layering them with salt in a beautiful crock we brought back from Calabria.

The salt draws moisture out of the anchovies, generating brine within hours. To keep the fish submerged in brine, you must weight them. The traditional procedure—which we follow, of course—calls for cutting an inch-thick (2½-centimeter-thick) disk of untreated wood slightly smaller in diameter than the crock. The wooden disk rests directly on top of the fish, and a weight goes on top of that. You could use a water-filled jar for your weight, but a river rock worn smooth by the current is traditional.

We don't scale the anchovies before salting them. The scales will come off when you rinse the anchovies prior to using them.

I can't claim that our home-cured anchovies are that much better than the excellent salt-packed anchovies from Sicily that many Italian markets carry in the United States. From a freshly opened tin, those anchovies are as moist, mild, and delectable as ours. But many stores don't know how to care for them properly. They sell the anchovies by weight from large tins to customers who only want a few, but the merchants don't keep the remaining anchovies properly covered with brine, so they quickly become rancid or dried out. No wonder many people think they don't like anchovies.

My mother and I do save a lot of money by curing our own anchovies—the fish cost almost nothing—but that is not our main motivation. We get great satisfaction from doing this project together, perpetuating a ritual that Calabrians have engaged in for generations. And we take enormous pride in bringing home-preserved food to the table.

Although anchovies can vary in size, you can figure about 3 dozen per pound on average.

2 pounds (900 grams) whole fresh anchovies
Approximately 1½ cups (8 ounces/225 grams) kosher salt, plus
    more as needed

CLEAN THE ANCHOVIES as directed on page 31. You do not need to scale them.

Choose a 2-quart (2-liter) earthenware or ceramic crock that is taller than it is wide so as to minimize evaporation. Make an ⅛-inch-thick (3-millimeter-thick) bed of salt in the bottom of the crock. Put a layer of anchovies on top of the salt, packing them snugly. Cover lightly with salt, using just enough to almost cover the anchovies. Press the salt in place with your hand. Repeat the layering of anchovies and salt, tucking the anchovy tails under if necessary so they don't poke through the salt. Finish with a slightly thicker layer of salt, using just enough so that you can't see the anchovies.

Leave the crock at room temperature for 24 hours, away from sunny windows where it might get warm. The salt will dissolve and a thin layer of brine will rise to the top. Top the fish with an inch-thick (2½-centimeter-thick) disk of untreated wood slightly smaller in diameter than the crock. Press firmly so the brine rises and completely submerges the anchovies. Top the disk with a 1-pound (450-gram) river rock or other weight that will not react with the brine.

Keep the crock in a cool, dark place, such as a pantry or wine cellar, for 3 months before trying the anchovies. Check weekly to make sure the anchovies remain submerged, as some brine will evaporate. Add more cold water if necessary to keep the anchovies submerged.

The anchovies are ready to eat after 3 months and will last for a year or more as long as they are constantly covered with brine.

To use, lift out as many anchovies as you need and rinse them well, then pat them dry. Replace the wooden disk and the weight in the crock and return the crock to a cool place.

ABOUT 6 DOZEN ANCHOVIES

Zucchine Seccate al Sole

SUN-DRIED ZUCCHINI

Calabrians preserve their abundant zucchini harvest in several clever ways. One method is to slice and dry them under the hot summer sun. If you visit Calabria in midsummer, you will see the drying trays set up wherever people have a little space behind their house. The relentless sun evaporates all the moisture, shriveling the zucchini slices until they look like pale dried porcini. Once dried, zucchini will keep for a year in the pantry.

In winter, we reconstitute them in water, then sauté them in olive oil with garlic and ground hot red pepper (page 303). After cooking, the dried zucchini have a springy texture and concentrated flavor reminiscent of mushrooms. Calabrians eat them as a side dish or add them to pasta with tomato sauce, but you could spoon them over sliced bread for a warm antipasto. They are a surprise to many Americans who know only about sun-dried tomatoes.

Save your biggest garden zucchini for sun drying, or ask a farmer at the farmers' market to supply you with the oversize ones that most shoppers don't want.

Large unblemished zucchini

Sheets of heavy cardboard

CUT THE ZUCCHINI crosswise into 4- to 5-inch (10- to 13-centimeter) chunks, then cut each chunk in half lengthwise. If the zucchini have obvious seed cavities with noticeable seeds, use a small spoon to hollow out the seed cavity. Slice all the zucchini crosswise about ¼ inch thick (6 millimeters thick).

Top the cardboard sheets with clean kitchen towels. Place the zucchini slices on the towels so that the slices aren't touching. Put the cardboard sheets on a table in a sunny spot outdoors.

Let dry for 24 hours, then turn the slices over and let dry for another 24 hours. Turn again and let dry for a third day. In hot, sunny weather, the zucchini should be completely dry in three days. If not, keep them under the sun, turning daily, until fully dry and slightly leathery.

Transfer to a paper bag or plastic food-storage bag and keep in a cool, dark area or in the freezer.

10 POUNDS (4½ KILOGRAMS) FRESH ZUCCHINI YIELDS APPROXIMATELY 10 OUNCES (300 GRAMS) DRIED ZUCCHINI

Variation

You can dry eggplants by the same process. If using slender Italian- or Asian-type eggplants, halve them lengthwise. If using large globe eggplants, quarter them lengthwise. Do not peel the eggplants. Cut into 4- to 5-inch (10- to 13-centimeter) chunks. Do not remove any seeds. Slice each piece lengthwise into strips about ⅜ inch (9 millimeters) thick. Arrange on towel-lined cardboard sheets, as for zucchini, and follow the same procedure for sun drying. The eggplants should be dry in 3 to 4 days, depending on the weather.

Peperoni Seccati al Sole
SUN-DRIED SWEET PEPPERS

Throughout the province of Cosenza, in late summer, people harvest the long sweet peppers from their gardens, thread them on sturdy twine, and string them up outdoors to dry. In Calabria's summer heat, the peppers quickly lose their moisture, becoming leathery and dry enough in a month or so to store for the winter. Even city people who don't have gardens will buy the fresh peppers, already strung, from a local market and dangle the drying *ristras* from their balconies. These are the same sweet peppers that, when fully dried and ground, produce *pepe rosso* (Calabrian Sweet Paprika, page 304), an essential ingredient in Calabrian sausage and some sauces. But in the province of Cosenza, and rarely elsewhere, home cooks keep many of their dried peppers whole. Like other natives of the Cosentino (the province of Cosenza), my mother and I add these sun-dried sweet peppers to braised rabbit (page 222) and use them in fritters (page 37). She also cooks them with potatoes in winter. Once rehydrated, dried sweet peppers have the sun-sweetened flavor of ripe red peppers but are even more concentrated.

TO MAKE SUN-DRIED SWEET PEPPERS, you need long, sweet Italian peppers, such as the variety that seed catalogs call "Sweet Italian." Farmers' markets are the best source for these elongated peppers, which have a more intense flavor and thinner walls than the square-shaped bell pepper. If you are growing them yourself, pick them when they are fully mature in size but just before they begin to change from green to red. If you let them ripen on the plant before drying them, they will make excellent *pepe rosso*, but they will not be good for cooking because the reconstituted flesh will be soft and tend to pull away from the papery skin.

Spread these underripe peppers on a sheet of cardboard large enough to hold them in a single layer without touching. Place them outdoors in a warm, well-ventilated area where they are not exposed to direct sun. You can put them on a table in the shade of a tree or under an awning, or even indoors by a warm window or in an airy garage. My mother makes a *ristra* with a heavy needle threaded with kitchen twine, stringing the peppers together through their stems. Then she hangs the *ristra* from a hook in a warm but shady spot.

Leave the peppers undisturbed until they become fully red, which may take up to two months. If rain threatens, bring them in until dry weather returns.

Sweet Italian peppers drying in my parents' garden in Oakland

In Calabria, the weather in late summer and early fall is hot enough to dry the peppers thoroughly. If you live in a climate where summer daytime temperatures are regularly 80°F (27°F) or above, you may also be able to dry them completely outdoors. They are fully dry when they feel leathery and almost crisp. More likely, the peppers will turn fully red before they are fully dry, and the weather will become too cool for the peppers to dry further. In that event, you will need to complete the drying inside, either in a dehydrator or in a warm, well-ventilated area.

To complete the drying indoors, remove the pepper stems and seeds and open the peppers flat. If your dehydrator has a thermostat, set it at 115°F (46°C). Keep the peppers in the dehydrator until

My father making a *ristra* of his homegrown sweet peppers

they are completely dry to the touch and leathery, about 10 hours, depending on how dry they were initially. Alternatively, put the flattened peppers on a tray and keep them in a warm area, such as above the refrigerator, until they are completely dry to the touch and leathery.

Let cool completely, then store in heavy-duty freezer bags in a pantry or in the freezer. They will keep for up to a year.

Pomodori Pelati
HOME-CANNED PEELED TOMATOES

My family has always canned enough of our homegrown San Marzano tomatoes to last us through the winter. I had never even tasted store-bought canned tomatoes until I began to teach cooking and needed to know what my students had to work with. Now that I've experienced the difficulty of finding high-quality canned tomatoes without undesirable additives (page 11), I'm even more motivated to can enough tomatoes for my winter needs—an amount that has grown along with my classes—and to encourage my students to do so. Working side-by-side with my mother, I put up about 100 quarts (100 liters) of tomatoes from my garden every year.

Until perhaps the middle of the last century, Calabrians were more likely to make *conserva* (sun-dried tomato paste, page 299) than to can whole peeled tomatoes. The *conserva* could be stored safely under a film of olive oil; the whole tomatoes had to be sealed in bottles, and glass was costly. Even today, Calabrians making preserves at home don't use anything resembling our Mason jars. They recycle the bottles they have, such as juice bottles and beer bottles. My grandmother, like other Calabrians of her day, used empty wine bottles and Coke bottles.

You might wonder how you get peeled tomatoes inside a wine bottle, and I can tell you, having filled hundreds of bottles as a child, that it isn't easy. My mother or grandmother would quarter the peeled plum tomatoes lengthwise, then I would feed one quarter at a time into the bottle. The bottles were sealed with corks and tied with an elaborate knot that my mother still recalls today. The knot kept the corks from pushing up when the bottles were processed. To remove the tomatoes, my grandparents had devised a long wire with a hook on the end. It was a pain to fill the bottles and a pain to pull the tomatoes out, but my grandmother wouldn't consent to canning puree, as her neighbors did. She preferred a chunky tomato sauce, and I do, too.

You don't have to use San Marzano or even plum-type tomatoes for canning. Any variety will do as long as it is fully ripe, even a little soft. Home gardens and farmers' markets are the best sources for dead-ripe tomatoes. If they're still a little firm when you buy them, leave them at room temperature for several days until they have fully colored up and softened.

Cleanliness is extremely important when canning. Make sure your tomatoes are well washed and that your jars, lids, tongs, and towels are pristine, too.

NOTE: The USDA recommends adding 2 tablespoons of bottled lemon juice per quart of tomatoes to prevent botulism. This is not Calabrian practice, and my mother and I have never done this. But if you are concerned that your tomatoes are not sufficiently high in acid, you should follow the USDA recommendation.

Unblemished vine-ripened tomatoes

RINSE THE TOMATOES WELL. Put 3 quarts (3 liters) of water in a 6-quart (6-liter) pot and bring to a boil over high heat. Prepare a large bowl of ice water. Immerse the tomatoes in the boiling water until you see the first sign of a split skin, 20 to 45 seconds, depending on ripeness. With a slotted spoon, remove the tomatoes immediately to the ice bath. When they're cool, slip off the skins and cut out the core. To remove the seeds, cut plum tomatoes (such as San Marzano and Roma types) lengthwise and scoop out the seeds with your fingers. If using large, round tomatoes, cut them in half horizontally, scoop out the seeds, then cut each half into large chunks. Plum tomatoes can be left as halves.

Drain the tomatoes in a colander for 30 minutes.

Pack the tomatoes tightly in 1-quart (1-liter) jars, following the Master Directions for Water-Bath Processing (page 273). As you pack them, prod them with the end of a wooden spoon to remove air gaps, but don't use so much force that you crush the tomatoes. Seal the jars and process the tomatoes according to the Master Directions, processing for an hour.

2½ TO 3 POUNDS (1⅛ TO 1½ KILOGRAMS) TOMATOES WILL FILL A 1-QUART (1-LITER) JAR

My mother peeling San Marzano tomatoes for canning

Homemade tomato *conserva* before I pack it in jars

Conserva di Pomodori
HOMEMADE TOMATO PASTE

In Calabria, even today, *conserva* is dried under the hot Mediterranean sun. Spread on a big wooden slab and brought inside at night, tomato puree dries to a thick paste in three to four days. When my grandmother was young, she and her neighbors around Verbicaro never put up whole tomatoes or tomato puree. They didn't know about water-bath canning. Instead, making *conserva* was the way they preserved their tomato harvest for the winter. Because it is so high in salt and low in moisture, it does not need to be processed in a water bath like canned tomatoes. Most Calabrians keep their *conserva* in crocks in the pantry, sealed with olive oil.

In my grandmother's day, people used *conserva* for their winter tomato sauce. They would sauté some garlic, then add a few tablespoons of *conserva* and some water and simmer until the *conserva* dissolved. Today, most cooks use *conserva* to add depth to sauces made with canned tomatoes, or to *ragù*.

Like many time-consuming kitchen arts, making *conserva* is not as common as it used to be. When my mother was young, every rural housewife made time for it. Although you can still see the big trays with their brick-red topping in rural Calabria, and sometimes on suburban balconies, many people have given up making it. When you do find it for sale, it is priced like gold.

Homemade *conserva* has a deep, mellow, caramelized flavor wholly unlike the acidic taste of canned tomato paste. I dole out this precious preserve by the teaspoon to add depth to braised lamb shanks or goat *sugo*. Often, after tasting these *conserva*-enriched dishes, guests ask me, "Why is this so good?"

If you know you will have three to four consecutive days of 100°F (38°C) weather, you can dry the tomato puree under the sun instead of in the convection oven. Follow the recipe in every other respect, and bring the tray in at night so it doesn't get damp.

Use only fully ripe, fragrant summer tomatoes for *conserva*, preferably from a farmers' market or home garden. It is not worth going to the trouble of making it with standard supermarket tomatoes. I use the San Marzano tomatoes my father grows, but you can use any type of ripe plum tomato or salad tomato.

When using *conserva*, always salt the dish after you have added the *conserva*, as the paste is quite salty.

10 pounds (4½ kilograms) very ripe tomatoes

¼ cup (35 grams) kosher salt

1 tablespoon extra virgin olive oil, plus more for topping jars

CORE THE TOMATOES. Cut them in half lengthwise if they are the plum type, in quarters if they are the large, round salad type. Remove the seeds with your fingers. Put all the tomatoes in an 8-quart (8-liter) stainless steel pot. Bring to a boil, stirring occasionally until the tomatoes release their juice. Boil briskly for 30 minutes to soften the tomatoes and reduce the juice.

Pass the tomatoes through a food mill fitted with a fine disk to remove the skins and seeds. Return the tomato puree to the same pot and set over high heat. Stir in the salt and simmer until the puree has reduced to about 1 quart (1 liter), 45 to 55 minutes. Turn the heat down as the puree thickens to prevent it from bubbling and splattering furiously, and stir often near the end to prevent scorching.

With the 1 tablespoon olive oil, lightly oil a 12- by 17-inch (30- by 43-centimeter) rimmed nonaluminum baking sheet. With a rubber spatula, spread the thick tomato puree in an even layer. It should cover the baking sheet.

Preheat the oven to 200°F (93°C) and turn on the convection fan. Place the baking sheet on a center rack and cook for 30 minutes. Remove the baking sheet from the oven and stir the puree with a rubber spatula so that it dries evenly and doesn't form a crust. Re-spread the puree with the spatula into a rectangle about ⅛ inch (3 millimeters) thick. Be fanatical about spreading it evenly; if any part is too thin, it may burn. Because of evaporation, the puree will no longer cover the baking sheet. With a paper towel, remove any bits of tomato that cling to the edges or exposed bottom of the baking sheet, or they will burn.

Return the baking sheet to the oven and continue baking until the tomato puree is no longer saucelike but very thick, stiff, and a little sticky, about 3 hours total. Every 20 minutes, stir and carefully re-spread the puree as before; the rectangle will become progressively smaller as water evaporates.

Let the *conserva* cool, then pack tightly in a clean jar with a spoon, tamping it down to make sure there are no air pockets. Level the surface with the back of the spoon. Cover completely with olive oil so that the paste is not exposed and refrigerate. After every use, level the surface of the paste and top with more oil so the paste remains completely submerged. It will keep in the refrigerator for at least a year.

MAKES ABOUT 1 PINT

Conserva di Peperoni
HOMEMADE SWEET PEPPER PASTE

As summer fades to fall and the sweet peppers in Calabrian gardens ripen to all-over red, traditionalists like my parents make *conserva di peperoni*. Like *conserva di pomodori* (page 299) or tomato paste, this thick, smooth preserve of sweet peppers and salt enhances dishes in the bleak winter months. A spoonful adds color and sweetness to tomato sauce, beans, salt-cod preparations, lamb or rabbit stew, and *pasta e fagioli* (pasta and bean soup). My mother sometimes puts a spoonful in the boiling water before adding polenta. Her mother would make a rudimentary winter pasta topping by sautéing garlic in olive oil, then adding *conserva di pomodori*, *conserva di peperoni*, and enough water to achieve a sauce.

Sadly, many Calabrians have abandoned the *conserva* tradition, now that their markets abound with produce all year. But nothing available in a jar or tube comes close to the concentrated taste of this condiment, and if you could find it, it would cost a fortune. It takes five pounds (2¼ kilograms) of ripe peppers to make a little more than a cup (250 milliliters).

When my parents were growing up, people still made *conserva di peperoni* on trays in the sun. Today, we use a convection oven, which is faster and more dependable in my coastal California climate. The method is easy. The only tedious part is passing the cooked peppers through the food mill to eliminate the skins. When my mother was young, they didn't throw away the pulpy residue from the food mill, the part that didn't pass through the screen. They would spread it on trays, dry it outdoors, and grind it for paprika.

---

5 pounds (2¼ kilograms) sweet Italian peppers *or* richly colored red
    bell peppers

2 tablespoons kosher salt

1 tablespoon extra virgin olive oil, plus more for topping jars

---

HALVE THE PEPPERS and remove the stems and seeds. Cut each half in half again crosswise, then cut into ½-inch-wide (12-millimeter-wide) strips. Put the peppers in an 8-quart (8-liter) pot with 1 quart (1 liter) water and the salt. Bring to a boil over high heat. Cook at a brisk boil, stirring often, until the peppers are completely soft and there is no liquid remaining, 45 minutes to 1 hour. Pass the peppers through a food mill fitted with the fine disk to make a thick, skinless puree.

Put the pepper puree in a 4-quart (4-liter) saucepan over medium heat. Simmer until reduced to 1 quart (1 liter), about 10 minutes.

With 1 tablespoon oil, lightly oil a 12- by 17-inch (30- by 43-centimeter) rimmed nonaluminum baking sheet. With a rubber spatula, spread the thick puree in an even layer. It should cover the baking sheet.

Preheat the oven to 200°F (93°C) and turn on the convection fan. Place the baking sheet on a center rack and cook for one hour. Remove the baking sheet from the oven and stir the puree with a rubber spatula so that it dries evenly and doesn't form a crust. Re-spread the puree with the spatula into a rectangle about ⅛ inch (3 millimeters) thick. Be fanatical about spreading it evenly; if any part is too thin, it may burn. Because of the evaporation, the puree will no longer cover the baking sheet.

Return the baking sheet to the oven and continue baking until the puree is no longer saucelike but as thick as tomato paste, about 2½ hours total. Every 30 minutes, stir and carefully re-spread the puree as before; the rectangle will become progressively smaller as water evaporates.

Let the *conserva* cool, then pack tightly in a clean jar with a spoon, tamping it down to make sure there are no air pockets. Level the surface with the back of the spoon. Cover completely with olive oil so that the paste is not exposed and refrigerate. It will keep for at least a year as long as you religiously top the surface with olive oil every time you remove some *conserva*.

MAKES ABOUT 1¼ CUPS (300 MILLILITERS)

Peperoncino

GROUND HOT RED PEPPER

Calabria's signature seasoning, *peperoncino* in a shaker jar, is on my dining table at lunch and dinner. Everyone has a different tolerance for heat, so I season dishes cautiously and let my family and guests add more *peperoncino* to taste. Whole dried cayenne peppers, available in Chinese and Latin markets, are the closest I have found to the dried *peperoncini* in Calabria. They must be dried further in a low oven to render them crisp enough to grind.

The ground *peperoncino* that you buy in Calabria has been sieved to remove the seeds. My mother and I do not do this at home, but you can sieve the ground pepper if you like.

½ pound small whole dried hot red peppers, about 2 inches long,
    such as cayenne, stem and cap removed

PREHEAT THE OVEN to the lowest possible setting, preferably around 140°F (60°C) but no higher than 160°F (70°C). Dry the hot peppers on a baking sheet in the oven for 4 hours, then turn the oven off and let the peppers remain in the oven overnight, or for about 12 hours. They will be dry and crunchy, and you will be able to hear the seeds rattle inside.

Remove them from the oven and transfer them to a blender. Do not let the peppers rest long at room temperature before grinding them or they may absorb moisture and lose some crispness. Blend as fine as possible. **Important:** To avoid inhaling pepper fumes, let the ground pepper settle in the blender jar for at least 5 minutes before removing the blender lid. Keep your face averted as you remove the lid. Transfer the ground pepper to a clean glass jar, and keep in a cool, dark place, or in the freezer. It will last for up to a year.

MAKES ABOUT 1½ CUPS GROUND HOT RED PEPPER

Pepe Rosso
CALABRIAN SWEET PAPRIKA

This mild seasoning adds sweetness and rich color to many Calabrian dishes, especially in the Cosentino, the region where I was raised. I use it liberally in Sun-Dried Zucchini with Calabrian Paprika (page 248), Dry-Cured Black Olives with Hot Red Pepper and Fennel (page 27), and numerous other dishes.

TO MAKE CALABRIAN SWEET PAPRIKA, you need long, sweet Italian peppers, such as the variety that seed catalogs call "Sweet Italian." Farmers' markets are the best source for these elongated peppers, which have a more intense flavor and thinner walls than the square-shaped bell pepper. For *pepe rosso*, they should be fully ripe and red all over.

Spread these ripe peppers in a single layer on a large sheet of cardboard. Place them outdoors in a warm, well-ventilated area where they are not exposed to direct sun. You can put them on a table in the shade of a tree or under an awning, or even indoors by a warm window or in an airy garage. My mother makes a *ristra* with a heavy needle threaded with kitchen twine, stringing the peppers together through their stems. Then she hangs the *ristra* from a hook in a warm but shady spot.

Leave the peppers undisturbed until they are fully dry, which may take one to two months. They should feel leathery and almost crisp. In Calabria, the weather in late summer and early fall remains hot enough that the peppers dry thoroughly outdoors. If you live in a warm climate, you may also be able to dry them completely outdoors. More likely, the weather will turn cool before the peppers are fully dry. If you do not have several hours a day at 70°F (21°C) or warmer, you will need to complete the drying inside, either in a dehydrator or in a warm, well-ventilated area. My mother places hers on top of the refrigerator.

To complete the drying indoors, remove the pepper stems and seeds and open the peppers flat. If your dehydrator has a thermostat, set it at 115°F (46°C). Keep the peppers in the dehydrator until they are completely dry to the touch and leathery, about 10 hours, depending on how dry they were initially. Alternatively, put the flattened peppers on a tray and keep them in a warm area, such as above the refigerator, until they are completely dry to the touch and leathery.

Let cool completely, then store in heavy-duty freezer bags in a pantry or in the freezer until you want to grind some for *pepe rosso*. They will keep for up to a year.

To make *pepe rosso*, the peppers must be dried further in a low oven to render them crisp enough to grind.

Preheat the oven to the lowest possible setting, preferably around 140°F (60°C) but no higher than 160°F (70°C). Put the dried peppers on a baking sheet in the oven for 4 hours, then turn the oven off and let the peppers remain in the oven overnight, or for about 12 hours. They will be crisp and crunchy.

Remove them from the oven and transfer them to a blender. Do not let the peppers rest long at room temperature before grinding them or they may absorb moisture and lose some crispness. Blend as fine as possible. Transfer the ground pepper to a clean glass jar, and keep in a cool, dark place, or in the freezer. It will last for up to a year.

Liquore al Mandarino
MANDARIN ORANGE LIQUEUR

When you visit someone at home in Calabria, you will practically be barred from leaving until you have shared a glass of *liquore* with your host. Within minutes of your arrival, out will come the serving tray set with tiny cut-crystal glasses and a bottle of fragrant and probably homemade liqueur. Urging visitors to have a *bicchierino* (a little glass) is part of Calabrian hospitality, and the same goes for restaurants, where waiters apparently find it astonishing that you might end your meal without a *digestivo.* No wedding, baptism, birth, or holiday passes without a celebratory round (or more) of *liquori.* Typically, at the end of the feast that marks all these occasions, the tray and the bottle make their rounds at the table. The men have the *liquore,* the women have *rosolio,* a similar concoction but sweeter and lower in alcohol.

Rural Calabrians have long preserved their orchard fruits in grain alcohol, first extracting the aromas via infusion, then straining out the fruit and sweetening the base with sugar syrup. Peaches, nectarines, strawberries, raspberries, prickly pear, citrus, and many other fruits are captured in the bottle this way. But Calabrians don't stop with fruit. They make *liquori* from fresh herbs, such as mint and wild fennel; flowers, such as roses, violets, and citron blossoms; coffee beans; hazelnuts; and even hot peppers. At the lovely Villa San Domenico in Morano Calabro, I sampled the owner's porcini liqueur and ginseng liqueur—peculiar beverages, to my taste, but a sign of the fondness Calabrians have for this after-dinner ritual.

My cousin Maria makes a *liquore ai cinque agrumi* (five-citrus liqueur) with the peels from orange, lemon, lime, citron, and mandarin orange. I have adapted her method to mandarins only, as citrons are difficult to find. Try to choose mandarin oranges with tight, not puffy, skins. If the skins are puffy and loose, pulling away from the flesh, you may have a hard time removing the zest in strips. If possible, purchase your fruit at a farmers' market where you can verify that it has not been sprayed with chemicals or waxed.

2 pounds (900 grams) tight-skinned organic mandarin oranges

1 bottle (750 milliliters) 151-proof grain alcohol, such as Everclear

2 cups (410 grams) sugar

WITH A SHARP vegetable peeler, remove the orange zest in wide strips, taking care to remove only the orange part and none of the bitter white pith.

Pour the alcohol in a 1-liter European-style canning jar with a rubber gasket and clamp lid, or any other jar of comparable size with a tight-fitting lid. Add the strips of orange zest. Close the jar and leave to infuse for one week in a cool, dark place, such as a pantry or wine cellar.

After one week, you can strain and sweeten the infusion. Place 4 cups (1 liter) water and the sugar in a 3- to 4-quart (3- to 4-liter) saucepan over low heat. Stir until the sugar dissolves and the syrup becomes clear. Remove from the heat and cool completely to room temperature. Proper cooling is important: if the sugar syrup is warm when added to the infusion, the finished liqueur will be cloudy.

Strain the infusion through a fine sieve. Stir in the sugar syrup and mix well. Decant the liqueur into clean bottles or jars. Seal with a cork or lid. Let mature for at least one week in a cool, dark place to allow the components to blend. The liqueur will keep indefinitely. *Mandarino* should be served chilled in small glasses, so refrigerate for several hours before serving. Keep opened bottles in the refrigerator.

MAKES 2 QUARTS (2 LITERS)

Limoncello Variation

Substitute 2 pounds (900 grams) organic Eureka or Meyer lemons for the mandarin oranges.

Fragolino Variation

Substitute 1 pint (450 grams) organic strawberries, hulled but left whole, for the mandarin oranges. In Calabria, people gather the tiny, intensely fragrant, wild woodland strawberries (*fragolini*), identical to French *fraises des bois*, for liqueur and *rosolio*.

Variation for Rosolio

To make *rosolio*, which is sweeter and less alcoholic than *liquore*, raise the water to 6 cups (1½ liters) and the sugar to 4 cups (825 grams).

Scorze d'Arance Candite
CANDIED ORANGE PEEL

My most requested recipe, these sugar-dusted, supple slices of orange peel are a homemade solution to the outrageously expensive (and not very tasty) candied orange peel in stores. I use this exquisite candied peel in Sicilian desserts, such as cassata and cannoli, and fold it into homemade ricotta ice cream (page 345) or into the ricotta filling for sweet ravioli (page 322). My daughter eats the peel like candy, and I have to hide the container in the freezer or it would be emptied in no time. The peel must be blanched five times to remove any trace of bitterness, but the painstaking method produces results finer than anything you can buy. The slices are pretty enough to package in a decorative jar as a holiday gift.

5 large navel oranges with thick peel, unsprayed

4 cups (800 grams) sugar, plus more for coating

2 tablespoons lemon juice

WITH A PARING KNIFE, cut the peel of each orange into strips roughly the shape of a marquise diamond, about 1 inch (2½ centimeters) wide at the widest part and pointed at the tips, slicing from stem end to blossom end and cutting all the way through the peel—the colored zest and white pith—but not into the juicy flesh. Remove each strip as you cut it; it will release from the flesh easily.

Place the peels in a 4-quart (4-liter) stainless saucepan and add 2 quarts (2 liters) cold water. Bring to a boil over high heat and boil for 2 minutes. Drain and repeat two more times. After the third blanching, drain the peels and return them to the pot. Cover with cold water and let stand until cool, then drain again.

With a paring knife, slice about half of the softened white pith off the peel, leaving a cushion of about ⅛ inch (3 millimeters). If you remove all the pith, the peel will be too thin and floppy. When you have pared all the strips, return them to the pot, and repeat the 2-minute boiling two more times, for a total of five times.

Put the sugar in the 4-quart (4-liter) stainless steel saucepan. Add the lemon juice and 2 cups (500 milliliters) water. Bring to a boil over high heat, stirring occasionally until the sugar dissolves, then reduce the heat to maintain a steady but not vigorous boil and cook for 15 minutes to thicken the syrup. Add the drained peels. Cook at a gentle simmer, stirring occasionally, until the peels look glassy and translucent, about one hour. To test, remove one strip and let it cool slightly. You should almost be able to see through it.

Remove the peels from the heat and let them cool in the syrup overnight. The peels will plump in the syrup, and the syrup will thicken considerably. The next morning, set a wire rack over a cookie sheet. Transfer each strip to the rack by hand, letting excess syrup drip back into the saucepan. Use your fingers to scrape excess syrup from the peels; they should not be dripping. Let them dry on the rack until they are no longer tacky, about 24 hours.

Oranges at a Vibo Valentia market that sells only local ingredients

Make a bed of sugar in a flat dish and press each strip in the sugar until evenly coated on both sides, patting the sugar into place. Return the strips to the rack and let stand at room temperature overnight to dry further.

To store, layer the peels in a plastic container with parchment paper between each layer so they don't stick to each other. They will last in the freezer indefinitely.

MAKES ABOUT 3 DOZEN

Mostaccioli (page 326) decorated with colored foil

Dolci
desserts

As a child in Verbicaro, I rarely had the pleasure of a homemade dessert because our kitchen had only a wood-burning oven. With no thermostat to control the temperature, it couldn't be relied on to produce uniform cakes or evenly browned cookies. On my birthday, when my mother would attempt to make a plain sponge cake in the oven, she would literally pray for good results and instruct everyone in the house to step lightly.

By the time I went to middle school, a *pasticceria*, or pastry shop, had opened in Verbicaro. On the way to school or on the way home, I would spend my pocket money on a pastry, temporarily appeasing a sweet tooth that persists today. My favorite treat, *il bombolone*, resembled a doughnut filled with pastry cream. Like an American child eager for Halloween, I could hardly wait for the next baptism, communion, or wedding, or the next important Catholic saint's day, knowing that the local women would prepare their best *dolci* and supplement with delights from the pastry shop.

More than any other Calabrian dishes, the region's sweets are intertwined with religion. Desserts are not part of the daily table, but almost every religious holiday has its associated pastry. For Calabrians of earlier times who lived lives of almost ceaseless privation, these religious holidays and their ritual sweets provided some of the year's few pleasures.

Because most of Calabria lacks the climate and landscape for dairy cattle, cooks developed a dessert repertoire largely devoid of butter, milk, and cream. Sugar was almost unknown in the region until the late 1800s, and was scarce and costly until after World War II; so most desserts relied for a sweetener on honey, available free to anyone who knew how to harvest it, or on *mosto cotto*, cooked-down grape must, or juice. Eggs, a valuable protein source, were rarely squandered on desserts. (Even today, if I put six eggs in my pastry cream, my mother says that four will do.)

Still, Calabria's inventive cooks managed to devise an impressive variety of desserts, enough to celebrate saints' days throughout the year and provide a groaning board at Christmas and Easter. For ingredients, they turned to dried figs and raisins; the aforementioned honey and *mosto cotto*; chestnuts, almonds, and walnuts; wheat flour; ricotta; citrus; and wines and homemade liqueurs. For fat, they had olive oil and lard. For aroma, they had the abundant wild fennel seed and black anise seed.

Many older Calabrian desserts are simple doughs shaped in numerous ways and fried in olive oil, reflecting the lack of baking implements and chemical leavening until modern times. People may not have had baking sheets and cake pans, but everyone had a pot for frying on top of the stove. These sweet fritters and their many variations include *anime beate* ("blessed souls," similar to cream puffs but with marmalade inside in place of whipped cream); *cannariculi* or *turdilli* (a fried ridged pastry with a honey glaze, page 316); *chiacchiere* (the same dough in a twisted ribbon shape); *chinulille* (sweet fried ravioli with a ricotta filling, page 322); *chinule* (fried chestnut ravioli with a honey glaze, page 319), and *ciambelline alla Calabrese* (a yeast dough with raisins, shaped into rings and fried). There are dozens more desserts in the same vein, many of ancient Greek origin.

Today, Calabrians have embraced the luscious pastries of Naples and Sicily, rich with pastry cream, chocolate, and sugar. Although you will find buttery pastries and cream-filled cakes in the region's pastry shops, as well as Neapolitan *sfogliatelle* (a flaky shell-shaped pastry) and Sicilian ricotta-filled *cannoli*, these sweets are relatively recent arrivals and not rooted in local tradition. Lacking the usual pastry ingredients and, until modern times, refrigeration, the region's cooks turned their talents to sweets that would last. Their creativity produced rustic but still beloved treats like *panicelli* (page 330), little packages of Zibibbo raisins and citron wrapped in citron leaves and baked; *mostaccioli* (page 326), sturdy honey and almond cookies with a seemingly infinite lifespan; and *crocette* (page 336), walnut-stuffed and baked dried figs, which I think of as Calabria's energy bars.

December is the month most rewarding to the Calabrian sweet tooth (which, it must be said, doesn't begin to compare to the famous Sicilian sweet tooth). Two weeks before Christmas, on December 13, Calabrians celebrate the *festa di Santa Lucia* with a dessert called *la cuccia*, a porridge-like dish of cooked wheat mixed with *mosto cotto* and nuts. It commemorates a miracle attributed to her, in which a ship full of grain showed up in Palermo, in Sicily, when the people there were starving and praying to Santa Lucia for help.

In the Cosenza region, where I am from, Christmas means *grispelle*, warm yeasted fritters drizzled with honey (page 324). (Made in a ring shape, they are *cud-durieddi*.) If I made *grispelle* at any other time of year, my family would think I had lost my mind—akin to an American making fruitcake in July. *Cannariculi* (page 316) are also traditional at Christmas in the Cosentino, as is *pitta 'mpigliata* (page 338), pastry rosettes with a filling of walnuts, raisins, and cinnamon.

Scalille (or *scalidde*), meaning "ladders," are Christmas fritters made with a dough similar to the *cannariculi* dough but shaped either to resemble a ladder, with two long parallel sides and shorter cross bars; or in a long corkscrew-like spiral made by wrapping a rope of dough around the handle of a wooden spoon, then dipping the spoon into the hot oil. According to Ottavio Cavalcanti, a Calabrian scholar with deep knowledge of the local food traditions, the ladder and spiral shapes symbolize the possibility of rising to heaven.

In the southern part of Calabria, in the region of Reggio Calabria, the Christmas dessert table will likely include *petrali*, half-moon turnovers filled with dried figs, nuts, chocolate, *mosto cotto*, orange peel, and candied citron and glazed with white or chocolate icing; and *pignolata* (page 316), tiny fritters about the size of chick peas glazed with lemon or chocolate icing.

For the feast of Carnevale, which precedes the forty days of Lent, Calabrians make *chiacchiere* and *cicirata* (page 318), using the same dough as for *cannariculi* but shaping it differently. The *cicirata* are the size of chick peas; the *chiacchiere* resemble little bowties.

For Easter, tradition-minded Calabrian housewives bake sweet breads decorated with hard-cooked eggs. The symbolic egg, with its promise of new life, recalls the resurrection of Christ. These festive breads are known as *buccellati* in the Cosenza region and as *cuzzupe* or *cuddure* in other parts of Calabria. Nowadays, some home cooks also prepare *pastiera*, a wheat-berry and ricotta tart that came to Calabria via Naples.

Most of the *feste*, or saints' holidays, are clustered in summer, for reasons that probably have little to do with religion. Every town has its patron saint, celebrated once a year in that town with an elaborate procession after Sunday Mass. A life-size statue of the saint is carried from the church through the town streets, with much revelry, then everyone goes home for a major lunch around one P.M. Because it is a saint's holiday, lunch ends with dessert, probably purchased from the local bakery that morning. Those who don't get to the bakery early can be out of luck.

You don't have to travel far in Calabria to find a *festa* on a summer weekend. Although these holidays have their roots in religion and maintain a religious veneer, they have become more secular in modern times. Today, a musical event of some sort takes place in the town square on the night before the *festa*, and towns compete to draw the most famous performers. After lunch on the day of the *festa*, all the town residents descend on the square for a *passeggiata*, or stroll, and vendors set up stalls selling *mostaccioli*, peanuts, ice cream, and children's toys.

Gelaterie (ice cream shops) flourish in Calabria, although most Calabrians don't consider ice cream a dessert appropriate for the end of a meal. It is, instead, a refreshment, eaten at the beach in summer or in the late afternoon on a sizzling day in the futile hope that it might cool you off. Most *gelaterie* make their product on the premises, with the accent on local ingredients and seasonal fruits. Calabria is the place to try ice cream made with figs, mulberries, prickly pear, ricotta, or licorice; or a granita from citron, fresh mint, almond milk, or watermelon. In Reggio Calabria, people even eat gelato for breakfast, tucking it into a brioche and enjoying it with their morning cappuccino.

The predecessor of modern sorbets and granitas is Calabria's *scirobetta*, a literal "snow cone" made by drizzling citrus juice or *mosto cotto* over fresh snow. In times past, Calabrian men would make their *scirobetta* with wine, while the women and children had a nonalcoholic version. I introduced my children to *scirobetta* when they were young, and even now, as teenagers, they love to scoop up newly fallen snow when we are in the mountains, top it with orange juice and sugar, and race to consume their primitive sorbet before it melts.

For the most part, everyday meals in Calabria end not with dessert but with fresh seasonal fruit: a bowl of cherries, fragrant peaches, plump grapes, or homegrown apples stored under straw so they stay crisp into winter. On a steamy summer evening, no dessert on earth could be as welcome or refreshing as the local watermelon, the slices heavy with cool, sweet juice.

Homemade Christmas desserts (clockwise from upper left): *Pitta 'mpigliata* (page 338), *mostaccioli con mandorle* (page 326), *cannariculi* (page 316)

Cannariculi

FRIED RIDGED PASTRY WITH WARM HONEY GLAZE

These petite, honey-glazed fritters are always on the abundant Calabrian dessert platter at Christmas. They are about the size of gnocchi, so depending on how many other desserts vie for attention, a diner might eat a handful of *cannariculi* or more than a dozen. In the province of Cosenza, the same dessert is called *turdilli*, and the honey glaze might be replaced with *mosto cotto* (cooked-down grape must).

Old Calabrian pastry doughs rarely include butter and are sparing with eggs, so this dessert is obviously a holiday indulgence. Some recipes call for Marsala or other sweet wine instead of white wine and rum. Some people add cinnamon, cloves, or orange peel to the dough, and some omit baking powder, but I like the puffy texture the leavening provides. My family's *cannariculi* are crunchy outside and soft within.

It is customary to shape the *cannariculi* on a wooden gnocchi paddle (see Resources, page 369) so they have ridges, although the ridges all but vanish when the dough is fried. At Carnevale, in our family and some other families, the same dough is used for *cicirata* (see Variation, below), from the word for chick pea in Calabrian dialect. The ropes of dough are cut into small pieces, fried and glazed as for *cannariculi*, and then piled into a sticky but irresistible pyramid that looks like a mountain of glistening chick peas. In Calabria's southernmost province, Reggio Calabria, the dessert is christened *pignolata* because the stacked fritters are thought to resemble a giant pine cone (*pigne*). Reflecting the influence of neighboring Sicily, with its elaborate sweets, *pignolata* is often glazed with a lemon or chocolate icing.

When the same dough is flattened like pasta, cut into pappardelle-like ribbons, and given a signature twist and fried, the result is *chiacchiere* (see Variation, below). A thick dusting of confectioner's sugar replaces the honey glaze. In some families, these are known as *bugie* ("lies"), perhaps because few people tell the truth about how many they have eaten. (Photograph on page 315.)

SUGGESTED WINE: Donnafugata "Ben Ryé," Passito di Pantelleria, Sicily
From air-dried Zibibbo grapes, this honeyed dessert wine smells like fresh apricots.
ALTERNATE: any *passito* (dessert wine from partially sun-dried grapes)

CANNARICULI DOUGH

4½ cups (1 pound 6 ounces/630 grams) unbleached all-purpose
    flour

1 teaspoon baking powder

¼ pound (1 stick; 120 grams) unsalted butter, melted and cooled

¾ cup (180 milliliters) white wine

¼ cup (60 milliliters) light rum or liqueur of your choice

2 tablespoons sugar

2 teaspoons vanilla extract

2 large eggs, at room temperature

Vegetable oil for frying

1 cup (250 milliliters) honey

FOR THE *CANNARICULI* DOUGH: Sift the flour and baking powder together into a bowl and set aside.

In a large bowl, combine the melted butter, wine, rum, sugar, vanilla, and eggs. Whisk until well blended.

Add the flour to the egg mixture one cup at a time, blending with a fork. Once you have incorporated all the flour, knead the dough briefly in the bowl with one hand until it is soft and smooth. It will be moist and a little sticky, but refrain from adding flour if you can. Cover the bowl and refrigerate the dough for 30 minutes.

To shape the *cannariculi*, work with a little dough at a time. Cut off a piece about the size of a cigar and roll on a very lightly floured work surface into a rope about ⅜ inch (9 millimeters) in diameter. (If you flour the board too heavily, you may have a hard time stretching the dough into a rope.) Cut the rope into 1-inch (2½-centimeter) pieces.

Lightly flour a gnocchi paddle. Put a piece of dough on the paddle. Using the index and middle fingers of your dominant hand, press down on the dough, then pull toward you to make the dough curl into a "C." The dough is soft, so you don't need to press hard. As you shape them, transfer the pieces to a tray lined with a kitchen towel, keeping them in a single layer so they don't stick to each other. Repeat with the remaining dough, lightly flouring the gnocchi paddle as needed to keep the dough from sticking.

Put 4 inches (10 centimeters) of vegetable oil in a heavy 6-quart (6-liter) pot and place over moderately high heat. While the oil is heating, warm the honey in a small saucepan over moderately low heat until it thins enough to drizzle; remove from the heat.

When the oil reaches 375°F (190°C), you can begin frying the *cannariculi*. Work in batches so you don't overcrowd the pot. Using a large, shallow stainless steel skimmer or a slotted spoon, transfer about 20 pieces of dough to the hot oil. They will puff immediately. Fry the *cannariculi*, keeping them constantly in motion, until they are golden all over, 1 to 1½ minutes. Transfer them to a tray lined with paper towels to drain briefly, then put them on a serving platter. Before frying the next batch, drizzle some of the warm honey over the *cannariculi*, coating them generously.

Continue frying and glazing the *cannariculi*, mounding them on the platter, until you have done them all. Let cool before serving.

MAKES ABOUT 20 DOZEN CANNARICULI, ENOUGH TO SERVE 16 TO 20

Cicirata *Variation*

Using the same dough, roll into ropes ½ inch (12 millimeters) in diameter. Cut the ropes into ½-inch (12-millimeter) pieces. Fry and glaze with honey as for *cannariculi*. When the *cicirata* are cool, mound them like a mountain and serve.

Chiacchiere *Variation*

Using the same dough, flatten with a pasta machine or a rolling pin into a ⅛-inch-thick (3-millimeter-thick) sheet, as for a pie crust, dusting with flour as needed to prevent sticking. With a fluted pastry cutter, cut the dough into strips about 1 inch (2½ centimeters) wide and 6 inches (15 centimeters) long. Cut a 2-inch (5-centimeter) slit lengthwise in the center of each strip. Pick up a strip, insert one end through the slit, and pull it through. Fry as for *cannariculi*. Dust heavily with confectioner's sugar while still warm.

Chinule
SWEET CHRISTMAS RAVIOLI WITH CHESTNUT AND CHOCOLATE FILLING

Chestnut trees proliferate around my hometown of Verbicaro, and the nearby towns of San Sosti and San Donato are famous for them. According to my mother, the trees are of two different types, which the locals can distinguish from the size and shape of the nut. *Castagne 'nserta* are the big fat ones that peel easily. *Castagne porcili* ("the pigs' chestnuts") are smaller and more difficult to peel, so they are usually left on the ground to fatten the pigs.

The chestnut harvest peaks around Christmas, inspiring several holiday desserts. These chestnut-filled ravioli, glazed with honey and served warm, are a typical Christmas pastry in and around Verbicaro. In addition to including boiled and pureed chestnuts, the rich, dark filling contains raisins, cocoa, chocolate, and cinnamon. The buttery dough is the same one used for *cannariculi* (page 316) and *chinulille* (page 322).

SUGGESTED WINE: Contesa "Shirin," Abruzzo
A late-harvest Montepulciano with a garnet color, baking-spice aromas, and a smooth, soft, elegant palate impression.
ALTERNATE: mulled wine

CHESTNUT FILLING

¾ pound (340 grams) unpeeled fresh chestnuts

⅓ cup (50 grams) raisins

¼ teaspoon ground cinnamon

1 tablespoon Strega or anise liqueur, such as anisette or Sambuca

1 ounce (30 grams) bittersweet chocolate, coarsely chopped

¼ cup (30 grams) unsweetened cocoa powder

¼ cup (50 grams) sugar

1 recipe *cannariculi* dough (page 317)

Vegetable oil for frying

1 cup (250 milliliters) honey

FOR THE FILLING: Place the chestnuts in a 3-quart (3-liter) pot and cover with 2 quarts (2 liters) water. Bring to a boil over high heat, then adjust the heat to maintain a simmer and cook until the interior is soft, 45 minutes to one hour. To test, remove a chestnut and cool it quickly under cold running water. With a paring knife, remove the hard outer shell and the thin brown skin underneath. Break the chestnut open and taste. It should be tender and no longer crunchy. Continue cooking if necessary. When they are done, drain the chestnuts and let cool in cold water.

When the chestnuts are cool enough to handle, use a paring knife to remove the outer shell and the thin inner skin. The skin may slip off easily, but sometimes it clings to the chestnut flesh; if so, pare the skin away, removing as little of the flesh as possible. Don't worry if the chestnuts crumble, as you are going to puree them. When all the chestnuts are peeled, put them in a food processor and blend until smooth. Transfer to a bowl and stir in the raisins, cinnamon, and liqueur and mix well.

In a 1-quart (1-liter) saucepan, combine ½ cup water with the chocolate, cocoa powder, and sugar. Bring to a boil over moderate heat, whisking until the chocolate has melted and the mixture is smooth.

Add the chocolate sauce to the chestnuts and mix until thoroughly blended. The filling should be smooth (except for the raisins) and a rich chocolate color. Set aside at room temperature while you prepare the dough according to the directions on page 317.

Divide the chilled dough in half. Working with one-half at a time on a lightly floured surface, flatten the dough with a rolling pin into a circle about 18 inches (45 centimeters) in diameter and ⅛ inch (3 millimeters) thick. Alternatively, flatten the dough with a pasta machine into a sheet ⅛ inch (3 millimeters) thick. Using a 3-inch (8-centimeter) round cookie cutter, cut as many circles as you can. Set the circles aside without stacking them. Gather the scraps of dough into a ball and re-roll them, cutting out as many additional circles as you can. You should get 30 to 32 circles from one half of the dough, enough to make 15 or 16 ravioli.

TO FILL AND FRY *CHINULE*: Roll 1 heaping tablespoon of the chestnut filling into a ball and place it in the center of one of the circles. Top with another circle. Carefully press the edges together with your fingers. Holding a fork horizontally, seal the rim by pressing gently all around with the tips of the fork tines. Be careful not to pierce the dough or the filling may come out when the ravioli are fried. Continue until you have assembled all the circles into ravioli, then place the ravioli on a tray lined with a kitchen towel. Repeat with the second half of the dough and the remaining filling. Place these on a tray as well. You will have a total of 30 or 32 ravioli.

Put 4 inches (10 centimeters) of oil in a heavy, deep pot over moderately high heat. When the oil reaches 375°F (190°C) put two or three ravioli in the hot oil. Fry until golden brown and crisp, 1½ to 2 minutes, turning them with tongs or two forks so they cook evenly on both sides. Transfer them with a wire-mesh skimmer or slotted spoon to a tray lined with paper towels. Repeat until all the ravioli have been fried, adjusting the heat as needed to maintain an oil temperature of 375°F (190°C).

TO SERVE CHINULE: Transfer the ravioli to a platter. If the honey is stiff, warm it in a small saucepan over moderately low heat until it is pourable. Drizzle the honey over the ravioli, coating them well. Serve warm.

MAKES 30 TO 32 RAVIOLI

Chinulille

SWEET RAVIOLI WITH RICOTTA AND CANDIED ORANGE

These deep-fried, sugar-dusted ravioli are best eaten soon after they're made, so you won't find them in Calabrian pastry shops. *Chinulille* are the province of home cooks, who prepare them most often at Christmas but for other special occasions, too. The candied orange peel in the ricotta filling is my own addition; it is not traditional, and you can omit it.

SUGGESTED WINE: Librandi "Le Passule," Val di Neto, Calabria
A medium-sweet passito with toasted almond, honey, and orange peel aromas.
ALTERNATE: Passito di Pantelleria

RICOTTA AND CANDIED ORANGE FILLING

1½ cups (335 grams) Homemade Ricotta (page 144), well drained,
    or store-bought whole-milk ricotta

½ cup (100 grams) granulated sugar

Grated zest of 1 lemon

Grated zest of 1 orange

1 tablespoon orange liqueur, such as Grand Marnier or Cointreau

1 teaspoon vanilla extract

1 ounce (30 grams) Candied Orange Peel (page 308) *or* store-bought
    candied orange peel, finely chopped, optional

1 recipe *cannariculi* dough (page 317)

Vegetable oil for frying

Confectioner's sugar for dusting

FOR THE FILLING: If using store-bought ricotta, place it in a cheesecloth-lined strainer set over a bowl and let drain in the refrigerator overnight.

With a rubber pastry scraper or metal bench scraper, press the ricotta through a fine-mesh sieve into a bowl. (I use a fine-mesh splatter screen, a flat screen that fits over a skillet and is designed to keep oil from splattering on the stove.) Sieving the ricotta makes it light and creamy. Do not use a food processor or the result will not be smooth enough. Stir in the granulated sugar, lemon and orange zests, orange liqueur, vanilla, and candied orange peel, if using. Mix well. Refrigerate until ready to use. The filling can be prepared a day ahead.

TO FILL AND FRY *CHINULILLE*: Follow the directions for flattening and cutting the dough and then filling and frying the *chinule* on page 320, using 1 level tablespoon of ricotta filling for each raviolo.

TO SERVE *CHINULILLE*: Transfer to a platter while warm. Dust generously with confectioner's sugar and serve immediately.

MAKES 30 TO 32

Bergamot: *Perfume on a Tree*

For the bergamot, the sunny coast of Reggio Calabria is home base. This rare citrus (*Citrus bergamia*) thrives in Calabria's southernmost province and virtually nowhere else on earth. Cultivated in a narrow coastal band between Villa San Giovanni and Gioiosa Ionica, the bergamot resembles a round or slightly pear-shaped lemon, depending on the variety. Based on DNA analysis, it is thought to be a cross between the sweet lemon (*C. aurantium*) and sweet lime (*C. limetta*).

Even when fully ripe, bergamot is too tart and bitter to use as a fruit, but its skin contains aromatic oils that are prized in fragrances. Most of the world's perfumes contain some essence of bergamot, and Reggio Calabria supplies almost all of it. Earl Grey tea owes its distinctive scent to bergamot, and *liquore di bergamotto* (bergamot liqueur) and bergamot candies are popular in Calabria. Some people make marmalade with the juice and skin, but it is an acquired taste. The bergamot aroma is floral and citrus-like, but the flavor has a bitter edge.

Bergamot was first planted in Reggio Calabria around 1750, and until the development of synthetic fragrances, it was hugely valuable. By the early twentieth century, the province had an established "bergamot bourgeoisie," families whose small bergamot gardens produced a very comfortable living. But lower-cost synthetics have brought hard times to bergamot growers, and many gardens have been uprooted in favor of housing.

Grispelle
WARM CHRISTMAS DOUGHNUTS

Calabrians make these deep-fried yeasted doughnuts primarily at Christmas time. My mother remembers her own mother getting up early on Christmas Eve day to make the dough so it would have plenty of time to rise. In the afternoon, while her six children were out playing and not underfoot, she would fry the *grispelle* in a pot in the wood-burning fireplace.

You can substitute russet potatoes for the sweet potatoes in this recipe, although you will probably need a little less flour, as the russet potatoes are drier. If you use sweet potatoes, look for the type with light brown skins and butter-colored flesh. Sweet potatoes with orange flesh—Garnet and Jewel types, for example—are too moist.

Grispelle, as my mother and I make them, are elongated fritters about the size and shape of slender éclairs. The name, also written as g*rispedde* or *crespelle*, comes from the Latin *crispus*, a reference to the crisp texture these doughnuts should have. In some homes, they are called *vecchiarelle*—little old ladies—because their wrinkled surface resembles the skin of an old woman. Other cooks shape the dough into rings before frying, in which case the fritters are called *cuddurieddi*. You can eat them as an appetizer straight from the fryer. For dessert, they are typically dusted with sugar or cinnamon sugar or served with honey for dipping.

SUGGESTED WINE: Feudi di San Gregorio "Privilegio," Irpinia Bianco, Campania
A botrytised passito from Fiano grapes, the wine has a honeyed concentration and an almond scent.
ALTERNATE: Sauternes

1 pound (450 grams) yellow-fleshed sweet potatoes (1 large or
    2 small), unpeeled

¼ cup (60 milliliters) lukewarm water

1 teaspoon active dry yeast

1½ cups (210 grams) unbleached all-purpose flour

1 teaspoon kosher salt

Vegetable oil for frying

Honey for serving, optional

PUT THE WHOLE sweet potatoes in a large pot that will hold them comfortably. Cover with 1 inch (2½ centimeters) of cold water. Bring to a boil over high heat and boil until the sweet potatoes can be easily pierced with a fork, 30 to 40 minutes. Drain them and set aside until cool enough to handle, then peel.

Using a ricer or a food mill fitted with the medium blade, pass the sweet potatoes into a large bowl.

Put the lukewarm water in a small bowl and add the yeast. Whisk with a fork until the yeast dissolves.

Add the flour and salt to the potatoes, then add the water with the dissolved yeast. Combine the ingredients with your hand until they come together into a sticky dough, then knead in the bowl, using one hand to steady the bowl and one hand to knead, until the dough is smooth and well blended, about 5 minutes. It will still be moist and a little sticky. Cover the bowl with plastic wrap and set aside until the dough doubles in size, about 1½ hours.

Put ½ inch (12 millimeters) of vegetable oil in a 10-inch (25-centimeter) skillet and heat over medium-high heat until the oil registers 375°F (190°C) on a candy thermometer.

Oil your hands lightly, then take a golf ball-size piece of dough from the bowl and stretch it between your hands into a thick "sausage" about 8 inches (20 centimeters) long and ½ to ¾ inch (12 to 18 millimeters) wide. The dough is pliable and will elongate easily. Carefully place it in the hot oil, then continue shaping and frying *grispelle* until you have four or five *grispelle* in the skillet. Cook until the underside is a deep golden brown, then flip the *grispelle* with tongs and brown the other side. Total cooking time is about 3 minutes.

Transfer the *grispelle* to a tray lined with paper towels. Repeat the shaping and frying until you have used all the dough. Add more vegetable oil if necessary to keep the level at ½ inch (12 millimeters). Serve the *grispelle* warm, with honey for dipping.

MAKES ABOUT 15 *GRISPELLE*

Mostaccioli con Mandorle
HONEY COOKIES FILLED WITH ALMONDS, COCOA, AND ANISETTE

Mostaccioli are Calabria's most beloved holiday cookies, made year-round for weddings, baptisms, festivals, and saint's days. They are also probably among the region's oldest sweets, judging from their primitive nature. At their most traditional, *mostaccioli* (also called *'nzuddi*) are made with nothing but flour and honey worked into a stiff dough, then rolled flat, cut into whimsical shapes, and baked into a rock-hard cookie (photograph on page 310). Calabrian children learn to suck slowly on these jaw-breaking cookies until they soften. Some people make them at home, but most purchase them from vendors who set up stalls at the religious festivals.

Mostaccioli are never frosted but are charmingly decorated with hatch marks and tiny squares of shiny colored tinfoil that you remove before eating. The shapes are limited only by the baker's imagination, but typically include horses and other farm animals, woven baskets, dolls, and little girls. The most common shapes are produced with molds, but the artisan *mostaccioli* maker, or *mostazzolaro*, creates many forms by hand, with only a knife, drawing his ideas from myth, legends, and daily life. In times past, a young man making his first official visit to his fiancée would take *mostaccioli,* often in the shape of a heart.

More modern interpretations of *mostaccioli*, like the recipe below, include spices, anisette, vanilla, eggs, and even some leavening in the dough to yield a more tender result. Baked in a log, then sliced on the diagonal, they resemble Tuscan biscotti in shape but have a spice-cookie fragrance and flavor. My own version, which I learned from an elderly friend of the family from Crucoli, incorporates a moist, dark filling of almonds, honey, and chocolate. This embellishment departs from the austere *mostaccioli* of tradition, but no one who tastes the results could complain. (Photograph on page 315.)

SUGGESTED WINE: Pervini "Primo Amore," Primitivo di Manduria, Apulia
Like raspberry liqueur but not cloying, this concentrated dessert wine has rich berry aromas that complement the cookies' chocolate and anise flavors.
ALTERNATE: late-harvest Zinfandel

DOUGH

4 cups (550 grams) all-purpose flour

½ teaspoon baking powder

¼ teaspoon baking soda

1 cup (250 milliliters) honey

2 large eggs

2 teaspoons orange juice

2 teaspoons anisette

2 teaspoons almond extract

½ teaspoon vanilla extract

FILLING

2 cups (285 grams) whole blanched (skinless) almonds

½ cup (125 milliliters) honey

¼ cup (25 grams) unsweetened cocoa powder

½ teaspoon cinnamon

½ teaspoon ground cloves

2 teaspoons grated orange zest

1 teaspoon vanilla extract

1 teaspoon almond extract

1 teaspoon anisette

4 ounces (115 grams) bittersweet chocolate, chopped into
      small pieces

EGG WASH

1 large egg

Few drops vanilla extract

MAKE THE DOUGH: In a bowl, stir together the flour, baking powder, and baking soda. Make a well in the flour and put the remaining dough ingredients in the well. Stir with a fork until the dough comes together, then knead it in the bowl with one hand, using the other hand to steady the bowl, until the dough is smooth, well blended, and similar in texture to a sugar cookie dough, about 2 minutes. Let stand for 15 minutes to allow the flour to absorb the moisture so it will be firm enough to roll.

Divide the dough in half. On a work surface, arrange two sheets of parchment paper, each large enough to accommodate a 14- by 6-inch (35- by 15-centimeter) rectangle. Dust the parchment sheets lightly with flour. Put half the dough on each sheet and, with a rolling pin, flatten the dough into a 14- by 6-inch (35- by 15-centimeter) rectangle about ⅜ inch (10 millimeters) thick. Use your hands, if necessary, to straighten the dough edges to make a neat rectangle. Don't worry about overworking the dough; it is very forgiving. Let the elongated dough rest at room temperature while you proceed with the filling.

MAKE THE FILLING: Preheat the oven to 350°F (175°C). Toast the almonds on a baking sheet until lightly colored and fragrant, about 10 minutes. Set aside to cool. Raise the oven temperature to 375°F (190°C).

Put the honey in a 1½-quart (1½-liter) pot and warm it over low heat until it becomes fluid. In a small bowl, combine the cocoa, cinnamon, cloves, orange zest, vanilla and almond extracts, and anisette. Add to the honey along with the almonds and chocolate. Bring to a simmer and cook, stirring, until the chocolate melts and the mixture is thick and well blended, about 1 minute. Let it cool until it begins to stiffen and is no longer syrupy, 1 to 2 minutes, but don't let it cool too long or it will become too stiff to spread.

Arrange the dough rectangles horizontally on the work surface, so that the 14-inch side is nearest you. Working quickly with a spoon, spread half the filling on the bottom half of each sheet of dough, staying about 1 inch (2½ centimeters) away from the edges. By lifting the parchment, carefully fold the top half of the dough over the filling to make a log about 14 inches long by 3 inches wide (35 by 8 centimeters). Peel away the parchment and press the edges of the dough together to seal it all the way around. Be sure to make a firm seal or the filling may leak during baking. With the palm of your hand, flatten the top of each log to prevent an air pocket from forming between the filling and the dough.

Line a 12- by 18-inch (30- by 43-centimeter) baking sheet with parchment paper. Transfer the logs to the baking sheet. With a fork, prick them decoratively, making about two dozen pricks in each log.

Bake for 20 minutes. While the cookies bake, prepare the egg wash by whisking together the egg, 1 tablespoon water, and the vanilla. Remove the baking sheet from the oven and brush the two logs generously with the egg wash. (You won't need it all.) Return the baking sheet to the oven and continue baking until the logs are caramel brown and firm to the touch, 5 to 10 minutes. Cool on the baking sheet for about 10 minutes, then cool completely on a rack. With a serrated knife, slice on the diagonal into cookies about ⅓ inch (9 millimeters) wide.

MAKES ABOUT 5 DOZEN

Citron: A Multipurpose Fruit

The coastal area from Tortora to Cetraro, a stretch of about 40 miles (65 kilometers) on Calabria's Tyrrhenian side known as the Riviera dei Cedri (the "Citron Riviera"), is one of the choice places on earth for citron production. This extraordinarily

valuable fruit—a single perfect one can fetch ten dollars or more—resembles a large, bumpy lemon, but it has no juice to speak of. Its thick, sweet peel is prized for candying and widely used in confectionery. (The green bits in American fruitcake are citron, dyed with food coloring; Italian confectioners leave the peel its natural color.) Perfumers use the distilled oil from the peel in scents and soaps. And to Jews the world over, the citron plays an essential role in the harvest festival of Sukkot.

During the seven days of Sukkot, observant Jews build a small outdoor hut and decorate it with palm fronds and citron (*etrog* in Hebrew). They take their meals in the hut as a reminder of the years their ancestors wandered in the desert. According to Jewish law, the citrons must be unblemished and from an ungrafted tree.

In July and August, when the citrons are still underdeveloped and green,

Fresh citron still on a plant in Santa Maria del Cedro, a town near the Abatemarco River, which flows down from Verbicaro. My parents spend every other summer at their house here, leaving me to tend their garden in Oakland as well as my own.

rabbis visit Calabria's citron orchards to choose the fruits they want. Citron trees resemble lemon trees, but they have vicious thorns that can bloody workers' hands. The trees are trained like grapevines on wire trellises about five feet off the ground, just high enough for the farmer to crouch under them as he works. If they are allowed to grow taller, they can suffer wind damage.

The farmer and rabbi stoop under the canopy of citron trees, while the rabbi inspects the trees to make sure they are ungrafted and then hand-selects the fruits he wants. The farmer harvests and boxes them, and they are shipped in time for the holiday. The citrons for candying are also picked at an underripe stage, before the fruit has changed from green to yellow. The remaining citrons will continue to mature, becoming larger, more fragrant, and more golden, until the main harvest begins in November. At that point, an individual citron may weigh almost two pounds (about 700 grams).

Growing citrons (*Citrus medica*) is backbreaking work, and many Calabrians are abandoning their orchards for better-paying jobs in construction. The trees want a great deal of pampering. They require steady temperatures, plenty of water, and protection from wind and frost. The fierce thorns can rip a farmer's hands or scar a perfect citron and make it unsalable for Sukkot. In a good year, the financial return can be generous, but not without struggle.

Many Calabrian pastry shops and even supermarkets sell candied citron halves. They are pale green, not the vivid green of dyed citron, and they are not sickly sweet. The pulp has been removed; only the thick peel is candied. Diced citron appears in desserts and sweet breads throughout Italy, such as Milan's *panettone* and Sicily's *cassata*, as well as in homemade Calabrian sweets like *panicelli* (or *panacieddi*).

Panicelli are palm-size bundles of Zibibbo raisins and small pieces of citron enclosed in citron leaves. The little packages are tied with a strip of raffia-like Scotch broom and baked until dry and perfumed. They last for months. When I was growing up, *panicelli* were my candy, and I have always been told that they originated in Verbicaro, my hometown. That claim makes sense, as Verbicaro was a prime growing region for Zibibbo grapes until emigration took its toll. Gabriele d'Annunzio, the early twentieth-century poet, praised the *panicelli* of Verbicaro.

Until modern times, *panicelli* were made mostly in local homes, by time-consuming methods. Many farm families in the Verbicaro and Diamante areas depended heavily on income from sales of their *panicelli*, and when these families emigrated and abandoned their vineyards, *panicelli* production all but ceased. In recent years, some artisan confectionery firms have revived production in recognition of the role *panicelli* once played in local life.

The old method calls for tying the ripe grape clusters together and dipping them in boiling water that has been filtered through wood ash. The ash leaves a fine coating on the sugary grapes, which protects them from insects during their stay in the drying shed. When sufficiently dry, the raisins are removed from the stems and rinsed, and any flawed ones are discarded. Then about twenty of the moist raisins are bundled with small pieces of citron in citron leaves, tied like a package, and baked. The heat melts the sugar in the raisins, helping them adhere, and drives the fragrance of the citron leaves inside.

Panicelli are a ritual confection in Verbicaro, one of thirteen dishes in the feast of Santa Lucia on December 13. They are usually accompanied by a glass of the sweet local wine.

"Peaches" with Pastry Cream

Pesche con Crema
"PEACHES" WITH PASTRY CREAM

The pastry shops on the Riviera dei Cedri (page xiii) sell these whimsical little cakes, which are filled with plain or chocolate pastry cream and decorated to resemble a peach. They are more refined than most Calabrian desserts, and I don't know their origin. Pastry cream was not part of old Calabrian dessert making because refrigeration was so late in coming to the region. Even today, *pesche con crema* are not a dessert any Calabrian would make at home. My mother and I developed the recipe only because we missed them so much in California.

Pesche do take time to make, but they require no special skill. If you work carefully, you can create a platter of "peaches" that will truly fool the eye. In Calabria, pastry chefs use Alchermes, a scarlet-colored liqueur, to give the cakes their peach hue, but as Alchermes is not available in the United States, I have opted for rum or liqueur tinted with food coloring.

Make the *pesche* a day ahead to allow the alcohol to penetrate and soften the cakes. To eat them, twist them apart, like the two halves of a peach. If you don't have access to real peach leaves, you can purchase decorative leaves made from sugar or chocolate from a baking supply store.

SUGGESTED WINE: Villa Schinosa Moscato di Trani, Apulia
An elegant, medium-sweet wine with flavors that hint of lemon curd.
ALTERNATE: Beaumes de Venise

PASTRY CREAM

2 cups (500 milliliters) whole milk

Zest (yellow part only) of 1 lemon, removed in large strips with a
    vegetable peeler

4 large egg yolks

¾ cup (150 grams) sugar

¼ cup (35 grams) unbleached all-purpose flour

3¾ cups (525 grams) all-purpose flour

1 tablespoon baking powder

3 large eggs

¾ cup (150 grams) sugar

½ cup (125 milliliters) milk

¼ pound (1 stick; 120 grams) unsalted butter, melted and cooled

Grated zest of 1 lemon

½ cup (125 milliliters) light rum *or* 6 tablespoons Italian
    maraschino liqueur (see Resources, page 368) plus 2
    tablespoons peach schnapps

Red and yellow food coloring

1 cup sugar, or more as needed for coating

Fresh peach leaves or decorative leaves (see recipe introduction)

MAKE THE PASTRY CREAM: In a heavy saucepan, bring the milk and lemon zest to a simmer. In a bowl, whisk the egg yolks with the sugar until thick and pale yellow. Add the flour to the bowl and whisk well.

Remove the lemon zest from the milk, then slowly whisk the hot milk into the egg mixture. Return the mixture to the saucepan and place over moderate heat. Cook, stirring constantly, until the cream thickens and begins to boil.

Transfer the pastry cream to a bowl. To prevent a skin from forming, place a piece of plastic wrap on the surface. Cool completely.

MAKE THE DOUGH: Sift together the flour and the baking powder into a bowl. Whisk the eggs in another bowl. Add the sugar to the eggs and whisk to blend. Whisk in the milk, butter, and lemon zest and mix until smooth. Add the flour mixture gradually, mixing with a fork just until you have a smooth, stiff dough. Let the dough rest for 5 minutes.

Preheat the oven to 350°F (175°C) and line two baking sheets with silicone baking mats or parchment paper.

Using a lightly mounded tablespoon of dough, roll the dough firmly between your palms to make a smooth, round ball about the size of a walnut. It is important to make the balls the same size, as you will sandwich them later. Place the balls on the baking sheets, spacing them about 1 inch (2½ centimeters) apart. You should be able to fit twenty-four balls on each baking sheet. Flatten the tops slightly with your fingertips.

Bake until the bottoms are lightly browned, about 15 minutes. The tops will remain pale. Cool them briefly on a rack.

While the cookies are still warm and have not yet hardened, hollow out a space for the cream filling. With a small, sharp knife, cut a circle about the size of a quarter on the bottom (flat) side of the cookie, taking care not to crack the edges. Use the tip of the knife to scrape out enough crumbs to make a hollow that will hold about 1 teaspoon of filling. (You can save the crumbs for garnishing another dessert, or discard them.)

Put the rum or the combined liqueur and schnapps in a small bowl. Add enough drops of red and yellow food coloring to turn the liquid a peach color.

Fill a shallow bowl with about 1 cup (200 grams) of sugar.

Fill the hollow in each cookie with about 1 teaspoon of pastry cream. Sandwich two cookies, flat sides together, to form a "peach." Press the two cookies together so the filling comes just to the edge, taking care not to crack or break them.

Using a pastry brush, generously coat one of the "peaches" with the tinted liquor. Let it rest for about one minute to absorb some of the liqueur, then roll it in the sugar. It should resemble a real peach, fuzz and all. Continue until all the "peaches" are colored and coated with sugar.

Refrigerate the "peaches" overnight in a covered container.

Just before serving, pierce each "peach" with a toothpick where the two cookies come together and insert the stem of a peach leaf. Alternatively, garnish with a decorative sugar or chocolate leaf.

MAKES 24 "PEACHES"

Myriad Sweets from Dried Figs

Of nature's many gifts of fruit, none is more prized in Calabria than the fig. These huge, generous trees grow with abandon on the Tyrrhenian coast, providing fruit that can be preserved for enjoyment all year. In earlier times, figs—both fresh and dried—contributed significantly to the peasants' diet, especially in the Cosenza region. Putting figs by for the winter was a time-consuming autumn task in many Cosentino households. My grandmother, with help from her children, would store one hundred kilos (about 220 pounds). Then as now, the prized fig for drying was the *fico dottato*, or Kadota fig, a thin-skinned white fig with few seeds.

When my mother was a child, many families in the Cosentino had a large wooden chest for storing dried figs. In fall, when the figs were so ripe they were dripping with syrup, the women would harvest them and arrange them on trays they had woven from local reeds. The trays would be placed in the sun until the figs shriveled and gave up their moisture—three to four weeks, depending on the weather. The sugar would leach out and crystallize on the surface, coating them with a fine dusting of white. My grandmother would braid some of these sun-baked figs on supple stems of fragrant myrtle to make wreaths or crowns, called *coroncine*. With others, she would make *spinapisci* ("fish spines") by threading fresh figs onto a sharpened reed through their necks in offset fashion—one fig to the left, one to the right—then baking them until dry. Or she would fashion *crocette*, or crosses, which my mother recalls helping to make.

For *crocette*, two dried figs are butterflied by halving them from the blossom end but not cutting all the way through the stem. Open like a book, with cut sides up, the two figs are crossed to form an "X." A piece of walnut or almond is placed on each exposed half, and sometimes a piece of candied citron or orange peel, then the "X" is topped with another pair of butterflied figs, cut sides down. The resulting cross is pressed firmly so the cut faces adhere, then baked until fully dry. *Crocette* could be kept airtight in the wooden chest all year and were the traditional Calabrian family's energy bars.

Crocette and *coroncine* remain much loved Calabrian sweets, and several Calabrian firms specialize in preparing them, beautifully packaged with doilies and ribbons, for the gift trade. These products are much more sophisticated than the fig confections of times past. The dried figs may be dipped in white or dark chocolate; or candied in sugar syrup with rum or grappa; or stuffed with pistachio cream. For *pallone* (a "ball" of figs), dried figs are caramelized in a syrup made from their

My mother, Maria, strings figs in the traditional ways to preserve them so we can eat them like candy in the winter months. Clockwise from top left: chocolate coated figs, *crocette*, *spinapisci*, *coroncine*. The myrtle leaves are on the right.

own juices and flavored with citrus peel, then several are wrapped together in fig leaves and baked. The firm of Colavolpe, in Belmonte Calabro, has led the way in transforming the peasants' humble candy into elegant gifts suitable for the export market.

Pitta 'mpigliata

ROLLED PASTRY ROSETTES WITH WALNUTS, RAISINS, AND CINNAMON

The pastry shops in and around San Giovanni in Fiore, a village in the Sila mountains between Cosenza and Crotone, specialize in this strudel-like pastry. Although bakeries make it year-round, the dessert is mostly closely associated with Christmas. Calabrians give each other *pitta 'mpigliata*, wrapped and beribboned, the same way Americans give fruitcake.

Near Crotone, the same dessert is known as *pitta 'nchiusa*. Both names roughly translate as dough rolled around a filling, but that plain description doesn't begin to convey how pretty these pastries are. Made from a 3-inch-wide (8-centimeter-wide) strip of dough folded over a filling of walnuts, raisins, cinnamon, cloves, and sugar, then coiled like a snake and baked with the filling exposed, *pitta 'mpigliata* resembles a multipetaled rose, or an American sticky bun. Although you can bake the rosettes individually, they are more often clustered snugly in a pan and baked side by side to form a sort of coffee cake. While still hot from the oven, they are drizzled with honey, which they soak up like a sponge. At serving time, they are pulled apart into individual rosettes. (Photograph on page 315.)

DOUGH

2 cups (280 grams) unbleached all-purpose flour

½ teaspoon baking powder

Pinch of kosher salt

1 large egg

¼ cup (2 fluid ounces/60 milliliters) olive oil

¼ cup (2 fluid ounces/60 milliliters) sweet white wine, such as
    sweet Muscat, *passito* or vin santo

2 tablespoons anisette, Strega, Sambuca, or rum, or a mixture

FILLING

3 tablespoons blanched almonds

1 cup (110 grams) walnut halves

1 cup (150 grams) raisins

2 tablespoons sugar

2 teaspoons grated orange zest

½ teaspoon cinnamon

¼ teaspoon ground cloves

1 cup (250 milliliters) honey, or more as desired

FOR THE DOUGH: In a bowl, sift together the flour, baking powder, and salt. Make a well in the center of this mixture and put the egg, olive oil, wine, and liqueur(s) in the well. Stir these liquid ingredients with a fork, then gradually incorporate the flour mixture. Knead the dough briefly in the bowl with one hand, steadying the bowl with the other hand, until the dough is smooth, silky, and well blended. Cover the surface of the dough with plastic wrap and let rest for 30 minutes. You can also make the dough several hours ahead and refrigerate until ready to use it.

FOR THE FILLING: Preheat the oven to 350°F (175°C). Toast the almonds until lightly colored and fragrant, about 10 minutes. Let cool. Coarsely chop the almonds and walnuts together. In a bowl, combine the chopped nuts, raisins, sugar, orange zest, cinnamon, and cloves. Toss together with a fork until well blended.

Divide the dough into 7 equal pieces. To make the base of the *pitta*, flatten one of the pieces of dough with a rolling pin into a very thin 10-inch (25-centimeter) round. Place the round on the bottom of an 8-inch (20-centimeter) springform pan so that the dough comes about 1 inch (2½ centimeters) up the sides of the pan. This sheet of dough will hold the rosettes together in the shape of a cake.

Working with one piece of dough at a time, roll each of the remaining 6 pieces into a thin rectangle 15 to 16 inches (38 to 40 centimeters) long and a little more than 3 inches (8 centimeters) wide, flouring the work surface if necessary to prevent sticking. Alternatively, flatten the dough into the specified shape with a pasta machine. With a fluted pastry cutter, trim the long edges so that the strip of dough is exactly 3 inches (8 centimeters) wide. Reserve and re-roll the trimmings to make a seventh rectangle of the same size.

Sprinkle ⅓ cup of filling lengthwise down the center of each strip of dough. With the palms of both hands, nudge the filling into a straight line down the center. Carefully lift the dough along one of its long edges and fold it over the filling, taking care not to squeeze out the filling. Line up the long edges of the dough but do not seal them.

Working from the end of the dough closest to you, gently roll the dough away from you into a neat coil. Try not to let any of the filling escape and be sure to keep the open edges open, not pinched together. Place the coil, folded edge down, on a work surface and secure the end of the coil by pressing it gently into the dough. The coil will resemble a flower, with the filling visible between the "petals." If necessary, gently pry open the petals a little to expose the filling. Place the seven rosettes in the dough-lined pan. They should fit snugly, which will prevent them from unwinding during baking.

Bake the *pitta* at 350° F (175°C) until golden all over, about 45 minutes. If the honey is stiff, warm it in a small saucepan over moderately low heat until it is pourable. Remove the *pitta* from the oven and immediately drizzle with about ½ cup (125 milliliters) of the honey. Wait until the honey is absorbed, then drizzle with more honey, a little at a time, until it is all absorbed. Let the *pitta* cool completely before serving.

MAKES ONE 8-INCH (20-CENTIMETER) *PITTA*, TO SERVE 7

Torta di Noci

ROSANGELA'S FLOURLESS WALNUT CAKE

I found the recipe for this featherlight walnut cake in my cousin Rosangela's hand-written recipe collection, which she shared with me when I began researching recipes for this book. Calabrian cooks rarely write down recipes, even for pastries. The only reason Rosangela had recorded some recipes is that when she married my cousin Alberto, she moved away from her mother. Of course, her notes had few specific proportions—just "a pinch of that" and "a handful of that."

This delicate, tender cake is made in homes throughout Calabria and is usually served with just a dusting of confectioner's sugar. A dollop of lightly sweetened whipped cream would dress it up. A nutty, not-too-sweet cake like this one is just what you want in mid-afternoon with a cup of espresso, or at the end of a meal with a glass of sweet Moscato or Malvasia or Shelley Lindgren's suggestions below. The cake will fall considerably as it cools, but it will be light inside.

Note that you will need a rotary cheese grater to turn the nuts into a fine, fluffy meal. A food processor would grind them to paste.

This cake is best eaten the day it is made.

SUGGESTED WINE: Marco De Bartoli "Vecchio Samperi," Marsala Superiore, Sicily
A premier example of Marsala, with a nutty, sherry-like quality that complements nut-based desserts.
ALTERNATE: Madeira or Amontillado sherry

---

8 ounces (225 grams) walnuts

6 large eggs

¾ cup (150 grams) sugar

Grated zest of 1 lemon

Pinch of kosher salt

Confectioner's sugar for dusting

Unsalted butter and flour for the cake pan

PREHEAT THE OVEN to 350°F (175°C). Toast the walnuts on a baking sheet until fragrant and lightly colored, about 10 minutes. Cool completely. Using a rotary cheese grater fitted with the finest holes, grate the nuts onto a plate. They should have the light, dry texture of fine meal. Set aside.

Reduce the oven temperature to 325°F (160°C). Butter and flour the bottom and sides of a 9-inch (23-centimeter) springform pan.

Separate the egg yolks and whites, putting them in separate large mixing bowls. With an electric stand mixer or hand-held mixer on medium speed, beat the yolks with half the sugar until pale yellow, thick, and fluffy, about 4 minutes. Beat in the lemon zest. Set aside.

With clean beaters, beat the whites on low speed with a pinch of salt to break them up, then raise the speed to medium and beat to soft peaks. Raise the speed to high and add the remaining sugar gradually. Continue beating to firm peaks.

Pour the beaten egg yolks over the egg whites. Sprinkle with one-quarter of the ground walnuts and fold gently. Fold in the remaining walnuts one-quarter at a time, taking care to preserve the volume of the batter and folding just until the nuts are incorporated.

Pour the batter into the prepared pan. Bake on the oven's middle rack until the cake is firm to the touch and golden on top and a toothpick comes out clean, 45 to 55 minutes. Cool in the pan on a rack for 20 minutes, then remove the sides of the pan and continue cooling the cake on the rack. Just before serving, dust the surface with confectioner's sugar, using a sifter or shaker.

MAKES ONE 9-INCH (23-CENTIMETER) CAKE, TO SERVE 8

A Fruit Lover's Eden

Amura e cerasi cchiù ndi menti e cchiù ndi trasi.
The more blackberries and cherries you eat, the more you want.

Despite living in California, America's fruit basket, I have never tasted fruits as good as those I grew up with in Calabria. Now that I return frequently as an adult, I can verify that the years have not embellished these early taste memories. Calabria's summer fruits really do seem to have an extraordinary intensity.

Any traveler to Calabria should make an effort to sample some of the more unusual fruits that thrive in the region. In season, they are available in farmers' markets and on backyard trees.

The *noce pesca gialla*, or yellow nectarine, has a thin, almost translucent skin and a silky-smooth surface. The fruit is entirely yellow, with no red blush, and has a scent that can perfume a room. Its flavor and fragrance are almost tropical, reminiscent of mango. A few California growers have now planted this fruit and are marketing it as a "mango nectarine." Look for it in July.

The mulberry trees that blanket Calabria attest to the region's once-thriving silk industry. The silk production has ceased, but fortunately the leafy trees remain. Fresh mulberries (*gelsi*), both black and white, have a blackberry shape, although the white ones are more elongated. They mature in early June and are a fleeting pleasure, with a season that lasts only a couple of weeks. They are extremely fragile and need to be eaten the day they are picked. These juicy, sweet berries make exquisite ice cream and jam, but no mulberry is as tasty as the one that goes from tree to mouth.

Fichi d'India, or prickly pears, grow like weeds in parts of Calabria, especially near the sea. They are the fruit of the cactus and have the spines to prove it. Around Capo Vaticano, some of the plants are as large as trees. They are wild, not cultivated, so the fruits, which mature in late summer, are unlikely to turn up in markets. People simply take them wherever they find them. The fruits have roughly the shape of a kiwi, with a hard, spine-covered skin that may be yellow, orange, or reddish.

My mother, who has a prickly-pear plant in her backyard, dons gloves to harvest the fruit. She brushes off the spines with a scrub brush, rinses the fruit in a bucket of water, cuts the ends off and then cuts a lengthwise slit. She peels the skin back from the slit and pops the fruit out whole. The interior is reddish-orange, moist, sweet, and juicy, with many soft, jelly-like, edible seeds. Today, most people eat *fichi d'India* fresh for dessert, but some make ice cream or jam with the pulp. To my surprise, some old Calabrian recipes describe how to batter and fry the skin.

The loquat, or *nespolo*, matures in June, along with cherries and mulberries. In the United States, it is an exotic fruit, but many Calabrians have trees of their own, so prized is the fruit. The loquat is about the size of a small apricot, round or oval, and golden-yellow when ripe. The skin is a little tough, but not inedible; some remove it, some do not. The flesh is moist and soft, like a cross between a grape and an apricot, and very sweet. Each fruit has two to four large, black, slippery seeds. The loquat is a hand-to-mouth fruit, typically served, like cherries, in a bowl at the end of a family meal.

Fresh loquats (here at the Vibo Valentia market) grow all over Calabria. I have a tree planted in my backyard for my kids, who love loquats.

Gelato di Ricotta Stregata
RICOTTA ICE CREAM WITH STREGA

A Berkeley, California, pastry chef, Mary Canales, introduced me to the idea of making ice cream with my homemade ricotta. I was happy with the recipe I devised until I tasted the ricotta ice cream at a *gelateria* on the boardwalk in Diamante, a popular beach town on Calabria's Tyrrhenian coast. The shop had flavored its ricotta ice cream with candied orange peel and Strega, an herbal Italian liqueur. I love finding the bits of candied orange peel in this exceedingly creamy gelato, but you could replace them with bits of chopped bittersweet chocolate or unsalted pistachios.

For the silkiest results, make this ice cream with Homemade Ricotta (page 144). Lacking that, purchase a top-quality whole-milk ricotta. Inferior ricotta will make grainy ice cream.

Because there is no egg in this ice cream, the texture does not remain velvety for long. If possible, serve the ice cream the same day you make it, either by itself or as an accompaniment to a warm slice of *crostata* (page 346) or fruit tart.

2½ cups (560 grams) Homemade Ricotta (page 144) *or* top-quality
   whole-milk ricotta

1 cup (200 grams) sugar

1½ tablespoons Strega liqueur

1 teaspoon pure vanilla extract

2 teaspoons finely grated lemon zest

1 cup (250 milliliters) heavy cream

2 ounces (60 grams) Candied Orange Peel (page 308), chopped,
   optional

IN A FOOD PROCESSOR, blend the ricotta, sugar, Strega, vanilla, and lemon zest until smooth. Scrape down the sides of the bowl and add the cream. Pulse to combine, then scrape down the bowl and pulse again until completely blended.

Transfer the mixture to an ice cream freezer and freeze according to the manufacturer's directions. By hand, fold in the candied orange peel, if using. Pack the ice cream in a freezer container and freeze until ready to serve.

MAKES 1½ QUARTS (1½ LITERS)

Crostata con Marmellata di Pomodori Verdi e Gelato di Ricotta Stregata

GREEN TOMATO JAM TART WITH RICOTTA ICE CREAM

The most common *crostata*, or tart, in Italy is the simple, lattice-topped jam tart, a pastry that practically every respectable Italian home cook knows how to make. The dough proportions vary slightly from household to household. Some use a little more or less sugar. Some add vanilla. Some omit baking powder, but I think the leavening produces a crisper crust.

You can fill the *crostata* with any jam or preserves you like, but green tomato jam intrigues people. I pair the tart with homemade ricotta ice cream, but you could use a premium store-bought vanilla ice cream instead. Should you have any *crostata* left over, serve it for breakfast, as the Italians do.

DOUGH

2 cups (280 grams) unbleached all-purpose flour

½ cup (100 grams) sugar

1 teaspoon baking powder

Pinch of kosher salt

¼ pound (1 stick; 110 grams) unsalted butter, chilled, cut into tablespoon-size pieces

1 large egg

1 large egg yolk

Grated zest of 1 lemon

Unsalted butter and flour for the cake pan

1½ cups Green Tomato Jam (page 275) *or* Fresh Fig Jam (page 277)

Ricotta Ice Cream with Strega (page 345) *or* store-bought vanilla ice cream

---

MAKE THE DOUGH: Put the flour, sugar, baking powder, and salt in a food processor. Pulse several times to blend. Add the butter and pulse four to five times, until the mixture resembles coarse crumbs. In a small bowl, whisk together the egg,

egg yolk, and lemon zest. With the food processor running, add the egg mixture through the feed tube. Process just until the dough begins to come together.

Turn the dough out onto a lightly floured surface and knead it gently, just until it comes together into a ball. Do not overwork it or the crust will be tough. Divide the dough into two unequal portions, one-third and two-thirds. With your hand, flatten each portion into a round disk about ½ inch (12 millimeters) thick. Wrap each disk in plastic wrap and refrigerate for at least one hour or up to 24 hours. If it's refrigerated for more than one hour, you will need to soften the dough slightly by removing it from the refrigerator about 30 minutes before you plan to roll it.

Preheat the oven to 375° F (190°C).

Lightly butter and flour the bottom and sides of a 9-inch (23-centimeter) spring-form pan. Place the larger portion of dough between two sheets of plastic wrap. With a rolling pin, flatten it into a 10-inch (25-centimeter) circle. Peel off the top sheet of plastic wrap. Invert the dough into the prepared cake pan, and remove the second sheet of plastic wrap. Nestle the dough in place so it covers the bottom of the pan and comes about ½ inch (12 millimeters) up the sides.

Spread the jam over the dough, covering the bottom evenly.

Place the smaller portion of dough between two sheets of plastic wrap. With a rolling pin, flatten it into a 9-inch (23-centimeter) circle. Chill for 30 minutes. Remove the top sheet of plastic wrap and cut the dough into ½-inch-wide (12-millimeter-wide) strips with a fluted pastry wheel or a sharp knife. Place these strips directly over the tart in a lattice-work pattern, leaving diamond-shaped spaces where the strips cross.

Fold the edges of the bottom dough over the ends of the lattice and press to seal the two doughs and make a border all around.

Bake until the lattice is golden brown, 25 to 30 minutes. Cool on a rack. Remove the sides of the pan and cut the *crostata* into wedges. Serve warm or at room temperature with Ricotta Ice Cream with Strega.

MAKES ONE 9-INCH (23-CENTIMETER) *CROSTATA*, TO SERVE 8

Gelato al Cioccolato con Peperoncino

DARK CHOCOLATE ICE CREAM WITH HOT RED PEPPER

When I saw this peculiar ice cream in a gelato shop in Scalea, I couldn't resist ordering it out of curiosity. After I tasted it, I told the server she had made a mistake: she had given me plain chocolate ice cream. "No, I didn't," she said. "Just wait. The heat comes at the end." She was right. The pepper is only in the finish, like a surprise ending. I tried repeatedly to re-create the ice cream at home but was never satisfied. Mine didn't have the same dense, creamy texture or intensity of flavor. Finally I went to the rear of the shop and asked what kind of chocolate they used. No chocolate, they said. Just cocoa. As I've since learned, Dutch-process cocoa produces a richer, darker color in the ice cream than non-Dutched cocoa and a profoundly deep chocolate taste.

---

1 cup (110 grams) unsweetened Dutch-process cocoa, preferably
    Valrhona (see Resources, page 368)

1 cup (250 milliliters) whole milk

6 large egg yolks

1 cup (200 grams) sugar

1 teaspoon vanilla extract

1⅓ cups (325 milliliters) heavy cream

½ teaspoon Ground Hot Red Pepper (page 303), or to taste

IN A BOWL, whisk the cocoa into the milk until well blended. The mixture will be thick.

In a saucepan, using a whisk or an electric hand-held mixer, whip the egg yolks, sugar, and vanilla until thick, pale yellow, and creamy. The mixture should form a ribbon when you lift the whisk. Whisk in the cocoa mixture.

Set the saucepan over medium heat and cook, whisking constantly, until the mixture visibly thickens, coats the spoon, and registers about 180°F (82°C) on an instant-read thermometer. Do not allow it to boil or it may curdle. Transfer immediately to a bowl and let cool for 15 minutes, then whisk in the cream. Refrigerate until cold. Stir in the red pepper and taste. The pepper's heat comes on slowly, so wait a moment before you decide to add more.

Freeze in an ice cream freezer according to the manufacturer's directions.

MAKES 1½ QUARTS (1½ LITERS)

Gelato alla Liquirizia
PURE LICORICE ICE CREAM

Calabrian licorice is prized by licorice enthusiasts the world over (page 350). I remember sucking on the tough, wild licorice roots as a child and loving their menthol-like taste. Pure licorice, derived from that gnarly root, is much more potent than the sweetened candy made with licorice extract. It is available in several forms, but I purchase it as small, pebble-like hard candies known as *liquirizia spezzata*. The candies melt in hot milk, forming the base for a silky ice cream that will delight anyone who adores licorice. The color is that of coffee gelato, the flavor subtle but unmistakable. Serve plain or with a drizzle of licorice liqueur.

½ ounce (15 grams) pure licorice, preferably Amarelli *spezzata* (see Resources, page 368)

1½ cups (375 milliliters) whole milk

4 large egg yolks

¾ cup (150 grams) sugar

2 cups (500 milliliters) heavy cream

PUT THE LICORICE in a plastic storage bag and pound it with a mallet or rolling pin to crush so it will melt faster in the warm milk. Put the crushed licorice and the milk in a 1½-quart (1½-liter) saucepan and set over medium-low heat. Bring to a simmer, then whisk constantly until the licorice dissolves, about 5 minutes.

In a medium bowl, using a whisk or an electric hand-held mixer, whip the egg yolks and sugar until thick, pale yellow, and creamy. The mixture should form a ribbon when you lift the whisk. Slowly whisk in the licorice mixture.

Return the mixture to the saucepan over medium heat and cook, stirring constantly with a wooden spoon, until the mixture visibly thickens, coats the spoon, and registers 180°F (82°C) on an instant-read thermometer. Do not allow it to boil or it may curdle. Transfer immediately to a bowl and let cool for 15 minutes, then whisk in the cream. Refrigerate until cold.

Freeze in an ice cream freezer according to the manufacturer's directions.

MAKES 1½ QUARTS (1½ LITERS)

Licorice: A Seductive Flavoring from Calabrian Soil

They say that its roots are so long they reach all the way to hell. The vigorous *Glycyr-rhiza glabra*, or licorice plant, has been a mixed blessing in Calabria for centuries. The invasive roots of this wild plant can make a plot of land impossible to cultivate. But those who take the trouble to harvest it can convert the root to cash.

Licorice root is found in other countries as well—in Turkey, Afghanistan, Greece, and Iran, among others—but Calabrian licorice is widely considered superior. It grows in the plains, preferring to establish itself near a river. If you have licorice root in your farmland, you have a problem.

In times past, when Calabria was a collection of feudal estates, the landowners would use peasants to dig out the roots when a parcel lay fallow. The roots were troublesome, so landowners were happy to let the peasants have them for free.

Originally, licorice's attributes were thought to be merely medicinal. It aided digestion, battled viruses, and eased coughs. But by the first half of the eighteenth century, confectioners had begun to convert the sweet root to candy, and the major licorice companies were born in Calabria.

Eventually, the feudal system collapsed and property fell into the hands of small landholders. These farmers could not afford the equipment needed to dig the licorice roots mechanically, so specialist companies arose to do the digging. These harvesting companies own the backhoes and other machinery necessary to rid a field of licorice root. The harvesters get the licorice and the farmers get a clean, plantable field.

The firm of Amarelli, established in Rossano in 1731, is considered Calabria's finest licorice producer. It is the only Calabrian licorice company that begins production with the root as opposed to an extract. Today, Amarelli maintains a licorice museum and invites visitors to tour the factory and see licorice being made.

The twiggy licorice roots are ground fine, then steam is used to extract their sugar and flavor. The resulting inky concoction is strained and evaporated until reduced to a paste of the proper malleable consistency—a critical judgment call that only a highly experienced worker can make. At that point, the dark, molten licorice paste is extruded in strands and polished with jets of steam to make it shine.

Finally, this dense black essence of the root is transformed into the candies that are beloved the world over. The intense, menthol-like flavor of these candies made from nothing but licorice root will surprise anyone accustomed to dime-store licorice ropes made with artificial flavors, corn syrup, and cornstarch.

Semifreddo al Torrone

SEMIFREDDO WITH ALMOND NOUGAT AND BITTERSWEET
CHOCOLATE SAUCE

Semifreddo—literally "half cold"—resembles ice cream, but it is frozen without churning. Whereas ice cream is usually scooped, semifreddo is molded (I use a loaf pan) and sliced. Its texture is softer than that of ice cream because the semifreddo contains beaten egg whites and whipped cream. I was motivated to create my own version after tasting some of the many different *semifreddi* produced at my favorite *gelateria* in Pizzo, a small fishing town on the Tyrrhenian coast, north of Tropea. Italians flavor *semifreddi* with espresso, hazelnut liqueur, lemon, strawberry, chocolate, or whatever strikes their fancy. Because Calabria is known for *torrone* (almond nougat), I folded some crushed *torrone* into a semifreddo and loved the results. I've added a layer of chopped *torrone* and chopped chocolate on top for crunch. A bittersweet chocolate sauce offsets the sweetness.

Be sure to use *torrone classico*, which is brittle, and not *torrone morbido*, which is soft. You will need a meat mallet or heavy cleaver to crush the *torrone*.

About 7 ounces (200 grams) Italian *torrone classico* (almond nougat)

3 large eggs, separated

½ cup (100 grams) sugar

¾ cup (180 milliliters) hot milk

2 tablespoons almond liqueur such as Amaretto

¼ cup (1½ ounces/45 grams) finely chopped bittersweet chocolate

1¼ cups (310 milliliters) heavy cream

CHOCOLATE SAUCE

½ cup (125 milliliters) heavy cream

4 ounces (115 grams) coarsely chopped bittersweet chocolate

SLICE THE NOUGAT into thick fingers, then place in a heavy-duty plastic bag and pound with a mallet or the side of a heavy cleaver until crushed. You should have no pieces larger than a petite pea, but stop short of pounding the nougat to powder, as you want the candy to contribute some crunch to the semifreddo. Set aside ½ cup of the crushed nougat.

Place the egg yolks and the sugar in a bowl. With a whisk or hand-held electric mixer, beat until fluffy and pale yellow, 1 to 2 minutes. Slowly add the hot milk. Put the mixture in a saucepan and cook over moderate heat, stirring constantly with a wooden spoon, until it visibly thickens and registers about 180°F (82°C) on an instant-read thermometer. Do not let the custard boil or it will curdle. Remove from the heat and let cool completely. Stir in the liqueur and all the crushed nougat but the reserved ½ cup.

Line a 9- by 5-inch (23- by 13-centimeter) loaf pan with a single sheet of plastic wrap, covering the bottom and all sides. Sprinkle the bottom with the ½ cup nougat and the chopped chocolate, spreading it evenly.

In an electric mixer or by hand, whip the egg whites to stiff peaks. In a separate bowl, whip the cream to firm peaks.

Gently fold one-third of the egg whites into the custard to lighten it, then gently but thoroughly fold in the remaining whites. Fold in the whipped cream.

Pour the semifreddo mixture into the prepared pan. Cover the pan with plastic wrap without touching the semifreddo surface. Freeze for 6 to 8 hours.

FOR THE CHOCOLATE SAUCE: In a small saucepan, bring the cream to a simmer. Put the chocolate in a bowl and pour the hot cream over it. Let stand for about 3 minutes to soften the chocolate, then whisk until smooth.

To serve, remove the plastic wrap covering the loaf pan. Put a platter upside down over the loaf pan. Invert and remove the loaf pan and plastic wrap. Cut the semifreddo into ½-inch (12-millimeter) slices and place on dessert plates. Spoon chocolate sauce around it. Serve immediately.

SERVES 12

Bagnara's Artisan Torrone

The picturesque fishing town of Bagnara, on Calabria's Tyrrhenian coast, has another specialty besides its sought-after swordfish. The *torrone*, or nougat, from Bagnara, made by a handful of small artisan producers in town, is held in high regard throughout Italy. Thought to be of Arab origin and introduced to Calabria via the Spanish, *torrone* has been produced commercially in Bagnara for at least two hundred years. Recipes and businesses pass from one generation to the next, in unbroken succession; over time, the machinery is modernized and the packaging updated, but the candy remains essentially as it was two centuries ago.

At the small firm of Cundari on the edge of town, Vincenzo Cundari perpetuates the craft he learned from his father. In the kitchen behind his tiny shop, egg whites and honey are whipped in a warm water bath for seven to eight hours, until they are thick, stiff, and fluffy. Toasted almonds are added to the mixer, then, working with a little at a time so the mixture stays hot and malleable, workers flatten it on work tables with rolling pins and cut the slabs into the traditional log shapes, or individual petite *torroncini*. A machine applies the chocolate glaze, then workers attach a thin sheet of edible paper made with rice flour or potato starch to keep the candy from sticking to its wrap.

Torrone production occurs largely in September and October, in time for the Christmas holidays. Firms like Cundari make the sweet in several permutations, and every *torrone* fancier has a favorite. *Torrone* may be chewy or crunchy, covered with white or dark chocolate, studded with candied fruit, or scented with orange essence. *Torrone gelato*, despite the name, is not frozen but a chewy *torrone* with candied fruit and a chocolate coat. *Torrone martiniana*—"poor man's *torrone*"—is the oldest type, made with only caramelized honey and almonds, no egg whites. It is the color of dark caramel and as brittle as praline.

Pizzo's Famous Ice Cream Truffle

Tartufo al Modo di Pizzo
PIZZO'S FAMOUS ICE CREAM TRUFFLE

The picturesque fishing town of Pizzo on Calabria's Tyrrhenian coast is a mecca for ice cream fans, who come expressly to taste a dessert developed there. The town's main square is lined with *gelaterie* (ice cream shops), all of them making the famous *tartufo* and claiming that theirs is the best or the only authentic one. As I discovered when I began trying to decipher the recipe, the shopkeepers are extremely competitive, even jealous, and disinclined to share any details with an outsider.

Pizzo's truffle mystified me for a long time. It is a molded ice cream dessert resembling a giant black truffle, with a cocoa coating concealing two layers of ice cream: a chocolate layer on the outside and hazelnut within. But the surprise is in the center, a molten fudge sauce that oozes like lava when you cut into the truffle. tHow, I asked myself, can a frozen dessert have a flowing interior?

In the interest of research, I sampled the *tartufo* at several of Pizzo's *gelaterie*. They varied only slightly, depending on the skills of the *gelataio* (the ice cream maker). "Play with the amount of sugar," one *gelataio* told me when I asked how to keep the fudgy center soft. No one would be more specific.

One July afternoon when a storm was brewing and few tourists strolled Pizzo's main square, I struck up a conversation with the proprietor of Chez Toi, who was standing outside his modest *gelateria* watching the ominous clouds gather. He insisted that I come inside to taste his *tartufo*. As soon as I sat down at one of his little café tables, the sky opened up and rain began pelting the street in a downpour so furious that it was impossible to think of venturing out again until it stopped. Owner Vittorio Riga, who had no other customers, eventually sat down with me and began revealing some of the *tartufo*'s secrets. He showed me his workroom, described how he shaped the truffles by hand, and confirmed that the fudge filling contained only cocoa, sugar, and water, although he would not reveal the proportions.

At home in California, preparing to experiment with the filling again, I had a stroke of luck. While researching the history of Pizzo's *tartufo* online, I stumbled on a document that Pizzo's artisanal *tartufo* producers had written jointly. To protect their livelihood from the many imitators making Pizzo-style *tartufi* in Diamante and other Calabrian beach towns, they had banded together to define the official dessert and propose certification for Pizzo's artisanal producers. (Only in Italy is ice cream taken so seriously.) The document did not give the recipe, but it did give ranges for the various ingredients, information that helped me devise a liquid-centered *tartufo* as good as any in Pizzo.

Although Riga showed me how he shapes the *tartufo* in his hand, I found this method awkward. Instead, I use a slope-sided glass custard cup lined with plastic wrap as a mold. Shortly before serving the *tartufi*, I unmold them, coat them with cocoa, and let them soften a little in the refrigerator so the ice cream will be silky and the filling properly fluid.

Even the Pizzo producers don't agree on the origins of their trademark dessert. Their document puts forth several theories. The most often repeated one attributes the *tartufo* to a Sicilian *gelataio* who opened a shop in the town and introduced the dessert in the 1950s.

Dark Chocolate Ice Cream with Hot Red Pepper (page 348), hot red
    pepper omitted

HAZELNUT ICE CREAM
½ pound (225 grams) hazelnuts
1½ cups (375 milliliters) milk
1 teaspoon vanilla extract
4 large egg yolks
¾ cup (150 grams) sugar
1½ cups (375 milliliters) heavy cream

CHOCOLATE FILLING
⅔ cup (75 grams) Dutch-process cocoa powder
½ cup (100 grams) granulated sugar

COATING
½ cup (60 grams) cocoa powder (not Dutch process), sifted
½ cup (100 grams) superfine sugar

Special equipment: Ten 6-ounce (180-milliliter) slope-sided glass
    custard cups

FOR THE HAZELNUT ICE CREAM: Preheat the oven to 350°F (175°C). Place the nuts on a rimmed baking sheet and bake, stirring occasionally, until they are fragrant and golden and their skins begin to crack, 12 to 15 minutes. While they are hot, transfer the nuts to an old, dry kitchen towel, gather the edges of the towel together into a bag, and rub the nuts vigorously inside the towel to loosen the skins. When you open the towel, you will find that many of the nuts have shed their papery skin. With your fingers, rub away as much of the remaining skin as you can. It's okay if you can't remove every last trace. Let the nuts cool before continuing.

Place the cooled hazelnuts in a food processor and grind them into a coarse paste, like natural peanut butter. Place the hazelnut paste in a 2-quart (2-liter) saucepan and whisk in the milk. Bring to a simmer over medium heat, whisking, then turn off the heat and let the mixture steep for 15 minutes. Stir in the vanilla.

In a medium bowl, whisk the egg yolks and sugar until the yolks are pale, the sugar has dissolved, and the mixture is thick and creamy, about 2 minutes.

Slowly add the warm milk to the egg mixture, whisking constantly until well blended. Then return the milk-egg mixture to the saucepan. Cook over medium heat, stirring constantly with a wooden spoon, until the mixture is thick enough to coat the spoon and reaches 180°F (82°C) on an instant-read thermometer, 3 to 5 minutes. Do not let it boil or it may curdle. Remove from the heat.

Transfer the mixture to a large, clean bowl and let it cool for 10 minutes. Whisk in the cream. Strain through a fine sieve into another bowl, pressing with the back of a spoon to extract all the liquid from the ground hazelnuts. Refrigerate the custard until cold. Transfer to an ice cream freezer and freeze according to the manufacturer's directions. Pack the freshly churned ice cream in an airtight plastic container and freeze for at least 3 hours before serving. You will have about 1½ quarts.

FOR THE CHOCOLATE FILLING: Place the cocoa powder, ⅔ cup (160 milliliters) water, and granulated sugar in a 1½-quart (1½-liter) pot. Whisk to combine and place over medium heat. Cook, whisking constantly, until the mixture reaches 190° F (88°C) on a candy thermometer, just shy of boiling. Remove from the heat and cool. When cool, transfer to a plastic container and place in the freezer until it is firm but not too stiff to scoop, about one hour. You can leave it in the freezer for weeks, if you like, but then you will need to thaw it until it is soft enough to scoop.

TO ASSEMBLE THE TRUFFLES: Remove the ice creams from the freezer and let soften enough so they can be easily scooped. If they become too soft while you are assembling the truffles, they will be difficult to mold; return them briefly to the freezer to firm them.

Line each mold with a sheet of plastic wrap that overhangs the rim by 2 inches (5 centimeters) all around. (You need enough overhang to cover the surface once you've filled the mold.) Press the plastic wrap against the mold so it adheres. Working with one mold at a time, put ¼ cup (60 milliliters) of chocolate ice cream in the center of the plastic wrap. With the back of a spoon, press the ice cream against the bottom and sides of the mold to form a shell of even thickness throughout. The shell should come all the way up the sides of the mold. Return the mold to the freezer for 15 minutes to firm the ice cream while you line the remaining molds with chocolate ice cream.

Again working with one mold at a time, remove a mold from the freezer and put ¼ cup (60 milliliters) of hazelnut ice cream in the center of the hardened chocolate shell. With the back of a clean spoon, press the hazelnut ice cream against the bottom and sides of the chocolate shell to create a similar shell of even thickness, with a well in the center. The objective is to create a "cup" with a layer of chocolate ice cream outside and a layer of hazelnut ice cream inside, with a hollow in the center to contain the soft filling.

Remove the chocolate filling from the freezer 1 hour ahead to soften. In the hollow of the ice cream cup, place 1 tablespoon of the chocolate filling. Return the filled mold to the freezer for 15 minutes, then remove the mold from the freezer and lift the edges of the plastic wrap to close the ice cream "cup" around the chocolate filling. To seal the filling completely, top with about 1 tablespoon of chocolate ice cream, spreading it over the filling so that the filling can't be seen. Place the overhanging plastic wrap over the surface to seal it. At this point, the *tartufo* can be returned to the freezer in its mold, or inverted, still in its plastic wrap, onto a plate or tray that will fit in your freezer. (Do not stack the *tartufi*.) Continue to form and freeze *tartufi* until you have run out of ice cream or chocolate filling. Freeze for at least 4 hours or overnight.

TO COAT AND SERVE: Combine the cocoa powder and superfine sugar in a wide, shallow dish and mix well. About 20 minutes before serving, remove the *tartufi* from the freezer. Working with one at a time, unwrap a *tartufo* and roll it in the cocoa-sugar mixture until generously coated all over. Put the *tartufi* on a tray and place in the refrigerator to soften for about 15 minutes before serving. Transfer to individual plates to serve.

MAKES 10 *TARTUFI*

Morino Riga, who showed me how to make *tartufo di Pizzo*, at "Chez Toi" in Pizzo

A bottle of homemade wine at a friend's house in Verbicaro. Most Calabrians to this day make their own wine.

Vini di Calabria
the wines of Calabria

U 'mgiari senza 'mbiviri e comu 'u nuvulatu senze chiovari.
A meal without wine is like a cloudy day without rain.

I grew up in a hill town known for its wine. Virtually everyone in Verbicaro had a few vines, enough to make wine for their own consumption. Some residents, like my parents, had more vineyard land and were able to make a living by selling wine or grapes. Every home had an underground *catuvo*, or wine cellar, where the wine barrels and bottled wines were kept. Periodically, my father and his friends would gather in each other's cool, dark cellars to sample and critique the wine and share a snack of bread and homemade *salumi*, or the crisply fried dried sweet peppers known as *peperoni cruschi*.

In my father's day, Verbicaro was best known for its dry red wine from the indigenous Magliocco dolce grape (my father knew it by another name: Guarnaccia nera) and for a dessert wine made from the Zibibbo grape, a type of Muscat. People from as far away as Naples would come to Verbicaro to buy wine.

My father and his neighbors pruned their vines in the *alberello* ("little tree") style, a method known to the ancient Greeks. *Alberello* vines aren't trained horizontally on trellises, like modern French or California grapevines. Instead they grow without supports and are pruned low to the ground, similar to the old head-pruned Zinfandel vines in some California vineyards. This method protects the grapes from the fierce sun and wind, while allowing air to pass through the clusters, keeping them dry and mildew free. It naturally restricts the yield, so the grapes develop more concentration. And because the vines stay low, they absorb reflected heat from the ground, which helps ripen the grapes fully and produce wines with substantial alcohol.

My father may not have understood all the viticultural arguments for the *alberello* method—he was simply growing grapes the way his father did—but it suits

Calabria's hot, dry climate. Many growers later turned to trellis systems to get bigger yields and accommodate mechanical harvesters, but a few—like Librandi and Odoardi—are returning to the more labor-intensive *alberello* method for their best wines.

My father and mother worked together in the vineyard, doing almost every task by hand. They hired men to help them turn the soil in the spring but otherwise they had no assistance and no machinery. When a crew was there, my mother would prepare a huge mid-morning meal for them. As a child, I always wondered how these men could eat so much food so early. Only later did I realize that they had been laboring in the fields since dawn.

Verbicaro's wine industry declined gradually over the twentieth century, the victim of Calabria's troubled economy and steady emigration. Many frustrated Verbicaresi, including my parents, simply walked away from their vineyards. Today, there is little commercial grape growing in Verbicaro itself, although there is a Verbicaro DOC (*denominazione di origine controllata*, or appellation), which encompasses a wider area. Even so, the DOC produces relatively little wine.

My parents' experience as struggling grape growers in the 1950s and 1960s stands in stark contrast to the energy, excitement, and optimism prevalent among Calabrian wine producers today. Visionary winemakers like Nicodemo Librandi, Gregorio Odoardi, and Roberto Ceraudo are bringing attention and critical acclaim to a region that has the longest wine history in Italy.

Calabria is the original *Oenotria* ("the land where grapes flourish"), a name bestowed by the Greek colonists who made this peninsula a stronghold of Magna Graecia. They found grapevines here and they planted more, especially in the coastal area between Sibari and Crotone. The wine from Krimisa (today's Cirò) was so esteemed that the Greeks used it to toast victorious Olympic athletes. Many wine historians believe that the Greeks introduced some of the grape varieties that remain important in Calabria today, such as Greco bianco and Greco nero.

The Romans expanded the vineyards in Calabria and exported the wine to other parts of their empire. Archeologists have turned up plentiful evidence of wine making in Calabria during Roman times, such as storage vats and amphorae, and writings of the Roman politician Cassiodorus praise the wine of the region.

During the Byzantine era, wine production persisted largely in the monasteries, as wine was essential to religious rites. Grapevine cultivation moved into the hills in this period, as people abandoned the coastlines for the safety of the interior, fearing both Arab invasions and malaria. By the 1500s, Calabria's wines were well known beyond its borders, with Scalea a major shipping point. Three centuries later, wealthy young Europeans on their Grand Tour were praising Calabrian wines in their letters and journals.

Disaster swept Calabria's vineyards in the late 1800s, as it did elsewhere in Europe, with the arrival of phylloxera. This voracious root louse devastated vines, especially in the province of Reggio Calabria. Infected sites had to be replanted with vines grafted onto phylloxera-resistant American rootstock. Grapevine production didn't recover until the 1920s.

Two world wars and the slow pace of modernization in twentieth-century Calabria afflicted the wine industry as well. Calabria lagged in adopting modern vinification technology, such as temperature-controlled stainless steel fermentation tanks, and temperature- and humidity-controlled facilities for aging.

Until the end of the twentieth century, few Calabrian grape growers bottled and marketed their own wines. Instead, the grapes were sold to local cooperatives, and the wine made there was sold in bulk for blending—used to add color and alcoholic strength to wines made in regions less favored by sun.

Today, that old system is in rapid transition, as forward-thinking Calabrian wine producers like Librandi, Lento, Ceraudo, Odoardi, and Statti have taken to bottling their own wines under their own names. Families that used to sell their grapes are starting small, independent wine making ventures, investing in modern winery equipment, and replanting vineyards using contemporary techniques. It has taken centuries, but Calabria is ready to recapture the stature it had during Greek times.

Refreshingly, several of Calabria's premier winemakers are showcasing the native grapes instead of, or in addition to, international varieties. Librandi, one of the few Calabrian wineries with strong export sales, exemplifies the region's renewed pride in these indigenous grapes. Although he never abandoned the native varieties, Nicodemo Librandi, a leading figure in the region, once believed that his winery's prestige lay in bottling international varieties such as Cabernet Sauvignon, Merlot, and Chardonnay—or blends of these varieties with native grapes. Today, the winery's vision has shifted. Librandi has sought out and planted many indigenous Calabrian varieties, including many that had been all but abandoned in favor of more productive types. The winery aims to identify and preserve the old grape varieties that have the most potential to produce great wines. Ironically, Calabria's historic reluctance to modernize its vineyards kept some of these grapevines from extinction, waiting to be rediscovered.

Calabria contributes only about 2 percent of Italian wine production, and roughly 80 percent of Calabrian wine is red. It ranks fifteenth among Italy's twenty regions in volume and will never be a big producer because much of the terrain is too mountainous for vineyards. The region's thirty-two thousand acres of grapevines (about thirteen thousand hectares) are found primarily along the coasts.

Twelve areas in Calabria enjoy Italy's prestigious DOC status, but some of the region's most intriguing wines don't bear the DOC designation. Some Calabrian producers, like winemakers elsewhere in Italy, find the DOC regulations too restrictive. They prefer to forgo DOC status for some of their wines in favor of the freedom to blend varieties that the DOC might not allow. Librandi's "Gravello," the winery's flagship red wine, merits only the lower-status IGT (*indicazione geografica tipica*) because it is a blend of Gaglioppo and Cabernet Sauvignon, the latter variety not permitted in wines entitled to the Cirò DOC.

Calabria is one of the last untapped wine frontiers of Italy, a region where ancient wisdom and renewed spirit converge to ensure a bright future.

CALABRIAN GRAPE VARIETIES

Pinning down names for the grapes used in Calabria's wines is like trying to nail down the wind. From one village to the next, the names change. Magliocco dolce, an important red grape, has at least thirteen aliases, each one favored in a particular location. And two different areas may use the same name for two different grapes. Only in modern times, with DNA analysis, have researchers succeeded in bringing some order to the chaos. The Librandi winery, in collaboration with Regione Calabria, the regional government, funded a massive research effort to gather and study the native grapes. The effort culiminated in an authoritative book, *Il Gaglioppo e i Suoi Fratelli: I Vitigni Autoctoni Calabresi* (see Bibliography, page 374), which is the source for much of the information I give here.

So with the caution that disputes persist about the proper names for the cultivars grown in Calabria, I list here the principal red and white wine grapes grown in the region for high-quality wine, using what I believe to be the most common name.

WHITE WINE VARIETIES

Greco bianco: Presumed (but not proven) to be of Greek origin, Greco bianco produces dry, aromatic white wines of high acidity that can age well. It is the main variety in the white wines of Cirò and Lamezia, although it is usually blended with other white varieties. It is also known as Guardavalle, among other names.

Greco di Bianco: In this case, the Bianco refers not to the Italian word for white but to the wine-growing commune of Bianco in the province of Reggio Calabria. It is the same grape as Malvasia delle Lipari, grown on Italy's Aeolian islands and made there into a sought-after dessert wine. Similarly, in Calabria, the Greco di Bianco yields one of the rarest and most ancient dessert wines in Italy and one of the great sweet wines of the world. Bottled as Greco di Bianco DOC, this luscious *passito* (dessert wine) delivers a heady scent of bergamot.

Mantonico bianco: Indigenous to Calabria, Mantonico bianco produces aromatic whites with good acidity. The variety is grown primarily on the southern end of the Ionian coast. Librandi uses 100 percent Mantonico bianco for its Efeso, a dry white wine with aromas of almond and fig, but other producers sun dry the grapes and use them for *passito.* The variety is sometimes confused with Montonico, a grape grown in Central Italy.

Other indigenous white varieties grown in Calabria include Guarnaccia bianca, Malvasia bianca, Pecorello, Trebbiano toscano, and Moscato bianco. Some growers have also planted Chardonnay, Pinot Blanc, and Sauvignon Blanc.

RED WINE VARIETIES

Gaglioppo: There are approximately eighteen thousand acres of Gaglioppo in Calabria, accounting for more than a quarter of the total wine-grape acreage. It is the prinicipal grape in the highly regarded Cirò DOC, but it also appears in the DOC wines of Bivongi, Donnici, Lamezia, Melissa, Pollino, S. Anna di Isola Capo Rizzuto, San Vito di Luzzi, Savuto, Scavigna, and Verbicaro. Typically, Gaglioppo produces a vibrant, medium-bodied red wine with medium tannins and aromas of cranberry, oregano, tomato, mint, and strawberry. Depending on producer style, wines from Gaglioppo can be rustic and earthy or modern and fruit forward. The *rosato* (rosé) made from Gaglioppo is a refreshing choice during Calabria's hot summers and a perfect match for the region's spicy seafood dishes.

Magliocco dolce: An important variety during Greek times, Magliocco dolce is increasingly recognized as a noble variety, yielding red wines of complexity. It produces more muscular wines than Gaglioppo, with aromas of plum and blackberry along with spicebox scents of clove, juniper berry, and white pepper. This is the variety to keep an eye on. Odoardi, Librandi, and Lento are producing excellent wines from Magliocco. Arvina, Guarnaccia nera, and Marsigliana are among its many synonyms.

Nerello: Several different cultivars bear the name Nerello ("little black one") in Calabria, usually with an identifying adjective to distinguish them (Nerello mascalese, Nerello cappuccio, Nerello paesano). In some parts of Calabria, the grape known simply as Nerello is the same as Tuscany's Sangiovese. Perhaps the most admired of these Nerello cultivars is Nerello mascalese, an up-and-coming variety in both Calabria and Sicily. Wines made from it exhibit aromas of rose hips and cherry, a muscular structure, and good acidity. In Calabria, Nerello mascalese is grown mainly around Lamezia and used in the Lamezia DOC and Sant'Anna di Isola Capo Rizzuto DOC wines. Nerello cappuccio is often part of the blend in the DOC reds of Lamezia, Savuto, and Scavigna.

Other indigenous red varieties grown in Calabria include Calabrese (the grape known in Sicily as Nero d'Avola), Greco nero, Castiglione, Prunesta, and Nocera. Growers have also planted some international red varieties, such as Merlot, Cabernet Sauvignon, Cabernet Franc, and Sangiovese.

CALABRIA'S DOC WINES

Most of Calabria's twelve DOC zones produce wines of relatively modest stature that tend to remain in Calabria. In quality terms, the two most important DOCs by far are Cirò and Lamezia, with Scavigna and Savuto gaining some renown thanks to the presence there of respected producer Gregorio Odoardi.

As for Cirò, this prestigious DOC in the Crotone province is the benchmark for Calabrian wine today, as it has been for centuries. Most of Calabria's wine exports are from this zone. The whites are made largely with Greco bianco, the reds and *rosato* with Gaglioppo. Cirò producers have been modernizing vineyard and wine making techniques, resulting in wines with fresher aromas, richer fruit, and lower alcohol than in the past. The red wines' soft tannins make them a suitable accompaniment to Calabria's spicy dishes, yet the wines are capable of aging. Roberto

Ceraudo, Fattoria San Francesco, Ippolito 1845, Librandi, Santa Venere, and Luigi Vivacqua are among the Cirò producers to watch for.

Lamezia, a DOC zone on the Tyrrhenian coast, produces red and white wines from many varieties and in high volume, but some wineries, such as Statti and Cantine Lento, are capable of outstanding quality. The predominant red grapes include Nerello mascalese, Magliocco dolce, and Gaglioppo. The Lamezia DOC whites are typically blends dominated by Greco bianco.

Traveling in Calabria provides the opportunity to sample wines from the lesser-known DOCs of Bivongi, Donnici, Greco di Bianco, Melissa, Pollino, San Vito di Luzzi, Sant'Anna di Isola Capo Rizzuto, Savuto, Scavigna, and Verbicaro.

Ingredient Resources

General

For a variety of Italian food products used in Calabrian cooking, including dried wild oregano, dried hot red pepper, tuna *bottarga*, Pecorino Crotonese, polenta, *guanciale*, and *lardo*:

www.amazon.com

BuonItalia
75 Ninth Avenue
New York, NY 10011
212-633-9090
www.buonitalia.com

Ditalia
1401 South Boyle
St. Louis, MO 63110
888-260-2192
www.ditalia.com

Salumeria Italiana
151 Richmond Street
Boston, MA 02109
800-400-5916
www.salumeriaitaliana.com

For Calabrian tuna, cheese, peppers, licorice, and other ingredients:

Rosetta's Amazon Store
http://astore.amazon.com/
wwwcalabriafr-20

Baking

For Valrhona cocoa powder and chocolate:

Chocosphere
P.O. Box 2237
Portland, OR 97062
877-992-4626
www.chocosphere.com

For unglazed quarry tiles:

Lowe's
800-445-6937
www.lowes.com

Cheese and Cheese Making

For liquid rennet and ricotta draining baskets:

New England Cheesemaking Supply Company
P.O. Box 85
Ashfield, MA 01330
413-628-3808
www.cheesemaking.com

For *ricotta affumicata*:

www.igourmet.com
877-446-8763

Liqueurs

For maraschino liqueur (*Luxardo Maraschino*):

BevMo!
www.bevmo.com

Meat, Fresh and Cured

For natural hog casings for sausage making:

The Sausage Maker, Inc.
1500 Clinton Bldg 123
Buffalo, NY 14206
888-490-8525
www.sausagemaker.com

For fresh pork belly:

Niman Ranch
Oakland, California
866-808-0340
www.nimanranch.com

For fresh rabbit:

Nicky USA
223 SE 3rd Avenue
Portland, OR 97214
800-469-4162
www.nickyusa.com

For baby lamb or goat:

Jamison Farm
171 Jamison Lane
Latrobe, PA 15650
800-237-5262
www.jamisonfarm.com

For Italian-style unrolled pancetta and *guanciale*:

La Quercia
400 Hakes Drive
Norwalk, IA 50211
515-981-1625
www.laquercia.us

For Italian-style *salumi*,
including *guanciale* and *'nduja*:

Boccalone Salumeria
Ferry Building Marketplace,
Shop 21
San Francisco, CA 94111
415-433-6500
www.boccalone.com

Calabria Pork Store
2338 Arthur Avenue
Bronx, NY 10458
718-367-5145
www.calabriaporkstore.com

Pasta and Pasta Making
For Calabrian *filej* (or *filei*)
and *paccheri*:

Todaro Bros.
555 Second Avenue
New York, NY 10016
877-472-2767
www.todarobros.com

For Rustichella d'Abruzzo
strozzapreti:

Market Hall Foods
5655 College Avenue
Oakland, CA 94618
888-952-4005
www.markethallfoods.com

For a ridged gnocchi paddle:

Fante's Kitchen Wares Shop
1006 S. Ninth Street
Philadelphia, PA 19147
800-443-2683
www.fantes.com

Sur La Table
800-243-0852
www.surlatable.com

Polenta, Calabrian Style
For Moretti's Bramata Bianca
(white cornmeal for polenta):

Market Hall Foods
5655 College Avenue
Oakland, CA 94618
888-952-4005
www.markethallfoods.com

Produce: Fresh, Canned, and Dried
For canned San Marzano
tomatoes:

Gustiamo
1715 West Farms Road
Bronx, NY 10460
877-907-2525
www.gustiamo.com

A. G. Ferrari Foods
14234 Catalina Street
San Leandro, CA 94577
877-878-2783
www.agferrari.com

For dried cranberry (borlotti)
beans:

Rancho Gordo
1924 Yajome Street
Napa, CA 94559
707-259-1935
www.ranchogordo.com

For fresh green and ripe olives
for curing:

Penna Gourmet Olives
3986 County Road NN
Orland, CA 95963
530-865-9810
www.greatolives.com

For dried sweet red peppers
(whole):

Italian Harvest
San Bruno, California
866-408-4457
www.italianharvest.com

For *peperoni cruschi*:

Zingerman's
422 Detroit Street
Ann Arbor, MI 48104
888-636-8162
www.zingermans.com

Seafood

For Norwegian salt cod:

Corti Bros.
5810 Folsom Boulevard
Sacramento, CA 95819
800-509-3663
www.cortibros.biz

For Callipo solid light tuna
in olive oil:

A. G. Ferrari Foods
14234 Catalina Street
San Leandro, CA 94577
877-878-2783
www.agferrari.com

For *bottarga*:

Gustiamo
1715 West Farms Road
Bronx, NY 10460
877-907-2525
www.gustiamo.com

Seasonings

For Calabrian paprika (*pepe
rosso*), hot pepper (*peperoncino*),
and wild fennel seed:

Italian Harvest
San Bruno, California
866-408-4457
www.italianharvest.com

Sausage Debauchery
www.sausagedebauchery.com

For dried Sicilian oregano:

Market Hall Foods
5655 College Avenue
Oakland, CA 94618
888-952-4005
www.markethallfoods.com

Vegetable Seeds

For wild fennel (*finocchio selvatico*) seeds, escarole seeds, "Sweet
Italian" and "Marconi" pepper seeds, "Principe Borghese"
tomato seeds, and *peperoncino*
(cayenne or Etna) seeds:

Seeds from Italy
P.O. Box 149
Winchester, MA 01890
781-721-5904
www.growitalian.com

Garden Edibles
www.gardenedibles.com
Specializing in vegetable seeds
from Southern Italy

Places to Stay, Eat, and Visit in Calabria

Please visit my Web site, www.cookingwithrosetta.com, for more suggestions on where to stay, eat, shop, and visit in Calabria.

Province key:

(CS) Cosenza
(CZ) Catanzaro
(KR) Crotone
(RC) Reggio Calabria
(VV) Vibo Valentia

Hotels

Grand Hotel San Michele
SS 18 Contrada Bosco, 8/9
Cetraro (CS)
Tel: (0982) 91012
www.sanmichele.it

Palazzo del Capo
Via C. Colombo, 5
Cittadella del Capo (CS)
Tel: (0982) 95674
www.palazzodelcapo.it

Villa San Domenico
Via Sotto gli Olmi
Morano Calabro (CS)
Tel: (0981) 399991
www.albergovillasandomenico.it

Porto Pirgos Hotel
Località Marina di
    Bordila S.S. 522
Tropea (CZ)
Tel: (0963) 600351
www.portopirgos.com

Agriturismi

Agriturismo Contrada Guido
Contrada Guido
Sellia Marina (CZ)
Tel: (0961) 961495

Agriturismo le Carolee
Contrada Gabella
Pianopoli (CZ)
Tel: (0968) 35076
www.lecarolee.com

Agriturismo Dattilo
Contrada Dattilo
Marina di Strongoli (KR)
Tel: (0962) 865613
www.dattilo.it

Fattoria il Borghetto
Locanda Capo Bianco
Isola Capo Rizzuto (KR)
Tel: (0962) 796223
www.fattoriailborghetto.it

Agriturismo le Puzelle
Contrada Puzelle
Santa Severina, (KR)
Tel: (0962) 51004
www.lepuzelle.it

Restaurants

Ristorante Pantagruel
Via Pittore Santanna, 2
Centro Storico Rende (CS)
Tel: (0984) 443846
www.pantagruelilristorante.it

La Locanda di Alia
Via Jetticelle, 55
87012 Castrovíllari (CS)
Tel: (0981) 46370
www.alia.it

La Rondinella
Via Vittorio Emanuele III, 21
87029 Scalea (CS)
Tel: (0985) 91360
www.la-rondinella.it

La Capricciosa
Via A. Viscardi
Firmo (CS)
Tel: (0981) 940297
Arbëreshe specialties

La Kamastra
Piazza Municipio, 3/6
87010 Civita (CS)
Tel: (0981) 73387
Arbëreshe specialties

Tari
Piazza Maggiore De Palma
Scalea Centro Storico
Scalea (CS)
Tel: (0985) 91777

La Taverna del Conte
Località Pietrarossa
Diamante (CS)
Tel: (0985) 876191

La Tavernetta
Contrada Campo San
   Lorenzo, 14
87052 Camigliatello Silano (CS)
Tel: (0984) 579026

Ristorante il Vecchio
Castagno
Locanda Tavernisi
88040 Serrastretta (CZ)
Tel: (0968) 81071
Chestnut specialties; superb
antipasti

L'Aragosta
Locanda Macchia
Marina di Nocera Terinese (CZ)
Tel: (0968) 93385
www.ristorantelaragosta.com

Ristorante Pimms
Largo Migliaresi
88038 Tropea (CZ)
Tel: (0963) 666105

Ristorante Dattilo
Contrada Dattilo
Marina di Strongoli (KR)
Tel: (0962) 865613
www.dattilo.it

Il Conte di Melissa
SS 106 Torre di Guardia
   Aragonese
Torre Melissa (KR)
Tel: (0962) 865386

Ristorante Max
Via Togliatti
Ciro Marina (KR)
Tel: (0962) 373009
www.maxpub.it

Ristorante da Ercole
Viale Antonio Gramsci, 122
88900 Crotone (KR)
Tel: (0962) 901425

Ristorante Medusa
Via Salomone, 243
Pizzo (VV)
Tel: (0963) 531203
www.ristorantemedusa.com

Ristorante a Casa Janca
Riviera Prangi,
   Localita Marinella
Pizzo (VV)
Tel: (0963) 264364

L'Approdo
Via Roma, 22
89811 Vibo Marina (VV)
Tel: (0963) 572640
www.lapprodo.com

Taverna Kerkyra
Via Vittorio Emanuale, 217
89011 Bagnara Calabra (RC)
Tel: (0966) 372260

Baylik
Vico Leone, 1/3/5
89100 Reggio Calabria (RC)
Tel: (0965) 48624
www.baylik.it

Wineries

Azienda Vinicola
Tramontana
Via Casa Savoia, 156
89135 Gallico Marina (RC)
Tel: (0965) 370067
www.vinitramontana.it

Cantine Lento
Via del Progresso, 1
88046 Lamezia Terme (CZ)
Tel: (0968) 23804
www.cantinelento.it

Cantine Spadafora
Zona Industriale Piano Lago, 18
Mangone (CS)
Tel: (0984) 969080
www.cantinespadafora.it

Cantine Viola
Via Roma, 18
87010 Saracena (CS)
Tel: (0981) 349495
www.cantineviola.it

Casa Vinicola Criserà
Via Militare, 10
89053 Catona di Reggio Calabria
   (RC)
Tel: (0965) 302683
www.crisevini.it

Ceraudo
Contrada Dattilo
Marina di Strongoli (KR)
Tel: (0962) 865613
www.dattilo.it

Fattoria San Francesco
Strada Provinciale ex S.S. 106
Loc. Quattromani
88813 Cirò (KR)
Tel: (0962) 32228
www.fattoriasanfrancesco.it

Librandi Antonio &
Nicodemo
S.S. 106 – Contrada da S. Gennaro
88811 Cirò Marina (KR)
Tel: (0962) 31518
www.librandi.it

G. B. Odoardi
Contrada Campodorato
88047 Nocera Terinese (CZ)
Tel: (0984) 29961

Santa Venere
Tenuta Voltagrande SP4
88813 Cirò (KR)
Tel: (0962) 38519
www.santavenere.com

Statti
Contrada Lenti
88046 Lamezia Terme (CZ)
Tel: (0968) 456138
www.statti.com

Terre di Balbia
Loc. Montino
Altomonte (CS)
Tel: (0481) 61264
www.terredibalbia.it

Verbicaro Viti e Vini
C.da S. Francesco
Verbicaro (CS)
Tel: (0985) 60292
www.verbicarovitievini.it

Vintripodi Cantine
Via Vecchia Comunale, 28
89121 Archi (RC)
Tel: (0965) 48438
www.vintripodi.it

Bibliography

Alois, Ester, Anna Amoroso, and Silvana Lombardi. *Chi màngisi 'nta l'anno: storielle di cibi e di feste.* Self-published. Castrovillari, 1989.

Andricciola, Pietro. *I Vini di Calabria.* Lamezia Terme: Calabria Mia, 2004.

Baccellieri, Carlo. *La buona cucina di Calabria.* Reggio Calabria: Falzea Editore, 1999.

Canadè, Teresa Gravina. *Una Calabrese in cucina.* Soveria Mannelli: Rubbettino Editore, 2000.

Cavalcanti, Ottavio. *Di cibo e dintorni.* Cassano Jonio: Istituto di Ricerca e di Studi di Demologia e di Dialettologia, 1995.

———. *Del mangier simboli.* Castrovillari: Editrice Il Coscile, 2005.

De Leo, Pietro. *In Calabria: Nature, Art, History.* Soveria Mannelli: CittàCalabria Edizioni, 2004.

Dodaro, Francesca. *Sua maestà il porco.* Cosenza: Edizioni Periferia, 2004.

Ferretti, Lya, and Piero Serra. *Cucina e vini in Calabria.* Monteruscello: Salvatore di Fraia Editore, publication date unknown.

Fotia, Giuseppina, and Salvino Nucera. *Sapori Antichi della Calabria Greca.* Reggio Calabria: Giuseppe Pontari Editore, 1996.

Multiple contributors. *Il Gaglioppo e i Suoi Fratelli: I Vitigni Autoctoni Calabresi.* Cirò Marina: Librandi Spa, 2008.

Imbesi, Bianca Paliologo. *Cucina Tradizionale di Calabria.* Rome: Gangemi Editore, publication date unknown.

Stella, Gian Antonio, and Vito Teti. *La Nave della Sila.* Soveria Mannelli: Rubbetino Editore, 2006.

Teti, Vito, ed. *Mangiare Meridiano.* Cosenza: Carical, 1996.

Vairo, Filippo. *Antichi sapori di Amantea.* Self-published. First ed. 1996; second ed. 2005.

Index

Note: Page numbers in **boldface** type refer to recipes themselves;
page numbers in *italic* type refer to photographs.

Verbicaro wines, 367

Verdicchio, 165

verdure. See vegetables; *specific vegetables*

Vestini Campagnano Pallagrello Nero, 197

Vibo Valentia, xvi–xvii

Villa Schinosa Moscato di Trani, 333

Vouvray, 35

Vrasciole alla Verbicarese, 194–95, *196,* **197–98**

Vruocculi ca' Savuzuizza, 109, **217**

walnuts
    Pitta 'mpigliata, **338–40**
    Rolled Pastry Rosettes with Walnuts, Raisins, and
        Cinnamon, **338–40**
    Rosangela's Flourless Walnut Cake, **341–42**
    Torta di Noci, **341–42**
Warm Christmas Doughnuts, *235,* **324–25**
Warm Seafood Crostini, **39–40**
water-bath processing, 273–74
wheat, growing of, 115–16
white Burgundy, 187
white Rhône, 175
Whole Fried Sweet Peppers with Anchovies, **241**
Whole Salt-Baked Sea Bass, 69, 103, 160, **181,** *182,*
    183, 189
Whole-Wheat Linguine with Anchovies and
    Breadcrumbs, **68–70,** 127
whole wheat variation of My Family's Everyday
    Bread, **125,** 128
Wide Noodles with Pork Ribs and Tomato, **88–89**
wild fennel, 215–16, 257
wild fennel seed
    about, 18
    Cracked Green Olives with Fennel and Hot Pepper,
        24–26
    Dry-Cured Black Olives with Hot Red Pepper and
        Fennel, **27–28,** 304
    Fresh Homemade Fennel Sausage Calabrian Style,
        75, 90, 101, 195, **211,** *212,* **213–15,** 217, 252
    Funghi Sott'Olio, 28, **283, 285**
    Melanazane Sott'Olio, 23, 216, **281–82**
    Mushrooms Preserved in Oil with Hot Peppers,
        Wild Fennel, and Garlic, 28, **283, 285**
    Olive Nere Secche con Peperoncino, **27–28,** 304
    Olive Verdi Schiacciate, **24–26**
    Pickled Eggplant Preserved in Oil with Hot
        Peppers, Wild Fennel, and Garlic, 23, 216,
        281–82
    Salsiccia Calabrese, 75, 90, 101, 195, **211,** *212,*
        213–15, 217, 252

wild greens, 256–57

wild mushrooms, foraging for, xv, 257–58

wild straberries, harvesting, 257

wine(s). *See* Calabrian wines; *specific wines and variet-*
    ies of wine

wineries, Calabrian, 366–67, 372–73. *See also specific*
    wineries

winter squash
    Butternut Squash Marinated with Garlic and
        Mint, **264–65**
    Zucca Gialla con la Menta, **264–65**

winter tomatoes, 249

yellow nectarines, 343

Zinfandel, 63, 88

Zucca Gialla con la Menta, **264–65**

Zucchine Ripiene con Ricotta, **246–47**

Zucchine Seccate al Sole, 248, 271, **291–92**

Zucchine Sott'Olio, 40, **286–87**

zucchini
    Baked Ricotta-Stuffed Zucchini, **246–47**
    Baked Zucchini Layered with Tomato, Mozzarella,
        and Parmigiano-Reggiano, **250–51**
    Ciambotta, **244–45**
    Parmigiana di Zucchine, **250–51**
    Pizza con Zucchine e Fiori di Zucchine, **137,** *138,*
        139
    Pizza with Grilled Zucchini and Stuffed Zucchini
        Blossoms, **137,** *138,* **139**
    Southern Italy's Summer Vegetable Stew, **244–45**
    Sun-Dried Zucchini, 248, 271, **291–92**
    Sun-Dried Zucchini with Calabrian Paprika, 23,
        233, **248–49,** 304
    Zucchine Ripiene con Ricotta, **246–47**
    Zucchine Seccate al Sole, 248, 271, **291–92**
    Zucchine Sott'Olio, 40, **286–87**
    Zucchini Preserved in Oil with Hot Peppers,
        Garlic, and Mint, 40, **286–87**
    Zucchini Seccati al Sole con Pepe Rosso, 23, 233,
        248–49, 304

zucchini blossoms
    Pizza con Zucchine e Fiori di Zucchine, **137,** *138,* **139**
    Pizza with Grilled Zucchini and Stuffed Zucchini
        Blossoms, **137,** *138,* **139**
    Zucchini Preserved in Oil with Hot Peppers, Garlic,
        and Mint, 40, **286–87**
    Zucchini Seccati al Sole con Pepe Rosso, 23, 233,
        248–49, 304

zuppa, 94